DRAMA OF OROKOLO

THE SOCIAL AND CEREMONIAL
LIFE OF THE ELEMA

An *Eravo* at Orokolo

DRAMA OF OROKOLO

THE SOCIAL AND CEREMONIAL
LIFE OF THE ELEMA

BY

F. E. WILLIAMS

OXFORD
AT THE CLARENDON PRESS

Oxford University Press, Ely House, London W. 1

GLASGOW NEW YORK TORONTO MELBOURNE WELLINGTON
CAPE TOWN SALISBURY IBADAN NAIROBI LUSAKA ADDIS ABABA
BOMBAY CALCUTTA MADRAS KARACHI LAHORE DACCA
KUALA LUMPUR SINGAPORE HONG KONG TOKYO

This reprint by arrangement with the
Administration of the Territory of Papua
and New Guinea

FIRST PUBLISHED 1940
REPRINTED LITHOGRAPHICALLY IN GREAT BRITAIN
AT THE UNIVERSITY PRESS, OXFORD
BY VIVIAN RIDLER
PRINTER TO THE UNIVERSITY
1969

TO
SIR HUBERT MURRAY

FOREWORD

THE area extending westwards from Maiva (Cape Possession) to the Fly Delta is ethnographically one of the least-known parts of the southern coastal zone of what was formerly called British New Guinea, now officially termed Papua. The present volume constitutes the eighteenth and so far the longest Anthropological Report rendered by Mr. Williams to the Papuan Government. It deals with the dominant people of the Papuan Gulf, the eastern half of the little-known area just referred to, and is particularly welcome in that it describes at length the ceremony or rather grand cycle of ceremonies constituting the *Hevehe*, which until a quarter of a century ago dominated the ceremonial and artistic life of the Elema people. *Hevehe* has now disappeared in most of the Gulf villages, and as will be seen from Mr. Williams's account certain features have dropped out even at Orokolo, the village in which the *Hevehe* he describes took place. This is perhaps not surprising, since the complete *Hevehe* cycle might normally last from ten to fifteen years.

In his present volume the author gives us practically two works: Part I (the first 138 pages) constitutes a short monograph of the social life of the Elema people, while Part II (over 300 pages) is devoted in the main to the description of a single institution, the *Hevehe* ceremony or group of ceremonies, of such artistic beauty that even Mr. Williams, who knows New Guinea so well, is constrained to write of them as ' a finer thing than I imagined any Papuans could do '.

Who then are the people of whom this is written, and what do we know of their physical and psychological background? They are almost the most western of the Elema group of that great congeries of tribes I have termed the True or Western Papuans, using the last word in its anthropological as opposed to its geographical significance. Physically, culturally, and in many mental traits, the Papuan Elema differ from the immigrant Papuo-Melanesians of South-Eastern New Guinea, though Mr. Williams sees in them traces of

Melanesian admixture not found in their western neighbours of the Purari Delta, with whom they share a number of cultural traits. Nevertheless, it seems to be true that both physically and culturally the Elema form a well-defined group within the great Papuan congeries.

The Elema culture as described in Part I of this book indicates a people among whom sorcery plays a considerable part, possessing no true class of chiefs, and whose religion—if it be necessary to define it briefly—might be said to be a mixture of animism and a cult of the dead, the latter at least as much an implicit background as an explicit series of beliefs and ceremonies. Thus the great *Hevehe* ceremony with which this book deals is directly far less concerned with the dead than with innumerable non-human spirits.

Even if the greater part of the volume were not devoted to ceremonies connected with the men's houses, *eravo*, the size and importance of these would immediately indicate that the Elema are a people living their life with a certain stateliness and spaciousness of ceremony, which in turn implies a satisfactory food-supply, with time for the organized pleasures of social life. That the Elema are extrovert, like all Papuasians, no one will doubt, but an interesting point arises here. Why did the folk of Orokolo, of one physical make-up and culture with their neighbours the Vailala, less than ten miles away, scarcely suffer from that mass hysteria which in 1919 and the succeeding years swept through the western Elema villages, being so acute at Vailala, where it began, as to become known as 'the Vailala Madness'? Mr. Williams, who has described the outburst, has also tabulated the factors that he believes were in the main responsible for the 'madness'. These were: (1) The effort to assimilate a body of new and difficult ideas, and a resultant mental confusion; (2) the loss of customary means of social excitement; and (3) a general sense of inferiority. ('The Vailala Madness in Retrospect', *Essays Presented to C. G. Seligman*, 1934, p. 377.)

Mr. Williams has also indicated the factors which saved Orokolo when he writes: 'It must be understood, however, that different villages are affected in different degrees.

Orokolo and the neighbouring village Iogu appear to have resisted the new influences successfully; and here all the paraphernalia of the ceremonies are to be seen as in the old days. Yet the next village of Arihava—only a mile or so removed—has been a veritable hot-bed of the cult, and is still one of its most active centres.' ('The Vailala Madness and the Destruction of Native Ceremonies in the Gulf Division', *Anthropology Report No. 4*, Port Moresby, 1923, p. 3.)

This fine volume is thus not only a record of the ancient tribal organization and ceremonial of the Elema but an indication of the value of the retention of these in the life of the people, a lesson to Government and Missions alike, for we may agree with the author that it was largely due to the intensity of foreign influence in Vailala and the malaise consequent thereon that the Gulf Madness arose.

The author emphasizes this lesson in the last chapters of the volume, in which the actual pragmatic value of the *Hevehe* is studied. Here is made one outstanding remark, which has not perhaps been made so explicitly before, though it was very much in Rivers's mind when he put forward the view that lack of interest in life was an important factor in the dying out of so many Melanesian populations.

'The interest of *Hevehe* is something different from that of everyday life; it rises high above day-to-day needs and their fulfilment . . . ; it is to its recreative aspect that I should without hesitation give pride of place. Native life is plentifully supplied with rest; but it is marked by a comparative absence of active recreation. In general terms, adults do not play.'

This is quite true; for the most part the 'native' has nothing to compare with the varied forms of diversion that the European has made for himself. Perhaps this is why cricket and cards have from time to time become positive curses in particular Papuasian communities. Lacking comparable organized recreation, the Papuasian with his more intense, though narrower, group interest has resorted to ceremonial, and this seems true of Papua for every group leading a reasonably unharried existence. The recreation entailed in the *Hevehe* festivities is obvious, 'the oft-repeated *Hevehe*

Karawa has all the attractions of a rag. . . . There is feasting and crowding together of people; the jollity of rehearsals and initiations; brilliant spectacles and pageantry—enjoyed by the onlookers and more still by the actors.' Who will disagree with Mr. Williams when he writes of the *Hevehe* that its greatest value is in the recreation it provides?

As already indicated, Mr. Williams sees a physical Melanesian element in the Elema. Among the beliefs of this people are a number that are also found among Papuo-Melanesians; some seem to be the result of diffusion, e.g. the close resemblance in certain features of the Elema *aualari* beliefs to the *kangakanga* of the Mekeo tribes, while the 'body cries' of the Elema bear an obvious relationship to the cries of exultation which among the Mekeo tribes are connected with their club-houses. Others are less easy to explain. The *vada* belief of the Koita has been shown by Fortune to exist among the Dobu Massim. This was sufficiently surprising, although the two peoples are both Papuo-Melanesians, though far apart in social organization and belonging to different immigrant waves. Mr. Williams now discovers the belief among the Elema. Such facts seem to point to an earlier and perhaps more thorough mixing of (true) Papuan and Melanesian cultural elements extending farther west than had hitherto seemed probable. Here prolonged investigation is needed. It is not the least of the high qualities of Mr. Williams's work that by implicitly posing such questions he indicates an important line that further research should take.

C. G. SELIGMAN.

PREFACE

THIS book is the 18th in the series of Anthropological Reports published by the Government of Papua. It embodies part of the results of eight working-periods, long and short, on the Gulf Division coast, totalling more than 21 months. Of these 16½ were spent among the Western Elema of the Orokolo district, where the ceremonies herein described are practised. The first of these trips was in 1923; the last in 1937.

The information was gained almost entirely through the Motu language, which in altered and simplified form has become virtually the lingua franca of the Territory. The majority of men at Orokolo can speak it to greater or less extent; and with any of the older generation who knew only their own language it was used as a medium of interpretation. English, which is exceedingly rare and mostly bad at Orokolo, was used hardly at all. Despite the length of my stay I developed no facility in speaking the Elema language itself, though I acquired some knowledge of its vocabulary and structure and was at least able to interpret statements and formulae when taken down verbatim. I must confess that, instead of making a determined attack on the language from the beginning, I preferred to spend my time adding to my ethnographical notes. This is a form of temptation to which I find myself very prone to yield; but, considering that Motu provided an easy, and largely direct, medium of communication, I am by no means convinced that my weakness did not pay me well.

The present work is devoted mainly to a description of one institution, a method of procedure which has some very notable precedents. The name by which the institution is known is the unfortunate one of *Hevehe*, a word which will be found so often in the ensuing pages that the reader will possibly grow to forget its outlandishness. It is pronounced with three short *e*s, the accent usually falling on the first, though it may shift to the second if a man wants to utter the word with emphasis.

The *Hevehe* ceremonies have not been dealt with previously, as far as I am aware, except very briefly by J. H. Holmes. His book, *In Primitive New Guinea*, gives less than four pages to the subject, and it is plain that he had a very inadequate idea of its extent. Speaking of that book in general, while it is to be expected that any two workers in the same area may see things somewhat differently, I feel bound to say that it caused me perplexity rather than gave me help in my investigations. This is largely due to the fact that all the different Elema tribes, as well as the neighbouring Namau people, were dealt with by Holmes between the covers of one book, and that somewhat indiscriminately; but beyond this, it is plain that in treating of the ceremonies he made little attempt to follow his subject through. I should acknowledge the probability that I have unconsciously derived a great number of leads from his work; but, except for that, my researches have been entirely independent. As for our respective results, any one might shrink from the task of trying to make them square.

The procedure of writing a book round a single institution demands an adequate setting of a more general nature; and I have endeavoured to furnish this, at the risk of too-great condensation, in the first 138 pages. But while the treatment there is necessarily somewhat mean, I have made the description of the ceremonies themselves almost as full as possible. I trust it is not too full for my purpose; for it is a melancholy thought that no reader is ever half so interested in a book as its writer was, and this, I fear, is doubly true of a work of ethnography.

The actual details of the ceremonies often demand explanation or interpretation, and I have continually paused by the wayside to offer it. But the cycle as a whole provides some scope for theorizing on a more ambitious scale, and in Chapter XXV some opinions are offered on what is the ultimate problem of social anthropology, viz. the nature or constitution of culture in the abstract.

While, however, I cannot pretend to be indifferent to the effect, if any, which this theorizing may have on my fellow anthropologists, I can say with candour that my main concern on this occasion is not with them, but with those others, administrative and missionary by profession, who have a more direct influence on the native's future.

Even a work like the present may claim to have its bearing on the application of anthropology; for it makes an attempt to evaluate the things it describes—a task which, in my opinion, applied anthropology should be prepared to face—and it discusses the problem of their extinction or continuance. I am well aware that I have been so much taken by *Hevehe*, a finer thing than I imagined any Papuans could do, that I shall inevitably appear in the light of its advocate. My main object has been to do it justice in description, in the hope that the reader also may come to admire it. If this result can be expected, if any eyes are opened to what primitive Papuans were able to achieve, then the present book will have done some service to applied anthropology and some to the cause of native welfare at large.

ACKNOWLEDGEMENTS

I desire first of all to express my appreciation of the attitude taken by the Papuan Government in regard to the publication of Anthropological Reports. It has undergone the expense as a matter of course, but that is not the point. There are some differences between the policy it pursues and the policy I recommend in respect of existent native culture, and what I wish to acknowledge is the fairness and generosity which has permitted the publication of my views.

Professor Seligman does me great honour by contributing a foreword. It is a responsibility in itself to follow the famous anthropologists who have made reputations in Papua, and the author of the present book is happy to think that he is carrying Professor Seligman's work a stage beyond its western boundary.

Once again I have to thank my magisterial friends who have done so much to assist me from the head-quarters of the Division. It is so long since my first trip to the Gulf that some of them have retired, and I cannot be sure that the following list is a full one: C. R. Muscutt, W. J. Lambden,

R. L. Dick, G. F. W. Zimmer, J. R. Horan, C. H. Karius, and R. A. Vivian. If I have omitted any names I make amends by thanking the magisterial service at large for their help and their good friendship; and, if I may particularize, I should thank Mr. Vivian specially for planting those bananas and sweet potatoes round the rest-house at Orokolo in anticipation of my wife's first visit to the Gulf Division.

At Orokolo itself there lives one of my first Papuan friends, Mr. Harry Coghill. To him and his late wife; to Mrs. Alan Sinclair and her late husband; and to Mr. Fred Burke, all of whom carried on the hard life of traders on the beach, I owe a debt of gratitude for their hospitality and good company.

To the members of the London Missionary Society who have been successively posted at Orokolo or Auma I am under obligation not only for their hospitality but also for practical help and the benefit of conversations on subjects in which we had a common interest. They are the Revs. H. P. Schlencker, R. A. Owen, G. Moir Smith, and Stanley Dewdney; and the same may be said of the representative of the Seventh Day Adventist Mission, Mr. R. Farrar (not forgetting the wives of any of them). To those who carry on the missionary cause to-day I would, besides remembering their kindness, wish all true success in the names of altruism and tolerance.

Lastly, I have, as usual, to thank my wife for her help in the preparation of this book, not only at the office table but on the windy beach of Orokolo.

F. E. W.

PORT MORESBY,
1 *October* 1938.

PUBLISHER'S NOTE

For technical reasons it has unfortunately proved impossible in this edition to reproduce plates 28, 29, and 31 in colour.

CONTENTS

CONTENTS xvii

CONTENTS   xix

LIST OF ILLUSTRATIONS

PLATES

FIGURES IN THE TEXT

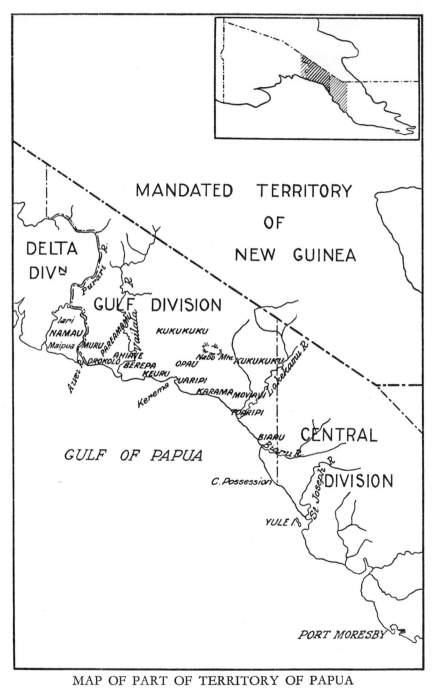

MAP OF PART OF TERRITORY OF PAPUA

(Scale: 1 inch = 40 miles)

THE STAGE

THE people of whom this book is written live in Orokolo Bay at the head of the Papuan Gulf, three days in a coastal boat from Port Moresby. The first day is spent in skirting the Dry Belt, a country of rolling hills against a mountain background. It is strongly reminiscent of Australia, with sparse eucalyptus and long grass scorched for the greater part of the year to a pale brown. The coast-line is varied and much besprinkled with reefs.

On the second day one reaches Cape Possession, and thereafter the characters of the Dry Belt grow less marked. The mountains recede into the distance and the grassy hills give place to broad forest-clad plains with only isolated mountain clumps. The scene is now more typically tropical; more verdant and less interesting. By a strange local dispensation of nature the seasons of rainfall are reversed. In the Dry Belt the trade-winds of the southern winter mean almost perpetually fine weather, whereas to the coast lying farther westward they bring its heaviest rains; and, as they blow head-on into the Gulf, the everlasting surf which they drive before them practically cuts off sea communication. For the coast is devoid of shelter; from Cape Possession to the Purari Delta it is bordered by 120 miles of beach, hardly broken except by the river mouths. The north-west, from October to April, is consequently the good season in the Papuan Gulf, both for natives and ethnographers, because of its fine clear weather and comparative calms. The ethnographer who outstays it may well prefer to walk home, as the writer has done thrice, rather than risk his notes, his negatives, and his life in a flat-bottomed punt amid the breakers.

Cape Possession is also an anthropological landmark. For it is here, leaving behind the Melanesian stocks who have occupied the south-eastern shores of the Territory, that we come upon the first unmistakable Papuans. It is true that the natives whom anthropologists have labelled by this

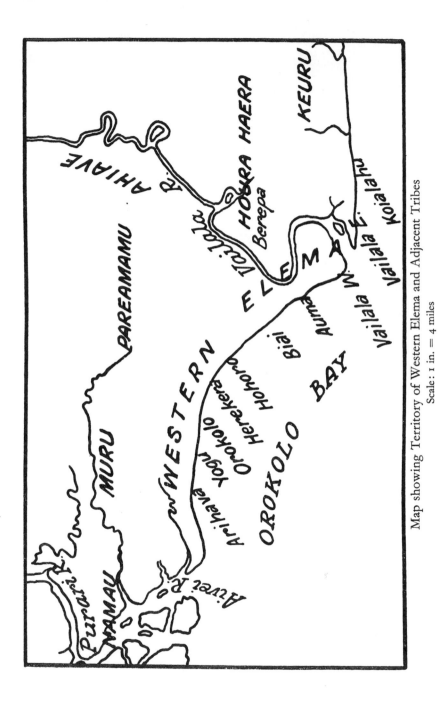

Map showing Territory of Western Elema and Adjacent Tribes

Scale : 1 in. = 4 miles

term and who occupy most of the island of New Guinea present a great deal of diversity, and we could not fail to notice it as we proceeded farther westwards. But our present journey will take us only so far as the first mouth of the Purari River, and the branch of the Papuan race which inhabits the country from Cape Possession to that point is sufficiently homogeneous and distinctive.

As a people they will be called the Elema. They live almost exclusively on the coast or near it, a belt of rich territory fringed with countless thousands of flourishing coco-nut palms. Behind these, on creek and swamp, grow the sago palms which furnish the people's main food, interspersed with areas of further coco-nut and areca, planted by forgotten gardeners, and tracts of virgin bush which still await the axe. This wide coastal strip fades along its northern edge into forested hills and swampy plains, unoccupied or sparsely inhabited by roaming Kukukuku. At its western extremity it ends abruptly at the Aivei, beyond which we come upon the Namau people who dwell numerously on the intricate muddy streams of the Delta.

The Village.

Our work will be almost solely in Orokolo Bay at the far end of the strip of coast that has just been described. The bay is some twenty miles across, from the spit of the Vailala to that of the Aivei, and it contains five main villages, Vailala, Auma, Orokolo, Yogu, and Arihava. These are already visible from the ship's deck, for they are built amongst the trees and coco-nuts almost on the beach itself. They stretch out wind-swept and untidy, some of them nearly a mile in length, while little hamlets are spaced here and there between them. When we have landed, say, at Orokolo, we find an irregular settlement straggling along the shore and some sixty yards in depth. Nowadays the village is fenced against the pigs; though it remains a question whether the fence serves more to keep them in or out. Several vacant spaces occur, open front and rear to beach and bush, so that the settlement takes the form of a series of enclosed rectangles, extremely elongated. Although Europeans

refer to Orokolo as one village, it is found in fact to consist of a number of separate but contiguous villages which
nowadays may be separated by fences but in the old days
certainly were not.

Within these oblongs the dwelling-houses are scattered
with small attention to order. The most that can be said is

FIG. 1. Two Styles of Western Elema Dwelling

that they usually conform to the rectangular layout of the
enclosure; though if any one cares to build his house on the
skew, as one or two have done, there is no authority to
stand in his way. The old-fashioned dwelling was hog-
backed, rising from rear to front, the roof culminating in a
high and forward-extending peak. This most picturesque
fashion alternated with another in which the front of the
dwelling was sheltered by a round, apse-like veranda. But
nowadays a third type with ridge-pole and gable ends, no
doubt attributable to indirect European influence, is surely
supplanting the other forms for the good reason that it is so
much easier to build. All stand on piles; they have veranda
platforms, small entrances, and dark, smoke-begrimed
interiors. Their timbers are bound in a very workman-
like manner with split cane; but the building-materials are
impermanent and the foundations of sand, so that some
houses are dilapidated and leaning. Yet with their walls of

dry sago midrib and their thatch of palm-leaf, ragged at the edges, they are always picturesque. When the subtle blend of browns is warmed and reddened by the evening sun, and when the smoke filters through the thatch to steal up among the coco-nuts and breadfruit trees, one must admit that even Orokolo, which is not a beautiful village as they go, has its own claims to beauty, and we may rejoice that the picture has not so far been spoilt by corrugated iron.

Some misguided sense of cleanliness causes the native to denude the sandy ground of all trace of grass, a perverse kind of diligence which increases heat, dust, and disease in his village and does nothing to enhance its beauty; though he makes some amends by sparing the flowers, degenerate zinnias and the like, where they grow, and by planting a few crotons and hibiscus. The whole scene, however, is somewhat bare. He might, if his tastes ran in that direction, make a far more effective staging for the ceremonies in which he shows himself to possess such an abundant share of aesthetic feeling.

The Men's House.

Dominating the whole scene and redeeming it from the ordinary is the men's house, the *eravo*. A huge structure, built on the lines of the old-fashioned house but enormously magnified, it covers a length of some 110 ft. and at the front reaches a height of more than 50 ft. The roof, which slopes upward from the rear, is supported on massive hardwood piles, and sweeps down almost to the ground on either side, a broad expanse of grey-brown thatch. With its soft colours and its innumerable shadows it is a peculiarly pleasing surface for the eye to rest upon.

The front of the building is completely covered in, presenting a broad, slightly convex façade, whose outline may be described as gothic if we allow for a little asymmetrical bulging. Its central feature is a narrow door, some 30 ft. in height. This door remains, so to speak, boarded up with layers of palm-leaf matting until, for one brief space in the life of the *eravo*, it is thrown open for the ceremony with which this book is to deal. At ordinary times an entrance at the base of it, rather less than man-high, serves for coming and going. A ladder of two or three steps, characteristically awkward and out of repair, gives access to this entrance and to the two narrow veranda platforms which flank it. They are sheltered by an ingenious kind of penthouse, while the high peak of the whole building extends forward to provide further shelter some 50 ft. overhead.

The *eravo* is hardly a pretty building; but, dwarfing all the surrounding structures, and with its head among the tall coco-nut palms, it possesses a very real dignity. Like some grey monster it lies couchant and silent, brooding over the affairs of the village or looking beyond them out to sea. Men may enter it as they please; two or three will be dozing in its cool interior by day, and at evening a dozen may gather to discuss a bowl or so of stew inside the entrance; guests of importance are entertained beneath its roof; and men may sleep there rather than at home. But the *eravo* is, on the whole, a place of quietness, virtually ignored by the men and women of the village and, except for occasional brief stirrings, mostly asleep. Yet at the appropriate moments it is galvanized into amazing activity and thronged about by a multitude.

Each has one or two attendants, smaller editions of itself, called *baupa eravo*. They are subsidiary men's houses (hardly more than twice the size of an ordinary dwelling). Normally the small *eravo* faces inland, whereas the *eravo* proper, with a wide dancing-ground free of coco-nuts before it, faces the sea from the opposite side of the village. The small *eravo*, always active and nearly always hopelessly untidy, is nominally a place for the boys; but it is patronized by men of all ages, and particularly so when, as is nowadays too often the case, the larger structure is missing from the scene. It must then fulfil, as best it may, certain of the functions which belong to the latter. But some—the most important—it cannot fulfil, so that when the true *eravo* is not there it means the absence of far more than a merely architectural feature in the life of the village.

The Elema Native.

The Papuans of the Gulf Division coast are, by general native comparisons, an attractive race of people—at least in

PLATE I

A village scene, Orokolo: showing dwelling-houses and two *baupa eravo*

the physical sense. They are tallish, lean, and well-made. Their skin is medium to dark brown and their features deeply chiselled; and while they are unmistakably 'Papuan' in their general cast of countenance they mostly lack the grosser characteristics—in particular the long hooked nose and pendulous lips—which are often associated with the term and have led so many explorers and journalists to discover the Lost Tribes in our Territory. Indeed, it may be hazarded that the Gulf coast natives as far as the Purari Delta show traces of Melanesian admixture, since the transition from east to west seems somewhat gradual, and it is not until we reach the Delta country that we encounter the 'Papuan' type in its extremer forms. However, the general contrast between Gulf native and Melanesian is clear enough; and it is pointed for us by the occasional presence of the Motuan crews of the visiting *lakatoi*. These men are distinguished from the local inhabitants by more than their tousled mops of hair and untidy clothes. We can recognize the Melanesian at a glance by his paler skin, his blunter nose, his semi-mongoloid eye, and his square ungraceful figure. The writer must confess to a sentimental preference (somewhat unusual, it would seem to be) for Papuans over Melanesians; and the above description might have been framed less unflatteringly. But in point of physical good looks at any rate the comparison between the Motuan visitor and the man of Orokolo goes wholly in favour of the latter.

Here, as elsewhere, there is many a miserable specimen; but the typical man bears himself with a touch of native swank and, however he may dawdle, walks like an athlete. You may see him returning from the day's work with a trade axe over his shoulder and his bow and arrows at the trail. He is naked save for a belt, a neat tight perineal band of bark-cloth, and one or two woven armlets. His hair is cut fairly close or perhaps allowed to form a two-inch mop. He wears no ornaments. The men of Vailala, Auma, and Arihava, however, are becoming increasingly addicted to the calico loin-cloth. They fancy themselves in these more modern garments and affect also coloured handkerchiefs, worn about the neck. It is in keeping with the conservative character of Orokolo and Yogu that they should have largely resisted these 'flash', exotic attractions and kept to their more scanty and more becoming traditional dress.

It is the unmarried youths, however, in whom we see the perfection of physical pride—tall, strapping, clean-limbed boys, still young enough to play games and hurl mock spears on the beach; their heads shorn close, except for a tuft at front and rear; with nothing in the nature of a shame-covering but a handsome, inadequate tassel of frayed fibre depending from the belt; and with their sleek young bodies all agleam with coco-nut oil. Boys formerly passed through several stages, marked by changes of dress, up to and after their seclusion, from which they emerged with white perineal bands. It was then, after the long inaction and systematic good feeding of perhaps nine months' internment, that the young bloods came out, oiled and reddened, in their finery and their long hair, to look for wives (though it seems that their minds and those of the girls concerned had usually been made up on the matter long before). Unfortunately, or so it seems to the writer, it is no longer possible to see youths to the same advantage in this flowering-time of marriage-ability, for seclusion seems now to have passed finally out of fashion in the villages of Orokolo Bay, and with it the special decoration worn by youths on their emergence. But, to be sure, they still take a pride in their appearance, and it is still a pleasure to look upon them.

When once a man is married he rather puts away vanity of personal appearance, except for occasions, and by the time he is really old he is usually content to be careless, though one can think of a few elderly fops who provide exception to the rule. We are dealing, however, with one of those societies in which age itself has a very pronounced dignity, and if the village elder's eye gleams with authority it does not matter if his body is dirty or if his uncombed hair shows a wisp or two of cobweb. Many of these rugged-featured old men who spit their betel-juice so explosively through the cracks in the floor are what we should call characters, with a bent towards the sterner mood. Not that they really direct village affairs in any very authoritative

PLATE **2**

A group of Orokolo girls. They wear pearl shells, dogs' teeth, and beads

manner, but they no longer feel they have to placate others. They do not try to exert authority—they do not need to do so; but they somehow wear the masterful look, quite unassumed.

Women and Children.

Women in the Orokolo villages are active and vociferous; it would be safe to say that they are generally happy, and they certainly have ample leisure. Their workaday dress is the skirt of frayed sago-leaf, old, brown, and ragged, except when they are in mourning for some relative, when they change it for a somewhat ridiculous-looking pair of broad leaves, worn front and rear, with the further necessary protection of a frayed sago-leaf perineal band. It is said that women's work is in the village and men's abroad. It is hardly the exact allocation of fields, but in the village itself one certainly sees the women more often at work, with their cooking, sweeping, net-making, feeding of pigs, and tending of babies. Their hardest work, however, is in sago-making, which they share with their menfolk, and they have the water and firewood to fetch. They are properly industrious, and you may see fresh girls, women in all stages of pregnancy, and skinny old hags bearing their share. But they are not overworked. They are mostly robust and well-fleshed; they sit about a great deal on their verandas or in the shade of the coco-nut trees; and their shrieks of strident laughter show that they do not find life too hard.

Orokolo women and girls are good-looking creatures. Old women, like old men, may cease to care, but younger wives and unmarried girls bear themselves very well and are thoughtful of their appearance. For any festal excuse whatever they bring out their new skirts of frayed sago, and these are the prettiest in the Territory. They are dyed in strips, dark brown, bluish grey, red and yellow, and some of these strips may be dyed in alternate colours from top to bottom, so that when all are assembled to form a skirt the effect is one of broad vertical bands alternating with very effective chequer-work. This is a charming dress for a brown-skinned girl, and one is happy to think that, though many youths have given up their neat perineal bands for flapping loin-cloths, the girls, whether from good taste, conservatism, or lack of pocket-money, have stuck to their native dress. But even so an increasing number see fit to change into calico, a more religious material, for Sundays.

Except on rare occasions the women wear no ornaments save armlets and ear-rings, but they have a unique and highly decorative manner of dressing the hair. Some time before a major festival you will see them busily barbering one an-other with broken glass or safety razor blades, a popular form of 'trade'. The hair, naturally black and woolly, is cut very short and largely shaved, but in such a manner as to leave a shining pate decorated with stripes, semicircles, chevrons, spirals of crisp black hair arranged in the prettiest patterns. Altogether, although a capacity for hard work is regarded as the first of feminine virtues, these young women do not miss the joy of life and are allowed full scope for the vanity which helps to make them so attractive.

Lastly there are the children, who, as in other Papuan societies, lead a life as free from responsibility as one could well imagine. Their parents treat them with indulgence. Their mothers carry them astride their necks or shoulders; their fathers dandle them on their laps or sit them on the sand between their knees; their small elder sisters make a fuss of them. As for education we should say, by European comparison, that they are subject to the direst neglect, though the indirect means of education are obviously there; for in the long run the boy and girl develop into the man and woman who fill their places in native society and get on successfully by doing as others do. In the meantime infants accompany their mothers to the sago-grounds or the beach, or, if for some reason they are left at home, lie bellowing and kicking with rage on the house-veranda until some passing interest replaces their disappointment. They amuse themselves under the houses by day and disport with greater vigour on the beach in the late afternoon. They first play at the serious business of life, with toy bow and arrows, spears, fish-nets, and brooms; they carry miniature loads of wood and beat imaginary sago on the sands; and before

long these little amateurs begin to show their usefulness.
Lastly there is the mission school to which they go not
unwillingly—though an occasional round-up is necessary—
to acquire the rudiments of religion and a literary education
on $2\frac{1}{2}$ days of the week.

The Village Pig.

Having thus paraded its human inhabitants we should not
leave the village without mention of that other species which
in the native view runs it so close in importance, viz. the
pig. Other living creatures—dogs and fowls—are treated
with scant respect. The Elema are not great hunters and the
dog is probably less valued for that purpose than as food
and as a purveyor of highly prized and ornamental strings
of teeth; while fowls are not kept as layers (most natives
revolt from the idea of eating a hen's egg), but are merely
killed for the pot. Neither come near the pig in numbers
or importance.

For the village pig is far more than living meat. He is the
living symbol of wealth, or as much wealth itself as the shell
armlets, frontlets, and pendants which are given in exchange
for him when he is killed. He is the means of cementing
friendship, of maintaining proper relations between kin;
and at every social and ceremonial gathering of importance
his dying squeals are pleasantly audible. (There is no doubt,
indeed, that the mere fact of having an animal ripe for
slaughter is sometimes the excuse for the ceremony.) The
pig, then, receives no small amount of attention. Dogs must
largely forage for themselves; but he is solicitously fed;
and despite what is generally acknowledged to be a somewhat unresponsive nature he may even get some petting.
As a piglet, member of a striped and dappled litter, he goes
squealing and grunting after his mother in the village. When
the litter are big enough to fend for themselves they are
turned outside, so that the fence may have its uses after all.
Sows in due course are served by bush boars, for the domestic
and the wild pig are precisely the same species. But though
they wander far afield their owners do not lose trace of them;
their ears are slit in various proprietary ways, and even if

they do not answer the evening summons for food, they can be rounded up when the approaching feast demands it. The population of pigs in and about the village is more numerous than that of human beings. One man will own a dozen, another five, another three, and so on. There are few with none at all. A large supply of them all round makes for social and ceremonial activity, and so they are highly prized. At the same time, and as a consequence, they give rise to a good many disputes and quarrels. Indeed, the principal sources of joy and dissension in the life of Orokolo males are their women and their pigs; and if in both respects the honours must be accorded to the women, it must be admitted that the pigs are not disgraced.

Bush and Garden.

The Orokolo environment divides itself obviously into three parallel regions: the village, the bush, and the beach. We have dealt at length with the first of these; let us now take a further glance at the immediate hinterland where the people gain their livelihood. They are predominantly, though not to the same extent as their neighbours on the west, dependent upon sago. The great coarse palms reach maturity at some fifteen years, when immediately prior to flowering they give the fullest yield of sago. But they grow in such profusion that the suckers seldom need to be planted out. In the Delta the whole work of sago-making, except for the felling, falls on the women. Here in Orokolo it is shared by the men. It is their work to split the trunk and scrape out the pith, while the women water and beat it in the trough, and then carry home the heavy block which is the result of their day's work. Man and wife between them will easily enough make 45 lb. of sago in a day from a section, say 2 ft. 6 in. long, of a well-grown palm. The whole palm might yield on an average 700 lb. These are very rough calculations, and results will vary very considerably according to the variety (at least eight are recognized and named) and, what is very important, the stage of maturity.

The actual technique is too well known to need full

description here.[1] It is rather a pleasant sight in the shady bush to see a family, or several families, brothers, brothers-in-law, and their wives and children, at work on the same palm. One or two men sit alongside the trunk from which the heavy bark has been prized off, and beat regularly with their scrapers, each blow grazing off some of the pith by means of the cupped end of the implement. It is hard, incessant work, requiring a machine-like swing and a good eye. The women, spattered from head to foot with sago and mud, stand at their sloping troughs, made of the broad branches of the sago palm itself, and with slender rods beat rhythmically at the pith which their husbands or brothers have scraped. From time to time they pour on water, and the sago trickles down the channel to the receptacle where it sinks and solidifies into a block. One or two adults are resting and smoking; small daughters are carrying water and doing odd jobs; and infants are amusing themselves after their own fashion. It is only the vile mud, the pestilential mosquitoes, and the horrible stench of rotten sago-pith that detract from the perfection of the idyll.

The other main source of livelihood is the garden. Unlike the natives of the Delta the Orokolo people have abundance of good ground and they are skilful if not very extensive gardeners. Apart from small patches cultivated by industrious individuals, the gardens of a considerable group, perhaps one village in the native sense of the word, will be grouped together. The whole is enclosed in a communal fence and divided laterally into strips by means of logs or saplings laid on the ground. Each such strip is then the temporary property of an individual. Its size is surprisingly small—say 8 yards by 60, a tenth of an acre.

Gardening is almost wholly men's work, and in the earlier stages, during the dry and hot north-west season, it is done in semi-communal drives. There is the usual sequence of operations: clearing the undergrowth (for the garden is made in heavy forest); felling or ring-barking the trees; fencing; burning off; laying the boundaries; and planting. Like so

[1] In all essential details similar to that used in the Purari Delta. See the writer's *Natives of Purari Delta*, Govt. Printer, Port Moresby, 1924, pp. 10, 11.

many undertakings, public and private, each of these has its appropriate and essential magic performed by the garden specialist; and thereafter the individual takes charge of his own plot, resting in confidence upon the foregoing magic and his own industry as a weeder to ensure a good harvest. It is only in the final digging up of the vegetables as they ripen that the women bear any part: all they ever do in this department of the food-quest is to visit the gardens and bring back a load—which incidentally is no light task.

The most picturesque of garden operations are the burning-off and the first planting, both of them carried out with some ceremony. The garden specialist himself kindles the first fire while the men and boys, their arms and legs decorated with bands and streamers of greenish-white nipa leaf, stand ready with their dry coco-nut fronds. These they presently light at the specialist's fire, which he has set going with the proper magic at the far end of the enclosure, and disperse to kindle the dry brushwood round it. Soon a vast cloud of smoke arises with spurts of red flame in its midst and sweeps down the length of the garden. The boys, advancing before it, shout and blow their shell trumpets, and seem like young black devils to spring from log to log in the very heart of the furnace. It is all over in a few minutes; and then, without stopping to see the flames finish their work, men and boys leap or scramble over the fence and rush in a body to the sea or the river, where they plunge into the water with a great hoot and a splash to wash the grime off their bodies.

For the planting-bee there may be a gathering of 100 and more men and boys. Each owner has laid out a varied assortment of plants on his own plot—shooting yams, off-sets of taro and banana, young bark-cloth trees, corn seeds, cuttings of coxcombs, crotons, and other plants used for decoration and magic. The specialist chews his medicine and spits on his digging-stick, makes a few preparatory holes, and then, with some whispered words, plants the first yam of the season. Upon this all the others start with a will on their own plots, assisted by the friends and relatives they have invited for the occasion. Work is almost fast and furious for an hour, but after that the energy fades away and

PLATE 3

Burning off a garden

the gardeners disperse, intending that the business, begun with a formal show of enthusiasm, shall be continued at a more congenial rate.

It would be possible to go on much further about the Orokolo native in the bush. There he collects the timber for his house-posts, the bamboo for his roof-timbers, and the cane to bind them together, the logs for his dugouts, the palmwood for his weapons, the bark for his clothes, and scores of other materials to furnish forth his material culture. It is there that he hunts the wild pig and the cassowary, though he is not a hunter from any economic necessity but only as opportunity offers or as ceremony demands (for the wind-up of every major ceremony is a hunt for the wild pig, and the thing cannot be brought to a satisfactory close until one is actually caught). His hunting-weapons are the bow and arrow helped out with the spear; his dog, often rather a miserable little animal, is nevertheless clever in the chase; and for an undertaking in which he so seldom engages he seems to possess an inordinate amount of magic.

The Sea and the Beach.

The Orokolo natives, however, are not as a rule far-penetrating bushmen, but people of the coast. Nor are they really at home on the sea. They have their small outrigger canoes for shark-fishing and in these the lone paddler will venture some miles from the shore. But of larger craft they possess very few. In the old days they would man long double canoes with paddlers and travel along the coast to Motumotu or even beyond Cape Possession to Yule Island, their object being to trade arrows and bamboo bows for the shell ornaments which had found their way from the Melanesians farther east. But they did not know the use of sails except in the form of a mat temporarily rigged on a couple of poles. The long expedition in which they now fairly often engage is a thing of recent times. First they adopted oars, copied from the whaleboats of traders and missionaries, and fitted their double canoes with fixed rowlocks. Then—and this is acknowledged to be quite a recent innovation—they began to copy the Motuan *lakatoi* which had for generations before

been bringing to their shores the cargoes of pots to be exchanged for sago. It is strange that this experiment should
have been so long delayed, but now there is a fairly well-
established series of expeditions running in the opposite
direction to those of the Motuans. The Gulf mariners sail
with cargoes of sago towards the end of the north-west
season, and nowadays may venture far beyond Port Moresby.
Their object is to trade, not for more pots, but for shell
ornaments; and they return—if they have got through—
with a great flourish and blowing of shell-trumpets, before
the south-easterly trade winds have got up too strongly.
They copy, or attempt to copy, the Motuan *lakatoi* in the
minutest detail; but their inexperience is shown by the great
proportion that come to grief. Time and again the *bevaia*,
as it is called, overloaded and grossly over-manned with
would-be travellers to the Papuan metropolis, sinks almost
before the journey has begun, and this despite a great deal
of magical preparation. So far the people of Orokolo Bay
are not so much mariners as enthusiastic learners. It remains
to be seen whether their enthusiasm will survive. During
my last visit it seemed rather to have dropped off.

Their ventures into the sea are for the most part only
waist deep. But it would be hard to find a people, unless it
be the modern kind of sun-worshippers, who spend more
of their time at the water's edge. We have observed the
endless beach which borders the Gulf Division coast.
Orokolo Bay has a fine sweep of slate-coloured sand broken
by only two or three small creeks, and at low tides about
150 yards in width. The rear is littered untidily with coco-
nut husks, nipa nuts, scattered driftwood, and other debris.
The front, swept clean by the tides, presents a broad expanse
of hard dark sand of extremely fine grain. It is the highway
from village to village, the sports ground for children, the
parade of youthful fashion, and the scene of evening repose
for every age. In the heat of the day it may be almost deserted
except for wayfarers, who may be seen sometimes trudging
along with a large green bough held up for an umbrella,
veritably men as trees walking; but in the cool of the late
afternoon it is thickly populated. Bands of small children

PLATE 4

Running a new dugout down to the sea. Several of these are lashed together to form the hull of the *bevaia*

play quietly—building themselves garden enclosures with nipa nuts, modelling *eravo* of wet sand, beating mock sago with the characteristic flail-like stroke of their elders, improvising toy canoes and sending them out to sea under sails of coco-nut leaf; or sometimes more noisily—pursuing the darting swallow with sticks, bringing down butterflies with handfuls of sand-shrapnel, or dodging and catching one another in some native round game. Now this pastime, now that, is in fashion. At one time all the larger lads are divided into groups, hurling mock spears at targets, end for end; at another they will be sauntering in twos and threes with sticks in their hands, inscribing crude and naïvely indecent pictures on the sand and writing their names in block capitals, not a few of them upside down; at another there will be a rage for that charming game in which they set up a row of sand-men like ninepins, one party against the other, and then stand off at a distance to topple them over with a fierce bombardment of snowballs made of hard wet sand. The only game of constant popularity is cricket, one of the gifts of the mission which has spread like wildfire. Boys from the merest children play in groups; the bat is home-made; the ball is thrown; the wicket is like a ploughed field; and there are usually neither sides nor scores. Yet the game goes on incessantly with shouts and cries.

On moonlight evenings the beach here and there may be alive with boys and girls, some of them youths and maidens, for this is a golden opportunity to mix love-making with horse-play. They move hither and thither, uniting and breaking, in indeterminate dark masses, their voices raised in a babel of song, shouts, and laughter. They are playing one or other of a variety of games which it is impossible for the onlooker to see or appreciate. Among them is the popular one of death and burial. The corpse is borne with chanting and wailing to the grave, a hole ready dug in the sand, and having been laid therein and partly covered, springs into life with a yell and scatters the shrieking mourners. The game does not appear to the actors as more than pleasantly gruesome.

But the beach, as we have seen, belongs to all ages. In

the afternoon you may see men walking, and women plod-
ding, home from their work. It is the latter mostly who bear
the burdens. Stooping from the middle and with necks
bent forward they carry on their backs, by a band which
encircles the forehead, bags swollen with sago or fresh
vegetables. Above this, maybe, is a large bundle of firewood;
and, surmounting the whole, a well-grown infant straddles
his mother's neck, his arms resting on her head and his
fingers clutched in her woolly hair. It is from the beach
again, which is always littered with drift-wood, that the
women usually obtain their fuel. Larger logs are marked
and appropriated as they are cast up, and now the women
who own them may be seen, bent low and with swinging
breasts, vigorously hacking them to pieces to be gathered
and stacked in great piles under their houses. Or we may see
them wielding their tall triangular fish-nets in the sea. If
there is an alarm, a shoal of small fish at any point, women
will come scurrying out of the village from right and left,
hastily adjusting as they go the small bags which hang from
their foreheads behind their necks. In a few minutes there
are a score of them raising and lowering the tall nets and
popping the insignificant result into the bags.

There is a great variety of fishing methods in Orokolo
Bay, and often mighty small result from any of them. In
fact it sometimes seems as if the people, men and women,
engage in them less as a serious business than as a fascinating
sport. Men stand resting on their spears, or slowly patrolling
the beach, for hours on end, their gaze fixed intently on the
waters for a sign. Now and again you will see one of them
madly pursuing his fish with long splashing strides: but I
have never yet been so fortunate as to see one speared by
this particular method. One of the most picturesque sights
in the bay is that of the fisherman perched solitary and high
on his pedestal, a section of tree-trunk upturned and cut
off at the spreading roots. Here he will stand in the broiling
sun, a fine statuesque figure, hardly moving except to turn
his head slowly and peer to right and left, while he holds his
bow half drawn with an arrow ready for the fish that never
seems to come.

PLATE 5

a. Making sand-men

b. The game in progress

The game of sand-men

As the sun declines the beach is dotted with villagers taking their ease—groups, couples (never, though, of love-makers), and solitary individuals chewing the cud. They sit on their haunches or lie in abandon on their stomachs, all with their faces seaward. The women leave the pots in which they have done their evening cooking to soak in the sea water or scrub them out with sand; and small babies, dangling without protest from one arm, are washed by their mothers in the wavelets.

Meanwhile, the sun is setting in a glory which can hardly be surpassed in any other bay, its colours reflected from the calm waters. The onlookers are not wholly oblivious of the beauty of the scene, for looking towards the glowing horizon in the west and thinking of the legendary region beyond it, they say, '*Ho-rovu Harihu bea here*'—'It is good weather in the land of the dead'. In the brief tropical twilight which follows one sees the black silhouettes of children still at play against a background of luminous blue. Fires spring up here and there, and fishermen begin to light their torches. But most of the people now return to their village and the beach is left to darkness and the shadowy forms of pigs at their everlasting rooting.

PLATE 6

A fisherman on his pedestal

PART I

THE ACTORS

I

NEIGHBOURS

Actors in a Drama

A KINDLY convention allows ethnographers to indulge in some superficial description as preface to their deeper and possibly drier studies. It is often the sugar-coating to a bitter pill; though they might argue that if they are to lead their readers nosing into other people's business they should effect some reasonably polite introduction before they begin; and further, if they hope to show their ethnographical pets in action, it is at least necessary to dress the stage. The Introduction is frankly of this sort.

It seems that those who engage in the study of society or culture are for ever being forced into the use of inadequate metaphors. It is bad enough in writing introductory chapters to speak of dressing the stage and so on; but when we try to penetrate deeper, to look through the society we are dealing with, the figurative language we are compelled to use seems still less equal to the occasion. The student can, it is true, according to his gifts and the amount of work he has done, see his society in the round or look right through it from this angle or from that; and he can, by the same token, see how this part bears upon that, and how one part actuates another. He may even visualize his society as a compact working whole. He is then tempted to use such words as 'organism' and 'machine', which seem to the present writer to present the systematic character of social relations and interactions with an over-emphasis which amounts to error.

The immediate aim just here is less ambitious. I shall not for the present attempt explicitly or consistently to bring the 'organism' into life, or set the 'machine' in motion. The ceremonies, when we come to them, will have to do the best they can to show how the whole, or at least a great part, of this particular culture can get into action.

In the meantime, it is proposed to examine Western Elema society for the most part structurally and statically. But even here, in seeking some compendious expression by way of title, one must fall back on metaphor. Thus one is tempted to call the first part of this book a sort of framework or interior structure about which one might build a series of façades, representing any one of a score of specific subjects— kinship, religion, sorcery, a particular institution, or what not. But unless our view is to remain superficial and unsatisfying we must be able to look through our subject and appreciate something of what is behind it; and since no architectural work permits of any such view, this metaphor, like most of the others, comes to grief.

To use another, which seems to promise better, one might call this first part The Anatomy of Western Elema Culture. In terms of this metaphor it is hoped that the reader may be prepared to follow a rather tedious process of dissection in order to see what our man is like inside. Apprehensions on the score of space have served to cut Part I down to a bare account which must dispense with life-giving examples; but when we have completed our dissection we shall at least pray that Part II will breathe life into the corpse.

But despite the temptingness of this more vivid figure of speech it has seemed easier, since we must discover titles for an Introduction and three ensuing parts and somehow make them consecutive, to fall back on the one first considered. The Introduction, then, is a dressing of the stage; and if it seems somewhat more elaborate than is usual it may be pleaded in excuse that the cycle of ceremonies which it is our main purpose to describe is essentially a Drama, with the bush, the village, and the beach for its Stage, and the whole community for Actors. It is the writer's really earnest hope that he can show in this book how well the thing goes off. To round the matter off the chapters of Part III, which contain some of his reflections, are called the Critique. Any one who has read through the drama must make his own judgement on it. But the writer confesses it would be an unwelcome surprise to him if the critique were other than favourable.

Our immediate concern is with the actors, and our task resolves itself principally into analysing the divisions, sub-divisions, and cross-divisions of Elema society. It would be easy going if we could start from the larger units and descend without interruption to the smaller; equally easy if we could do the opposite. But neither method, of course, works out. The former is the writer's preference, which it is intended to pursue as far as possible. But there are many principles of division and therefore many cross-sections—of locality, of lineal descent, of age, friendship, occupation, authority, and so on. We shall have to follow these, not nearly as far as they lead, but far enough to prepare for understanding our chosen subject.

There can be no doubt that in many directions this analysis goes farther than is really necessary for the express purpose in hand: that is to say, there can be no pretence that everything written in the first part is relevant to the subject of the ceremonies which fills the remainder of the book. *Pace* the Functionalists I still believe that some parts of a culture may have no practical bearing on other parts, or on the whole; and in the first six chapters no doubt there are many things mentioned which have no bearing on *Hevehe*. But it seemed an opportunity to make a job of the thing, and so Part I has expanded into an account of Western Elema social organization, admittedly sketchy but more or less all-round.

The Elema People

The coastal people from Cape Possession to the mouth of the Purari clearly constitute one ethnic group. But they do not possess among their various component groups sufficient sense of unity to have thought of a common name. So we are confronted by the familiar difficulty of choosing or inventing one.

Holmes called them the 'Ipi People' or 'Ipi Group' in contradistinction to the Namau of the Purari Delta, having

written of both in the same book.[1] For the latter name there
was some good justification, since the natives of the Delta
were known as Namau to their eastern neighbours[2] even if
they never used the name of themselves. But 'Ipi Group'
was a sheer improvisation into which Holmes felt himself
forced for lack of anything better. It has never, as far as I
am aware, been used by any one else, and is simply founded
on the fact that many of the names of the component groups
—Moreáripi, Beraripi, Kaivipi, &c.—end in these particular
syllables.

To European residents of Papua the people at large are
known as 'Gulf Natives', because they inhabit the coast of
the Gulf Division, one of the Magisterial units into which
the Territory is divided. The term 'Gulf Boy' is unfortunately not without reproach, though the reputation which
attaches to it, bandied about by thoughtless people who have
little or no experience of the natives to whom it applies,
seems to the writer far worse than it need be. It is hoped
incidentally that this book may do something to redeem it.

But the above name is at any rate hardly distinctive enough
for our purpose, and it is therefore proposed to adopt the
third choice available, viz. 'Elema'. This word has been
used, presumably for generations, by the Motuan sailors
who still make their annual trading expeditions to the Gulf.[3]
It embraces the whole coastal population of the Division,
though I suspect it to be a rendering of the word *Hereva*
which appears in *Hereva-Haera*, the name of the particular
group living in and about the village of Orokolo.[4] Although, as Holmes observes, the people at large do not use
'Elema' as a name for themselves, the same objection might

[1] J. H. Holmes, *In Primitive New Guinea*, Seeley Service, 1924. *Ipi* means 'base'
or 'origin'.
[2] These neighbours, however, more often called them Hurava Haera—'Western
Men'. To show how hard it is to nail down these tribal and ethnic names, it may be
mentioned that 'Namau' is applied to the Western Elema by the tribes living farther
eastwards.
[3] See Seligman's *Melanesians of British New Guinea*, chapter viii.
[4] I have heard *Hereva*, as the old name for Orokolo, pronounced *Kereva* or
Kerema. In the last form it is the name of the present Government station of the
Division.
This may be a case of the same name cropping up at different points along the
coast, or else Kerema has there resulted from a mispronunciation of Kairuma, the
river on which it is situated.

be raised against the other names put forward, and it seems that on the whole this has the best claims.

Elema will therefore stand for the population from Cape Possession to the Purari River. As we shall be dealing intensively with the inhabitants of Orokolo Bay at the far extremity of this coast, these may be distinguished as the Western Elema; for even the people of this particular bay, homogeneous as they are, acknowledge no inclusive name of their own.

The ethnic neighbours of the Elema can be placed on the map as follows:

First, on the west, live the people of the Purari Delta who, despite close contact, speak a wholly different language and are readily distinguished in other cultural respects as well as by their smaller physique. For these we may retain the name Namau.

Second, on the north, are found the tribes, semi-nomadic, elusive, and still to some extent hostile, who belong to the Gulf Division hinterland. These will be referred to as Kukukuku. This quaint name is said to be a term for 'bushmen' in the language of some tribe or other of the coast. Whatever its origin it has come to be used very generally in Papua, covering a wide territory and a multitude of differences, and as a general name it will do well enough in the present connexion. Comparatively little is known about the people who bear it, and they seldom come into contact with those on the coast.

Lastly, on the east lie the littoral populations of Kevori and Maiva with whom the Elema have been in fairly constant touch.

Thus distinguished from their neighbours, we find the Elema people to share one language and, in broad outlines, one culture. Their environment, from end to end of the coast, and their general economic relations with it, are largely uniform. Descent is patrilineal; marriage patrilocal; and throughout there is the same kind of relation between affines and between nephew and maternal uncle. Everywhere there are (or were) men's houses typifying a social life in which the sexes were to some extent segregated, and a ceremonial life from which the women were almost wholly debarred. Boys underwent a period of seclusion, and males were classed in age-groups according to its date. The cult of the bull-roarer was common to all, as well as various other ceremonies which, while differing in very essential points, were distinguished throughout by the use of elaborate masks. With these and many other points in common, therefore, the Elema may fairly be spoken of as one people.

The Tribes

The whole people is divided into some dozen territorial units which may be called tribes. These speak mutually intelligible dialects. The Orokolo men, for instance, can understand the Toaripi at the opposite end of the coast, though they complain that the latter speak with their tongues between their teeth and chatter and twitter like birds. (I have not recorded what the Toaripi think of the speech of Orokolo.) In the old days it would appear that tribes sometimes made war upon each other. But within the tribe itself, although its members were much given to fighting, there were no deliberate killing expeditions.

Some of these tribes are known by distinctive general names, at least to their neighbours. But such is the confusion —different names being given to the same tribes by different neighbours, and the tribes usually possessing no certain designations for themselves—that I have solved the difficulty out of hand by using those of representative villages. These from west to east are as follows: Orokolo, Muru, Pareamamu, Berepa, Ahiave, Keuru, Opau, Uaripi, Karama, Toaripi, Moviavi, Biaru. This list, especially as regards the eastern end, could be added to, and the units no doubt subdivided; but with that kind of work we are not in the least concerned. Nor, except incidentally, shall we need to mention cultural differences between the tribes. The writer has thrice done the length of the coast and has worked at different times in each one of them.[1] But in the midst of general homogeneity the differences are such that to write upon them would mean

[1] With the exception of Ahiave.

a very big book, if not a thoroughly confusing one. Our attention will be concentrated upon the first tribe named.

Although, in order to bring it into line with the others, I have in this place called it the Orokolo tribe, using the name of one representative village, it has already been seen that the tribe contains several large village groups; and, as it will be necessary from time to time to distinguish between these, we may best continue to speak of the whole as the Western Elema.[1]

Main Village Groups

Each of the tribes has a number of larger or smaller villages. In past days it appears that they were less numerous than now; the large settlements were separated by long stretches of unoccupied beach. But with the coming of the White Man's Peace there is a growing tendency to punctuate these no-man's-lands with small hamlets which have in these times no reason to fear unneighbourly tribesmen or raiding Kukukuku.

The five main village groups of the Western Elema bear modern names which would seem to have come into being to suit the convenience of the white man. Arihava is the name of a particular track leading into the bush. It has been given to the whole mile-long settlement because in the very early days a trader occupied a site where the track took off from the beach. Orokolo means 'leaf of the *oro*', viz. the broad-leaved tree which grows in profusion on the beach. (It was not a local name for the whole settlement. Some attribute it to the poetic fancy of an early missionary; others, more plausibly, say it was a name given to the village, under some misunderstanding, by the Motuan sailors.)[2] Auma is

[1] Present population, Western Elema, 1937—4,465 (males 2,398, females 2,067).

Arihava	1,409
Yogu	216
Orokolo	986
Off-shoot hamlets	409
Auma	302
Vailala, East and West	1,143

[2] Orokolo was the name of a small tributary of the Aivei leading to Muru. It may have once been used by the Motuans for their *lakatoi*, as they often penetrated the Delta; but many years ago, we are told, it was barricaded by sago-leaves against a fleet of raiding Maipuans, and these practical measures together with the appropriate magic converted it from a stream into a sago-swamp.

E

the name of the little headland; and Vailala, of the river. Yogu alone seems to have been established in pre-European usage.

The natives had general names for the people occupying these settlements. Arihava belongs to the Hareamavu or Moreari Haera;[1] Orokolo to the Hereva Haera; Auma to the Haruape Haera; and Vailala to the Aita Haera. It is not worth trying to pursue the etymology of these. The whole tribe draws its legendary, or perhaps even its historical, origin from Popo,[2] a former village some two or three miles inland from Arihava, the tall coco-nuts which still grow there being attributed, no doubt wrongly, to its founders.[3] A variety of legends, garbled and irreconcilable as narrated by different informants of Arihava, Yogu, and Orokolo, tell of the origin of mankind, the foundation of Popo, and the final scission between the Hareamavu and Hereva groups. One characteristic version of the last episode is that the division followed on a quarrel between two brothers, one of whom attempted to seduce the other's wife while he was away fishing. The quarrel led to a faction fight, and when that was finished the parties agreed to go their ways. They thought they could detect some differences in their respective languages and this was a further reason for separating. Thus the Hareamavu have in course of time found their way to Arihava and the Hereva to Orokolo. My informants, belonging in this case to the former group, professed in justification of their story to detect some differences between the speeches of the two: the Orokolo men in fact talked rather too loudly. I am not personally aware of any difference whatever. The Western Elema of Orokolo Bay speak one dialect, and any village differences are not worth mentioning.

---

[1] Hareamavu is applied (1) to the whole of Arihava, and (2) more particularly to the western end of it. In both senses it is acknowledged by the people themselves. Moreari Haera or Moreáripi is a nickname given to the Arihava people by those of Orokolo. I am unable to discover any meaning for it. It is presumably the same word as Holmes's 'Morea-ipi' which he uses to cover both Arihava and Orokolo. Strictly speaking, this is an error.

[2] Pronounced *Paw-paw*.

[3] Popo may well have been a sea village, for the coast of Orokolo Bay has evidently been making ground in recent times, and the population, who are so attached to beach life, have moved forward with it. Indeed the sites of the present villages were mostly, within living memory, under the sea.

Although the five villages belonged, linguistically and in all other respects, to one and the same culture there is nowadays to be seen a very significant difference. This consists in the degree in which they have been affected by European influence; and one has no hesitation in believing that the difference came into being chiefly through the movement known as the Vailala Madness.[1] Further reference to this movement will be made in a later chapter. It is enough here to say that while it swept through Vailala, Auma, and Arihava, it left the intermediate villages of Orokolo and Yogu almost wholly unaffected. However much these latter have been modified, in common with the others, by the influence of missionary, trader, and Government, they were at least spared the devastation of that spectacular and ugly movement of eighteen years ago. By comparison Orokolo and Yogu stand forth as strongholds of the old customs; and it is in these two villages alone that there seems to remain any prospect of viewing the major masked ceremonies with which we are concerned.

The great bulk of the writer's field-work was done while he camped in Orokolo, whence the villages of Arihava and Yogu as well as a number of the hamlets are within easy distance. Camps were made for shorter periods at Auma and Vailala, so that the whole tribe has been laid under contribution. But it is upon Orokolo that our interest will be mainly focused.

Eravo-*communities:* Karigara

What we have been calling the village is, as already mentioned, subdivided into a number of smaller contiguous villages, called *karigara*.[2] To take Orokolo as our example, it is found to be divided into the following (west to east): Harelareva, Ovarova, Hopaiku, Hururu, Mirimurua, and Kavava. Nowadays these may (or may not) be separated by

---

[1] See the author's *The Vailala Madness and the Destruction of Ceremonies in the Gulf Division*, Anthropological Report No. 4, Government Printer, Port Moresby, 1923; also 'The Vailala Madness in Retrospect', in *Essays Presented to C. G. Seligman*, Kegan Paul, 1934.

[2] The same native word, *karigara*, may be used also for the whole settlement, though one suspects that this use is post-European.

fences, while more permanent marks exist in the shape of coco-nut palms; though, to be sure, when it comes to the point of defining *karigara* boundaries the authorities consulted are vague individually and in discussion argumentative. But while there may be dispute—as unimportant as it is insoluble—about a few yards of ground there is none regarding the allocation of individuals to this *karigara* or to that.

The *karigara* is an important unit. It might be spoken of as a community. Not that its daily life is in any strict way separated from that of the neighbouring communities, but in all festive or ceremonial concerns its members stick together inasmuch as they give mutual assistance and support: whether related or not—and in point of kinship the *karigara* may be a very mixed crew—they contribute in the all-important business of providing food. The ownership of land follows a deeper-lying division than the one we are discussing, but in the use of it, especially in the yearly garden, the *karigara* once more acts together: the typical arrangement is for all the members to unite in clearing and fencing one large area, individuals being then allotted their plots within it.

In this and other enterprises, such as building and loading a trading vessel or celebrating *Kovave*, the *karigara* tends to act together; and it is evident enough that to some important extent its members feel together. They entertain towards each other, individually and collectively, a sentiment which, without trying to analyse it here, we may call again by the familiar name, Group Sentiment. It seems unlikely that any one would deny the existence of anything so obvious; and if we grant that it exists, we must also grant that it does not exist for nothing. I feel bound to believe that the conduct and attitude of members towards one another and their conduct towards outsiders are both in their different ways conditioned by the sentiment which binds them in a self-conscious unity. That sentiment, as I have elsewhere suggested, may be called the sentiment of Fellowship.[1] Whether the unity of the group be based on locality, kinship, coevality,

---

[1] See the author's *Papuans of the Trans-Fly*, O.U.P. 1936, chapter xlv.

or common interest and occupations, it gives rise to a sense of sympathy which is perhaps most simply explained as an extended feeling of self. It is not intended to develop this view any further here, and certainly not to maintain that this is the only sanction of morality and law. But it seems to me the best explanation for that not solely primitive condition which we call clannishness, and clannishness is typically strong among the Western Elema. In the broad sense of the word it may characterize any kind of social grouping, and, to return to the subject of locality as a principle of organization, it seems that among the Western Elema it is nowhere more obviously evinced than by the *karigara*.

Properly speaking each *karigara* should have its own *eravo*, distinguished by a personal name, and it is this *eravo* that symbolizes its unity. Members are fancy-free in the matter of building-sites provided they do not encroach unduly on the open space before the great men's house. They can hardly be said to cluster in its shadow, but rather build at a respectful distance—for it is undesirable that women should dwell too close to an edifice which belongs to a life apart from theirs. But the succession of towering *eravo* is what really marks the succession of different *karigara,* so that these units may be referred to as *eravo*-communities.

The *eravo* as we have seen is the daily meeting-place of the men, or of such as choose to go there; and it is the duty of their womenfolk to supply pots of ready-cooked food each afternoon. There may be only three or four each ordinary day, but a member of the community whose wife failed to do her share would get a bad name as one who always ate at home. By night a larger number of men will sleep by their *eravo* hearths; and of course on the occasion of a major ceremony the building may become the scene of crowded and strenuous activity. We shall be constantly referring to the *eravo* in the later parts of this book. Enough has been said here to show that it is identified with the whole *karigara* community. The great ceremony which we are to describe is a function of both. It is got up and carried out on the responsibility of the *karigara* acting through its *eravo*.

The Eravo *and its Sides*

Some detailed description of the building will be necessary for an understanding of the *Hevehe* ceremonies, and it may as well be given at this point, particularly as the very nature of its construction leads to a minor social division which is really local in character.

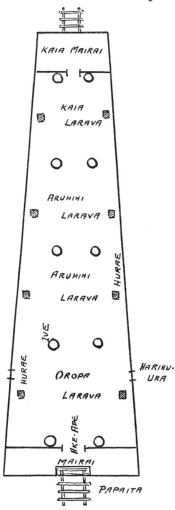

Fig. 2. Plan of *Meouri Ravi* (length of building, 99 ft.)

The central pillars (*ive*), usually five pairs of them, stand in parallel lines, the space between forming a passage from front to rear. These pairs of *ive* mark off the interior into four divisions called *larava*, each with a hearth (*hurae*) on either side. The foremost, lofty and spacious, is called *oropa*, the front; the two in the centre, *aruhihi*, the middle; the last, *kaia*, the rear. The *oropa larava* is where men sit and talk; the others are ordinarily no more than sleeping-places, by day quiet and deserted.

The entrances at front and rear are called *ake-ape* (literally 'track-mouth') and *kaia ake-ape* respectively. The former is placed at the base of the tall door (*dehe*) which is only opened at the final stage of the *Hevehe* ceremony.

At each end is a veranda platform (*mairai*). At the rear this is sheltered by the extension of the roof, which is there only about 12 ft. above it. In front the projecting peak (*eravo apo*, i.e. *eravo*, 'bow' or 'bow-point') is too high up

PLATE 7

Carrying an *Ive*, or *Eravo*-post

Setting up the post

to afford real shelter,[1] so the front wall is brought forward at the base on either side forming a pair of penthouse verandas (*kivori*). Beneath them are two windows commonly closed with coco-nut-leaf matting and called *heveheape ake-ape* ('*hevehe*-mouth doors'). Finally, at the base of the side walls on each side and some 30 ft. from the front are two little entrances about 3 ft. square which go by the intriguing but unexplained name of *harihu-ura*, 'spirit-holes'. They are so to speak emergency exits or entrances, being used when those at front and rear are placed under tabu during the ceremony.

The *eravo* being elevated on a host of heavy piles, some 5 ft. from the ground, is reached ordinarily by a rickety ladder of two or three rungs. For the final stages of the ceremony this is replaced by a stoutly constructed ramp, the *papaita*.

It will be noted that the *eravo* is a long building symmetrically divided by the central passage into two 'sides' (*kai*), and this fact in itself divides the occupants into sides. There is nothing like a Dual Division in Western Elema society, and there is certainly no division into the Right Side and the Left. In fact these terms are not used in the present connexion. A native commonly has to stop and think which is his *mai-ore* (right hand) and *mai-keva* (left hand), but he does not need to ponder as to the direction of the Aivei and Vailala Rivers, and it is these latter terms which he uses for the *eravo* sides. You belong, in your particular *eravo*, to one or the other; and as most *eravo* face the sea you belong to the Aivei side if your hearth happens to be on the right. When, as has occurred in one or two comparatively recent instances,[2] the new *eravo* is built facing in the opposite direction, then the right side of the old transfers to the left side of the new, and vice versa. Each sticks to its own, Aivei or Vailala.

The division into two sides is neither important nor strict. If one grows over-crowded, members may shift across to hearths on the other. Nor can the divisions be made to correspond with the groups which we shall have presently

---

[1] In the Western Elema *eravo* proper this does not project far forward as in those of the Purari Delta. But *baupa eravo* often assume the Namau for.m
[2] This was the case with Meouri Ravi: see diagram, p. 36.

to consider; you will find *bira'ipi* and *aualari* represented on either side without any discrimination. Further, there is no superiority of one side over the other, and although of the two *eravo* chiefs, belonging to the respective sides, one will probably be the more influential, there is no telling on which side you may find him.

In spite of all these negative facts there does exist a sense of duality in the *eravo*. As we have just indicated, each side owns its chief called *eravo amua*, and each, further, possesses a functionary, the *apa haro haera*, who takes precedence on that side in the *Hevehe* ceremonies. There would seem, however, to be little trace of rivalry. The tendency is rather to aim at mutual balance; and this is shown by the habit of exchanging food. At any function in which the *eravo* has co-operated the guests are fed first and sent away, and then the hosts foregather in their own *eravo*, like native gentlemen, to eat afterwards. On such occasions the comestibles —pots of stew, coco-nut, betel, and so on—are ranged down either side of the passage in the *oropa larava* by the men who belong to that side. They are nominally for exchange, though it is not to be thought that individuals need be particular to eat only food from the opposite side when, having got rid of their guests, they fall to at the end of the day. But the form of exchange is observed, and it is justified by the plea that it makes the two sides *iki beveke*, i.e. well-disposed or literally 'good-livered'.

Apart from these nominal exchanges of food I can think only of a few ceremonial occasions on which the sides are, as it were, drawn up against each other. One is when the drum-tabu which follows any death in the village is brought to an end. The husband or nearest of kin to the deceased must give his consent, and he himself formally beats the first drum after a silence of say half a year. On that occasion there is the usual exchange of food, and the *amua* of the side opposite to that of the deceased is expected to present one or more ornaments to the chief mourner. Further instances in which one side is set off against the other will be met with in the description of *Hevehe*.[1]

[1] See pp. 184, 304–6, 311, 365.

PLATE 8

Ori Ravi, Orokolo. The forward part (*oropa larava*) has been some years in this unfinished condition

The division between the two sides of the *eravo* is so unimportant functionally as hardly to be worth dwelling upon except as an example of what may well be an incipient form of local division. It is possibly an echo of the much more strongly marked division which is found in the Purari Delta; but the writer is inclined to repeat the suggestion which was hazarded in that connexion,[1] viz. that the division into halves may be regarded as reflecting a natural tendency. Such a division, which may be in the first place no more than arbitrary (e.g. when a small migrant group builds its first *eravo*), may harden into a definite one, with an *esprit de corps* for either side and a little emulation between the two. While there is no such thing as an all-pervading Dual Division among the Western Elema, yet every one of their *eravo* develops that Dual Division in little. When a communal house is bisected in the architectural sense it may follow merely as a natural result that its occupants will 'take sides' accordingly.

The Bira'ipi *Clans*

We now take leave of the purely local principle of division and proceed to consider a further series of groups which are founded partly on locality and also partly on the principle of descent. Before dealing with these, which I shall call the *bira'ipi*, it is necessary to anticipate by enumerating a series of larger divisions, the *aualari* groups, which are in their present constitution purely lineal; viz. *Kaia, Ahea, Hurava, Purari, Miri, Baiu, Auma, Vailala, Nabo*, and *Kauri*. These highly important divisions will be considered in the next chapter. They are named at this point in order to help in the understanding of the *bira'ipi* clans with which we are concerned at the moment.

Neither the *karigara* names nor those of the *eravo* are much in use, the latter even less so than the former. Indeed the particular *eravo* names were often enough unknown to Orokolo villagers at large, and sometimes even to members of the *eravo* in question. (If they appeared to be better acquainted with them at the end of my work than at the

---

[1] *Natives of the Purari Delta*, p. 103.

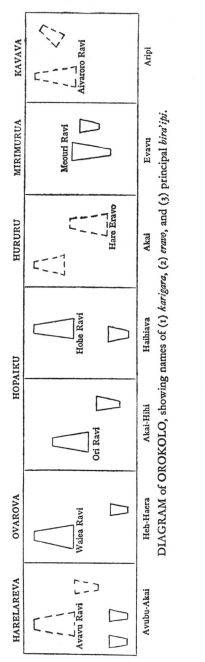

HARELAREVA	OVAROVA	HOPAIKU		HURURU	MIRIMURUA	KAVAVA
Avavu Ravi	Waiea Ravi	Ori Ravi	Hobe Ravi	Hare Eravo	Meouri Ravi	Alvaroro Ravi
Avubu-Akai	Heh-Haera	Akai-Hihi	Haihiava	Akai	Evavu	Aripi

DIAGRAM of OROKOLO, showing names of (1) *karigara*, (2) *eravo*, and (3) principal *bira'ipi*.

Akai
(*Purari*)

Evavu (*Baiu*)		Aripi (*Hurava*)	Hairi (*Purari*)		Haihiava (*Kauri*)	Laribairu (*Purari*)		do.	do.	Haihiava (*Vailala*)	Evavu (*Auma*)		Huruvu (*Kaia*)	Hairi (*Purari*)
Hairi (*Ahea*)		Heh (*Ahea*)	Haihiava (*Kauri*)		Haihiava (*Kauri*)	Birahiru (*Purari*)		do.	do.	Akai (*Ahea*)	Birahiru (*Purari*)		Akai (*Nabo*)	
Hairi (*Ahea*)		Akai (*Purari*)	Huruvu (*Kaia*)		Haihiava (*Kauri*)	Larihairu (*Hurava*)		do.	do.	Akai (*Ahea*)	Beraripi (*Ahea*)		Mareapavura (*Auma*)	Haihiava (*Purari*)
Akai (*Purari*)		Heh (*Ahea*)	Heh (*Purari*)		Haihiava (*Kauri*)	Birahiru (*Purari*)		Akai-Hihi (*Nabo*)	Akai-Hihi (*Nabo*)				Pakemana (*Kauri*)	Haihiava (*Hurava*)
Akai (*Purari*)		Aripi (*Hurava*)	Heh (*Ahea*)					Akai (*Ahea*)	Akai (*Ahea*)				Akai (*Nabo*)	Aripi (*Hurava*)

DIAGRAM of the SEVEN ERAVO, showing (1) *bira'ipi* and (2) *awalari* of hearth-holders.

PLATE 9

Waiea Ravi, Orokolo. The front wall has still to be thatched and the door closed in

beginning, this was undoubtedly due to my own irrational preference for the *eravo* name as against that of the village.) Much more popular than either among the natives themselves was the name of the clan, or rather that of the first, or representative, clan to whom the village and its *eravo* belonged. Thus each *eravo*-community was commonly referred to by the name of one certain *bira'ipi* (though, as will be seen, it is nearly always a composite unit, with representatives of a number of *bira'ipi*).

Now the native, albeit a master of its actual content, is not always so interested in the theory of social organization as to possess generic names for social units. From beginning to end of the writer's work in Orokolo there was this difficulty and minor source of irritation. The native's own way of framing the relevant question is usually no more than *De haera?*—'What man are you?' And the answer to this may be either the man's *aulari* group or what we are calling his *bira'ipi*. For purposes of exposition, however, it is plainly necessary to give each kind of group a distinctive name.

The word *bira'ipi* was applied to the smaller kind of group, which we are here discussing, by sufficient informants and with sufficient confidence to justify our use of it. Its derivation from *bira* (male, husband, man) and *ipi* (base or origin) indicates the nature of descent within the group, which, like that of the *aualari*, is of course patrilineal. An alternative name is *pupu-lare*, or *pupu*-name. The word *pupu* means forbidden, untouchable, sacred; or, more concretely, the tabu-sign or mark of property, e.g. the leaflets tied into a knot and affixed to the trunk of a coco-nut. It is commonly used to indicate the sanctity and immutability of tradition; but here, somewhat less plausibly, it has been explained as referring to the exodus from the original village of Popo, when the several groups set up sago branches or other *pupu*, i.e. marks of ownership, on the territories they had appropriated.

Although this legend savours of rationalization its implicit suggestion seems highly probable, viz. that the actual names of the several *bira'ipi* belonged really to localities.[1] At

[1] It may be that the names of the localities derived in some cases from those of

any rate they tend to do so now, although their representatives may be scattered. Thus, if we look at the diagram of Orokolo we find that each of the seven *karigara* has its recognized *bira'ipi* name (in one case the *karigara* is divided, east and west, between two *bira'ipi*). Arihava, a larger place, is divided among eleven *bira'ipi*; Yogu, a much smaller one, between two only. The names are as follows:

Arihava (west to east). Lavai'ipi, Hoirahiru, Haurahiru, Birahiru, Marea, Pakemana, Huruvu, Kaivukavu, Larihairu, Mareapavura, Aripi.

Yogu. Hairi, Maipi.

Orokolo. Avubu-Akai, Heh-Haera, Akai-Hihi (or Korova-Ravi), Haihiava, Akai, Evavu, Aripi.[1]

These stand in common use for definite places, viz. *karigara*, as well as more strictly for the people, the *bira'ipi*, to whom the places nominally belong. If we look more closely into the population of any one *karigara*, however, we shall probably find it composed of members of a number of different *bira'ipi*. A convenient way of doing this is to enumerate the hearths in the *eravo* itself, each of which belongs to a related group of men within the *karigara* (see diagram). Thus in Aivaroro Ravi (Kavava) which is commonly referred to as Aripi, we find that of 8 hearths only 1 (the foremost on the left) is Aripi; of the remaining 7, 2 are Akai, 1 Haihiava, 1 Pakemana, 1 Hairi, 1 Mareapavura, and 1 Huruvu. Other *karigara* are somewhat less mixed, and two of them, those of Ori Ravi and Hare Eravo, claim to be purely Akai-Hihi and Akai respectively. But generally speaking the *karigara*, or *eravo* community, comprises representatives of a number of *bira'ipi*. The 56 hearths in the 7 *eravo* of Orokolo[2] are distributed, very much at random, as follows: Akai, 24 (of these 8 are Akai-Hihi and 6 are Avubu-Akai); Haihiava, 7; Hairi, 5; Heh, 4; Evavu, Aripi, Birahiru, 3 each; Huruvu, Larihairu, 2 each; Pakemana, Mareapavura, Beraripi, each 1. All of these, with the sole exception of the

---

the first settlers. Thus the ancestor of Haihiava Haera is said to be Haihiava Akorevira (man-child); of Heh Haera, Heh; and of Kaivukavu Haera, Kaivukavu Akorevira. This, however, may be rationalization again.

[1] Aripi proper is in Arihava. The Orokolo Aripi is named after people who came from there.   [2] Only four *eravo* proper are now standing (1937).

last, which hails from farther east, have their nominal head-
quarters in some *karigara* or other in Orokolo Bay. What
their remoter origin was we cannot say, but it seems clear
that those *karigara* which now bear their names were at any
rate their dispersion centres in more recent times. Indeed,
there is abundant proof of this in the circumstantial accounts
of small-scale migrations or house-movings. Thus it appears
that the immediate origin of the *bira'ipi* is a local one.

It might be expected that these *bira'ipi* groups would
turn out to be subdivisions of the *aualari* groups already
enumerated. This is in part the case, but the rule by no
means works out. Thus of the three Akai *bira'ipi* in Orokolo,
one is Akai proper, while the other two are distinguished
as Akai-Hihi, and Avubu; but all claim expressly to be
Akai. Yet one is *Ahea aualari*, one *Nabo*, and one *Purari*.
Similarly, while members of Haihiava *bira'ipi* are usually
Purari, some are *Vailala*; those of Evavu *bira'ipi* are in some
cases *Auma*, in others *Ahea*, and in others *Baiu*; and so on.
All we can say is that the members of most *bira'ipi* clans
tend to belong to one *aualari* group or the other. But when,
as has frequently happened, they change their *bira'ipi* affiliation they still hold fast to their *aualari*. Hence arises the
overlapping of the two classifications.

Altogether it seems that the *bira'ipi* classification is less
fundamental and more changeable than that of the *aualari*.
It is suggested that groups of the former kind have their
origin in local aggregations, perhaps typically of kinsmen,
but in some cases composite. Once established, the local
bond tends to become a lineal bond. For in the transfer of
individuals and families from one *eravo* community to another, the *bira'ipi* affiliation tends to be retained. There are
many causes and instances of such migration and merging
into new *eravo* communities, e.g. not infrequent matrilocal
marriage, or the remarriage of a widow who brings with her
an infant child or children, or the flight from vengeance after
some quarrel or offence in the original community. Such
immigrants and their descendants commonly retain their
old *bira'ipi* connexions, and their *bira'ipi* name with it; and
thus, since small movements of the kind indicated have been

so common, we may account for the composite character of most *eravo* communities.

On the other hand, with generations of residence, there is a tendency for the fact of stranger origin to be forgotten, particularly so when the strangers are in a very small minority. Then we see a submerging of the old *bira'ipi* name. I have heard it expressly stated that the children of stray individuals in an *eravo* community should be classed with the *bira'ipi* of the majority; that is to say, brought into the fold. By the same token and in a still looser fashion all the men of any one *eravo* community are ready to be called by the name of the leading *bira'ipi* in it, although they may still retain connexion with their own *bira'ipi* proper.

The given local group becomes a descent group. It scatters for one reason or another, and the fragments of this and other groups combine into new local aggregations which in time take on the character of descent groups themselves. Without speculating as to priority of origin one can see that the border-line between the local and lineal principles of grouping is a very hazy one, and that in cases like the present the one easily fades into the other.

II

KINSMEN

The Aualari *Groups*

HAVING dealt with these somewhat fluid groups, the *bira'ipi*, which represent a transition from the local to the lineal principle, we may now pass on to note the division of our society into a number of groups whose membership is governed purely by descent. These are the *aualari* groups already mentioned. Among the Western Elema they are ten in number, and a corresponding division runs through the whole Elema people. As we go east the *aualari* groups may appear under new names; and a few are added, while others disappear. But in the main they are to be identified with those of the Western Elema.

The ten picturesquely named *aualari* groups are:

1. *Kaia*, the Sky.
2. *Ahea*, the Sea.
3. *Hurava*, the West.
4. *Purari*, the River Purari.
5. *Miri*, the Beach.
6. *Baiu* (the *ma-hevehe* at the Aivei Mouth).[1]
7. *Auma*, the small headland of that name.
8. *Vailala*, the River Vailala.
9. *Nabo*, the Nabo Mountains.
10. *Kauri*, the East.

The first of these, *Kaia* (also called *Havora'ipi* and *Huruvu*), is really divided into two, the *Akea Haera* and the *Ipi Haera*, i.e. the 'Above' and 'Below' people respectively. But despite this difference in mythological antecedents they may be treated as one. Among the others it is evident that *Ahea* has some affinities with *Hurava*, and *Purari* with *Miri*.

On a few odd occasions Western Elema informants have spoken of an eleventh, viz. *Muru*. But this lacks the essential characters which we shall find to belong to the *aualari* group,

---

[1] For *ma-hevehe* see Chapter X. There seems to be no geographical equivalent of *Baiu* as of the other *aualari*.

being only cited as possessing certain distinctive patterns
for the *hevehe* mask: it is scornfully dismissed from the category of true *aualari* by those who know. Nevertheless a
tendency to include another *aualari* and to name it after a
distinct tribe or place gives some support to the idea that
the groups may have had mostly a local origin. With the
obvious exceptions of the first two their names would be
quite in keeping with this interpretation; but, while the
writer thinks it is probably true, he has no intention here of
entering a welter of conflicting and unreliable evidence in
the endeavour to establish it.[1]

Whatever their origin may have been, the *aualari* groups
of the Western Elema now possess no local significance
whatever. Their representatives are scattered in smaller
units and families throughout the length of Orokolo Bay,
just as they are beyond it down the whole Elema coast. In a
large village you will find samples of the whole ten; in an
eravo you may find representatives of half a dozen or more.

The expression '*aualari* group' is once more an arbitrary
one, for there exists no native word for the group as such.
If you put the question, '*Ave aualari de?*', 'What is your
aualari?', you may receive as an answer one of the names
listed above, or the name of a mythical ancestor, or again
the name of one of the principal associated totems. Any one
of these indeed would be sufficient for identification, but I
found it impossible to frame the question in such a way
as to be sure of getting the name of the group itself, for the
simple reason, already stated, that the native possesses no
word for this particular social unit. In a previous publication
I spoke of them as 'sections';[2] but as that word, however non-
committal, has come to be used in a specific sense elsewhere
in anthropology, it is proposed here to adopt a designation
which, if somewhat clumsy, is at any rate distinctive.

Children belong to the *aualari* group of their fathers.

---

[1] The Keuru and Uripi tribes, whose *aualari* groups are identifiable in the main
with those listed above, acknowledge one, 'Opau', which is not found among the
Western Elema. I have no evidence that Opau is an upstart *aualari* like *Muru*, but
it is perhaps an example of the local origin of this kind of group.

[2] *Bull-Roarers in the Papuan Gulf*, Anthropology Report No. 17, Government
Printer, Port Moresby, 1936, p. 11.

There would seem to be no evidence that descent was ever anything but patrilineal. Holmes, who uses the Toaripi form of the word, viz. *ualare*, etymologizes it into *ua* (woman, wife) and *lare* (name), an analysis which he considers 'historically illuminating' because it reveals the fact that 'the totemism of the Ipi tribes' (which he has presented in its patriarchal form) 'emerged, or evolved, from a one-time matriarchal form'.[1] It is the present writer's opinion that these derivations are false; and if so the conclusion drawn from them, which has nothing else to support it, falls to the ground. As for the Orokolo word *aualari*, there is no reason to suppose that it is a corruption of the Toaripi form *ualare*. It might just as well be the other way about; or they might have a common origin which was different from either. At any rate the Western Elema word *aualari* would seem to have nothing to do with either 'woman' or 'name'.[2] It would be difficult to find a more thoroughly patrilineal organization anywhere; and, to repeat, there is no reason to imagine that it was otherwise in the past.

An understanding of the *aualari* groups is of the first importance for an appreciation of the *Hevehe* ceremonies, but it is not intended to deal with them fully at this point. It will be found that they have an intimate connexion with Western Elema mythology; indeed it may be said that each of the ten groups possesses its own body of myths, its own traditional ancestors and heroes. Furthermore each group has a large and heterogeneous following of 'totems', of species or material objects which belong to it by reason of association with the several myths. In fact it is the ancestor, hero, or totem, rather than the group itself, to which the term *aualari* applies. Lastly each group has, at any rate to some considerable extent, its own methods of private magic which are found once more to derive their force from association with the *aualari* myths. It is thought better to reserve these subjects for a later chapter, and to rest content here with noting the *aualari* as a fixed number of patrilineal

---

[1] Op. cit., p. 145.
[2] *Lare*, name, is expressly distinguished by Orokolo informants from the *-lari* in the word under discussion.

groups to which the whole of Western Elema society is apportioned.

The Patrilineal Kinship Group, Larava

We have seen that the much more numerous *bira'ipi* groups cannot be treated as neat subdivisions of these *aualari*, for there is some amount of overlapping; nor can we can say that they are constituted wholly on a basis of descent. But whereas the kinship bond of the *aualari* group at large is wholly fictitious, that of the *bira'ipi, qua* kinship group, may be to some extent a real one.

To come now to a finer division, it was observed that each of the hearths in any *eravo* acknowledged a *bira'ipi* name; and it is found in any normal instance that the hearth-holders all belong to that *bira'ipi*; further that they trace a common descent to some recent ancestor. We thus come to a consideration of real kinship.

The hearth itself is called *hurae*. The hearth-holders as a body of kinsmen are said to constitute a *larava*. There is little doubt that this word, like *ravi*, which appears in the name of practically every *eravo*, hails from the Namau. There, in the Purari Delta, the men's house, or, as it is called, the *ravi*, is a much larger and longer building, and it is divided on either side into a series of alcoves, themselves called *larava*.[1] The alcoves are formed by low partitions running from each pair of central posts to the main wall on either side, the central space remaining as a long passage. Each compartment has its own hearth and belongs to a small patrilineal unit. Now in the Elema *eravo* there are usually no such partitions, and therefore no *larava* in the corresponding sense; though, as we have seen, the word is used, by what seems an obvious misapplication, for the longitudinal sections of the whole building, both sides included. But it also stands, in a manner reminiscent of Namau usage, for the members of the kinship group who are accustomed, or at least entitled, to sleep round the hearth.

With typical vagueness it is often extended to include all

---

[1] See *Natives of the Purari Delta*, chapter vi.

the descendants of perhaps one great-great-grandfather; and it may well be that these occupy several different hearths, even in different *eravo*. While it seems plain, then, that its origin is what I have indicated, we may use the word in its larger sense.

Another expression for this group of patrilineal kinsmen who possess clear knowledge of their common origin or at least entertain no doubt of it, is *hekore haruapo*, 'one navel'.[1] I have never heard any satisfactory explanation of this vivid phrase, but if any one reads an obstetrical meaning into it there seems no reason to take it as further evidence of an original state of matriarchy.

As a contemporary group the *larava* may contain the following kinsmen, in the classificatory sense:

	Singular	Collective
Grandfathers	*birari*	*birari-ura*
Father's elder brothers . . .	,,	,,
Grandmothers (on paternal side) .	*wari*	*wari-ura*
Father's elder sisters . . .	,,	,,
Own father	*oa*	
Father's younger brothers . .	*oa-hera*	*oa-hera*
Father's younger sisters . . .	*lau-hera*	*lau-hera*
Elder brothers	*akore-apo*	*huhuhoaha*[2]
Younger brothers	*akore-heare*	*maraita*
Elder sisters	*mori-apo*	*marita-hoaha*
Younger sisters	*mori-heare*	*maraita*
Own sons	*akore*	*akorevari*[3]
Elder brother's sons . . .	,,	,,
Own daughters	*mori*	*marita*
Elder brother's daughters . .	,,	,,
Younger brother's sons and daughters	*meavo*	*meavo-hura*
Grandchildren	,,	,,

It is highly important to recognize that these terms, whether in the singular or the collective form, may be used very vaguely. Not only do they extend far beyond the *larava* even in its widest sense, but they are constantly used in regard to the members of the whole *aualari* group, the *bira'ipi*

[1] It may be noted that *larave* [*sic*] means navel-string.

[2] In full *huhu(v)o-hoaha*. This term and *maraita* were used in a much wider sense for the secludees of the batches respectively preceding and following one's own.

[3] *Akorevari* is also an inclusive term for sons *and* daughters (in full, *akorevari morita-ira*).

at large, and even fellow members of a village. Nothing is commoner indeed than to hear men speak of fellow villagers as 'brothers' when their *aualari* and *bira'ipi* are different, and when they are totally unable to establish patrilineal or any kind of kinship whatever. The common inclusive term for kin is *apo-heare*, literally 'senior-junior'. It is extremely elastic.

While the actual terms of kinship are used in this very generous and sloppy manner, there nevertheless exists a strong sense of kinship in the narrower sense, and we may say that its limits coincide, in a vague fashion, with those of the rather vague unit which we have called the *larava*. It is perhaps truistic to observe that within this group there are various degrees of intensity in the sense of kinship according to its nearness, reaching their maximum in the mutual loyalties of father, son, and true brother.

The *larava* may be called the unit of exogamy provided we remember that its boundaries are conveniently indistinct. The *aualari* group is never represented as exogamous in theory, though such statistics as I have gathered show that only a small proportion of marriages take place within it. Neither is the *bira'ipi* group exogamous, provided the contracting parties belong to different *eravo* communities. But the *larava* is represented as such by native theorists or moralists. It is true that the breaches of the rule—and I have recorded a number—do not seem to be regarded in any serious light, and in certain cases there seems a tendency on the part of some at any rate of the elders to encourage them. This may happen when an *eravo* community or a hamlet is comparatively homogeneous in its patrilineal composition and when in any particular family there is a preponderance of female children. The father of a girl or girls who has no son is loath to see his daughter carried off, perhaps to some distant village, when there is no prospect of replacing her by a daughter-in-law; moreover, apart from practical considerations, he is fond of his child and wants to keep her near. In such circumstances he is not averse to her marriage with a kinsman, and in the absence of any real objection in other quarters such marriages are not uncommon. It may be said that such practical and sentimental considerations often come into conflict with the principle of exogamy, and sometimes win.

The solidarity of the *larava* is best, or at any rate most spectacularly, revealed in the village brawl, called *hihiri* when it is a matter of words only, *hahari* when it turns to one of sticks (there are no stones). A quarrel between individuals need not implicate their kinsmen provided they merely argue at a distance—and such quarrels are often no more than long-range bombardments, each combatant sitting on his house veranda. But if it is a stand-up argument there is likely to be a ring; and if one or the other strikes a blow, then the respective kinsmen may be caught up in the whirl of a faction fight.

Sympathy is thus often determined by kinship, but of course it is not always so. A man may commit some offence and fail entirely to enlist the support of his kinsmen in the resultant brawl. It is the not-uncommon outcome of such a situation for the offender to pack up and leave his village, and not a little of the dispersion of *bira'ipi* groups which we previously noted has been due to such flights from a community which is in part vengeful and wholly unsympathetic. Nor can it be said that the near kinship group is always at peace within itself. Examples of quarrels, infidelities, and violence are not wanting to show that even brothers may fall apart. But such inter-kin dissensions are regarded as especially deplorable and it is obvious that in any really serious form they are exceptional.

The kinship group identifies itself with the individual member in the important duty of finding him a wife: they get together the shell ornaments—things of vital concern to Elema natives—which go to make up the bride-price, and the bride's kin on their part get together the almost equivalent ornaments which are given in return. It is true that the immediate families are the most deeply interested parties, but the *larava* groups on either side are concerned. The marriage is a bond between them, and they show their interest and goodwill in this typical way, by an exchange of gifts.

The ownership of land is nominally vested in the *bira'ipi*.

But in effect it is subdivided among the various *larava*; and if, as happens often enough, the *larava* itself subdivides, the ownership of its land undergoes a further partition. The head of the group is in nominal control: but the actual use of the land is freely given, as when the whole *eravo* community, irrespective of kinship, makes its common garden on a chosen site which belongs to one of its constituent *larava*.

It would be possible to enumerate further points illustrating the unity of the *larava* kin group—co-operation in the provision of death-feasts, in the initiations of juvenile members, in trading expeditions, in sorcery feuds, and so on. But it would not do to over-emphasize the solidarity of kin in Western Elema society, or to seek to isolate it unduly from other kinds of organization. The *larava* merely plays its part along with other institutions, sometimes predominant and sometimes wholly subordinate. In the *Hevehe* ceremonies it will be found sometimes to be swamped in the larger unity of the *eravo*.

The Family

For the ultimate kinship unit, the social cell or molecule, viz. the family, there is no one word in regular use. A man will speak of his wife and children as *arave lau akorevari*, 'my mother-and-children' inclusively. This is a recognized phrase; but another, which is sometimes used to cover the whole family group, viz. *harokokore*, is one of those words upon which informants disagree. There are no lexicographers to lay down rules among the Elema, and it can only be said that *harokokore* is used by some to mean 'man, wife, and children', by others to mean simply 'wife'. It is said to be an old-fashioned word, still used in the language of the Muru tribe. At Orokolo it seems to pass mostly as a humorous synonym for *uva*, wife. But the absence of a set phrase for 'family' does not, of course, imply that the native is unaware of it as a clearly defined unit. We have already had difficulty in naming the larger groups, but they exist and function and are recognized. The individual family, whether named or not, is a unit which every one can grasp.

It is normally monogamous though hardly so strictly monogamous as was claimed by Holmes. Comparing the Elema favourably with the Namau (whose polygamy was 'synonymous with unbridled sexual passion' and whose social and moral life was 'a foul quagmire of sexual bestiality') he found among the former tribe a 'sacred law of monogamy'. The sacredness, and indeed the law, must, I think, be questioned. If in the course of fifteen years he discovered only two breaches of it, it must have been either that he did not look for them or else that the practice of polygamy came suddenly into vogue after he had left the country. For in the Annual Report of 1920-1 appears a tabulation of polygamous marriages throughout various taxable parts of the Territory, and the tribes of the Gulf Coast come second on the list. Whatever the explanation of this discrepancy may be, bigamous marriages are not regarded nowadays with any disfavour. I noted fifteen incidentally between Arihava and Auma.[1] Allowing for others that were not noticed, the proportion certainly remains a small one, but it cannot be said that there is any social disapproval involved. It is the not uncommon choice of a widow to add herself to the household of a man already married; and more than this, it was recognized as permissible, if somewhat unusual, for a youth on emerging from seclusion to marry two girls simultaneously.

Both wives, where there are two, usually live (at peace or otherwise) in the same house with their husband. But jealousy between polygamous wives being fairly common, the monogamous husband is prone to profess that he would not take another spouse if he had the chance. In the vast majority of cases, then, the household consists of husband, one wife, and their children. But since building is slow work and the materials rather perishable we find many households giving temporary or permanent shelter to other relatives— brothers and their wives, daughters and their husbands,

---

[1] Only two cases of husbands with three wives were noted, one in Pareamamu, one in Vailala.

widowed parents, or orphan children, and so on. There are several hearths or sleeping-mats in each, and these become the recognized places of the various members of the household.[1]

Marriages are mostly permanent and a man and his wife get on well together provided she is faithful, a good worker, reasonably obedient, and punctual with his meals. 'Wife-beating' is common enough, but we must not imagine a man belabouring his woman into submission. The beating consists at most of an angry blow or two, or perhaps a kick with the sole of the foot, and the wife does not take it lying down but breaks into shrill abuse, paying him back with her tongue. She may go to the length of absenting herself for a period, taking refuge with her own people; and if there are continued disagreements she can leave her husband permanently and the union is severed by the restitution of ornaments. A good many women, boiling with indignation and displaying a bruise or weal, sometimes severe but sometimes hardly visible to the naked eye, have appeared before me at different times to make complaint against their husbands. Without possessing any magisterial authority I make a point of hearing the 'case' for other reasons, and usually dismiss it finally with words of comfort and a stick of tobacco. Amid a variety of more or less trivial causes the most frequent is certainly a breakdown in the cooking arrangements.

More serious misdemeanours, those of sexual infidelity, find their way eventually to the Magistrate at Kerema. In native custom they commonly led to violent retaliation against the male concerned,[2] while the wife might be severely handled by an enraged husband, though she was not necessarily divorced. As Holmes has pointed out, sexual regulations among the Elema are much stricter than those of their next-door neighbours the Namau. There is nothing to compare with the temporary exchange of wives and their

[1] The native, amid conditions not on the whole encouraging to privacy, shows a liking for a little place all his own; even in the *eravo* boys like to build cubby-holes to which they mount by precarious ladders.

[2] Adultery is made a criminal offence for natives in Papua, the justification being that punishment by the Government precludes violent retribution.

common prostitution (practices which are socially approved in the Purari Delta), but on the other hand a very strict standard of marital fidelity.[1] This is not to say that the rules are always kept, but it accounts for the rather high degree of sexual jealousy evinced by males, and, further, for the promptitude with which busybodies report what they think to be misconduct. Perhaps the immediate conviction on all sides, regardless of sound evidence, that such reports are true, argues a general belief that women are much more seducible than is overtly supposed.

The mother normally cooks for the family and there are no fussy restrictions on commensality. The children, brothers and sisters, will eat together from the same bowl, but as they grow up they separate at meals as in other less important things. Youths and maidens even of the same family would hardly submit to eating in each other's company under any circumstances; while, as for lovers, the method of approach so popular among ourselves would be regarded as simply hateful. Husband and wife, however, having got over their shyness, may share the same dish; though a husband who eats too often at home is condemned —not for uxoriousness, which is nobody's concern, but for failing to bring his food with him to the *eravo*.

The sons of the household live with their parents until they grow big enough, at about the age of 12, to move to the *baupa eravo*. Henceforward they will sleep and eat there, carrying pots of food across from their mothers' fire-places just as do the men of the *eravo* proper. Under these conditions boys show more independence of the family than do their sisters. They work willingly enough at men's tasks on occasion, but spend a great deal of time loafing with their fellows in the *baupa eravo*, or in aimless expeditions to the bush. The boys of like age in the *eravo* community thus form a small band of mates whose mutual loyalty, determined by constant association from childhood, will

[1] Occasional expeditions of Goaribari natives from the R. Kikori elude the Government regulations and find their way to Orokolo Bay. The purpose of these expeditions is to prostitute the Goaribari wives for shell ornaments, and, however high the standards of sexual morality observed among the Elema themselves, the visitors may be said to do a roaring trade.

last them, whether real kinsmen or not, throughout their lives.

Towards their children both fathers and mothers show a good deal of indulgence, especially in their early years. Of deliberate training there is obviously very little; of chastisement administered with a sorrowful hand with a view to moral correction, none at all. If a father occasionally uses corporal punishment upon his children it is of the same sort as he gives his wife, though somewhat less severe; that is to say, hardly more than one angry blow or a shove, accompanied by a sudden brief burst of scolding. He then redirects his attention to whatever matter of adult interest was previously occupying it. One never sees a father using the metaphorical iron rod. He would hardly know how to do so. From childhood the boy begins to enjoy that peculiar private independence of will and action which seems to characterize the primitive society, however hidebound by custom. Fathers do not order their children about; and no full-grown native is ordered about by any one. So foreign to his mind is the idea of personal control by one individual over another that it is practically impossible to get one man to speak for another in the latter's absence, even to guess what he will do. The answer is always 'His desire; He himself'. Of all those who might be called chiefs among the Western Elema there is none who can bring himself to say 'This or that will be done'. No more will a father commit himself about the conduct of his boys, so that the schooling in personal independence (negative, as it is, rather than positive) begins early. Direct coercion of individuals is not thought of; least of all physical coercion.

Unlike their brothers, the daughters of the household continue to live in it up to the time of their marriage. They are thrown much more into the company of their mothers and other women of the household or the immediate neighbourhood, for there is nothing to correspond to the men's club-house. On the whole they lend their aid very willingly in cooking, sago-making, fishing, and all the other domestic tasks of women, and yet find ample leisure for lolling on the beach in one another's idle company.

Marriage and Affinal Relations

We may postpone considering relations with the maternal kin until after dealing with those set up by marriage, for the most important of the former, viz. that between nephew and maternal uncle, may be viewed as following on from the relations between brothers-in-law or between brother and married sister.

Every female—bar serious disability—and practically every male in due course marries and thereupon enters a new system of relationships. Apart from his responsibilities as a prospective parent the husband has now to deal with the kin of his spouse.

There are no severe restrictions upon marriage among the Western Elema. We have noted the somewhat elastic idea of *larava* exogamy together with the fact that it may be disregarded without any serious social results. Several cases of marriage between second cousins in the patrilineal line have been recorded, but none between first cousins. On the other side there is no actual prohibition of marriage with the mother's kin at large, but no examples of marriage with the mother's near kin. A girl may marry her classificatory *aukau* (maternal uncle), but certainly not her true mother's brother; and there is no marriage between true cross-cousins. As for positive regulations in respect of kinship, they are entirely absent. There is no predicting where a boy or a girl will find a mate, and parents refuse to admit any foreknowledge until arrangements have been actually set on foot. If you ask them they will simply answer, 'Who can tell?' I do not know of any case of a marriage forced by parents.

There are, however, tendencies to restrict marriage to age-mates and—very vaguely—to certain local communities. The first of these restrictions has the general support of public opinion. Girls, though never themselves secluded, fall into corresponding groups with the boys. They are commonly spoken of as *hii haruapo*—'the same perineal band'—with the batch of boys who underwent seclusion and received their *hii* at approximately the same time; and this expression persists though seclusion and the presentation of *hii* have practically died out. It was generally expected that the boys, who married soon after their emergence, would find mates among their coevals. This is what generally happens, and thus the available girls are snapped up. Widows may marry older men; but a girl who married out of her age-group might be 'laughed at on the beach'.

The effect of locality upon marriage resolves itself into a natural tendency to find mates near home which is re-inforced, as we have seen, by the common desire of parents to keep their daughters by them. There is admittedly no rule in the matter. A young man who brings a bride from a distance rather gets credit for it. They say he is a strong fellow with lots of pluck, and his achievement is regarded as something of a victory over the other village. The people of this other village, however, are not so pleased. They have lost a girl. 'But', they say, 'wait till next time, and one of our boys will make it square.' There is a sort of rivalry in the matter, and mostly quite good-humoured. But it may lead to a rough and ready exchange or balance between com-munities, such as those of Auma, the several *karigara* of which were ready to tally up recent marriages one against the other.[1]

Courtship, with these very light restrictions upon it, goes on mainly by day in the bush where youths make assigna-tions or waylay their sweethearts. The beach, even by night, is too exposed, for lovers are extremely bashful in the public eye. There is no 'necking' to be seen at Orokolo; in fact any kind of love-approaches in the open would be regarded as unseemly and ridiculous. The beach, therefore, is only useful to lovers for showing off at a distance and for a little fugitive making of eyes; perhaps also on certain moonlight evenings when the tide is low and youths and girls may come into closer contact in the uncertain light and under cover of mob games and horse-play. But their love-making by night is mostly conducted in the girl's house. The youth knows her sleeping-place and, previously invited, he climbs up when the village is asleep, which is usually quite early. Such courting is spiced with adventure, for a wakeful father may

---

[1] I did not put this idea to the test anywhere else.

demand an explanation; but it is declared on all sides to be very common, so that we can only conclude that parents are often accommodating or else very heavy sleepers.

Sexual freedom before marriage is not socially condoned, though this is not to say that the rule against it is not frequently broken. Even if we are not ready to take the admissions or boasts of various boys at their face value, the recorded cases of prenuptial pregnancy, together with the disapproval and scandal which accompany them, prove on the one hand that the rule is a stringent one, and on the other that, however stringent, it is evaded. The mistake, here as elsewhere, is that of being found out.

Lovers exchange presents. The boy makes gifts of betel, tobacco, pocket-knives, and so on; the girl may or may not return them in the shape of a nose-bone or some other pretty trinket. But if she is in the habit of accepting his presents she has virtually accepted his suit. The boy confides— probably indirectly, for he is afflicted intensely with *maioka*, or shame—in his parents, and they make formal representations to the parents of the girl. If they are willing—their daughter having confirmed their assent—they agree to receive the *obo-eva*, or preliminary payment.

The actual giving of this preliminary payment, called *maiepakive*, establishes a betrothal. It may consist merely of a rooster, one or two ornaments, and a few pots of food, or it may be much more pretentious—a full-sized pig and quite a number of ornaments. It may, again, be paid in several instalments. But after the first payment the girl is pledged to the boy; she has been publicly betrothed. Henceforward she is supposed to entertain no other lover; and she should be discreet, going to fetch water in company with her mother rather than alone. The deed of *maiepakive* is done nominally when the boy is an *erekai-akore*, or 'belted boy', that is, while he is still wearing the light belt of *oro* bark with a pubic tassel, and before he has acquired a *hii* or perineal band. He is now at liberty to enter his seclusion (or in these modern times may go off and sign on for a year or two's labour) in the fair confidence that his girl will remain constant in her affections.

The *obo-eva*, which may mean the 'seeing ornaments',[1] i.e. the payment which brings the matter before the public eye, is given to the parents of the bride, or whoever stands as her guardian. These ornaments are a direct payment. Unlike those of the larger payment which is to follow, none of them are refunded to the givers, nor are they distributed among the bride's kinsmen at large. When once they have been handed over the girl is expected to help her future husband's parents at sago-making and other such work.

Until a year or so ago the preliminaries to marriage were pleasantly spectacular. His seclusion over, the boy emerged together with his mates in the well-fed, befeathered, and mop-haired beauty of a *hoaho-akore*. During the few weeks that followed he and his mates, one after the other, would claim their brides. That is to say, each would go to the house of his betrothed by night and lead her off to that of his parents. She went as a rule willingly, for on the one hand she was pledged to go, and on the other, perhaps, she found the young man in his pride and finery quite irresistible. No ceremony whatever attached to his removal of the young bride. She was made at home by the bridegroom's mother, while he went off to sleep in the *baupa eravo*. Not until the *hoaho-akore* had turned themselves into *are-bira*, that is to say, when several weeks later they had put aside most of their decorations and bound up their mops of hair, did the young husbands assert their sexual rights: to do so prematurely would mean that their hair would fall out. Thus personal vanity overcame desire. But when they had agreed, more or less simultaneously, to bind up their hair, there was no fear that one would outshine another, so a young man might tell his bride to accompany him to the garden, and in the bush there took place what was supposed to be their first act of intercourse. Nowadays, when the practice of seclusion may be said to have ceased, individual marriages pursue the same course, but there is no longer the social mating season with its picturesque accompaniment.

The betrothal and preliminary payment are regarded as

---

[1] *obo* is the Uaripi word for 'eye'; the Orokolo form is *obohae*, which may mean, not very prettily, the 'egg of the eye'.

good form, giving satisfaction to the bride's people from the beginning. But it seems always to have been recognized that these may be dispensed with; a youth may abduct a girl, and the first thing her parents know about her marriage is that she has disappeared. No father or mother, however, takes this sort of thing lightly. There is a morning uproar in the home and a louder one when they discover where the girl has found shelter. It sometimes happens—I have recorded a number of cases of the kind—that the parents, supported by kinsmen, bring home their daughter with execrations and blows. But the matter is usually settled in the long run; payment is made, and this sort of marriage is as permanent as the other.

The bride having been brought home in one way or the other to the husband's house, his kinsmen now begin to get together the ornaments—called generally the *eva*—which are to constitute the payment proper. This is the main responsibility of the father, or the nearest senior male relative; but items are added by others, by the mother and by uncles, brothers, and sisters; and these together add up to far more than the contribution of the father. When, after a fortnight or so, they have been accumulated in sufficient quantity, they are tied to a long pole—and a very pretty show they make—and thus carried by a party of women to the bride's house and delivered to her parents. The bride herself accompanies them but the young husband bashfully makes himself scarce, nor need any males join the party except for a couple to carry the live pig which forms an important part of the bride-price.

The ornaments on the pole fall into two shares, which may be marked off by two loops of dogs' teeth, a longer and a shorter. Those constituting the former share have been contributed by the kinsmen of the bridegroom, and are to be divided among those of the bride, who will in due course return an exact equivalent. Those constituting the latter have been contributed by the bridegroom's father himself (or the person who stands in his stead) and are destined for the father of the bride. For some of them he will make a like return; others he keeps outright. The pig, or maybe more than one, is a direct payment for which no return is made.

The kinsmen of the bride come presently to take their share. They may be seen gathered round the pole, which has been set up before the house, critically examining the ornaments, or perhaps sitting round the mat on which they have

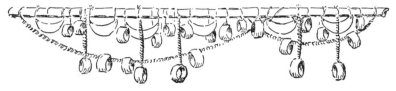

FIG. 3. *Eva*–bride-price on Pole

The loop of dog's teeth on left marks off the ornaments for exchange. That on the right marks off those to be kept by bride's parents

been laid in a pile. They consist of conus shell armlets (*huaiea*); crescent pearl shells (*aitave*); frontlets (*apakora*) made of overlapping white shell disks; dogs' teeth (*maki*) pierced at the root and sewn neatly in a line; boars' tusks (*huka*); and strings of small white shells (*movio*). The major ornaments, *huaiea* and *aitave*, vary much in size and finish, and are valued accordingly; also in their degree of uncleanness, which is a matter of no moment. *En masse*, despite a certain griminess (which indeed does not always detract from their appearance) the ornaments have their own richness and beauty—the dead white of the circular armshell, the iridescent half-moon of the pearl, the overlapping disks of the frontlet in nicely graded crescendo and diminuendo, and above all the serried line of dogs' teeth, in soft browns and creams of polished ivory.

His shell ornaments are things of intense interest to the native. Not that he often wears them. Indeed you will hardly ever see them on a human being except at a formal presentation. They are hoarded in pots (concealed in a corner of the house) or kept under lock and key of a trade box. They are possibly treasured all the more for the absence of display. At any rate they are the wealth of the people in its most concentrated form, and we shall see how often the bestowal of them, or their transfer from one to another, forms the culminating point of a ceremony.

Now the kinsmen of the bride are carefully picking them over or sitting back and looking at them with narrowed eyes. They have brought ornaments of their own, and these they presently extract from their bags. Very deliberately they unfold the packing of dry leaf, and compare the contents with the particular specimens which, knowing the value of their own, they have selected on sight as suitable for exchange. Armshells are flicked with the finger-nail to see if they ring true; *aitave* are turned this way and that; *apakora* are laid side by side and the disks counted. A man does not want to be done; and on the other hand he does not want to make an unfair bargain. He wants to give value for value; and, as exchanges can be no more than approximate, he will eventually take up a piece and lay down his own with an air of 'Near enough!' There is a good deal of conversation and a great deal of passing from hand to hand, so that one is amazed that the ornaments of bride's and bridegroom's kin do not become hopelessly mixed. But at long last the pieces to be given in exchange are laid down on the *aroa*, or string bag, which is spread out on the mat. It has been stretched tight by a half-circle of cane, and the ornaments are now attached to the mesh, while those which no one has come forward to take, or any which are rejected because of flaws, are put inside it for return. Meanwhile those which were meant specially for the bride's father he has himself taken charge of. He has stowed them away in his pot or his box; but he will have extracted a few of his own, not the equivalent of all he has received, to add to those on the *aroa*.

This business of distributing and assembling ornaments takes at least some few days at the home of the bride's father. Her escort of women meanwhile have returned; but she remains with her father until the *aroa* has been made ready. Then she makes a rather special toilet and dons her best *mae*, or sago-leaf skirt. Her father gives her an armshell or two to wear and hangs some dogs' teeth to her ears and some ornaments about her neck. These are her *karave-ve-eharu*, or 'neck ornaments', her dowry, a gift from her parents which remains her personal property. They have also prepared a substantial and practical trousseau (*haruku*) or paraphernalia —viz. fish-nets (*keve* and *iviri*), pots (*eraa* and *haida*), a coco-nut bowl (*hekako*), a coco-nut spoon (*arita*), &c., all stuffed as far as may be into a capacious string bag (*ouraa*); and to these housekeeping essentials they probably add a sucking pig and a puppy. Thus, amid an escort of girls and women who carry the various items of her *haruku*, she goes off with her *aroa* on her back to take up life as a fully recognized spouse, paid for and fitted out, in her husband's village.[1]

It will be seen that the larger portion of the *eva* tied to the pole is accepted on the understanding that the equivalent, ornament for ornament, will be returned tied to the string bag *aroa*. It is thus to that extent a case of equal exchange. To seek an economic justification for it is obviously futile: its function, like that of many other exchange presents, is presumably to declare and establish goodwill between the two groups of kin who are brought into relation by the marriage.

There are no further collective presents between the kin-groups, but they continue between the parties most closely concerned, viz. the married couple on the one hand and the woman's brothers on the other. The brothers-in-law are reciprocally *akira*, and on various ceremonial occasions, as at *Hevehe* and *Kovave*, the wife's brothers will give her further ornaments, which she and her husband repay with pigs. Between the reciprocal *akira* it is thought desirable to maintain good feeling, and although there are occasional breakdowns and estrangements, the relations nominally remain what they should be. There are no avoidances to be observed, and *akira* treat one another in a perfectly ordinary manner. One helps the other, e.g. in house-building, or they may join in making sago from a tree which belongs to one of them. In the not infrequent cases of matrilocal marriage they become neighbours, and they may share the same dwelling.

---

[1] On the remarriage of widows a smaller payment is made by the second husband to the kinsmen of the first, i.e. to the individual or individuals (or their heirs) who actually gave the *obo-eva* and that part of the *eva* for which there was no refund.

PLATE 10

The bride-price, *Eva*, and some of the donors

A bride returning from her
father's house with ornaments
given in exchange

The Maternal Kin: Aukau *and* Arivu

Now when in due course a child is born, matters take a fresh turn. Gifts from brother to sister and return gifts of pigs will not stop, but the wife's brothers are now laid under a new obligation: they are *aukau* to the child, whom they

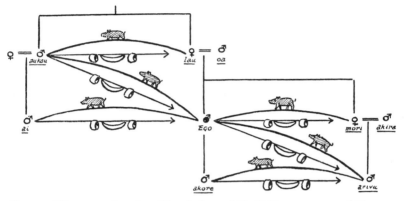

Fig. 4. Diagram showing Circulation of Shell Ornaments and Return Presents of Pig

call *arivu*, and they must make presents in future to the *arivu* as well. The terms are classificatory, but there is one of the brothers who becomes *aukau-havahu*, i.e. the 'proper' *aukau*, and it is his special business to give presents to the child. If, as must often be the case, the woman has no brother, or not enough brothers to cope with an increasing family of children, then one or other of her kinsmen, sometimes of the older generation, will undertake the duties of *aukau-havahu* to each individual child. The ornament gifts are always acknowledged by counter-gifts of pig or pig-meat, and the direction remains constant. It is the uncle (*aukau*) who gives the ornaments, and the nephew (*arivu*)—or his parents for him in his earlier years—who gives the pig.

In the case of a girl-child the *aukau* continues to give presents only up to her marriage. From that point the present-giving duty towards her is taken over by the girl's brothers as we have already seen, and the same cycle begins in another set of circumstances, those brothers becoming eventually *aukau* to the girl's children.[1]

In the case of a boy-child, however, the *aukau*, or some one representing him, continues to give presents and receive pigs up till his *arivu*'s death. If the *aukau* predeceases the *arivu* (as, being a generation older, he must probably do), the obligation falls on the shoulders of his son, i.e. the boy's *ai*. *Ai* is a reciprocal term used by male cross-cousins; and the exchanges continue between the two; one *ai* gives ornaments, the other pigs, and always in the same old way. The mother's brother gave ornaments to his sister's son; so the mother's brother's son continues to give ornaments to his father's sister's son.

The diagram on p. 61 will show how these gifts, which are virtually obligatory, serve to keep the shell ornaments in circulation.[2]

The mother's kin, of her generation, are referred to as *aukahura*, a collective term for *aukau*; of one's own generation, as *aiape*, collective for *ai*. And just as there is a desire, duly reciprocated, to keep on generally good terms with the people of one's wife, so there is a desire, reciprocated once more, to keep on good terms with the people of one's mother. It is, so to speak, an inherited *entente*. Your father and mother were always giving pigs to your mother's brothers and getting ornaments in return; so you continue the tradition of giving pigs to, and receiving ornaments from, the same group of people—your father's affines and your own maternal kindred.

This relationship may, it is true, come to an abrupt end as the result of a quarrel, for the Western Elema, like other people, can be extremely huffy, and no matters are better calculated to provoke recriminations than the quality of ornaments and the size of pigs. But normally it goes on till you are dead. Then it is brought formally to an end by a final gift of ornaments, this time, and for the first time,

---

[1] The last gift of an *aukau* to his female *arivu* is spoken of as *eva-hoa-koarapakive* (ornaments-finish-cut-off). Now that she is married she must look elsewhere.

[2] The counter-gifts are not always whole pigs; they may be joints, quarters, &c. At any rate the pigs are given to be eaten: there is no actual circulation of live animals among the Elema.

in the opposite direction. When a man dies his younger brother is responsible for getting together his *haro-eharu*— his 'head-things' or head-ornaments. They consist largely of the property of the dead man himself, but are added to by those of his kin who feel called upon to help. The ornaments contributed by these latter are eventually repaid in kind, but those which belonged to the deceased are kept, and this final gift is said to 'cut off', to put an end to, the exchanges between a man and his *aukahura* and *aiape*. It is spoken of as a repayment for all the ornaments which they have given him during his life. Of course it does not represent more than a small fraction of them, for they have been continually repaid with pigs. But it is a symbolic payback, and thus represents a posthumous termination of the relations between a man and his maternal kindred.

Upon the death of a woman the *haro eharu* is paid, not to her *aukahura* but to her brothers. This, it will be observed, is in logical keeping with the fact that it is her brothers who, since her marriage, have undertaken the duty of giving her presents.

Native sociologists sometimes put another interpretation on the *haro eharu*, particularly in the case of women. They regard it, not as a restitution or payback, but as a placatory payment to the community from which the deceased woman originally came. It is to buy off their suspicions of sorcery as the cause of death. There is no doubt that members of both communities have this consideration in view, and it may actually represent the origin of the custom, the other explanation, viz. that of repayment, being only subsidiary. But it may be noted that in cases of matrilocy the *haro eharu* is still paid over, and there is no doubt—whatever its origin may be—that it stands as the final rite announcing the close of gift-exchange relations. The estate, so to speak, is clear of debt.

To return to that important person in Western Elema life, the *aukau*, we find that he is called upon to officiate in a whole succession of ceremonial duties. The presents which he gives are bestowed in connexion with them—at ear-piercing, nose-piercing, initiations to Bull-Roarer and

Kovave, at seclusion, and at *Hevehe*. Nor when the youth has passed through all these ceremonies do the gifts of ornaments cease. They go on almost to old age. Fathers putting their sons through one ceremony or another may receive ornaments appropriate to their age from their own *aukau* or *ai* (just as elderly women may receive them from their brothers). The opportunity is found at the 'prize-giving' with which the major ceremonies come to an end, for every such ceremony means the killing of many pigs.

The *aukau* is expected to perform certain duties in connexion with these ceremonies as his *arivu* passes through them; he is the surgeon who sticks the septum on the nose; he presents the new bull-roarer; and so on. And he is acknowledged as the boy's mentor. It is true that the duties are performed somewhat perfunctorily and sometimes altogether scamped; while his moral advice may be confined to the harangues (sometimes directed less at the *arivu* himself than at his parents) by which present-giving and other rites are accompanied. But when circumstances are favourable, when, for instance, the *aukau* does not live too far away, he may see a good deal of his nephew. The latter is expected to help him at his work, and there are cases to show that he will stand by him in a brawl. It cannot be said, however, that the *aukau* in the normal instance possesses any authority over his *arivu*. That, such as it is, belongs to the father. I have noted only one case in which an *aukau* took it upon himself to chastise a child, and (as a direct result) it was one of those few cases where the friendly relations of two *akira* closed abruptly in a disgraceful row.

Altogether it may be safely said that personal relations, attitudes, mutual services, and the rest, between *aukau* and *arivu* fade into insignificance compared with the vital matters of ornaments and pigs. Life in the home and community is largely self-sufficient. A man is first of all son of his father, brother of his brethren, member of his *eravo*. He may perhaps see his *auka hura* only on rare occasions, and then he treats them much like any other seniors. But he must 'keep good' with them, because of this all-important business of exchange.

The function of the exchange in a social sense (it lacks any economic justification) is apparently to maintain good relations between the individuals and groups concerned. And yet it would almost seem that the position has been reversed. Exchange of gifts, from being a means to social concord, has attracted so much attention and aroused such intense feeling that it has become definitely an end in itself. If it is true that you exchange gifts in order to remain friends, it is also true that you must remain friends in order to exchange gifts. Shell ornaments and pigs are two great passions of the Western Elema, as of so many other Papuans. And while *aukau* and *arivu* may be fond of one another, their mutual indispensability does not rest on sentimental, but on other, grounds. It is true, in a sense, and no insult either, to say that ornaments are more than uncles, pigs than maternal nephews.

The Place of Kinship in Social Organization

In this and the preceding chapter we have been speaking of kinship and locality as principles of social organization, and we shall go on to consider still further principles as they find illustration in the present social setting. It seems evident that in different societies the various principles may have different weight, and it seems the right moment to indulge in a brief digression in order to declare the opinion that kinship, to which so much importance is commonly attached by anthropologists, carries in this particular society rather less weight than would appear usual. It may be that the Western Elema will be considered atypical; but the writer's experience with other primitive societies in Papua largely confirms his own impression, unorthodox and even presumptuous though it may be, that kinship as a principle of social organization and as a determinant of social conduct is sometimes ridden too hard.

The list of relationship-terms has in this book been relegated to an appendix. The only comments I feel inclined to make will refer to a thesis which, even in its extreme forms, has, I believe, some respectable support, viz. that each different relationship-term indicates a certain attitude together with its appropriate conduct, towards the persons of whom it is used.

Now in some cases this is obviously the case, particularly at what we may call, in the kinship sense, close quarters. But the farther outwards the classificatory term extends the hazier its implications become, until they are practically lost to view. This much would be generally admitted: one's true elder brother (*akoreapo*) is nearer than one's first cousin in the patrilineal line, and one's first cousin nearer than one's third, fourth, or fifth. They are all called *akoreapo*, but the mutual loyalties involved decrease, as one might well expect, as the relationship recedes into genealogical distance.

But in Western Elema society we find the term *akoreapo* (elder brother), as likewise *akoreheare* (younger brother), employed in a manner which we may almost call indiscriminate. It is, indeed, used constantly for all the fellow members of one's community, regardless of their descent; and it may be used without a thought for kindred on the mother's side as well as the father's. The term *ai* (cross-cousin) is only an alternative for *akoreapo* or *akoreheare*. Again and again an informant has spoken of such-and-such a person as his 'brother', and then, when we have sifted out the connexion, has added casually, 'Of course he is my *ai* also.' Among all the people, then, whom an Orokolo native calls *akoreapo* or *akoreheare* there is some very considerable diversity of attitudes involved; some are true patrilineal kin with whom the speaker identifies himself most closely and towards whom he feels the strongest loyalties; some are matrilineal kin with whom relations are more artificial, having to be sustained by mutual gifts of a specific kind which are never made between patrilineal kin; and some are not kin at all but bound to the speaker only by neighbourliness.

Again it might seem that there should be a distinct difference between one's attitudes toward *akoreapo* and *akoreheare* respectively. This is indeed the case within the family or the narrow kinship unit; they are attitudes of deference and superiority respectively. But within the wider circle of those whom a man calls generally *apo-heare*, i.e. senior-plus-junior kinsmen collectively, it is very frequently found that he hesitates when it comes to a question, not knowing whether such and such an individual is his *akoreapo* or his *akoreheare*; or perhaps he first speaks of him as the one and then discovers on reflection, or by appeal to some one else, that he is the other. Such uncertainty does not argue any carefully observed attitude in accordance with the term, since the man in question obviously does not know which of the theoretical attitudes he should adopt. The truth is, of course, that he simply does not think about it.

Again the terms *akoreapo* and *akoreheare* are used in a thorough-going classificatory sense; that is to say the son of your father's elder brother is your *akoreapo* even if he is born after you, and vice versa with the son of your father's younger brother. But the attitude of deference and superiority which you use respectively towards your true *akoreapo* and *akoreheare*, your own brothers, are not carried on to an *akoreapo* who is your junior and an *akoreheare* who is your senior merely because they are known by these terms. The difference in years is sometimes quite considerable, and if a man's *akoreapo* is a youngster, then he treats him, generally speaking, like any other youngster, and throughout life continues to use the advantage which his extra years have given him.

As another instance we may take the term *birari* which means both grandfather and father's elder brother. The one, granted his personality is equal to it, will be one of the real rulers of the *eravo* community, a right reverend; the other will be merely the father's contemporary, one of the men of the village. The relationship-terms are identical, but one's respective attitudes toward the relatives in question will be strikingly different. When we come to the conduct of the *Hevehe* ceremony we shall see how wide the difference is.

Similarly the *meavore* stands for grandchild and for younger brother's child. One's elder brother's and one's own children are *akore*; they are more or less contemporary with the children of one's younger brother and the attitude is therefore similar towards all of them. While the last-mentioned

are classed under the same term as grandchildren, they are
not of necessity treated like grandchildren. Nor is the
younger brother's wife treated like the son's wife, although
both go under the same term, *evera*.

Lastly, as a *reductio ad absurdum* of the claim that a relationship always indicates a specific line of conduct, we have the
universal practice of calling one's daughter and her husband
by the same term, *mori* (daughter); one's elder sister and
her husband by the same, *moriapo* (elder sister); and one's
younger sister and her husband by the same, *moriheare*
(younger sister).[1] Apart from the fact that we are dealing
with a society where the lives of the sexes are so widely
separated, we may note that the attitudes of father to daughter, or brother to sister, on the one hand, are fundamentally
different from their attitudes towards the women's husbands. It is one of fondness or loyalty in the first instance;
in the second, one of much more distant friendship and
looser attachment, sometimes, indeed, with an admixture of
antagonism.

The distribution of relationship-terms of any society must,
of course, have something to account for it, and no doubt
indicates in an important way the general structure of that
society. But it is suggested that their present use may rest in
no small degree upon their past history and origin—problems which are for the most part quite beyond solution—
and that it is unreasonable to attempt to correlate each and
every one of them with specific social attitudes at the present day.

Altogether, the present writer can say with confidence
of this society that it is not so overmastered and hidebound
by ties of kinship as some other societies are, or as primitive
society in general is usually said to be.

---

[1] Not to mention f.eld.s. and f.eld.s.h. = *uwari* (grandmother); f.y.s. and f.y.s.h. =
lau (mother); m.eld.s. and m.eld.s.h. = *uwari*; m.y.s. and m.y.s.h. = *lau*; w.s. and
w.s.h. = *moriapo* or *moriheare*.

III

FRIENDS AND AGE-MATES

Friendship, Informal and Formal

IT seems generally true that human relations in primitive
society are more stereotyped than in ours. But of course
—and one feels almost glad to observe it—the personal
attraction of individuals towards one another, independent
of any formal bond, is by no means absent. As one of the
means of uniting people, therefore, we should not, in our
examination of a primitive society, omit the fact of ordinary
human friendship. For natives may have certain preferences
for individuals outside any unit, kinship or otherwise, just
as they sometimes may feel antipathy to individuals within
the unit.

The Elema word for friend is *kake*. It is commonly used
as a form of greeting to the comparative stranger with
whom you wish to be on good terms, but it may stand for
something far more permanent. Just as individual natives
form attachments to the foreigners—armed constables, cook-
boys, even anthropologists—who come into their midst,
so they form attachments to one another, whether kinsmen
or not. They hit it off well, visit, chew betel together; and
such friendships may last through life. One thinks of the
two old widowers, almost the oldest men of all the Western
Elema, Heveheapo and Mapu, who used to come on private
visits from Orokolo and Arihava respectively and stroll
about in one another's rather silent but mutually contented
company.

But there is an undoubted tendency for friendship to be
formalized or confined to formal, ready-made relations. If
you ask a man to name his special friends he will almost
invariably name certain of his age-mates, his *hii-haruapo*,
'men of the one perineal band', also called his *bira-kake*.
This, in itself, shows the strength of the bond between
age-mates. But, before turning to the principle of age or
seniority, we should observe two special kinds of friendship

which are independent of it, as of other principles such as kinship or locality.

Resemblance Friends

The first is the Friendship of Resemblance. I have met with precisely half a dozen examples of this in all, and only as a result of stumbling luckily on the small feast which marked the beginning of one of them. A father in Arihava had been struck by the likeness between his son and a lad of Yogu who happened on the previous day to be in the former's village. He had sent a message to the parents of the Yogu boy expressing his desire to make him his son's *kake*, and in due course the boy had presented himself at Hoirahiru and received an *aroa* with seven armshells, three pearl shells, and an *apakora*. A return feast was made that afternoon at Yogu and the boys were thenceforward *kake*.[1] It goes without saying that both the ornaments and the feast were repaid in kind.

Such Resemblance Friends are also called *papare haruapu* or 'one moon'; for their likeness, such as it may be (and I admit it did not seem very striking in this case), is attributed to the supposed fact that they were begotten in the same month, or in other words that their mothers had been impregnated by the same moon. Henceforward they are pledged to mutual hospitality and help, though there are no further formal exchanges between them. It is said that one will give things to the other without asking or expecting payment; but it may be taken for granted that the balance is kept pretty even between them, for otherwise, the native sense of reciprocity being what it is, their relationship would come to an early and acrimonious end. Each individual is said henceforward to have two fathers, and when they marry, each will refer to the other's spouse as *uva*, 'wife', though this is merely a form and entails no marital rights whatever. Lastly, when one or the other dies, his *kake* will

---

[1] Chance namesakes, as well as namesake godparent and godchild, call one another *kake*. In the former case there are no mutual obligations; in the latter none except the quaint one by which the godparent provides edible leaves as diet for the nursing mother.

go into mourning. It is somewhat as if the one becomes a 'brother' to the other (or a 'sister', since the pair may be girls); but there is no true kinship at the bottom of the affair. In two of the six cases that came to my notice the Resemblance Friendship was established between children of the Orokolo tribe and children of the Uaripi tribe.

Hereditary Friends: Okeahi

The second kind of formal friendship is much commoner and more important. It is nominally between individuals, and they call one another *okeahi*. The friendship here becomes virtually hereditary. I have seen no case of the actual initiation of one of these partnerships, but it is said that an individual, so to speak an odd man out, may approach one of the visitors at a dance and make him hospitable gifts of tobacco, betel, and food. In this manner they first become *okeahi*, and much more substantial gifts follow to cement their friendship. In due course their sons will probably become *okeahi*; and if each has more than one son, then they may pair off, thus increasing the number. By no means every man can boast an *okeahi*; but there is a wide network of these relationships, and because of their hereditary nature one *larava* will come to supply *okeahi* for another. In those cases that I have noted the partners belong respectively to different *eravo*, and further, to different *bira'ipi* and *aualari*; so that the *okeahi* relationship is a means of binding individuals together which is independent of locality and kin.

Native informants have suggested a derivation for the word. It should be remarked that it is often abbreviated as *oke*, and that *oke* means, paradoxically, 'enemy'. The *oke-haera* proper were those, such as the Arihava bushfolk and the Keuru tribe, against whom the Western Elema in times not so very distant made killing expeditions. The *oke* is then the enemy and the foreigner. The suggested interpretation of the suffix as *hahi*, a 'journey' or a 'trading expedition', is plausible enough; and if it is true, then *okeahi* may have meant originally the 'friend from foreign parts', the enemy with whom you have made a trading alliance.[1] Now-adays, indeed, your *okeahi* are mostly nearer home, but they are still other than your kin or neighbours.

Although the fathers have been *okeahi* before, each partner-ship, unless it is to lapse, must be initiated afresh by the sons as they grow up to be young men. The first gift may take various forms, but the typical one is the spectacular *hoera kora*, or 'taro tree'. This consists of a thin tree-trunk, which may be 60 ft. long, loaded on either side with bundles of the taro which grow to such splendid proportions at Orokolo. The trunk is flanked by bamboo poles attached by cross-pieces, and makes a load for 70 or 80 men who have come to help from various *eravo*. The taro on one such *hoera kora* I estimated at about 700, and there were haulms of bananas and bundles of sugar-cane as well, the whole having been got together by the *eravo* of the *okeahi* who was making the gift. Made gay with croton, dracaena, and new white *hii* fluttering from arrows as flagpoles, the whole imposing contraption is borne along the beach to the *eravo* of the *okeahi* who is to receive it. The bearers, as many as can find a place to put their shoulders to, struggle and stagger under the weight. If they actually collapse, or if the bamboo poles crack and finally break in the middle, all the better. No one is in command; every one is telling every one else what to do; the man with the loudest voice may suc-ceed in suggesting new tactics, or some practical-minded individual rushes off amid the tumult to get some more poles and show the others by his example how or where to make repairs. Thus, amid immense vociferation, with transient rages on the part of those who cannot make their good advice heard in the din, but with great good humour on the whole, the *hoera kora* is finally deposited on a series of forked stumps before the *okeahi*'s *eravo*. Here the bearers are enter-tained with food, drink, and betel, and when they have gone the taro is distributed among the *eravo* members, the various arrows and bark-cloth *hii* being taken by those for whom they are intended: for this gift, though nominally from one

---

[1] For trading partners in the case of the *lakatoi* the word *pavora* is used. This may be Motuan in origin.

okeahi to the other, is in effect from *eravo* to *eravo*. It will be returned in due course, perhaps next season, with very careful regard to equality.

Between the individual *okeahi* there are further exchanges of gifts and services—as in canoe-making, house-building, *eravo*-building; in the making of *hevehe*, *eharo*, and *kovave*; and in the provision of *hapa*, i.e. effigies of totemic birds, fish, and fabulous creatures which are hung for decoration over the entrance of a new *baupa eravo*. An *eravo* member who has the pig to give away may call on his *okeahi* to make such a mask or figure when it is required, on the understanding that he himself will do the same and receive a pig on another occasion. But, as we noted in the case of brothers-in-law, a man does not in any real sense depend on his *okeahi* for everyday services; he is largely self-sufficient and there are other and nearer sources of help if he needs it. The *okeahi* relationship is thought of by the native as one of food-exchange rather than mutual help. It appears to be another case of extending the range of friendship, of strengthening one's own position through alliances which are established and maintained by gift-exchange.

Age, Genealogical and Biological

Apart from purely casual friendships and those of the formal kinds that have just been discussed, we saw that a man's particular friends are mostly found among his age-mates; and this leads us to a consideration of age as a factor in social grouping. Throughout Elema society this factor is of great importance, resulting, as it were, in a stratification by years which is seen clearly in the family, in the larger lineal group of the *larava*, and in the *eravo*.

Seniority and juniority may be either genealogical or biological. The relationship-terms stick by the former principle: that is to say, e.g., the son of an elder brother is *akoreapo* to the son of a younger brother, even though born after him; and in such crucial matters as that of land inheritance or the succession to *eravo* chieftainship, it is this genealogical seniority which is in theory the determining factor. But there is ample evidence that the two principles are not infrequently in conflict. Within the single family, of course, no such conflict can arise because the principles coincide. But beyond the family it may sometimes happen that an *akoreapo* is actually much younger than his *akoreheare*; and then, as was observed in another connexion, any deference due from one to the other in ordinary dealings does not follow from their kinship relation, but contrariwise, from their disparity in years. In the case of an *eravo* chief[1] or a land controller, however, genealogical seniority gradually comes into its own. While the individual is young his functions, such as they are, devolve upon some older member of the *eravo* or of the land-holding group (which is typically the *larava*); but as he grows in years he may gradually assert himself (the age at which he does so depending on his personality), until his genealogical rights prevail and he may be tacitly recognized as a chief or as a controller of the group lands though still a young man.[2]

Age-groups and Age-grades

It is not genealogical age, however, with which we are here concerned, but actual age; and in the present chapter we are less interested in differences of actual age than in equality, or coevality. For, quite irrespective of kinship, we find among the Elema a definite classification by age-groups. This classification is—or was—based to some extent upon the practice of seclusion. Every two or three years (the periods were not strictly regular) all the *eravo* in the tribe, and even those beyond it, secluded their adolescent boys more or less simultaneously. The boys then received their first *hii*; and so the members of any such batch were spoken of as *hii haruapu*—'one perineal band'.

It is hardly necessary to distinguish the age-group from the age-grade. Every individual is born into an age-group and belongs to that group throughout his life. On the other hand he passes through all the age-grades one after another provided he lives long enough. These latter are fairly clearly

[1] See p. 90.
[2] I have noted cases where seniority, both genealogical and biological, was overridden in the succession to *eravo* chieftainship, i.e. where a younger brother superseded an elder.

distinguished and in some cases are made obvious by changes in costume. They are as follows :[1]

1. *Akore hekai*: Little boys, naked.
2. *Akore ikua*: Small boys from about 6 years; narrow bark belt and small pubic tassel of frayed bark.
3. *Erekai akore*: 'Belt boys', from about 12 years, belt (*erekai*) of bark with a larger pubic tassel, or properly with tassels front and rear.
4. *Miro akore*: 'Parrot Boys', during seclusion lasting from 6 to 12 months about the age of 14 or 15; perineal band of *hii*, bark-cloth.
5. *Hoaho*: 'Bachelors', wearing finery and large mops of hair during a few weeks after emergence from seclusion.
6. *Are bira*: 'Young men', or 'young husbands', upon binding up their mops of hair, and in most cases marrying.
7. *Haera eapapo*: 'Big Men', i.e. old enough to be of importance, say from 35 years.
8. *Oapau*: Old men.

Age-grouping, in a somewhat rough and ready manner, begins long prior to seclusion, in fact with the *akore hekai*. It is noticeable that from very early years children of the same age tend to flock together. So trite an observation may be justified by the fact that this tendency seems even more marked in Orokolo than among our own children. Thus the *akore ikua* play rounders, or whatever game is in vogue, among themselves; farther down the beach the same game is being played on a larger scale by a group of harder-hitting *erekai akore*; and so on with many and various other occupations. Now when these older playfellows began to show the ordinary signs of adolescent change it was thought time to seclude them. Not every community made provision for seclusion, so that it was often convenient for boys of one community to be interned in the *baupa eravo* of another. But the tendency was for all youths of similar age throughout the settlement to go up together.

Seclusion

Since seclusion seems to have died out finally in Orokolo it is not necessary to spend overlong in describing an institution

---

[1] Females pass through corresponding age-grades. (1) *Mori hekai*; (2) *Mori ikua*; (3, 4, and 5) *Mori hari*; (6) *Uavari*; (7) *Uavari eapapo*; (8) *Lau eapapo*. For males, a term *mekehaku* properly embraces grades 1 and 2: it is equivalent to 'youngsters'. But it is often extended in a semi-humorous way to include all the younger males (grades 1 to 6).

which, despite interesting and picturesque features, can no longer be said to form part of the existent culture. The first step, however, was to construct a high-walled enclosure (*hirita*) in rear of and adjoining the *baupa eravo*. This was to be the home of the secludees for the ensuing six months or more, perhaps even a year. They made their entry together. Their respective *aukau* cut off their *erekai* and presented them with new white *hii*, first throwing the *hii* in the air and catching them, while they uttered their private spells to ensure that their nephews grew into fine tall fellows. They gave them the usual injunctions against stealing, disrespect of their elders, and so on; and cautioned them more particularly to refrain from philandering during their seclusion, and to be careful to keep out of the sight of women. If they neglected these precautions then they could not expect to put on weight or grow creditable mops of hair.

The last sentence contains in a nutshell the overt purpose of seclusion. Here, as elsewhere in Papua, every native has the idea, as fixed as it is clear, that seclusion makes for growth of hair and body; and that alone, in the native view, is the reason for the institution. The boys anoint themselves generously with coco-nut oil, one spraying it from his mouth over another while the latter turns slowly on his feet, as if on a revolving pedestal, so as to get the full benefit of it, atomized and well distributed. Their bodies are smeared with red ochre (*paira*), whence is said to come their nickname of *miro akore*, or 'parrot boys'. These applications are not cosmetic, for the boys never leave their *hirita* by daytime to be admired: they are expressly fattening. As their seclusion advances their *paira* may be changed for *aro*, or charcoal; for if a boy is not making satisfactory progress under one treatment, then it is proper to try another. Their food tabus—shrimps, crabs, catfish, lizards—resolve themselves into sympathetic magic; the risk is that the boys may turn out shrivelled, ugly, or horny-skinned.[1] If they must

---

[1] Since the boys spend their time so idly in seclusion and thereby draw down the disapproval of some Europeans on the institution, I once suggested to the Orokolo natives that they might improve the shining hours in the *hirita* by making copra. The suggestion was not approved, though only one man could give me a reason against it. He reminded me that in the process of copra-making the meat of the

PLATE 11

Two *Erekai Akore*. One is spraying the other with coco nut oil from his
mouth

Two *Miro Akore* in seclusion. They are beating bark-cloth (*hii*)

(particularly during the earlier stages) avoid even indirect contact with young women, it is because of the risk to their growing hair; for anything that has even the remotest con-nexion with sexual intercourse will cause it to fall out. Thus it is that they must be fed and tended either by old bachelors and widowers or by old women and little girls (the boys' sisters), all of whom are beyond suspicion of sexual activity.[1] When their hair is long enough, each is formally presented with a comb; but the combing is done by a *haera dedehi*, 'a man without a wife', because of the same risk. Once they have reached this stage it is true they are allowed to make love to their sweethearts by night; for by now, it is said, they have made good growth and established themselves. But until their emergence they still observe the rule against showing themselves to womenfolk by day. They may roam at will in the bush, where they can always hide from an approaching female. But passing through the village in full daylight is only possible under cover of a *hara*, i.e. a pair of plaited coco-nut fronds hinged along one side, a queer disguise, which gives the secluded boy the appearance of some gigantic cocoon shuffling along on one of its points. There is no harm in his seeing young women—he easily does so through the meshes—but he must remain unseen himself.

The reason for this hiding is plainly and consistently stated; it is to enable the secludees, when they finally emerge, to create surprise. After a purifying bathe they are decorated within the *eravo*; and thereupon descend[2] in their full glory to tour the village in single-file procession and to receive at the hands of their *aukau* the *maki hii*, or ceremonial bark-cloth bands edged with dogs' teeth. The women, young and old, are delighted to see them again after so long an absence and (whether really or in make-believe) are astounded at

coco-nut dries and shrivels in the shell, and that was the last thing they would have happen to their boys in seclusion.

[1] Only males could enter the *hirita*. Women handed food in through a little covered window.

[2] In the Uaripi and Opau tribes (where seclusion is still practised) it is the custom for the *aukahura* to carry the secludees down in litters called 'canoes'. These 'canoes' bear mythological names derived from the *aukaus' aulari*. They are subsequently filled with food and sent back to the houses of the respective *aukau*.

their size. Mothers, it is often averred, can hardly recognize their sons. For some weeks thereafter the youths parade or lounge about the village as *hoahu*, and any one who has seen these splendid specimens of young manhood can understand the pride which the village takes in them and they in themselves.

The native rationale of seclusion as a means of forcing growth may not perhaps be so wide of the mark. It is certain that the boys spend their time in almost complete idleness. They amuse themselves by beating out new *hii* and plaiting armlets—neither of them very arduous occupations—or by wandering in holiday mood about the bush. Meanwhile they are fed often and well, being denied nothing save the few entirely unimportant foods which for magical reasons are unsuitable. It may well be that such treatment helps to build up flesh. But whether it does or not, the Orokolo native thinks it does. He admires size and plumpness (although he inclines to be lean), and the only reason he can ever think of for seclusion is that it makes the boys big.

Since I have found the same explanation wherever I have dealt with seclusion in other Papuan societies I am disposed to attach a good deal of importance to it. Irrespective of any validity from the physiological point of view, and whatever the origin of seclusion—which latter is a question entirely beyond our scope—it seems that this is the only conscious motive, other than mere conservatism, for its continuance.

Age-mates as Friends

It may, however, fulfil certain other functions of which the people who practise it are unaware; and one of these may be that of binding together more firmly each batch of age-mates. Within any one *eravo* the secludees are thrown together and kept together very closely for maybe a year; and as they may roam in the bush by day or anywhere they please by night, they are prone to forgather with others in a like situation from near-by *eravo*. They form themselves into a care-free band, and not infrequently get into some minor mischief[1] which, like that of University students, is strangely tolerated by the public. In this way they become chums or mates; and friendships developed in the close quarters of the *hirita* or in the escapades of fellow larrikins may last a lifetime. Even an old man will be able and pleased, if you ask him, to enumerate his *bira-kake* within certain limits. It is plain that an *esprit de corps* has survived the passage of time.

The age-group is called *birakau*[2] generically, and each succeeding one is distinguished by a nickname. It is plain, however, that the system of age-grouping was stronger and more definite towards the eastern end of the coast; among the Western Elema certain of the usages met with would seem to be hardly more than echoes. Thus the nicknames seem always to have originated in the Toaripi tribe, whence the knowledge of them spread more or less quickly, and not always perfectly, right along to the Aivei. All youths who were secluded about the same time adopted the nickname as it came along. Thus they might be 'Haha', or 'Ori Roro', or 'Kevaro' (which mean 'Sago Thorn', 'Bird's Nest', 'Lightning'), and so on. It is impossible to give fully the results of a most intriguing search into the origin of these names. I have recorded thirty-four, going back perhaps eighty or ninety years, and for the most of them a beginning is discoverable in some still-remembered joke, some youthful boast, or humorous incident.[3] At Motumotu, or wherever the name originated, it was often adopted by youngsters long prior to seclusion; but they kept it of course throughout life. As the knowledge of it passed along it was applied, sooner or later, to their coevals; and thus an age-group came to be known by the same nickname from end to end of the coast. Namesakes (who are met with as commonly as among ourselves) could be distinguished by prefixing

[1] I have recorded several cases of pig-stealing by boys in seclusion, the pigs being killed, cooked, and eaten in the bush. Needless to say this is beyond the pale of minor mischiefs.

[2] Uaripi, *miratau*: Karama, *migiatau*; Toaripi, *hiatau*.

[3] The most recent are significant of modern interest. Proceeding backwards into the past: (1) '*Puse*', 'copra bag'; (2) '*Raisi-ipi*', 'Rice at the bottom of the Bag'; (3) 'Blanket'; (4) 'Singlet'; (5) 'Cement'; (6) '*Auri*', 'Iron'; (7) '*Lauari*', 'Flash, good-looking'; (8) '*Peni*', 'Pencil'.

their personal names by that of their *birakau*.[1] It must be said, however, that, whereas the sequence of the back numbers is sufficiently well remembered at Motumotu, it becomes rather vague, even with the more recent numbers, by the time we reach Orokolo.

Just as the knowledge of *birakau* names tends to fade out towards the extreme west, so do we find increasing vagueness regarding the mutual obligations of *bira-kake*. In the Uaripi tribe I recorded some picturesque and amusing incidents illustrating the *birakau's* solidarity. When one of their number by chance fell into the water from a canoe it was incumbent upon all his *bira-kake* who happened to be witnesses of this ignominious accident to plunge in after him. When one member of the *birakau* was overheard quarrelling with his wife, his fellow members would club together and spend the night talking and chewing betel under his house; and in the morning husband and wife, both withered with shame, or perhaps sharing in a good joke, had to provide a pig. But these are not Orokolo customs. Joint action among *bira-kake* was there wholly informal. They might be called on to bring in the timber for a house, or to gather sago leaves and thatch in the course of a day's working-bee, or to lend their strength in hauling a canoe-log to the beach; and they were of course entertained with a feast if they did so and could count on reciprocal services on a future occasion. But, even so, such services tended rather to lapse as the years passed by; and for any major enterprise requiring man-power *en masse*—such as raising an *eravo* pile or carrying a *hoera-kora* or dragging down a *lakatoi* log—every able-bodied man would turn to, irrespective of age-groups. Nevertheless, in the heyday of young manhood *bira-kake* do show a tendency to stick together. They make a good cheerful crew of paddlers, for instance; and if one of them 'signs on' for indentured labour, his mates are very prone to sign on with him.

It is interesting, though not perhaps very significant, to

[1] My cook, a middle-aged hunchback named Hure, was distinguished from the many other Hures of Motumotu by being called 'Karai' Hure, Karai being the 13th *birakau* back from the present. The word is said to come from Karaidiba, the name of a plantation on which a number of his age-group worked as indentured labourers.

PLATE 12

Two secluded boys passing through the village in their *Hara*. Behind, a *baupa eravo* with the *hirita* in rear

Boys of the 'Puse' (inner two) and 'Raisi-Ipi' (outer two) age-groups

note that age-mates, like Resemblance Friends, call one another's wives *uva*. Once again it is a mere form of address; a man has no claims of any kind upon the wife of his *bira-kake*; though it is worth observing that the girls of any age-group, who by a mild stretch of language are referred to as *hii haruapu* with the boys, are expected to marry within it. That is to say the *birakau* is an endogamous unit. This hardly amounts to a strict rule, but certainly represents the norm. When seclusion was practised maidens married off when their age-mates emerged; and they still marry their age-mates even though seclusion has virtually ceased. It is regarded as somewhat ridiculous for a girl to marry a boy of the group following her own; indeed it is more than that —an infringement of the tacit proprietary rights of her male age-mates as a collective unit.[1]

I have known a case—certainly an unusual one—in which father and son came to blows and the former's age-mate rushed into the fray to help him. But it does not appear that the *birakau* was the sort of group that stuck together against groups otherwise constituted. It is impossible to name any specific functions of the age-group as such except in connexion with the rites of seclusion; and I do not think the bond of coevality compares in strength with the bond which unites kinsmen or neighbours. But it nevertheless remains as one of the principles of cohesion in Elema society. It can at least be said that those who have passed through the various stages of life together usually maintain their friendship to the end.

The Decay of Seclusion

It has been several times remarked that among the Western Elema seclusion seems practically defunct. Up till three or four years ago it still survived in Orokolo, but during my last trip (1937) only one *eravo* in the whole tribe was keeping the custom, and that was at Biai, one of the small colonies of Orokolo scattered along the beach. It is too early to

[1] A mere lad had compromised a girl of the previous age-group while I was at Orokolo. She was pregnant and he was named as responsible. This was unwelcome and embarrassing to all. As I was about to move down to Kerema he attached himself to me and eased the situation by flight.

declare that it is gone for ever, but present-day inhabitants of Orokolo show no active inclination or desire to revive it; while the large settlements of Arihava, Auma, and Vailala have dispensed with it these eighteen years and more.[1]

Arihava, Auma, and Vailala threw out seclusion, together with a great many other customs, as a result of the Vailala Madness. Orokolo and Yogu, which remained immune, have allowed it to die gradually. It was found that secluded boys sometimes broke bounds completely; disappeared during the night; and set off down the coast in search of work. Their elders simply shrugged their shoulders. So far from being deeply perturbed they seemed to think it rather amusing. Even when seclusion was definitely in vogue it struck the writer that boys to no small extent did as they pleased. For instance, an *eravo* chief named Hito-vakore informed me that, his *eravo* members having decided on seclusion, he had told the youths themselves to collect the timbers for the *hirita*, a job which falls to them in the ordinary course. But, he said, they had not yet done so in spite of repeated urgings. Weeks went by, and when I finally took my departure there was still no sign of a *hirita*. I believe neither that Hitovakore urged his boys very hard nor that they listened at all attentively to him when he did urge them. It is thoroughly in keeping with that absence of real authority which we have noted[2] that the boys should choose their own time for beginning; and it is equally in keeping that they should now decide for themselves whether seclusion is to survive or not. There can be no doubt that changing conditions militate against the institution, and chief among them is the opportunity for labour with the white man. This amounts to necessity if we regard the reluctance to make copra in sufficient quantity at home as fixed and incurable. For the imposition of a tax[3] means that

[1] It may be remarked that in the Uaripi tribe it is still vigorously alive.
[2] p. 52.
[3] The tax (which nowhere exceeds £1 per head) is payable by males between the ages of 16 and 36. The proceeds go into a Native Trust Fund and are expended solely on objects calculated to benefit the natives themselves, e.g. education, medical services, &c. Needless to say the calculation of a native's age is a matter of guess-work; but it has been an accepted rule that boys still in seclusion should be exempted. Unfortunately a well-meaning but perhaps too strenuous young patrol officer some

young men must find money; and the quickest way, as it seems to them, of finding it is to 'sign on'. Not only this motive, but a desire to see the outside world lures the impatient youth away from his village, and thus seclusion is apt to be evaded.

The decay of a picturesque institution will always affect an anthropologist with some degree of melancholy, if it does not sting him to fury. But in this case it seems to the writer that the institution, although a very striking one, was never very important in the sense that much depended on it. It is probable that the division into age-groups will grow progressively less distinct; and possibly the bond which unites *bira-kake* will be the weaker for lack of that period of six months or more when the youths depended so completely on one another's company. But the age-groups and the sense of fellowship between age-mates will survive this set-back even if it has weakened them; while as for the rest of Orokolo culture I cannot see that the loss of seclusion has seriously disturbed it. Obviously there are some institutions more firmly embedded, more deeply implicated in the total mass. But seclusion has disappeared, or seems on the point of disappearing, without effecting any vital change. Its disappearance will be a loss to the culture, an ornamental feature gone, but the culture can flourish without it.

years ago cleared out a number of *hirita* and made the inmates fork out £1 each. This left an erroneous impression that the Government was against seclusion. It is surprisingly hard to disabuse primitive minds of such impressions.

IV

PEOPLE OF IMPORTANCE

ELEMA society is remarkably democratic. One is inclined to say outright that in it all men are substantially equal; that there are no masters and no servants; no definite system of rulership; and no 'social class'. But perhaps these statements are too categorical. It may be true that our major civilized institutions, in so far as they answer to fundamental needs or tendencies, will be found to have their counterparts in every society, however primitive. And so we do of course find rulership of a sort, even though its functions are very indefinite; and it might be claimed that we come upon the beginnings of social class, since differences in wealth and rank, more or less hidden as they are, affect social attitudes even in Orokolo. But it may certainly be said that these institutions or distinctions are, as we find them, hardly more than embryonic.

The Old Men

We shall deal with rank and wealth later on in this chapter. In the meantime, and contrariwise, we may give our attention to a kind of organization which is highly developed in Western Elema society but has lost much of its force in civilization, viz. that of stratification by age. We have already dealt with this subject in the foregoing pages, but with the emphasis on sameness of age, or coevality. Here we shall consider rather the fact of difference. For in Elema society it may be stated as a general rule that the older strata become, in a social sense, progressively more important, until in the oldest men of the tribe we meet with something like a ruling class. It soon becomes obvious that they are not rulers in any save an indirect and indefinite manner; and further, that they cannot constitute a class in the accepted sense, since every individual in the normal course rises to the top. But in Western Elema society as it was, and as it still is, it remains true that the oldest men constitute the

PLATE 13

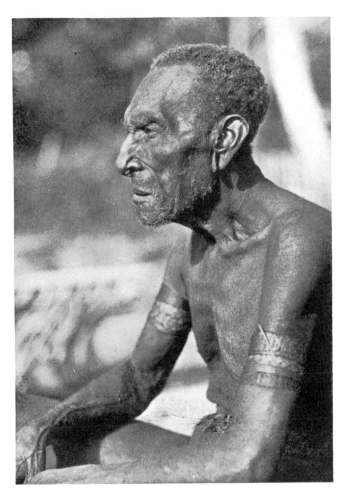

Lahoe, the oldest man of Orokolo Bay

stratum which enjoys the greatest privileges and wields the greatest power.

The progression in importance is in the case of males very obvious.[1] From little boys who don't much matter, they become youths who attract attention transiently, and then *are bira*, young married men who provide the muscle of the community as its workers and, in the old days, its front-line fighters. Gradually they drift into middle age and come to be called *eapapo*, 'big' men. The relative insignificance of the younger men is shown by the common practice of lumping them all together as *mekehaku*, a term which is properly applied to little boys. Thus, though the pick of the community in manly strength, they are still 'youngsters' in the tolerant view of the *haera eapapo*, the 'oldsters'; and they show a realization of their position by a becoming reticence. But once they have by general consent passed into the ranks of *haera eapapo* they are no longer afraid to raise their voices in council: not that there is anything in the nature of a true council, but they have gained assurance and carry weight, and they are treated with increasing respect by their juniors and consideration by their elders. The word *eapapo* continues to be applied to them with gathering emphasis as the years pass. Literally it means 'large', but, in this connexion, 'important', or merely 'old'; and so some of the skinniest, frailest, and smallest men in the tribe are known, in this honourable sense of the word, as its biggest.

The old men, as a somewhat ill-defined class, constitute what is called the *avai*.[2] This is another of those words which appear in a number of different meanings remotely but significantly connected. It is probably, like *larava*, derived from the Namau language, where it signifies a group of kinsmen, roughly equivalent to the occupants of a *larava*[3] or, more strictly, one generation within that group. Among the Western Elema the same word (or what informants declare to be the same, though they are unable to

---

[1] Less so with females: old women, past work, child-bearing, and desirability, do not stay the course of social promotion so well.

[2] Distinguished from *avae*, 'breast'.

[3] See *Natives of the Purari Delta*, pp. 68–70.

establish a connexion) is used in two senses. First, it may stand for fixed property—land, coco-nuts, areca palms, bread-fruit, &c.—i.e. the real basis of the wealth and standing which are held and inherited by the near-kin group. Second, it may stand for the vaguely select body of old men whom we are considering. There seems little doubt that these are various meanings of the same word, which is the centre of a muddled nexus of ideas—kinship, generation, property, and power.

The *avai* in the sense we are considering has no fixed constitution. It might be said to include all the old men of Orokolo Bay and even beyond. Membership is not restricted expressly to the oldest *birakau*, nor is there any rite of admission. A man waits for an invitation from certain of its members, and then he merely sits among the group when they assemble in their informal way for some ceremony or occasion in the *eravo*. For the *avai* is not convoked like a parliament. Those of the old men who happen to live near or who have been invited come as they please; they sit down, take their ease while younger men work, and enjoy the best of everything. They are, at that time and place, the *avai*, and no unfit person dare intrude upon them.

It is said that of a number of brothers, whatever their age, only the eldest may sit with the *avai*. This, however, is by no means a regular rule. I suspect it is invoked only in those cases where, for some personal reasons, the eldest brother has adopted a jealous, dog-in-the-manger attitude. But such cases show that no man can enter the select company without the unanimous approval of its members.[1] Presumptuousness would be speedily punished by sorcery. For the *avai*, if not sorcerers to a man, possess a quite incalculable *ahea*, or heat, and there are assuredly sorcerers among them—or so every Elema native believes—and, whether sorcerers or not, they can easily, through certain influential connexions, set the powers of sorcery in motion.

We shall meet the *avai* so often in the second part of this book that a mere summary of their privileges and

---

[1] For a ceremonial introduction to the *avai*, not admission, but a mere presentation, see p. 272.

functions will suffice at this point. To them alone belongs the right of admission to the *eravo* when at certain periods it is under tabu. There they may sit undisturbed in the cool and the quiet, enjoying one another's society, and (if it crosses their minds to do so) their common sense of superiority. They meet also on external occasions: for instance certain members may assemble by invitation at specially large-scale death-feasts, to sit in a group and sing. And whenever these old men are gathered together there is good food to eat, and they get the best of it. One cannot fail to be impressed by the simple delight in food evinced by a relatively primitive people whose delights are so much less varied, or whose appetites so much less jaded, than our own; and it is consequently the highest privilege of the *avai* that they should be the 'eaters', while the rest of the community are the 'workers'. So they are fed first and given the titbits of the pig, the liver and other tender morsels. It would be in the last degree inadvisable to offer a slight to any member of the *avai* or to send him away hungry.

It is most of all in the conduct of *Hevehe* (when we shall see more of them) that the old men appear as a specially privileged class. Except on ceremonial occasions there is little in their behaviour, and nothing in their appearance (save their age), to distinguish them from their fellow villagers. Some few old men take a conspicuous pride in their appearance—perhaps as an echo of a more dressy period in Orokolo history than the present; but there is no badge of membership whatever for the *avai*, and the majority of old men are inconspicuously indifferent.

There are neither election, formal meetings, nor decrees. The *avai* is a sinecure senate in which privileges plainly outweigh responsibilities. It has no positive authority and represents gerontocracy in only an indirect sense. Yet its indirect influence is a very important one; for the old-timers of the *avai* are, more than any others, the trustees and champions of tradition. The continuance of the old order (and this is specially apparent in such a matter as the intricate ceremonial of *Hevehe*) depends not only on their unanimously conservative attitude, but even (since *Hevehe* occurs so seldom) on their memory. In these times of change, those who desire change will call them die-hards. But we should give them the credit of standing by their great conviction, which is summed up in the belief that what their grand-fathers did was mostly right.

In defence of this conviction they exert the prestige which age has given them and keep in reserve the forces, or imagined forces, of sorcery. The *avai-ve-ahea*, magical power of the old men, is feared by all; and it may, in popular belief, be used not only against those who infringe their rights, but against those who intentionally or unintentionally commit a breach of custom—particularly some custom in connexion with *Hevehe*. Sorcery is thus found to assist here in the preservation of *Hevehe* ritual, though, as we shall see, it is a two-edged sword and can operate with equal effect against it, thus counteracting itself.

Though the trend of their politics is sufficiently obvious it would not be true to say that the old men are impervious to modern ideas. At least they are often disposed towards compromise—in which they are more reasonable than some of the younger generation who are all for subversion. When in years to come the youngsters of to-day wear grey beards and sit in the *avai* (if there is one), it is not inconceivable that they themselves will have changed their attitude for some-thing a little more conservative; though then, perhaps, there will not be the same things to conserve. In the mean-time, while the present body of benign but formidable old men survives, the most rabid young iconoclast is held in check.

Chiefs

Apart from this somewhat amorphous system of rule by old men, there is a more clearly defined though still undevel-oped system of hereditary chieftainship. The chiefs—if they may be dignified by such a word—are called *amua*; and here is yet another instance of identity of terms in the Elema and Namau languages, though the *amua* of the former people can hardly be said to compare with those of the latter in power and dignity.[1]

[1] See *Natives of the Purari Delta*, pp. 111, 117, 118.

Each *eravo* normally has two *amua*, one for the Right and one for the Left. They are both called *eravo amua* and nominally their rank is equal, for as we have seen the division of the *eravo* into two sides is an unimportant one, neither side taking precedence over the other. It is nearly always found, however, that one of the two men predominates to some extent, so that the whole *eravo* in question is commonly spoken of as his. This predominance may be based merely on personal character, or it may have its origin in a prior hereditary connexion with the community, or rather the land.

For there is another kind of chief, called the *karigara amua* ('village chief') or *kekere haera* ('land-man'), who is properly a descendant of the *eravo*-founder, i.e. of the first settler who owned or controlled the village land on which it is built and the bush-land on which it still depends. Usually one or other of the *eravo amua* is at the same time *karigara amua*. But this is not always the case. Waiea Ravi, e.g. the most vigorous of those that now stand in Orokolo, kept the chiefly capacities separate from one another; it had its *amua* of both Right and Left, while a third person, actually a younger man but one who might be said to take precedence of both of them, filled the position of *karigara amua*. This is an unusual but not a solitary instance.

There is no genuine chiefly class among the Elema. Any man, whatever his *aualari* or *bira'ipi*, has it in him to be a chief. It has always been a common practice to break away and form colonies, usually on some distant land belonging to the emigrants. Any who does so probably succeeds in attracting some other families to his small settlement. It grows by multiplication and addition; makes its own *baupa eravo*; and finally its true *eravo*. The original leader or senior male of the colony becomes its *karigara amua* from the outset; and when eventually an *eravo* rises, the two sides of it may by common consent fall to two men of different *bira'ipi*, senior men of different elements in a composite community. They are the *eravo amua*.

Succession is hereditary in the male line, passing from elder brother to younger brother and back to elder brother's son; though I have noted a few cases where the elder brother, through disinclination or unfitness, stood down in favour of the younger. It is not that he makes any formal abdication; rather he neglects his duties, such as they are, or absents himself until the younger brother gradually takes precedence. It is in general keeping with the principle of age-stratification that the younger man who happens to be in the direct line should have to wait till the death of his paternal uncles before he is known as the *amua*. Although the above rule is not without exception, it is typically the old men in the chiefly *larava* on either side of the *eravo* who are its chiefs in effect.

There is no ceremony of installation, merely a tacitly recognized change; and, lest the institution of chieftainship should be thought more developed than it is, it may be remarked that very often the members of a community will be found in doubt as to who, among several possibilities, is the true *amua*. Here, indeed, as elsewhere, when asking the name of the chief in such and such an *eravo*, I have been given that of a man dead and in his grave.

The duties of *amua* are not easy to define, but some light will be thrown on the Elema ideal of chieftainship by an examination of the word itself. As already suggested, it probably derives from the Namau language; but in that of the Elema it may also mean kind-hearted, hospitable, generous. The Elema have a simple physical psychology by which they allocate all emotion, desire, and thought to the liver, *iki*.[1] Of the two sides of this organ the right (*mai-ore*) is the seat of kindliness, sociability; the left (*mai keva*) of the angry passions, strong talk, unsociability. Not being cannibals the Elema had to base their knowledge of internal anatomy largely on the analogy of the pig, and there is some confusion in their ideas, even some uncertainty regarding the respective sides to which the different kinds of mental experience belong.[2] But the majority favour the allocation of good emotions to the right and the bad ones to the left. They have noted the frequent disparity in size and

---

[1] Thus the terms *iki vere*, desire; *iki heaha*, bad temper; *iki beveke*, good temper; *iki heroe*, compassion; *iki ore*, knowledge; *iki kekere*, thought, belief; &c.

[2] To make matters worse they became sadly mixed up as to right and left hand.

shape between the two lobes of the pig's liver, one being well developed, while the other is small and 'crooked'; and the predominance of one or the other kind of temper is described accordingly. Whether it is bigness or smallness or crookedness that makes for predominance of the relevant passions is just the point on which informants are most uncertain; but in the midst of this uncertainty it is agreed that the good side, right or left, large or small, is *iki amua*; and the man whose liver so to speak secretes the corresponding thoughts, emotions, or desires, is an *iki amua haera*.

It seems probable that this is a secondary meaning of the word; but, whether or no, it is just the qualities indicated that are expected of the true *amua*. He should be above all generous; and since generosity is to no small extent measured by display, he should by implication be comparatively wealthy, in fact ready and able to make a big splash at a feast —the sort of man who owns many pigs and is not loath to kill them.[1] He should also be hospitable; his first duty is to greet the stranger, to entertain him in the *eravo* with betel and tobacco, and call upon the women to cook food. Accordingly also he should be a home-keeper. It is not expected of him to be always in his village—he is probably an industrious gardener and often away; but he should not be a wanderer, one of those who go off to spend half their time in a hamlet along the beach. He has his duty to village and *eravo*; and to be absent over-long is a kind of disloyalty.

The *amua*, whether of *eravo* or village, gives the word for feasts, for the beginning of gardens, for ceremonies, and so on.[2] But he does not give orders and expect obedience. For the most part he merely voices collective decisions which have resulted from a good deal of random discussion.

[1] A man who is not in any sense chief of *eravo* or village may be called *amua haera* by virtue of wealth and generosity. Thus the L.M.S. missionary, Mr. S. H. Dewdney, was so called, both because of qualities which at any rate deserve the name, and more particularly, because of the size of the mission establishment.

[2] Some *eravo* recognize an *oharo kirea haera*, i.e. one who instructs (*kirea*) the others, an intermediary who passes on to them the words (*oharo*) of the *eravo amua*. Tahia (see p. 199) was said to be the *oharo kirea haera* for the two old men Ma-hevehe and Koraguba. Tahia, however, was a very influential man himself and any 'strong talk' he gave to the *eravo* was mostly original rather than passed on. Cf. the *iki amua* of the Namau (*Natives of the Purari Delta*, p. 116).

If he attempted to give orders without such previous discussion he would throw the community into a state of
indignant surprise; and we may count upon it there would
be discussion enough afterwards. For all are anxious to
thrash things out and agree.

If there is any feature in the social life of the Elema which
has impressed itself forcibly upon the writer it is this desire
for unanimity. How it is reached in the absence of formal
proceedings remains rather a mystery. But it is evident that
any enterprise involving the whole *eravo* should have the
support of all members before they feel satisfied about
beginning it. Differences of opinion are at first very freely
expressed, but these have a way of resolving themselves
into a common purpose. Schism is strongly deprecated,
and minorities—unless they are so set in their opinions as
to secede altogether—commonly sink their objections rather
than be different. It is true that some *amua* (as we shall see
later on) do exercise a strong personal influence, and in the
midst of a ceremony can virtually take command of it. Such
men can and do raise their voices to good effect; for although
ranting is expressly a habit which belongs to the other side
of the liver, it is admitted that the *amua* should be capable
of strong talk on occasion. But it is generally true that he
acts as little more than the mouthpiece of a community
which in some mysterious manner has already made up its
mind.

Amua dispense the food at *eravo* feasts; they give and
receive invitations in the name of their people for feasts,
dances, or undertakings (such as raising an *eravo*-post or
hauling a canoe) which require much man-power; and their
invitations or acceptances generally meet with a good response, though less out of respect for their authority than
from a desire to move and act in a body.

Such real authority, then, as the *amua* possesses is dependent on his personality more than inherent in his rank. It is
hardly too much to say that he is a figure-head. Finally it
may be remarked that he receives no tribute and wears no
insignia. His reward—for what he does—is his *lare eapapo*,
his 'big name'.

Ceremonial Functionaries

There are certain hereditary offices in the *eravo* which belong to ceremonial rather than secular chieftainship. The first is that of the *kwara-haera* (curator), or *eravo kariki haera* (the hand-maker, or 'handy-man' of the *eravo*). Both expressions refer especially to his responsibility for the *hohao* or *kaiavuru*,[1] those staring, anthropomorphic plaques of carved wood that are set up in the *larava*; for he it is who looks after them and cleans them—on the rare occasions when they receive any such attention. The word *kariki* does not imply that he has actually fashioned them, for they are probably generations older than he is; it is a very general expression for 'making', 'attending to', 'fixing up'.

The office of *kariki-haera* is hereditary in the ordinary patrilineal way. Sometimes it may be fused with that of the *amua* on one side or the other, but more frequently it is held independently; and the necessary qualification is the possession of certain magic used for the benefit of the *eravo* as a whole. Although its purpose is the common weal, this magic is the jealously guarded possession of the *kariki-haera* alone; and needless to say he passes it on, like his office, only to his rightful successor.

The magic deals in particular with hunting; with *eravo* architecture; and with the purification, the ceremonial tidying-up, of the interior of the building after *Hevehe* and *Kovave*. For the first purpose he uses his magical rapport with the *hohao* who have special influence over hunting, being themselves spirits of the bush. By virtue of dream-communications he is in a position to give warnings or tips; and before the hunt he stands the bows and arrows of the hunters against the *hohao* and fumigates them by burning his scented leaves and medicines in a broken pot. Such ministrations precede every communal hunt, though it should be remembered that communal hunts are rare occurrences. (Nowadays, I believe, they are never undertaken on any scale except for the purpose of rounding off a ceremony.) For his work as hunting magician he receives

---

[1] See pp. 155, 385.

no extra portion of the catch or other tangible reward. If the expedition succeeds he is *maea-peraia*—glad in his body; if it fails, he is *maioka*—ashamed that his work has gone for nothing.

In the important business of building the *eravo* he does not appear as an architect but as one who knows the spells to be used at certain crucial moments, e.g. in sinking a pier or laying the first floor-joist. They are highly secret, sometimes referring to that most mysterious of beings, *eravo-ve-uvari*, the *eravo*-grandmother herself, who dwells in the ground beneath the building.[1] The magic is necessary to protect it from the fury of the winds or from subsidence in the sandy soil. The fact that *eravo* too often acquire a threatening lean despite the *kariki haera*'s efforts only provides argument for renewing and redoubling them next time.

The third business, that of cleaning the *eravo* interior at the end of a ceremony, we shall see performed in connexion with the *Hevehe*.

It may be remarked that these functions are not always fulfilled by one and the same man. Sometimes they are the prerogatives of different men, each with magic of his own. But in any case they are unremunerated. The magician enjoys the prestige which his single-handed labours bring him in a highly esteemed profession. That provides one of his motives. The other is his desire to benefit the community of which he is a member.

There remain two *eravo* functionaries to whom attention should be drawn, viz. the *apa-haro-haera* or 'Drum-Head-Men', also called *Oropa-haera*, or 'Front-Men'. Their functions belong solely to *Hevehe*; but, since *Hevehe* is a recurrent cycle, their office is a permanent one in the *eravo* and is usually handed down according to the normal rules of succession. They are called *apa-haro-haera* because the *hevehe* carry *apa*, or drums, and they are their leaders; *oropa-haera*, because, during the long period while the *hevehe* masks remain in the *eravo*, theirs occupy the places of honour, one on either side of the entrance in the *oropa larava*. While there is an *apa-haro-haera* for each *eravo*-side, one of them will

[1] See p. 159.

be found on occasions to take precedence. It is not the precedence, however, of Right over Left or vice versa, but one determined by personal influence.

We shall see a good deal of these functionaries (whom we shall henceforward call Drum-Leaders) when we come to deal with *Hevehe*. In the meantime it may be noted that their duties are much like those of *amua*. It is their business to see that dancers who come as guests of the *eravo* are plied with food and drink, tobacco and betel; they have to supply pigs for the *eravo* as a whole on certain occasions in connexion with the ceremony; and they must see to it personally that the old men of the *avai* receive the delicacies which are due to them. To miss one of these distinguished visitors, to send him away slighted or unsatisfied, would, if it did not bring down more direct vengeance, at least give the *eravo* a bad name. The Drum-Leaders are for the time being the chief guardians of its reputation for liberality.

Their duties are thus somewhat more specific than those of *amua*; and in the matter of pigs they are not inexpensive. As compensation they have the honour of the front places and of leading the procession when the *hevehe* emerge. A *Hevehe* attracts a great deal of attention up and down the coast, so that its acknowledged leaders are satisfied with their meed of fame.

Men of Substance

While it is possible to name chiefs and ceremonial functionaries and to give some account of their duties and privileges, it must be repeated by way of caution that these are not very clear-cut or well-recognized offices. The danger is that even such an analysis as has been attempted may give a false idea of the situation. If we say again, however, that there is often some uncertainty among the members of a community as to who their office-bearers are at a given time, it will be enough to show that chieftainship or rulership among the Elema is really still at a very elementary stage.

The distinctions of social class are still more elementary. In the accepted sense of the expression it is virtually absent;

at any rate there is no sign of its more unpleasant manifestations. Generally speaking there is no snobbery; no condescension, snubs, or raised eyebrows; nor on the other hand obsequiousness or social fright. Such complementary attitudes, in so far as they are found at all, are determined by difference in age, which is plainly not in point.

It might be expected that the *aualari*-groups, with their different mythological antecedents and their prerogatives in magic, would be graded in some sort of social hierarchy. But such is not the case. There is no leading *aualari* group; none is more blue-blooded than another. Nor is there any fixed aristocracy of birth. The eldest son of an *amua* will (probably) in his turn become *amua*; but, until then, he is in no sense a chief, and neither he nor his brothers are in any way privileged. Further, as we have seen, a man who sets up on his own may come to be called an *amua* whatever his antecedents. While individuals vary strikingly enough in respect of social importance there is no ready-made social gradation; and it has simply never occurred to the Elema to divide themselves into cliques, assuming a social superiority on the one hand and kow-towing to it on the other.

It is not that the Elema native is incapable of learning this lesson from a superior civilization. Indeed we may detect the beginning of class distinction in the tendency of the mission-educated native to believe himself a cut above the mere villager. With his glistening white loin-cloth and with his lesson-book under his arm, the station mission boy is not always, one suspects, guiltless of a feeling of superiority, and now and again there is some evidence of antagonism. But on the whole it is rather surprising that this feeling of superiority, in so far as it exists, should be so free from offensive manifestations.

In the face of what has been said it might seem wasted time to search for class-distinctions in Elema society as untouched by European influence. But we shall find at least glimmerings of it in the relative status given by wealth and the secure membership of a community.

It is true that in a place like Orokolo differences in wealth are not readily apparent. At ordinary times there is little display, and wealth certainly does not imply luxury. All live at very much the same standard and all have enough. It is indeed said that a fine house is befitting to an important man, so that he may offer shelter to many friends and kinsmen at a feast; but this is only one of those glib rules that break down when we look for examples. Many important men remain content with small, ramshackle houses; and the size and good building of a dwelling are not so much a sign of wealth (since similar materials are available to all) as of its owner's industry.

Even those very special forms of condensed wealth, viz. the shell ornaments (*huaiea, aitave*, and *apakora* in particular), remain for the most part hidden away in pots and boxes as if—and this is partly true—their owner wished, like a miser, to keep his riches as dark as possible. But here, though they are not worn on the person, there comes a time when they are fittingly displayed, viz. at those recurrent ceremonial presentations in which the natives take so intense an interest. Then the uncle or the brother who makes the gift likes to do so with liberality and so enhance his good name. If, on the other hand, he fails to make a creditable showing he is afflicted with *maioka*, or shame; he feels small; and he may have to endure the actual taunts of those directly or indirectly associated with the gift, for there is no convention of polite silence on such matters.[1] The ideal thing, since the principle of reciprocity holds here as strongly as elsewhere, is both to give and to receive on a lavish scale; but failing equivalent return, a man has his reward in the respect, or even fame, which liberality, or the mere display of wealth at appropriate moments, will bring him.

Such a one is *eharuari-haera*, literally 'a man of many things',[2] a phrase which refers as well to other kinds of property, more materially useful. The *eharuari-haera* owns many pigs; many fruit-bearing trees and palms—sago, coco-nut, and areca; and he can lay claim to wide lands: in fact he has a generous share of that kind of property which

---

[1] Except on the part of the person who is at the moment receiving the gift. The giver has the whip hand of him then.

[2] *eharu-uaria*, 'many things', i.e. items of property.

is subsumed under the term *avai*.[1] And this leads us to the
other of the two considerations which, as it seems, entitle
a man to be regarded as one of real substance, viz. the fact
of long-established membership of the community.

In a version of the Iko myth[2] known to certain people of
Yogu the hero appears under the name of Meravakore,
while the man (or really the men—for it is the common
mythopoeic habit to treat of a village or tribe as an individual) with whom he is associated is called Avaiakore.
These expressions, which might be interpreted 'Bush-boy'
and 'Property-boy', are names rather than terms in general
use; but they serve to point the contrast. For Iko came as a
stranger; he was *ita-lahua-haera*, 'a man of another place';
and as an orphan, destitute and landless, he was *haera
merava*, a 'wild man'. The people who received him on the
other hand were permanently settled, with their *avai*, in the
sense of property, behind them; and though they welcomed
him and profited by his visit they eventually cast him out.

The term *haera merava* is one of contempt. *Ira merava*
means bush-pig; and the man to whom this epithet is
applied is one who, like that animal, scratches for a living.
It is a term which can be used with devastating effect in a
quarrel. In Elema society there are very frequent changes of
residence by individuals. The new-comer, whatever his
reasons for moving, is commonly welcomed, given the use
of land, and made to feel at home. He digs himself in quite
comfortably. But if subsequently he falls out with some of
the more permanent members of the village, his stranger
origin will not be forgotten. As a last insult it may be flung
in his face with the word *merava*. This is a common situation
in the myths. The heroic traveller settles, marries, and
becomes a father. Then for some trifling reason he falls
out with his wife, and she turns on him with this bitter,
unanswerable word. Cut to the heart, the stranger husband
sulks awhile, then packs up secretly and goes off on his
heroic travels again.

There would seem, then, to be some discrimination
against the comparative new-comer. He has no well-

---

[1] See p. 86.   [2] See p. 118.

established place in the community. He is not exactly 'one of us' who have a stake in the country. And this instability of membership, together with the comparative poverty which often goes with it, may be said to constitute a ground for social discrimination, inconspicuous as it is, which is independent of European influence.

Specialists

The native is an all-rounder and a highly competent one; and in all essential points—building, sago-getting, fishing, &c.—his household is economically self-sufficient. For only one important commodity are the Elema people dependent on trade: they get their cooking-pots by exchange of sago from the Motuan *lakatoi*. Apart from this, every man and woman, generally speaking, knows how to go about the tasks of daily life and how to make the necessary tools.

It is obvious, however, that individuals vary in skill. This is not so much the result of differences in technique (for there are no monopolies, no trade secrets) as of those incalculable gifts of muscular precision and artistic sense. Thus there are acknowledged experts in certain practical departments such as adzing canoes, hollowing drums, carving *hohao* or *erekai*, constructing masks. They are called *evera-haera* or *mai-ore-haera*, which means 'men with skill of hand'. It is significant that the individual who is good at one of them is usually good at all.

Such skill may be turned to account. For instance the man who hollows out one of the small dugouts used in shark-fishing—rather a ticklish business when it comes to the last touches with the adze—expects to receive the first shark caught as a present, to be remembered at the cutting-up of subsequent sharks, and to use the canoe on occasion himself. But there is no set scale of payment, and the *evera-haera*, who, from his nature, rather likes using tools, is ready to help his kinsmen and fellow villagers for nothing. So, e.g., in the case of the *hevehe* mask: every man is capable of making his own; but when it comes to the more intricate points he is glad enough to sit back while some better hand among his voluntary helpers is equally glad to take on the work.

So much for the experts, practical and artistic. There is a much wider range of specialisms in *maho*, or magic. But just as every man is his own carpenter, so for the most part he is his own magician. He has his *maho* for fishing, planting coco-nuts, wooing women, and most other ordinary purposes. He keeps it to himself, for he wants to surpass his neighbours and cannot allow them to share his secret of success; though despite the bewildering variety of magic and the reticence of its owners, it is found that the same magical names (in which consists the essence of the spell) appear often enough in the repertoires of different men who think they hold them safely as monopolies.

While every man has a good stock of magic to draw upon, it by no means covers all his activities; and it is readily admitted that, where he has none, he does without. Thus some men have magic for building houses, and some have none; but the latter sort build without any apparent misgiving. Only if, one after another, his houses show too early a tendency to lean or fall to pieces will the builder bethink himself of the advisability of laying his foundations with magic. He may then approach a near kinsman, perhaps an elder brother (for even brothers may withhold magic from one another), and ask his help. If he has none to give, then the builder may, for an arm-shell and a pearl shell, buy a formula from some one else.

While all are magicians to some extent, some have achieved reputations in particular directions, such as for catching *larovea* fish, shooting cockatoo or hornbill, causing rough seas or thunder, hunting bush-pigs or destroying the village pigs of their neighbours, &c.; and some again, in the native sense the most learned of the tribe, have a general reputation and stand correspondingly high in public esteem.

While the great bulk of this magic is used for private purposes, whether good or ill, there is not lacking a ceremonial or public magic used in the interests of the whole com-

his patient and has located the source of illness, he proceeds
to whatever treatment in his repertoire is indicated.

He is much resorted to, and by dragging out the causes
of illness in such convincingly concrete forms he does some
useful service to his impressionable patients, notwithstanding the great scope which the system allows for roguery.
His fees are paid in shell ornaments—from one or two to half
a dozen—and he may do very well; though it must be
understood that he is in no way dependent on his profession
for a living. He is the same sort of all-rounder as any other
native, and does his daily work as they do. Medicine is
merely a lucrative side-line. The doctor's fees are called
kau-kavare, or 'tooth payment', because, what with everlasting sucking and contact with dangerous illness, his teeth
become loose and fall out. It is also claimed that they are
a fair return for his trouble, in particular for the frequent
fasting which is an essential preliminary to treatment in that
it enables the operator to work up 'heat'.

Sorcerers

Should the doctor find the patient's health growing worse
in spite of all his efforts he will dismiss the case as profes-
sionally *ultra vires*: the sickness is caused by some sorcery
which is too powerful for him to deal with. He should then
return his fees, which he has received in advance. But
rather than pursue a course so unacceptable to himself he
may suggest quite another line of treatment: he offers to
discover the identity of the sorcerer. This may lead to
diplomatic approaches, suitable bribes, and further treatment by the sorcerer (if such can be found) whom it pleases
to admit responsibility. But if, as is likely enough, the
patient is really a dying man, the doctor who attended him
unsuccessfully in the first place will have earned his money
well by showing to whom the patient's eventual death must
be attributed, thereby enabling his relatives to proceed to
vengeance. If a doctor thus offers to treat with the sorcerers,
it is because he poses as one of them himself. For the
sorcerers are popularly imagined to form a great combine;
and, while some doctors profess to restrict themselves wholly

to the healing art, it is generally thought—and generally admitted by the doctors themselves—that they are members of it; in fact that they are equally well acquainted with the art of magical killing.

Now every man is, if only because of native gullibility, a potential sorcerer; and there is no doubt, generally speaking, that the older the man the more likely he is to be accounted one. Most would rebut the charge with indignation. But there are certain individuals who, without resorting to open advertisement, still contrive to establish a reputation, and make no real secret of a profession which may bring them a great deal of power and profit. The subject of sorcery, together with that of magic at large, is one of huge proportions. On its ideological side it becomes involved in confusion, with unendingly diverse and conflicting theories which mean sore distress of mind to a conscientious ethnographer until he realizes that the confusion is not to be straightened out; that there are in fact many methods and many explanations which cannot be reconciled. Where the whole business is secret and underhand, and where imagination is overfed by suspicion and fear, we should hardly expect to find among the people in general, or even among the profession in particular, a neat and logical arrangement of ideas. The writer hopes to deal more adequately elsewhere with Western Elema magic and its implications. All that can be attempted here is to point to one or two leading ideas and show the position of the sorcerer in society.

The common inclusive term for sorcery is *harea*, and it means the magical art of killing or doing other things harmful to society or the individual. We shall here adopt the common native view, and think of the *harea haera* at his worst, as one who can and does use magic to kill his fellows. The commonest method, in popular fancy, is that of pointing, or stabbing from a distance (*huhareavakive*). The sorcerer, who is in hiding or has actually made himself invisible, stabs at his victim with some implement, a bamboo knife or a miniature fighting-stick (*kaipau*). He averts his head, and delivers the thrust covertly from under his own left arm. Thereby he manages to introject the *eroe*, the foreign article, which will bring about fatal illness unless it is removed. Some informants believe that the *harea haera*, who wrenches his *kaipau* away after the thrust with as much effort as if he were extracting a spear, drags out with it the victim's *ove* or soul.

Another general term for the sorcerer is *harihu haera*, which may be derived from his association with the ghost (*ove harihu*) of his victim. For sorcerers are known to be ghouls, who dig for the newly buried corpse's bones, fragments of liver, finger-nails, and so on; and it is said they do so in order to gain possession of the dead man's soul. The relics, either carried as charms about the person or rendered down and imbibed like a dose of medicine, serve both to make their owner invisible and to help him in locating further victims. Some attribute these effects to the relic's intrinsic qualities; but it seems to be the more general opinion that they are achieved by the deceased's ghost which the sorcerer now has in his power and uses as a servant, the relics being no more than vehicles. Yet the ghost, thus pressed into service, may prove a rather doubtful associate. It is prone to attach itself embarrassingly to the sorcerer's company, so that he must take measures to be rid of it, or else run the risk of betrayal; for the *ove* may reveal itself to the expedition of diviners when they draw close to his place of hiding and thus put them on his track.

The phrase *harihu haera*, however, is more plausibly derived from *harihu* in another of its meanings, viz. that of the spirit familiar, usually a bush creature (representing its species) which makes itself known to the sorcerer either in a dream (*ivahi*) or during the fasting which is part of his novitiate. This *harihu* is thenceforward at his service, and it is somehow embodied in the *marupai*, the dwarf coco-nut, delicately carved and given the semblance of a small pig's head, with eyes, nostrils, and open mouth. There are *marupai* innumerable in the Elema village, and most of them may be said to be little more than trinkets. But with the proper medicines stuffed in its mouth and with the spell and the *harihu* to aid its flight, the sorcerer's *marupai* can defy every law of nature and probability.

Then there are the *hara-harea* allegedly named from the *hara* or coco-nut-leaf bag. Their methods are somewhat specialized and they work in company. One waylays the victim on the track and shoots him; others come behind to jump over his dead body in turn, to cut it up, extract what is wanted, bundle the disjointed corpse into a *hara*, and hang

FIG. 5. *Marupai*
3 ins. approx.

it to a tree-branch; and then comes the third party to piece everything neatly together, bring the man to life, and send him back to his village, externally sound but without a soul. He has no recollection of his assailants; he is stupefied; and that night he lies down to die.[1]

Lastly, to bring this already much shortened account of sorcery methods to a close, there are the *maea-hiri haera* or 'body dirt' sorcerers, whose method consists of what has been aptly called 'personal-leavings magic'. The substitute for the victim is provided in the form of a discarded armlet, a fragment of his bark-cloth perineal band, or something of the kind which has been impregnated with the sweat and grease of his body; and this is subjected to the familiar treatment with spells and potent vegetable medicines and finally boiled in sea-water. When the bamboo in which the mixture has been placed explodes or blows out its stopper, the sorcerer knows it is all up with his victim.

Amid all the variety of practice and theory of which these few illustrations have been given it is found that the sorcerer

[1] This is the Western Elema version of the widespread method of supposed sorcery known by the Motu-Koita word *vada*. See Seligman, pp. 170–1.

always relies on certain leaves and barks, both for use in his magical mixtures and for his own internal consumption. Ginger (*upi*) is an essential; and the others, mostly strong-smelling and strong-tasting barks, are all thought to generate *ahea*, that is heat and potency, in the body of the sorcerer, a condition which he transfers to his implements and materials by spraying them with saliva. From this practice the sorcerers may be called *kora-iru-haera* or 'tree-bark' men; and from the subjective effect which it produces upon them both sorcerers and doctors (who must prepare themselves in the same way) are known as *maea-hekeheke haera*, i.e. 'body-prickling' men. The supposedly essential condition of *ahea*, or heat, is to a large extent, no doubt, an imaginary one associated with the hot taste of the medicines; though the writer has seen such surprising behaviour on the part of those who have been chewing them that it seems possible some may be intoxicating. There is no doubt on the other hand that the reeling, staggering, collapsing, and the rest of it are to no small extent assumed or self-encouraged. The *kora-iru-haera* is letting himself go with a vengeance. Further the effect of the medicines, nasty as they are, is increased by a day or two's rigorous fasting, without which the necessary furnace of *ahea* could not be stoked up. Incidentally it may be remarked that, in so far as the sorcerer really exists and really practises, such preparations seem to argue some genuine belief in his powers and at least show that he works at his job.

I shall not at this stage enter into the subject of spells and dramatization. They will be dealt with in very general terms in the next chapter. We may go on here to discuss the position of the sorcerer in Western Elema society as a kind of specialist.

Belief in, and fear of, sorcery seem to vary somewhat in intensity among different Papuan societies. But it might be difficult to find a place where they were more deeply ingrained than in the villages of Orokolo Bay. Here as elsewhere every death can be attributed to sorcery—though it does not rest heavy on the native's intellectual conscience to make a generalization in one breath and in the next to dash it with an exception. Thus an informant may declare that So-and-so died of sheer senility—*hare kariderai*, 'his sun is no more', or *beahovea kariderai*, 'his time is up'; but if the old man happened to be his father one may be sure that he would not take so detached a view. It may be safely said, then, that every death is attributed to sorcery by some one or other, and this being the case the relatives of the deceased are deeply concerned to discover who was responsible so that they may pay him back in his own coin. There are some elaborate methods of divination: the corpse itself may take charge at the funeral and lead the bearers a merry dance until it forces them to the very door-step of the sorcerer; and one may still see the *bubuita dakea*, an expedition of earnest young men armed with bows and arrows and *marupai*, and seemingly intoxicated with ginger and *kora-iru*, go forth in single file to search for the *harea haera* and his confederates in the recesses of the bush.

Sometimes the imputation of sorcery leads to violent retaliation; but the bereaved relatives are usually content to take their time and use counter-sorcery, and they are prone to express themselves content when the next death among the sorcerer's kinsmen appears to have restored the balance. Bitter feuds, however, may arise between groups, usually at some distance; and as death, in the course of years, claims one man or another, it is regarded either as a requital or as a further point gained for the side. Under such conditions as these the sorcerers enjoy a very great prestige. In popular imagination they are thought to constitute a secret guild, widespread and maleficent; a sort of powerful underworld whose members forgather in the remotest parts of the bush (a somewhat unnecessary precaution, since they can easily make themselves invisible), there to plan together and confide their successes to one another.

The existence in popular belief of this phantom army of sorcerers enables some individuals to pose successfully as members of it. The *harea haera* presumably feel the same confidence in their spells, their manual procedure, and their medicines, as do the innocent magicians; but they can hardly share the popular notions regarding their powers of invisibility, of shooting *marupai* from their hands, or of travelling at supernatural speed; while their supposed hob-nobbing together to exchange confidences seems hardly less remote from probability. Despite a belief in their own magic it remains obvious that sorcerers are to a very large extent impostors, trading on the superstition of their fellows.

Their profits arise from fees (in shell ornaments) for sorcerizing the enemies of others; fees for annulling their own sorcery; fees for discovering the sorcerer in any particular case or informing against him (for they are sup-posed to be in the know); fees for bribing off other sorcerers in the confederacy; and fees for initiating learners to their secrets. They thus contrive to make themselves compara-tively well-to-do, though hardly to the extent that this imposing list might lead one to believe. For, needless to say, the trafficking with sorcerers is in reality the merest fraction of what it is supposed to be.

To sum up, every man, particularly every old man, can be credited with sorcery and is in danger of being accused of it; and a proportion of men accept the imputation and play up to it. To what extent these few actually put their sorcery (if they have any) into practice can never be accu-rately known. But it is quite enough for them to pretend, By virtue of this pretence they constitute a highly powerful clique of specialists. They are at once the *élite*, and the most feared and ill-famed, of the magical profession.

V

DEAD MEN

IN the two remaining chapters of Part I we shall attempt an analysis of Western Elema religion, a task made more than difficult by the vagueness, laxity, and confusion of native ideas on the subject. While it may seem that we are here branching off on a somewhat new line, we have not entirely taken leave of the field of social organization. For in the larger sense Western Elema society extends beyond the generations of the living and beyond their habitation in space. It includes also the disembodied population of bush and sea and of places purely fabulous, comprising those members of society, in fact, who lived in the near or distant past and who continue to enjoy a spirit immortality.

Spheres of Religious Interest

This supernatural world, dating from a vast antiquity and extending indefinitely into the future, is the principal sphere of Elema religion. It does of course have numerous points of contact with merely mundane existence, or we should be unable to substantiate the claim that it is bound up with social organization. But it is important to record the impression that it is, like religion to most professing Christians, largely a thing apart. The native's thoughts do not often touch upon what we could call religious things, and he is far from being obsessed by them. It is only at certain times —much less regular, though no doubt more frequent, than with most Christians—that his attention is withdrawn from the things of the earth in which he moves. They are occasions of ritual and magic; and even then it seems obvious that routine has largely dispensed with the emotional and cognitive elements that might justify us in calling them religious. When we come to examine the *Hevehe* we shall constantly be brought into touch with this spiritual world. But, so far from being a wholly religious festival, I feel bound to say, after the most earnest endeavours to under-

stand and evaluate it, that I do not think it even a deeply
religious one. Since, however, it is so rich in reference,
whether understood and felt by the participants or not, to
what may be called their religion, we should be called upon
to study that aspect of their culture if only in order to
understand it.

Western Elema religion is not without its animatistic
elements, hardly to be described as forming a substratum,
but rather bobbing up from time to time beside more highly
developed beliefs. It is a 'pre-animistic' leavening. Of this
—from the very nature of the concept—we must expect no
clear account from the native himself. There is plainly,
however, a notion that certain things and people possess a
supernatural power, whether inherent or transient; and this
is not ascribed to any spirit personality, nor does the notion
per se involve any belief in spirits.

If we sought among the Western Elema for a counterpart
of *mana*[1] we should find it approximately in the notion of
ahea, or magical heat. This word is transferred from the
purely physical heat of fire or sun to that of the magician
who is in a state to do something beyond ordinary human
powers. In this sense, viz., as the prerequisite of potency,
we have already seen it ascribed to the native doctor, as if
he had to work himself up to fever heat before he began to
bring into action those other factors on which his magic
depends. But it is also a quality inherent in some things.
Thus the old men of the *avai* possess their permanent *ahea*;
and it belongs also to the bull-roarer, the *kaiavuru*, and the
sorcerer's charm, *marupai* (though in these last-mentioned
cases it can be ascribed by deeper-thinking informants to
the spirits immanent in those objects). More directly it is
found in those secret leaves and barks (*kora-iru*) which
magicians use; and in the ginger (*upi*) which they chew with
the express purpose of making themselves 'hot'. It is not
difficult to understand, since we use the same metaphor in
some connexions ourselves, that the word for 'heat' should

[1] Cf. the notion of *imunu* among the Namau. *Natives of the Purari Delta*, pp. 243–5.
The writer wishes to record his complete disagreement with Holmes's interpretation
of this word, apparently derived from one of his mission boys. See Holmes,
pp. 154–5.

come to be used for keenness, *élan*, striking-power, a potency above the ordinary.

Another word is carried over from everyday affairs to denote a kind of supernatural dangerousness. It is *aiha*, which basically means no more than fierce or bad-tempered. A man who is easily roused and who cannot stop his tongue when once a quarrel has started is an *aiha-haera*, and as such, incidentally, a public nuisance. And the same quality of touchiness, a sort of irascibility in the supernatural sphere, belong to those things—the bull-roarer, the *marupai*, the sorcerer's *hika*, or bamboo medicine-container, &c.—which we have characterized as *ahea eharu*, or 'hot things'. They are charged with power, and those who handle them without authority may expect a shock; or they are fierce and liable to snap.

Again the idea of certain phenomena of nature belongs partly at least to the animatistic stage. The squall, the thunder-clap, the earthquake, are things to be dreaded, and in an almost personal form. But, while there are spirits in Elema religion, it is not thought that any spirits expressly bring about these phenomena; there are no gods of earthquake, wind, and fire. It is true that such visitations may be brought about by magic wherein the names of beings who may be called spirits are used; but for the most part they are thought to happen of themselves. So with disease; it is regarded as some kind of baleful entity which exists in its own right. It may come on the wind; and an epidemic may be driven out of the village by a demonstration, with drum-beating and hooting. There is not (though some informants of the more ingenious sort have suggested it) any generally accepted spirit aetiology.

But while animatistic notions show themselves if we look for them, it is with Elema religion in its more explicit form that we are concerned, and here we immediately enter the realm of spirits—legions of them. They fall into two general classes, (1) Spirits of the dead, or ghosts, (2) Spirits in their own right; thus virtually constituting two spirit worlds, which despite some overlapping and confusion of terms are readily distinguishable.

The duality of religious interest resulting from this classification is to be observed in many cultures, with greater emphasis on one side or the other. Among the people we are discussing it may well be that the former, involving something like a cult of the dead, has greater sentimental importance; but it seems plain that the latter exerts a wider influence on the culture at large. Ideologically it is of fundamental importance, standing as the basis of the totemic (*aualari*) organization and providing the essence of magic. It will be found that the *Hevehe* ceremony in Orokolo Bay touches but lightly on the spirits of the dead, whereas it is fairly wrapped up in the theory of independent spirits.[1]

The remainder of this chapter will be devoted to the relations between the living and the dead; in the following one we shall attempt to deal with the more baffling subject of the second category of the spirit world.

Death and Burial

The dying Orokolan lies in his house surrounded by expectant women. The news of his death gets round quickly and the number of women rises to a throng. They discard their skirts of *mae* and substitute two broad green leaves, front and rear, worn over a perineal band. It is an unbecoming, even slightly ridiculous, costume; but some of the younger sort manage to carry it off with a touch of style. The wailing, continuous at first but later punctuated by increasing intervals, may last for as long as twelve hours. Meanwhile the corpse has been laid out on a concave board, half of a broken canoe. It is dressed for burial with a new white perineal band or a fresh skirt; its face may be painted; a lump of cooked sago is wedged under its chin; and a coconut placed in its hand. With the onset of death the body has lost its *ove* or soul—maybe abstracted by the guilty sorcerer; but it retains enough of life to urinate or to distort its face

---

[1] *Hevehe* is one of those words which appear in a variety of different meanings in different parts of the Elema coast (see Chapter IX). In the Karama tribe (where I made a short study of it fifteen years ago, using the results in *The Vailala Madness*, Anth. Rpt. No. 4), the external features of the ceremony bear considerable resemblance to those seen in Orokolo Bay, but the ideological background is there furnished mainly by the ghosts or spirits of the dead.

into a brief grin if the sorcerer, or even his wife, should enter the house of mourning. For this reason, it is said, sorcerers never attend the funerals of their victims and warn their wives to deny themselves the feminine satisfaction of wailing in company.

The grave (*kapu*) has been dug by old women (it is thought of as an unwholesome business for which they are fitted), and the funeral procession, wading across the creek to the burial ground in the rear of the village, is made up almost entirely of females. Among the last stragglers goes the widow, who has stripped herself naked as a sign that she has been faithful to her husband. Except for the four bearers of the coffin few men go to the graveside, unless the deceased be a person of importance. They watch the procession out of sight from their verandas.

Nowadays a great many villagers give their dead a Christian burial, the service being read by the missionary or one of his teachers; and it is doubtful whether the one or two picturesque ceremonies mentioned here will be practised any longer. But it was the former custom for the deceased's nearest patrilineal kinsmen to take a bow and arrows to the grave, and, before the body was laid in it, to cause the stiff fingers to twang the string; then he shot an arrow into the bush.[1] This was a means, or a gesture, of spreading the *ove* on its way to the land of the dead. After that he caused the deceased's fingers to tap on the membrane of a drum. It was the last time that any drum could be sounded in the village, until, perhaps some six months later, the appropriate ceremony brought the tabu to an end.

The corpse lay supine, with its feet towards the sea. In earlier times it was lightly covered with earth, only as far as the neck, the head being merely protected with matting. After decomposition the skull was taken up, cleaned, painted, and kept in the house of the widow or son until in

---

[1] Among a number of burials which I attended I saw this ceremony performed only once (1931). Two arrows were shot away into the bush, one northwards and one eastwards. The only intelligible reason for the second was that the deceased had spent his youth at Auma, which lay to the east. Even the man who did the shooting was rather at a loss for an explanation. It was already then a moribund custom. The land of the dead is by general consent in the west.

due course it was reburied. But only the oldest surviving members of the tribe have seen this done. Burial customs have yielded to government and missionary influence; and, whereas formerly the dead were interred in the village itself with the aforementioned accompaniments, they are now disposed of more expeditiously in a burial ground beyond the creek.

Subsequent mortuary rites and practices, however, have remained much as they were. Despite the church service it is still the custom to protect the grave with elaborate precaution against ghouls, viz. the sorcerers who desire to possess themselves of those parts of the corpse which will aid them in their nefarious work. Every grave is therefore surrounded by a strong fence, perhaps furnished with spikes or covered with dry thorny sago-fronds, which are nasty things to deal with in the dark and will moreover make a tell-tale noise if they are disturbed. It is always said to be the practice for brothers or other near relatives to stand guard over the grave for some days after burial, and I might have recorded this as a real custom had I not visited a new graveside by night in order to put my informant to the test. Needless to say there was nobody there. For the comfort of the deceased himself some ripe coco-nuts are left by the fence, sometimes with one or two bunches of bananas; while beside the grave there is placed a fire-stick to light him on his way. Formalists will add a few roast fishes.

Mortuary Feasts

The succession of mortuary feasts must be lightly dealt with. The first of them, a minor one, follows immediately on the burial; but those who have had contact with the corpse cannot partake to any extent, for the contamination of death (a direct notion, which does not imply any malignancy on the part of the spirit) is still about them and compels them to take solid food on pronged sticks instead of handling it with their fingers. The more cautious will forgo all solid food for a time and content themselves with *ma-ahea*, literally 'hot water' but really a soup of boiled sago, which they can eat with a spoon.

In the meantime preparations are made for the first

important feast, the *hehe eapoi* which will take place in a
week or so's time. On a small platform, rigged for the
purpose across a corner of the deceased's house, various
items of food are left ostensibly for his *ove*, such as pork,
sago, bananas, crabs; and about it is arranged a display of
'His things' (*areve eharu*), e.g. a new bark-cloth band, his bow
and arrows, feather head-dress, string bag, belt, lime-gourd,
&c., often set off in these days by a brand-new loin-cloth of
coloured calico. This may be seen by the many who enter
the house on the day of the *hehe eapoi* or Mourners' Feast
(*hehe* being a general term for the kinsmen and neighbours
of the deceased, more particularly for those who have helped
in one way or another at the funeral). It is on the day following the *hehe eapoi* that the widow or widower, as the case
may be, and any close relatives who care to follow their
example, assume the principal signs of mourning. The
widow smears her body from head to heel with mud (*bea*)
which dries pale grey, almost white. The widower blackens
himself with charcoal (*aro*) and begins to let his beard grow.
Both thereafter remain in seclusion, women observing it
more conscientiously and for a longer period than men.

The payment of *haro eharu*[1] may take place simultaneously
with the *hehe eapoi*, or subsequently, as a separate performance. It is followed at a long interval by *horo eapoi*, the 'sand
feast', made to those women and girls who have carried
clean sand from the beach and piled it on the grave to fill
up any hollows and make a mound. This minor feast,
which is sometimes omitted altogether, may be a survival
from the days when mortuary rites were more elaborate and
when it was actually necessary to fill up the graves after the
removal of the skull.

The second major feast, called *la huakive* or 'the spraying
on of coco-nut oil' (the spraying being done from the mouth),
brings the principal observances of mourning to a close.
The widower washes off his *aro*, the widow, her *bea*; and the
former offers his chin to his *akira* (deceased wife's brother)
to be plucked. Seclusion comes definitely to an end, and the
widower, who has been a grim figure with his blackened

[1] See p. 63.

PLATE 14

The creek behind Orokolo; women wading across in a funeral procession

A mortuary feast, the *Hehe Eapoi*

skin and his weapons always in his hand (he is on the look-out for the sorcerer), now appears before the village in gala dress, his hair teased into a mop, his body glistening with oil, and an *aroa* of handsome shell ornaments hanging from his shoulder. These last are a return gift for the pig which the widower has given his *akira* for plucking his beard.

The last feast,[1] which may be long delayed, is *maea-hiri-a'airovakive*, 'the burning of body dirt', when various personal belongings of the deceased, such as his mat, his old *hii*, &c., are finally got rid of.

Life after Death

The most illuminating, for our present purpose, of the above-described rites are the offering in the house and the display of the deceased's property. The former is called *ivua-eapoi*, food for the 'house of the dead' (*ivua-uvi*). Good food, of course, is not lightly thrown away, and this is meant for human consumption; it will be eaten by the principal mourners who are secluded in the house and by those who during the earlier stages give them the solace of their company. But it is also, and significantly, called by another name, *ove-ve-eapoi*, 'food for the ghosts'. Informants usually deny that they use any sort of formula in putting their food on the platform, and there is no reason to doubt them. In fact it is likely that the rite is largely performed as routine, its religious import being often absent from consciousness. But they can supply a formula to this effect:

> Spirit of the dead, your food is here; (spirits of) kinsmen, all of you, here is your food.[2]

It is explained that the word *apoheare*, the inclusive term for paternal kinsmen, refers in the present context to those who have departed this life; so that the food in its capacity as offering to the dead is meant not only for the recently deceased inmate of the house but for an indeterminate body of his earlier-deceased kin who are present as guests, so to speak, at the *hehe-eapoi*. I have not heard it suggested that

---

[1] The feasts are all provided in the village where the deceased lived, by the widower for the death of a woman, by brothers and sons for the death of a man. The whole *eravo* contributes in either case. [2] *Haera ove eve eapoi maia; apoheare e koko eve eapoi.*

they make any inroads on the food itself; so far as they are concerned it is no more than a sign.

Similarly a formula—though, I imagine, never uttered in such cumbrous form—can be given for the display of *areve eharu*:

> Your bow, your bag, your belt; your pearl shell, arm-shell, feathers; your perineal band, axe, knife, dogs' teeth—these your things, take them and go, your ornaments and your property.[1]

I have heard a much more pretentious formula than this purporting to reproduce, with the necessary adaptation in names, the valediction of Kapai to his nephew Iko. The story of the hero Iko,[2] amounting with its many episodes almost to a saga, is one of the most widely known in Elema mythology. At the end of a long series of adventures he quarrels with a rival named Ipavu, whom he worsts in a hand-to-hand struggle. Ipavu's people, among whom Iko is at the time a guest, think their leader has been killed (though he has only been knocked senseless), and in revenge slay Iko, cut him up and eat him. But while Kapai, his *aukau*, is mourning alone in the rear of the *eravo* he is astounded to see the slain hero enter and walk down the length of it. 'But you are dead!' he cries; and, when Iko assures him otherwise, he brings out and shows him the morsel of human flesh, the tit-bit which he has received as one of the *avai* but has put aside uneaten. Iko at this stage must have been something more substantial than a mere *ove*, for presently Ipavu and his people come in and kill him again. This was enough for the hero.[3] He made no further public come-back, but went off alone to Horovu Harihu beyond the sunset. There on a desolate beach he sheltered beneath a stranded tree-trunk and subsisted on raw fish. When he did come back again it was covertly and by night. He confided to Kapai the secret of sorcery which would enable him to kill Ipavu; and then, collecting his weapons and belongings, a burning fire-stick and some ready-baked fish, he departed

---

[1] *Ave apo, ave aroa, ave erekai, aitave, huaiea, orikoro, hii, ira, hoi, maki—ave eharu avi-aukia, baupa eharu.*

[2] Iko appears under several names in different versions of the myth belonging to different *aualari* (see p. 43). Kapai, who is his *aukau* in the version here referred to, appears elsewhere as a young man, his *arivu*, under the name Urau.

Though, as some tell the story, he was killed three times.

PLATE 15

A widow wearing her mud before the *La Huakive*

A widower after the *La Huakive* with his *Aroa* of ornaments

to the land of the dead never to return. It is the farewell of Kapai, spoken under these circumstances, which is said to provide the pattern for the formula used in settling up a dead man's belongings, and this mythological precedent which gave rise to the rite itself.

Although I have heard this story in many forms I have never heard it expressly said that Iko was the first man really to die, i.e. to leave the land of the living for ever. But he was at any rate the first man to go to Horovu Harihu. Thanks to his creative powers it was converted from a desolate shore to a blessed region of coco-nut palms and gardens, though there is a less desirable quarter to which those who die by sorcery are condemned. The first to arrive there was Ipavu, the rival, for Kapai had carried out his instructions faithfully. When the victim, now an *ove*, travelled to the west he was met on the track by Iko who, feeling himself injured, declared that he would not suffer his company and sent him off along that other path which so many, likewise victims of sorcery, have followed after him.[1]

This however is an eschatological refinement which the majority of natives are content to slur over, even if they know of it. I have recorded no distinctive name for Ipavu's portion of the west, and if it were generally accepted that such a place existed, it could hardly do without one; for it would follow from the prevalent belief in sorcery as the cause of death that it must carry a far greater population than the more favoured portion of Iko. General belief, in fact, makes no distinction between the two places. The land of the dead is open to all and the name Horovu Harihu covers the whole region. It is thought of as a pleasant place, especially when at sunset the world beyond the horizon seems to glow with supernatural colour. A variant name seems to express more intimately the idea of a home from

---

[1] Like many other mythical stories this has become confused in the minds of some people with Christian teaching. A highly intelligent and well-informed man named Baii gave me a full account of Iko's life and death, but said that he went to some favoured region in the sky, whereas Ipavu went to Horovu Harihu in the west. Iko met him on the path (as he has done all who have died subsequently) and in the character of 'judge' sent him to the land of the wicked. All who committed adultery, stole, sorcerized, &c., went there afterwards; those who had lived righteously joined Iko in the skies.

home: it is Hurava Oro Miri—'the Western Beach where the Oro trees grow'.

Although it is possible to set down these ideas fairly clearly, it is not to be supposed that the ordinary individual has a very clear notion of the hereafter, much less that it is often in his thoughts. I have been many times struck by the poor responses to questions about the life after death. 'What becomes of the dead?' 'We do not know. How can we tell?' That is the commonest of first reactions, and it is not assumed. There are many men who can simply go no farther, and not a few who do not even know the common names by which the land of the dead is known. Relevant beliefs are with most Elema natives vague in the extreme. They have not been formulated for general acceptance; and the confessed ignorance which is so common reflects, I believe, the large measure of indifference which most feel on the question as it concerns themselves.

The Effect of Death on the Community

The death of neighbour, kinsman, or friend is mourned according to the place he held in others' affections and his importance in the community. It is obvious that, of those who flock to the wake, many are not greatly perturbed; their tears may flow merely as the result of emotional infection and are quickly dried. But it is equally obvious that individuals closely associated may grieve very deeply; and even among the more or less perfunctory mourners it is fair to suppose that grief is quite as real as among Europeans at a funeral. The common contemptuous idea that natives are incapable of real sorrow, as of other refined emotions thought proper to civilization, is too absurd to need refuting. And the suggestion that their funerary tears are hypocrisy can only be accepted if we apply it also, for instance, to our own black neckties. Both are regarded as the proper thing; and we are equally unable to tell what density of emotion fills the mourner's heart, whether it beats behind a black necktie or a smear or two of mud. One may guess that it is about the same.

But whatever their grief or lack of it, it seems plain that a people like the Western Elema take much greater relative notice of death as an event in the community. Not only does it set in motion a whole series of feasts, but it acts as a brake on certain other activities though they involve the whole community. The drums may not be sounded, and anything connected with the drum must halt. Thus the tremendous momentum of the *Hevehe* may cease in a moment, and it is impossible to take any further action in connexion with it until the deceased's nearest of kin is ready and disposed to remove the tabu by formally tapping the drum himself. The unconscionable slowness of the cycle is mainly due to this cause. As for the rationale of it, I have never heard, despite a good deal of cautious fishing, that the tabu has anything to do with the spirits of the dead, as if the drum-beating might offend them; it is always explained as due to the living mourner in deference to his grief. While he secludes and blackens himself it would be indecent to engage in festivities; and the community does not dare to risk offending his feelings.[1] These would undoubtedly find vent in the kind of wordy uproar, called *hahari*, which can so easily take a turn towards violence, and they would always have sorcery to fall back upon. The obstinacy of some mourners in delaying the drum-beating is a frequent source of irritation and complaint among the rest of the community, and, needless to say, it is the ethnographer's despair.

Attitude towards the Dead

While the individual dead are mourned for a long period it may be said of the dead in general that once disposed of they are largely out of mind. This is by no means wholly the case; and there has been a tendency, apparently modern but still predominantly 'native', to bring them more to the forefront.[2] But it can at least be said that Elema religion is relatively free from that ever-present fear of the dead which one ventures to call an unfortunate

---

[1] I know of only one case where the tabu was disregarded and it ended in a *débâcle*. See p. 228.   [2] See pp. 123, 124.

feature of so many primitive cultures. They are not viewed as naturally malignant, and are not made the cause of disease.

The ghost is supposed to hover about its home for a while before leaving for Horovu Harihu or—as so many would say—wherever its destination may be. If some unusual noise is heard in the house of the dead it will be put down to the *ove*, which is perhaps protesting that its food has not been set on the platform. To the somewhat nervy ears of the widow, sitting in her dark corner, the squeak of a rat is no other than the voice of her husband; but there is no barricading of doors or covering of the floor-cracks with matting. *Ove* are not ordinarily visible, though they may sometimes be seen, soon after death, as a beam of light which leads the watching brother or son to the house of the sorcerer. And I have heard it said that they may take the form of such nocturnal creatures as *ovurara* (owls), *hakare* (moths), and *hohoro* (fireflies). But these last are at most only temporary forms, and they certainly do not represent a general belief.

Without possessing any set theories on the subject, however, the native behaves sometimes as if he believed the dead, even the long-ago dead, to maintain contact with their former homes. We have noted that departed kinsmen are supposed to be present at the *hehe eapoi*; and we shall see later that in a ceremony called *ivaiva*[1] the ancestors of the *eravo* may be called on, with an offering of food, never to desert the building or their descendants who occupy it. But neither at *hehe eapoi* nor, in ordinary circumstances, at *ivaiva* is the food-offering to be construed as an act of conciliation, as if the *ove* of the deceased were to be dreaded. It is, on the contrary, a rite of attachment. The food given symbolically in the form of the feast is given out of consideration and fondness for the dead; it is for their entertainment and comfort—or at least this is professedly the motive when thoughts of the dead rise to the surface of consciousness; and when an *ivaiva* is addressed to the departed ancestors the old man who pours out the stew on the ground

[1] See p. 229.

speaks mainly of his desire that they should abide with their people.

There are, indeed, some traces of another kind of attitude. They are seen notably when the *ivaiva* is performed in connexion with the trading voyage of the *bevaia*. Then the names of certain more recently deceased persons are uttered, particularly those of former *bevaia-haera*, or captains; and they are adjured to let the voyage proceed successfully. The anger of offended spirits is at least one of the causes of those disasters which so often overtake the Western Elema as mariners. But this, to repeat, is not the prevailing attitude. It is as a rule something more benevolent.

As an aid to understanding the attitude towards the dead it is worth recording a very significant observation made to me by certain informants well qualified by age and knowledge to speak. It concerned the contrast seen in some connexions between spirits of the dead and spirits in their own right as providing the ideological background of custom: in respect of one and the same practice it may be found that some men refer to the former, others to the latter. What these informants said was that the emphasis on spirits of the dead (in certain magico-religious contexts) was a new-fangled thing. Their way was the old original way, and they dealt rather with the old original spirits. There is no means of verifying such a statement, but no particular reason to doubt it; and I am inclined to attach a good deal of weight to the opinion of these old men because it falls into line with what has been a very obvious trend in some quarters.

The opinion must not of course be misread. There is no reason to suppose that interest in and concern for the spirits of the dead are in themselves anything new: the mortuary rites above described presumably date from far back in tribal history,[1] and the concern and interest spoken of are implicit in them. But my informants wished to say that they had of late increased in strength; and this is plainly the case in those large sections of the tribe which were directly affected by the Vailala Madness. If this movement in its religious aspect can be summed up in a phrase it was a 'cult

---

[1] And probably had their beginnings in a much more distant past.

of the dead'. For they were continually regaled with showy offerings of food; the ministers of the cult were in constant communication with them; and their return *en masse* to their old home was once confidently expected. Even now there are occasional revivals of this expectation,[1] the fitful flaring of a fire that seems dead but still smoulders; and even in those sections of the tribe which resisted the Vailala Madness from the beginning it is reasonable to suppose that some of its doctrines should have had their effect. Orokolo and Yogu have been in fact more influenced by this movement among their neighbours on the east and west than they themselves appreciate; and one of its effects upon them is seen in this increased interest in and concern for the spirits of the dead.

Whether, even taking into account these modern influences, Western Elema religion can be said to embrace a 'cult of the dead' depends of course on the meaning attached to that phrase. It seems in the writer's judgement perhaps too high-sounding for the often perfunctory attentions and fleeting thoughts with which the dead are honoured. This chapter, however, may be concluded with reference to a somewhat impersonal but real and important attitude towards the dead in general as representing the past history of the tribe. Without employing any such phrase as 'ancestor worship' one may say nevertheless that the Western Elema have a deep reverence for their ancestry, their *birari*. It does not even imply a knowledge of their names (which commonly goes back no great distance). But it involves the conviction that they, who set up the present established way of life, were right in everything they did; and the oft-repeated justification of conservative practice is that it is *birari mai*—'the fashion of our forefathers'. It may be called simply *overa mai*—'the ancient way'; or, by a stronger phrase, *birari pupu mai*—'the sacred, untouchable way of our ancestors'. However stubborn this attitude may be, however misguided and ungracious it may seem to those who honestly desire to help the native on, it must nevertheless, in strength

[1] One occurred in 1936 (1937) when the beach at Arihava was beflagged to welcome the 'steamer'.

of conviction and depth of feeling, command some tribute of respect. Those who may have a new religion to teach and who find this reverence for the past to be an obstacle may well reflect, as they tear it down, that it also deserves to be called religious. It is to be hoped—and happily it is not impossible—that the new faith will be held with as much sincerity as that old faith in the wisdom of ancestors.

VI

THE IMMORTAL STORY FOLK

Souls, Ghosts, and Independent Spirits

WE may now turn to the second domain of Western Elema religion, viz. that of the independent spirits. While the two domains between which distinction has been made are largely separable, it is not surprising that there should be some border-line confusion; and this immediately becomes apparent in the various terms used for one kind of spirit or the other. There are not a few of them; nor is it in the nature of the case possible to distinguish them all clearly from one another. A glossary of spirit terms, each with its orthodox meaning, is unfortunately out of the question.

In the first place, however, there is the term *ove* which may be used very generally and loosely to cover the whole spirit field. Literally it means (1) shadow or reflection, or (2) the soul of a living being. (It does not appear which of these is the original; needless to say neither the native nor any one else can answer this question, which is happily without importance.) As soul the *ove* is diffused throughout the body, having no substance or shape. The body, *kurua*, is sometimes spoken of figuratively as *ruru*, the mask, the same word as is used for *hevehe* and *kovave* masks, or for those temporary disguises in which the characters of the myths so often appear. Thus the body is thought of as a mere husk or garment of the soul, and with the latter's departure it dies; though here there is some latitude, for in certain circumstances, e.g. when a sorcerer has gained possession of it, a man deprived of his *ove* may still go on living after a fashion; he can at any rate do without it for a while.

An interesting variant is the word *hae*, which, however, is generally acknowledged to be a modernism, popularized by the doctrinaires of the Vailala Madness.[1] It means

---

[1] In its complete form the doctrine embraced *haera hae*, *haera-ve-ove*, and *haera harihu*, all three immanent in the body. To try to obtain sensible definitions of these

commonly 'egg' or 'seed', but stands also for the inner substance or core: thus *kora-ve-hae* is the central part of a tree-trunk as opposed to the softer exterior and the bark. In this literal sense the *hae* is the essential inner part of a man, and his body merely the outer covering. There is no need, however, to draw any distinction between *hae* and *ove* as meaning 'soul', except to say that the former, a modern word, is more strictly limited to the living.

Ove on the other hand is used both for the soul of the living and for the spirit of the dead, or ghost. It appears also in the forms *haera-ove*, 'human ghost'; *ove haera*, 'ghost-man'; and *ove heaha*, meaning 'bad spirit'. The last mentioned does not imply any general belief in the malignancy of ghosts; it is a term of abuse, the offensiveness of which may be fully understood when it is said to conjure up the vision of a rotting corpse.

While *ove* is thus used very commonly for ghost (as well as soul) several of the older men of the tribe declared at different times that the original specific term was *harihu* or *haera-harihu*. This, it will be noted, appears in the phrase Horovu Harihu, the Land of the Dead. But it would appear to have been largely superseded in current usage by the looser term, *ove*.

So far we have been speaking of souls and spirits of the dead. Now, with this word *harihu*, we are carried over into the domain of independent spirits; for, unfortunately, it is another of those words which bear a number of meanings only distinguishable by their context. Despite what the best-informed witnesses declare to be its original meaning, it is nowadays used much more commonly for the independent spirits of the bush. These may assume the living forms of any kind of creature—lizard, snake, animal, or bird; and the word *harihu* is used for the sorcerers' familiars, whose spirits inhabit their *marupai* charms and go unseen on their errands.

Another expression for the independent spirits is *ove-*

is to waste one's time. There is no doubt that they had their origin in some triune notion of Christianity—body, soul, and spirit; or perhaps even Father, Son, and Holy Ghost.

hahu, always rendered 'spirits of the *bush*', though I cannot find that *hahu* means 'bush' or has anything directly to do with it.[1] This is a vague term which I have heard extended to include spirits of the dead when they are thought of as roaming in the bush; but this is a licence which most agree in calling incorrect. *Ove-hahu* are properly independent spirits.

A third expression is *kora marita*, 'tree maidens' or 'dryads', though there is no insistence on their sex. They inhabit the big trees or hollow trunks in disembodied form, or again they may show themselves in the guise of living creatures.

Harihu, *ove-hahu*, and *kora marita* are largely interchangeable terms, though there seems to be some difference in sentimental connotation. The two former may convey a suggestion of the sinister; the last, a pretty phrase, is practically devoid of it. All are spirits of the natural environment, particularly the bush and the rivers. They are ordinarily unseen by humans; but privileged individuals, magicians, are in active rapport with them. Numerous personal experiences are claimed by such men, though they mostly keep them to themselves because of their value for magic. Those, however, who can be prevailed upon to speak will tell of chance encounters in the bush; of strange noises followed by a fleeting glimpse of some shy creature; of some reptile which behaves curiously, or perhaps has a head at each end; or of an apparition seen while a gardener or hunter dozes at midday. The man so favoured by fortune gets on speaking terms with the spirit, learns its name (which he thenceforward keeps a deadly secret), and through the agency of dreams (*ivahi*) receives helpful warnings and advice, especially in the matters of hunting and fishing. He speaks of the spirit as his *kake* (friend) or even *uva* (wife); and retains his hold over it by keeping it in his *marupai*; or he may fashion one of those plaques called *hohao* and set it up in the *eravo*, partly as image, but more as the spirit's dwelling-place. It hardly matters whether such stories are true or false. Some of them indeed

---

Hahu-leikive means to go into the bush on a hunt, so that the *ove-hahu* may mean 'the hunting spirits', i.e. the spirits useful to hunters.

are pretty obvious fabrications; but they are very widely believed because they are in keeping with the wide belief in an unlimited number of such independent spirits, mainly inhabiting the bush.

There is a somewhat special class of creatures, more often thought of in material terms but also capable of a spirit existence, which inhabit the sea and great rivers. These, the *ma-hevehe*, we shall have much to do with at a later stage. They are merely noted here as hardly to be included with the *ove-hahu*, yet, like them, supernatural and independent of any human antecedents.

The distinction which has been drawn between the two categories of the spirits, confused though it may be by some common terms, is by no means an arbitrary one. It is expressly said of the *harihu*, *ove-hahu*, *kora marita*—whatever term is used for them—that they are not, and never were, spirits of the human dead. The latter are *ou erarura haera*, 'born from the womb'; and, however ancient they may be, belong to an era which is by comparison a recent one. The independent spirits date from the very dawn of time. Both categories are called *birari*, 'ancestors'; but they are *birari* of different orders. The spirits of the dead were once flesh and blood; they are ancestors merely legendary, historical, or recent. The independent spirits were from the outset supernatural; they derive from the era of the myths.

How then did they come into being? To account for them we shall have to go back to the subject of the *aualari* which we left in Chapter II. We may now pursue it—very hurriedly—through the fields of mythology, totemism, and magic; and we shall find that it eventually leads us to some explanation of these independent spirits of the natural environment.

A Digression on Gods

Before doing so, however, it is desirable to make a passing reference to Holmes's chapter on 'Gods, Spirits, and Ghosts', in which he sums up Elema religion. When living among the people of Orokolo, he writes, he 'continually heard them using the term *Harihu* as the name of the spirit whom they revered as the Supreme Being of their tribe'. 'Harisu, or Harihu', he continues, 'was supposed to be the god of hosts, the supreme chief or head of all other gods, and it was said that it was his sole right to preside over the councils of other gods who in relation to him were as sub-deities. . . .' 'There was also a belief in the existence of an evil god, a Satan, named Karisu, who had controlling authority over all evil spirits.' Again, 'Among the Ipi tribes it was generally assumed that the far-away things, the undefinable things, were created by a god named Ualare.'[1] And so on with the presumably lesser 'god of the mountains', 'god of the sea', 'god of war', &c.

All the present writer can say is that he has been unable to find any trace of these Judaic-Olympian conceptions among the people of Orokolo Bay. *Harihu* has been adopted at Orokolo, like *Ualare* at Toaripi, as the mission word for God—a perfectly legitimate measure. But it appears just as perfectly plain that it is not based on any conception of a deity or deities in the pre-European culture. The various meanings of *Harihu* have been already touched upon. *Karisu*, which is obviously the same word, is used for ghost, or spirit of the dead, at Karama. *Ualare*, or *aualari*, we shall go on to consider, and we shall assuredly not find that it is the native God of Creation. I shall therefore discuss these quotations no further, except to say that the ideas expressed therein are denied by the wisest and soundest of native informants, who state plainly that they know only one 'god', viz. the God who has been shown to them by the mission. Holmes has toned down his interpretation by stating that his use of the term 'god' is 'in deference to modern expression and not in keeping with Papuan thought, which had not reached the conceptions we associate with the word'.[2] It should be toned down much further; for apart from the question of their attributes or powers, the 'gods' whom he names simply do not have any individual existence in native thought. The words stand rather for a numberless legion of spiritual beings, and vaguely conceived at that.

[1] *In Primitive New Guinea*, Seeley Service, 1924, p. 178. *Ualare* is the Toaripi form of the word *aualari*. See p. 43.   [2] Op. cit., pp. 178–9.

The present writer cannot, therefore, avoid expressing the opinion that Holmes's chapter on 'Gods, Spirits, and Ghosts' would have been far sounder for the omission of the first word and all that concerns it.

The Aualari: Myth and Totem

It was seen in Chapter III that the whole of Western Elema Society is divided into ten patrilineal units, thoroughly mixed up with one another in the geographical sense, to which we gave the name *aualari* groups. It was admitted there that this name was an arbitrary one. The word *aualari* does not in native usage refer to the group itself, but rather to the mythical persons or things specifically connected with it—mythical ancestors, heroes, lesser characters, and various objects of nature.

By way of approaching the magico-religious aspect of this organization we may first take note of a somewhat trivial point. Each *aualari* group possesses one or two distinctive *maea-ihura*, or 'body cries', in which the names of its ancestors or leading mythical characters appear. They are used in moments of triumph, danger, excitement, or exhaustion. Thus, as he transfixes a pig, or confronts an enemy, or even as he throws himself down after working in the heat, the *Kaia* man may cry, '*Oa Havora !*'; or the Ahea man '*Oa Laho!*'; and so on. Women use similar and mostly corresponding cries, as for instance when they land a big fish or as they scream at one another in the heat of a quarrel; and their cries are phrased in a way which reveals the meaning of the *maea-ihura*. It is not a cry for help or one of pious gratitude, but rather one of elation, a boast. It means, 'What a woman am I!' or 'See whom you have to deal with!' Thus the *Ahea* woman cries, '*Oa Laho ve mori!*', 'I am the daughter of Father Laho!'; the *Nabo* woman, '*Ira Nabo ve mori!*', 'I am the daughter of Ira Nabo!'; or the Vailala woman, '*Lau Lavara-ve mori!*', 'Child of Mother Lavara !'

The *maea-ihura* used by men are as follows; most of them being prefixed by the word *Oa*, 'Father':

Kaia: *Oa Havora* (monitor lizard); *Biai-ve-Akore* (son of the python).[1]

---

[1] The same name *Biai* is applied to the rainbow, a *Kaia aualari*.

Ahea: *Oa Laho* (a bird, the shag); *Oa Berare* (a large gull).

Hurava: *Oa Laho; Oa Berare; Ahea Arava* (*ahea*, sea; *arava*, a large fish, the bonito?).

Purari: *Aua*[1] *Kaiva* (the coco-nut); *Maiu Kivavia* (a kind of pepper fruit).

Miri: *Aua*[1] *Kaiva; Oa Ive* (the *oro* tree).

Baiu: *Oa Baiu* (the crocodile?); *Hevehe Ope* (*hevehe*, sea monster; *ope*, a kind of fish).

Auma: *Oa Evoa* (the mangrove, *ova*); *Oa Kari* (the fish named *mara'ope*).

Vailala: *Oa Hiraki* (the bush pig); *Ori Kako* (the friar bird or leather-head).

Nabo: *Oa Irava* (the hornbill); *Ira Nabo* (pig of the Nabo Mountains).

Kauri: *Oa Apu* (a kind of snake); *Oa Harapa* (a hawk).

The interpretations above given serve to introduce the connexion between the *aualari* groups and Elema mythology. The *maea-ihura* do not necessarily embody the literal everyday names of the species to which they refer: *La*, not *kaiva*, is the word for coco-nut; *ira*, not *hiraki*, for pig; *baiva*, not *irava*, for hornbill; and so on. But to every such name there is attached a body of myth, and the connexion with animal, bird, fish, plant, or natural phenomenon is to be discovered therein, being indeed recognized by those, or at least a proportion of those, to whom the myth belongs. We shall see presently how this connexion is established in native ideology.

The mythology of the Western Elema is rich and, to say the least, complicated. It is complicated especially by the fact that, so far from one set of myths serving the whole people, each of the *aualari* groups possesses its own. While these are in strictness, and to a very large extent in fact, independent, there is naturally some considerable fusion and confusion: indeed some incidents in the careers of different *aualari* characters are suspiciously similar, so that here and there it seems that we are following the adventures of the same personality under different names. But the mutual independence of *aualari* myths remains a fact of outstanding significance. No individual could boast—nor would he think of boasting—that he was master of them all. On the contrary they are often treated with exaggerated secrecy. In

---

[1] Always so pronounced in this instance.

broad outlines, it is true, they are widely known, for young
and old will gather about the fires on the cold south-east
nights and listen to the story-teller while they crack and
devour *okari* nuts. But even so a man should tell his own
stories. And the most significant parts of them he will pass
over. Such are reserved for the intimates of his own family.
Many passages are wholly secret; above all, like veritable
hidden treasure, those true names upon which depends the
efficacy of magic. For it is just this jealous desire to mono-
polize magic that accounts for the secrecy. In this way, then,
the myths of one *aualari* group remain separate from those
of another; and within the *aualari* group itself the versions
become divergent and irreconcilable as they are split up
among clans, families, and individuals. The writer has
amassed a considerable volume of myth, but no story of any
consequence has been told in company: it is always from
one individual, or at the most a select one or two who belong
to the same local unit of the same *aualari* group, that one
hears the myth in anything like entirety. It goes without
saying that there are many discrepancies between different
versions.

The stories are unconscionably long-winded. More than
once at the end of a session I have cried 'Enough for the day!'
and left the narrator with a subtle smile on his face, partly
of malicious amusement at having worsted me, and partly
of pride in the sheer length of his story. The tale is one of
miracle and fantastic adventure mixed with the homely doings
of ordinary human beings. The heroes of Elema myth were
prodigious travellers, and they were for ever meeting people.
But they and the people they met are represented as speaking
and thinking in thoroughly human fashion; and if their
changes of outward form and their manner of progress,
through the sky or under the sea, were often miraculous,
they made friends and enemies, feasted, murdered, raped,
seduced, joked, and deceived, much as do the people of
to-day, though rather more vividly and on a grander scale.

But while eminently human in their conduct, the characters of the myths are constantly identified in some manner
with natural objects or species; so much so that it is a

profitable exercise for the ethnographer to go through the story after he has recorded it, asking what this or that person really is. He will be disappointed often enough; but again and again it is found that such-and-such a character is a kind of tree, a bird, a crab, a star—any one of a great number of things which are, so to speak, personified by the myth-makers. Whether or no their previous behaviour has given any hint of what is to come, it is the very common end of the mythical characters, major and minor, to be meta-morphosed into the things of nature. Certain transient changes for the sake of disguise have been a common feature of their previous existence. For this sort of thing the word is *maea-koerari*—to change your body by way of a trick; and no incident is commoner than that of adopting the *ruru* or mask, whether of bird, snake, or what not, and thus appear-ing for the time in a convenient disguise. But the eventual change, not necessarily mentioned in the narrative, is of a more permanent kind. It is *maearai*, a transformation of body, a metamorphosis.

Thus Kaiva becomes the coco-nut, Hiraki the pig, and Irava the hornbill; and the list is endless. To mention a few random examples, Keko turns into a bamboo; Hitovea into a black cockatoo; Mairau into a cassowary; Kari into the *mara'ope* fish; Epe into the crocodile; Hirihi and Ikikavape into little crabs; Ovaro and Mairo into kinds of taro; Lavora into the spathe of a *haio* palm; Eoe into a submerged rock in the Vailala River; and so on interminably. According as these characters appeared in this or that myth, so the species or the objects into which they were metamorphosed are permanently identified with the group to which the myth belongs. They are in fact its *aualari*, or, as we might choose to call them, its totems.

It is not only by metamorphosis that the *aualari* come into being: mere association is sufficient. If Lavai, the Vailala hero, lived in an *uri* tree then the *uri* is a *Vailala aualari*; and if various kinds of banana and yam grew up from the burial-place of Oa Irava, the *Nabo* man, then these are *Nabo aualari*. Further, and in keeping with what seems obviously a local origin of the groups, it is found that persons or creatures who appear in the myths as belonging to this or that part of the Gulf region are allotted to the *aualari* corresponding. Thus the old woman who lives on the upper Purari is a *Purari aualari*, though she may figure in the myths of more than one different group; and the rock-girls of Auma Point are *Auma aualari* though they entertain the hero of an *Ahea* or a *Vailala* myth. The outstanding belief, however, and the one which goes far to explain the further difficulties which we shall encounter, is that of metamorphosis. The main characters in the myths turned into things; and in some hazily understood manner they are still identified with them.

The *aualari* are thus practically innumerable. It would be almost possible to distribute among the ten *aualari* groups all the most significant species and varieties of the Western Elema environment, even down to insignificant creatures like rats (the long-nosed variety is given to *Miri*, a short-nosed to *Kauri*), frogs (*Kaia*), grasshoppers (different varieties belong to *Ahea* and *Nabo*), mosquitoes and flies (*Vailala*), and lice (*Baiu*). While this classification stops a long way short of completeness and is sometimes the subject of dispute, it remains a fact that each *aualari* group possesses an imposing list of 'totems'—birds, animals, fish, reptiles, insects, and plants. Even the varieties of coco-nut, banana, taro, and sago are allotted to them in the same way.

The Aualari: *Myth and Magic*

As for the attitude towards the *aualari* species or variety as such, it contains no element of religious respect. There are no food tabus or other avoidances for the generality of men. The *Kaia* man does not spare the monitor lizard whose skin will cover his drum any more than the *Vailala* man would refrain from smacking a fly. It is only those who practise the relevant magic who may abstain for reasons of their own, as an *Ahea* fish-magician, for instance, may refrain from eating most of the thirty-odd varieties which happen to be his *aualari*. But such a sacrifice would hardly commend itself to the bulk of *Ahea* men.

The ordinary man feels for the most part only a mild pride of ownership towards his *aualari* species. Any deeper sentiment is founded on such interest as he feels in them, or any of them, as a maker of magic. For every man is at least to some extent a magician. His efficiency depends first and foremost on his knowledge of the relevant passages in the myth, in particular of the secret names under which the heroes of olden times performed their exploits. The rationale of this method will not be dealt with fully here;[1] but it may be summarized, I suggest, in the phrase 'Magic of impersonation', the magician of to-day securing his success by actually impersonating, by pretending to himself to be, the mythical hero, and by re-enacting, however sketchily, that particular exploit which is parallel to his present purpose. For this impersonation it is necessary to know the esoteric names not only of the hero but of the things he deals with in his heroic fashion, so that they may be assumed by the magician himself or applied to the things—bows, arrows, dogs, pigs, coco-nuts, sago, canoes—whatever they are, which he happens to be dealing with.

It is found accordingly that each *aualari* group possesses a series of special names for the bow, the dog, the pig, and the trading-canoe; further, for coco-nut, banana, sago, &c., these latter not corresponding with the different varieties of the plants in question. Such names are not taken in vain; they are semi-secret, being the common property of the *aualari* group as drawn from its mythology, and they are used for the relevant magic. It is true that individuals may know and apply to these things magic names which derive from *aualari* other than their own, for there is buying and selling, giving and stealing, of these as of more material commodities; and, further than this, there are many secret names and many secret episodes in the myths, the knowledge of which is held and bequeathed more or less privately by individuals or small kin groups, being too precious for common use even within *aualari* bounds. But these considerations do not alter the fact that each *aualari* group possesses in the main its own reservoir of magic drawn from its own mythology.

[1] See the writer's 'Trading Voyages from the Gulf of Papua', *Oceania*, vol. iii, no. 2, 1932.

Magic in general is called *maho*; and the mythical characters whom a magician impersonates are *maho-haera*, Magic People. He himself is merely *maho-ore-haera*—one who 'knows' *maho*. There is no confusion between these two expressions. The *maho-haera* belongs to the far-away past. The *maho-ore-haera* is obviously of the present; but by identifying his magical process with the mythical performance of the *maho-haera*, his *aualari*, he employs a precedent and prototype which at least make him confident of success.

The Immortal Story Folk

As far as magic is concerned it does not appear that the *maho haera* are necessarily thought of as still existent. Some forms of expression do contain an appeal; but they are not usual. The typical form is, 'I am so-and-so' (an *aualari* character), 'and I do this' (as he did it). Nor in other connexions does it seem that belief in the immortality of mythical characters is universal or strongly held. But while some informants have shrugged their shoulders, and some have denied it outright, not a few have declared that the people of the myths really are immortal; and we must, I believe, accept this as at least a partly realized assumption. It forms the ideological background for practices which are without it unintelligible.

The people of the myths are called *lau-haera*[1]—the Story Folk. That they really lived and achieved marvels in their time is never doubted. And, although the modern native in his more rationalistic moods may speak of them as gone for ever, there are nevertheless still times when their existence is plainly assumed. Those Elema philosophers who have actually propounded the theory of immortality—and it is their theory, voluntarily offered, not mine—explain it in this way: the Story Folk changed themselves at the end of the mythical epoch into various creatures, or sometimes inanimate things, of forest, air, and sea. They thus enjoy a kind of immortality in the species or in some permanent work of nature. But they also exist in some spirit form (of which we cannot expect any definite formulation), as if

---

[1] Or *lau-hira-leipe-haera*, presumably meaning 'the people made in Story'.

they merely incorporated themselves in the living creature or merely haunted the rock or stream. There are abundant cases of alleged encounters and resultant association with spirits of the bush—not ghosts but independent spirits in anthropomorphic form; and those who at other times and at large profess disbelief in the existence of such spirits are always ready to accept these tales as true.

They are happily oblivious to their own inconsistency. The belief, then, although it may be denied, is still there, latent.

To quote the tribal philosophers once more, they pull things together neatly enough by explaining that the *lauhaera* actually *became* the *harihu*, or *ove hahu*, or *kora marita*. The independent spirits who still haunt the Elema environment are, in fact, no other than the Immortal Story Folk.

PART II

THE DRAMA

VII[1]

THE *KOVAVE* CEREMONY

The Mask

ONE might look along the beach of Orokolo Bay at noon and find it almost deserted. But at odd periods in the course of the year the midday solitude is likely to be broken by a few lonely figures of altogether outlandish appearance. To any one who sees them for the first time they are a vision certainly astounding and probably delightful. Each wears a mask of graceful outline, semi-conical, and rising to a tall point. It is furnished with round eyes and projecting ears and mouth, the latter perpetually open and lined with fierce teeth. Beneath this head-piece appears a voluminous mantle of cream-coloured bast, neatly trimmed at thigh-level; and beneath this again, a pair of well-turned brown calves which bear the whole superstructure in a very lively and even dainty manner. The figure is undeniably an artistic success. The designs on the head-piece, picked out in black, grey, rose-pink, red, or yellow on a white background of lime, are symmetrical and bold; and while the whole effect is (as it is meant to be) rather comical, it has enough of terror in it to make the proper impression on small boys. The figure is never still; if it appears to stand, its feet are restlessly and rhythmically on the move. It never merely walks; it advances in a springy kind of trot, the mantle of bast rising and falling with each step. Two naked arms are visible. They may carry bow and arrows (full-size or miniature), but more often a light and serviceable stick.

While we are admiring the grace and dignity of this preposterous figure, we shall be surprised to see it break into a

---

[1] The greater part of this chapter appeared in the *Illustrated London News* of 12 June 1937, pp. 1092-6, and 25 August 1934, pp. 290-2.

run—and very imposing it is at that moment. But the run quickly develops into an ungainly sprint, when the figure is bent forward, ostrich-like, its bast feathers flying in the wind, and its human arms and legs showing every sign of supreme effort. If we glance up the beach we shall see the reason for this sudden transformation. A band of small children are scampering in a kind of gleeful terror for the shelter of the village fence. The masked figure does not deign to pursue them far; he slackens his pace, shakes his bast mantle into position with a hitch of the shoulders, and resumes his pompous way along the water's edge. Presently he turns into the village and, mounting the ramp that leads up to a *baupa eravo*, disappears into its interior.

The figure thus described is a *kovave*.[1] It belongs to one of the two varieties of masked figures which appear in the spectacular ceremonies of the Gulf, and for which *Kaiva Kuku*[2] has become the popular name. The other variety is that of the *hevehe*, very different in appearance. It is to the latter kind of mask, and all that concerns it, that the present book is devoted; but it seems desirable at least to sketch *kovave* as something which, while independent of the greater ceremony, is in some ways closely similar to it. To attempt to deal fully with both would inevitably confuse the picture, so our dealings with the lesser kind of mask will be restricted almost entirely to the present chapter. Let us go back to the beginning of the ceremony and follow the *kovave* through its brief cycle.

A Sketch of the Kovave *Cycle*

Since each community bears the ever-present responsibility of a batch of growing youngsters, it must from time to time arrange for their initiation into the mysteries. Thus it comes about that a prosperous community will call out its own *kovave* every few years. First there is a secret expedition

[1] Throughout this book the capital letter will be used for the ceremony or cult, the small for the material object used in connexion with it. Thus *Kovave* stands for the ceremony or cycle of ceremonies, *kovave* for the mask; similarly, *Hevehe* for the cycle, *hevehe* for the mask; Bull-Roarer for the cult, bull-roarer for the actual object.

[2] I am not sure of the origin of this expression. It is used for all the masks of the Elema by the Motu, but it does not sound Motuan.

PLATE 16

A *Kovave* before the *Baupa Eravo*. It is carrying the *hovahi* rod (see p. 146)

A *Kovave* on the beach

to the bush to procure the rattan cane of which the skeletons of the masks are made. The whole ceremonial cycle is a strange mixture in which sincerity contends with make-believe; but here at the cane-cutting we see the former attitude unmistakably predominant. As each man cuts his cane he utters the traditional name of his *kovave*, the name which his father and his grandfather used before him, and calls upon it to leave the forest and live for a space in the village, for the time has come to reveal the mystery to his son. '*Arulavai!*' or '*Meravakore!*' or '*Lepulela!*', he may cry, 'Come to our village. I have a pig waiting for you.' On the return of the expedition the cane is smuggled into the *eravo* by night, unseen by women or children.

Then in the privacy of the men's house it is split and fashioned into trim frameworks, and these covered with bark-cloth. The traditional designs are embroidered upon them, and it is essential that *Arulavai*'s face should wear precisely the same patterns on this occasion as it did when he last appeared. It is all leisurely and sociable work, and weeks may elapse before the masks are ready for the actual initiation.

Now the *kovave*, with head-piece and bast mantle complete, but as yet unpainted, are conveyed overnight to a clearing some distance behind the village. We shall find this clearing a scene of great activity on the following day. To enter fully into the kinship obligations connected with *kovave* would mean a long digression; it is enough here to say that in the typical case the boy's father undertakes the bulk of the material preparations, but that his maternal uncle bears at least a nominal share in them, and is further called upon to lead him to the actual initiation. Now the uncles are seen performing their first duty; they are painting the masks. If we look closely into the matter we shall probably find that other willing hands are doing the painting while the maternal uncles are chewing betel. It is ostensibly their work, and no more. Nobody cares, however; the day is one of bustle, jollity, and a good deal of confusion; and while the young men are adding the final touches and fitting the masks on one another's heads, the old men, real rulers of

Gulf society, enjoy their privilege of eating while others work.

At about four in the afternoon everything is ready. The completed masks are borne off down the track towards the village by young men full of mischief. It is a fine lark. They hide in the dense undergrowth holding the masks in readiness. One youth perhaps prepares to climb a coco-nut palm to provide a diversion. Gradually silence supervenes and all is expectancy.

Now in a few moments we hear sounds of a party approaching from the village. The maternal uncles have gone off to bring their nephews and already they are on their way to the scene of the revelation. The boys themselves are supposedly ignorant of what is in store for them, though there is some likelihood that they see through the benevolent deceits which are meant to keep them so. 'Come along with us', their uncles say, 'we want you to climb for some betel-nut'; and as the party proceeds along the narrow track they make boisterous conversation in order to distract their nephews' minds. 'That fellow is stealing coco-nuts!' they shout, as the coco-nut climber comes into view; and while the children innocently peer ahead there is a sudden startling uproar; the men leap from their ambush with howls and yells, and each initiate finds a *kovave* mask clamped on his head. Jostled and buffeted, the astounded youngsters are borne along at a run, some struggling and kicking, some actually in tears. But it is all over in a few moments. The cheering mob has already reached the open space, and the initiates are unmasked. Now they stand somewhat embarrassed while the noise and laughter subside. The laughter is not at the novices but rather of the kind that we indulge in when we have emerged from a good rough-and-tumble. The old men are not visibly roused; they have seen this sort of thing too often to be much amused.

When all have got their breath sufficiently they proceed to the fitting. They break up into little groups surrounding the several novices in their new masks, while the maternal uncles perform their next duty, that of trimming the hitherto ragged ends of the bast mantle to a suitable level. Where the

novice is a small boy, a full-grown man will wear the mask
for him (embracing the youngster meanwhile underneath it)
so that the length of the mantle may be properly judged;
for it is to be worn subsequently by men of full stature.

The trimming completed, the new initiate stands alone
and submits to a homily from his maternal uncle. We find
as a matter of fact that the uncle often spares his nephew
the embarrassment and himself the trouble. But this is the
proper occasion for any of the relatives interested to air an
opinion or a grievance; and thus the initiate may be made
the nominal butt of a harangue. Even if he is the real object
of the speaker's indignation, he does not care; it is true he
cannot answer back, for *kovave* do not speak; but it is likewise true that his blushes are invisible, and by this time he is
beginning to feel at home in his new mask and no doubt a
little important.

Finally the young initiate must try a few steps. It is
amusing, but also rather touching, to see the smallest boy,
his heart no doubt bursting with pride, as he circles about
in a mask many sizes too big for him. No applause greets
his success, but correction from every side and shouts of
good-humoured laughter accompany his mistakes. But the
trial is very brief, and most of the boys can do their steps as
to the manner born, for they have played at *kovave* scores of
times in imitation of their elders.

When the last boy has been put through his paces the
masks are left at the place of initiation and all return to the
village. That evening a long springy ramp is constructed,
leading from the ground to the entrance of the *eravo*, and the
night is spent in singing the appropriate songs. To-morrow
at dawn the *kovave* are to make their formal appearance,
being worn by the initiates themselves.

Soon after day-break, while we are waiting in the village,
a chant is heard in the distance, mostly in monotone but
with a strange catchy rhythm. It is sung by the escort of the
first *kovave*; and presently we see a band of befeathered and
beweaponed youths carrying numerous streamers of fresh
green coco-nut leaves emerge from the bush and turn along
the beach, running fast as they sing. Once opposite their

eravo they suddenly extend, and disclose in their midst the first of the *kovave*. He enters the village, takes a turn or two about the open space before the *eravo*, and then trots sedately up the ramp. If the wearer be a young boy, he will be staggering so with fatigue by this time that it is necessary for a man to shepherd him along and help him up the final slope.

One by one or in groups the remaining *kovave* come in. They are doffed by the initiates as they arrive and set up in their places in the *eravo*; but before the last have come in, the first are already out on the beach again. Men and youths are waiting their turn, and henceforward for many days you will see *kovave* coming and going; the mask hoisted on to the wearer's shoulders in the *eravo*; his stately progress down the ramp; a brief restrained evolution—a sort of hint that the *kovave* is so light-footed that he might almost dance; a hitch of the mantle like a ruffling of feathers; then out on to the beach to parade for half an hour in the blazing sun and occasionally give chase to little boys.

This is where we first encountered our *kovave*, and for a month or more we shall continue to see him and his fellows patrolling the beach. Meantime preparations are going on for the winding up of the ceremony, for the dispatch of the *kovave* to their homes again. These preparations mean principally the accumulation of food for a feast, and of ornaments for presentation to the new initiates and to those who stand as 'fathers' or 'mothers' to the several *kovave*. The gift transactions are too intricate to be dealt with here in detail; as far as the initiate is concerned it will suffice to say that in the typical case he is decorated with armlets, pearl-shells, and other ornaments by his maternal uncle, who will receive in return a pig, or part of one, from the initiate's father.

The presentations take place in the late afternoon, when the efforts of the perspiring women in the open-air kitchens have come to an end, and a long row of pots, filled to the brim with hot *papaa*, stand ready before the *eravo*. Now the *kovave* issue one by one and cross the village to another *eravo* where stand the maternal uncles of the initiates. Each *kovave* carries a ladle, fashioned from coco-nut shell, which he

PLATE 17

Kovave in a village at Muru

mutely displays before the avuncular eye. It is the invitation to eat. And each *kovave* having shown his spoon receives a light staff or wand called *hovahi*, prettily decorated, which he brings back to his *eravo*, with intent to make good use of it later that evening.

Now follows the presentation of gifts. In native eyes this is the moment of supreme interest, the climax of the whole ceremony. Once again it is an occasion for the free airing of opinions, and one may see the donors work themselves into what seems like a fury, while the recipients, loaded with ornaments as they are but looking very sheepish, are obliged to listen in silence.

The presentations over and the pots of food distributed there follows an episode of a more frivolous kind. It is now within an hour of sundown. The tide is out and there is a broad hard beach, and we already see the crowd beginning to line the landward side of it. Now the *kovave* come out in full strength, following one another on to the beach, where they aline themselves along the water's edge in extended order at some twenty paces' interval. There they stand, facing landwards, in readiness for the trial of speed, *kovave* against man. Meantime a crowd of young men—they are from a rival village—have formed up at one end of the line, and they now advance abreast down the beach. They pass the first few *kovave* without issuing a challenge, but suddenly one of their number darts forward, and immediately the nearest masked figure, with brandished stick, is flying in pursuit. Another and another give the challenge, until all the *kovave* are seen in full fluttering career, each after his own man. Where the runners are equally matched the result is a foregone conclusion, and the *kovave* are gradually outstripped; but sometimes they get close enough to use their sticks.

It is all a sporting contest and should be a friendly one. But, alas, friendly contests too often end in strife where many natives are gathered together. These are rival villages; old victories of the *kovave* are recalled; the reluctance to give challenges on this occasion is a cause for derision; there are shouts and jeers; and finally the *kovave* disappear in the midst

of a thousand furiously angry men, partisans of both sides
who have 'rushed the grounds'. So many are armed, with
bows and arrows, clubs and trade axes, that we have all the
materials for a first-class riot; and in earlier days it could
have ended in no other way. But now there is a sprinkling
of village constables and councillors, and some of them at
any rate are calm enough to work for the cause of peace:
so that within an hour of the beginning of the race the crowd
has dispersed and the *kovave* are all safely back in their *eravo*.

There are further episodes that evening which must be
dismissed very briefly. Some of the *kovave* have planned a
raid on a neighbouring *eravo*, and having stolen into it while
its occupants are asleep they poke and belabour them with
the long *hovahi* rods which they received earlier in the day.
The resultant alarm is the signal for a general muster of
the mask-wearers together with all the men and boys in the
village; then to the sound of drumming and singing the
kovave, making some show of resistance, are hedged in by
a barrier of poles borne by the villagers and gradually pushed
back into their own *eravo*. Later on that night the masks
leave the *eravo* for the last time and are secreted in the bush
near by for the events of the morrow.

For the last twenty-four hours a score of pigs have been
lying under the village houses. They are securely trussed up
and save for an occasional grunt or scuffle they brood over
their predicament in silence. But their hour is now at hand.
At seven o'clock in the morning an expectant crowd has already collected and the first pair of pigs are carried out and
laid on the ground before the *eravo*. The round note of a
single shell trumpet is heard, turning to a throbbing discord
as others join in, and presently, in answer to this summons,
the two leading *kovave* are seen entering the village from the
bush. They are now armed with full-sized bows and arrows,
and as they near the *eravo*, without abandoning their almost
majestic style, they are seen to be peering about in order to
locate their respective pigs. The wearer of a *kovave* has only
a limited field of vision, for he looks through small holes in
the bark-cloth covering of his head-piece—so that his
movements are sometimes laughably slow and deliberate.

PLATE 18

A *Kovave* shooting its pig

But, now, having sighted his pig, he leaps over it in his stride; turns about and leaps over it again; and then, halting before it, fits an arrow to his bow. Strong men are chosen to wear the mask on this occasion, for it would be unseemly for the *kovave* to fail. But it is, of course, a sitter; he shoots one arrow and then makes off, leaving his victim in the throes of death. One after another all the *kovave* come in and dispatch their pigs. If one by chance fumbles his arrow and drops it, he does not stoop but calmly feels for it with his foot and picks it up with the help of a more or less prehensile great-toe; if the shot is not fatal, he will have to leave it to one of the bystanders to joggle the arrow humanely in the wound until the animal expires.

When all the *kovave* have disappeared there follows the work of singeing and butchering. The pigs, some of them enormous specimens, are disembowelled and cut into halves or quarters, and all this occupies the rest of the morning. At about 3 p.m. the shell trumpets sound again, and the leading *kovave* reappear. Some elderly men have come forward to make the distribution, and two of them succeed in lifting the forepart, with head and legs, of a tremendous pig, and placing it in the arms of the first *kovave*; and the *kovave*, by a truly remarkable feat of strength, succeeds in staggering off with his burden. Others who receive lesser portions make off at a great pace, and so the procession continues for an hour or more, the *kovave* in some cases returning several times, till the last of the meat has been taken.

If we follow the procession, we shall find a crowd of men and boys on the track some two hundred yards away from the village. Sides, quarters, chines of pig lie everywhere, amid tousled masks thrown carelessly on the ground. Everyone is talking; some are cutting up the meat, and others are already carrying away their shares. To avoid the details of the distribution we may say that the maternal uncles are carrying off the payment for the ornaments which yesterday they gave to the initiates.

But we must hurry back to the village in order to see one of the last episodes. There is evidently something in the wind; men, women, and children are mounting their verandas rather hurriedly, and the youths are arming themselves with bundles of short sticks, moving furtively meanwhile among the piles of the houses or peering from behind coco-nut palms. In a moment the cause of this apprehension appears in the form of two *kovave*. Fairly galloping—that is the only word—they sweep through the village and immediately the small boys' sticks begin to fly from all directions. The *kovave* themselves are provided with the same sort of missiles, and, as they are virtually in armour, they adopt the offensive. For a few minutes the battle rages, the *kovave* pursuing the boys and being themselves pursued, and it is no wonder that the villagers choose to watch the fray from their verandas.

But very soon the stock of ammunition has given out; and the *kovave* return more sedately to the front of the *eravo*, where one of the old men is awaiting them. He presents them with a firebrand. It is a parting gift, and (as the women are supposed to believe) it will serve to kindle their torches for the journey homeward through the forest. Taking it without ceremony they now return to the spot where the other masks have been thrown down and the butchering is still in progress.

Some of the younger men are carrying the masks, rather battered and bedraggled by now and already bereft of their feathers (the most valued part of their make-up) to the creek, one hundred yards or more away. Here they are thrown carelessly in a great heap, on the muddy bank, and while the buzz of conversation continues round the carcasses of the pigs, some one takes a firebrand and unconcernedly thrusts it into the pile. By rights it is the firebrand which those particularly aggressive *kovave* received after their final raid on the village; but in point of fact it may be any merely convenient firebrand; and the old man whose duty or privilege it is to apply the fire may be far too busy watching the dismemberment of a pig. It seems almost a case of getting it over, and undoubtedly the most deeply impressed among those who are there to watch the fiery passing of the *kovave* is the solitary European. But while flames are devouring the dry cane and bark-cloth with its beautifully executed decorations, and while he is watching, a little disappointed at the lack of ceremony, an old man comes down the path and stands before the burning pile. Then he raises his voice in a high clear exhortation. '*Meravakore, Avaiakore*', he cries, naming the two chief *kovave* of this particular celebration, 'Go back now to your homes in the bush. We have fed you: do not be angry with us. When other strong men of our village have pigs for you, they will sound the shell trumpet. Hearken and come again.'

The *kovave* are the spirits of the bush. They are the innumerable characters of tribal myth who once, in the prime, were living creatures, of human or more than human character, and who now dwell spiritually and immortally in the depths of the forest. They have paid their visit to the village; now they have gone to their homes in the big trees. But they will be listening for another summons; and when there is a new generation of fat pigs in the village the conch shells will sound again and the cycle will recommence.

Its Interpretation

The foregoing brief sketch, which might easily be expanded to the size of a book, will have to suffice for *Kovave*. As one of the two mask ceremonies of the Western Elema it is generally acknowledged, or at least thought, to have its actual home in Orokolo Bay. But there are various counterparts to it along the coast. (1) First, on the west, there are the *kanipu*[1] masks of the Namau, often flat-faced but otherwise similar to the *kovave*; these have the special function of guarding the coco-nuts when they are under tabu. (2) A series of ceremonies precisely similar to *Kovave* in costume and conduct belongs to the Berepa and Keuru tribes, though there the masked figures go by the name *harihu*. (3) Among the Uaripi tribe[2] and at Opau the mask is different in character. The head-piece is squarish, and the mantle extends to the feet, so that the movements of the wearers are no longer

[1] See the writer's *Natives of the Purari Delta*, pp. 204 ff.
[2] Among the Uaripi the *Kovave* is also practised under that name and with the Orokolo type of mask. This is acknowledged as an importation from Western Elema.

light and dainty. The *harisu* (as it is called at Uaripi) or *haruhu* (as at Opau) moves rather like an extremely portly and sedate old woman, or like a church dignitary in his robes. (4) At Karama the counterpart of the *kovave* is called *harisu*. But here the costume is different once more, the mantle being now of banana-leaves; and the wearers are again found to play the role of guardians of the coco-nut groves, as they did in the Purari Delta. (5) Beyond Koaru, in the Toaripi, Moviavi, and Biaru tribes, the corresponding masks are called *Oio* and *Oioi*.

Except for the last-mentioned, of which I have very little information, it may safely be said that all these ceremonies have much in common despite considerable differences in procedure and form of mask. The name *kovave* defies interpretation; but the others, including possibly *kanipu*, are obviously the same as the Western Elema word *harihu*. As we shall see, in another connexion, it would be extremely unsafe to assume identity of meaning from identity of name; but in this case I think it may be safely asserted that the main idea of the above-named ceremonies throughout is the entertainment and placation of the spirits of the bush. That this is so in the case of *Kovave* needs no further proof. It is not a matter of assumption, but is the native's own explicit theory of the ceremony in its religious aspect; though it must be said to contend with a thoroughly rational view in which *Kovave* is a man-made device for tricking the women and children. Of these two attitudes first one and then the other takes the lead; but I have no hesitation whatever in saying that the rational, mundane view is on the whole an easy winner.

A word must be spoken here of Holmes's description and interpretation of *Kovave*. The few facts recorded in his book are so completely at variance with present-day practice in Orokolo Bay that the only conclusion I find possible is that he was writing of some ceremony in another Elema tribe and applying to it the name *Kovave* by mistake. Thus he speaks of initiation as taking place within the *eravo*, or 'temple'; of the part played by the bull-roarer, the boy receiving 'two or three whacks across the chest' with it; of the bestowal of a plaited girdle by the maternal aunt; and so on.[1] Now *Kovave*, by that name, belongs to Orokolo Bay, and there are no such performances connected with it at present, nor do my informants, some of them contemporary with Holmes, recollect anything of the kind in the past. Whether Holmes actually saw what he describes, or whether he merely took down a description from informants, does not appear. In any case one is not in a position to deny that such a performance took place somewhere; but the present writer is forced to doubt strongly whether it took place in Orokolo Bay, and whether it could have been called *Kovave*.[2]

But all kind of doubt vanishes in respect of Holmes's interpretation. He goes on to speak of *Kovave* as a 'tribal deity',[3] as 'a god supposed to reside in the mountains',[3] and, finally, as 'the god of the mountains'.[4] On the contrary and as a matter of fact, the *kovave* are individuals, each with its own name and characteristics, and they are innumerable. The writer can only conclude that these facts escaped Holmes's observation and that his interpretation of *Kovave* as 'god of the mountains' is on a par with his interpretation of *Harihu* among the people of Orokolo as the 'Supreme Being of their tribe', their 'god of hosts'.

The other kind of mask ceremony practised by the Western Elema, viz. *Hevehe*, also has what may be called its counterparts in the Purari Delta and down the coast. But there is some confusion among them in practice and theory. Our business in this book is with the *Hevehe* ceremony as performed in Orokolo Bay, and no reference will be made to the similar ceremonies in other parts except in so far as they may help towards understanding it.

Having stated that there are two kinds of mask ceremonies among the Western Elema, one must repeat with

---

[1] *In Primitive New Guinea*, pp. 120-2.

[2] The only plausible explanation which old informants are able to offer is that Holmes may have witnessed an initiation to *Kovave* which was actually performed within the walls of the *eravo* because wet weather made it impossible to carry it out in the bush. Some few cases are recalled in which this was done. And it is said that *Kovave* and Bull-Roarer initiations have actually taken place simultaneously under these conditions. This, however, was purely a matter of convenience. The two institutions are wholly separate.

[3] Ibid., p. 120.   [4] Ibid., p. 178.

emphasis that, while they possess certain similarities, they are mutually independent, and totally so. *Hevehe* and *Kovave* do not follow one from the other. Each is a performance with beginning, middle, and end, complete in itself. For all the bearing which it has on *Hevehe* the description of *Kovave* might have been omitted from the present work. But apart from the similarity which it bears to the vastly greater undertaking with which we are concerned, our excuse for including an account of it is that the practical considerations which we shall discuss at the end of the book apply equally to both.

VIII

SUPERNATURAL INMATES OF THE *ERAVO*

WE have seen something of the *eravo* as a club-house and sleeping-quarters for the village men; but it is much more than that. As we pass through the low doorway that gives entrance to the front part of the building we may well experience a sense of withdrawal from everyday affairs. In contrast to the sandy glare of the village one finds here cool and semi-darkness; and, if the building is unoccupied, a curiously muffled silence. With its lofty arched roof, its pillars, and the long nave-like passage between them, it has reminded many visitors of a church; and this impression may remain even after they have learnt something of its purpose. At certain times none would deny the *eravo* an air of real solemnity; amid its other functions it is un-mistakably a place of religion.

The Hevehe

But if it is an old-established *eravo* we shall not find the great space of its interior unoccupied. It is literally thronged with strange shapes depending by rattan canes from the roof. They are themselves structures of rattan cane, long, narrow, ovoid, and flat. On the bark-cloth with which each of them is covered there appear a great number of bold and effective patterns, picked out in delicate colours, those at the base resolving themselves into a highly decorative form which unmistakably portrays a face. From the apex of the structure there projects a tall spike swathed in painted bark-cloth; behind and beneath it hangs a voluminous drapery of shredded bast, pale straw-coloured. Scores of these queer figures occupy the space on either side, shoulder to shoulder, their ample skirts reaching to within a foot or so of the floor.

They are the *hevehe* masks. A breath of cool air passing down the central passage may lift a stray wisp of bast, or may cause one of the masks to revolve slowly in a half-circle; but mostly they hang quite motionless. They are biding their time. In Avavu Ravi, where the writer saw them in the open at the finale of the ceremony, there were 122; in Waiea Ravi, after a conscientious but difficult count in a dim, crowded interior, he found 139.

These *hevehe* are obviously, then, the real inhabitants of the *eravo*; indeed it seems clear that the building has assumed its unique form for the direct purpose of accommodating them. And it is obvious, if only from the vaguely sanctified atmosphere in which they dwell, that they are more than mere masks; in fact it will be found that they have some highly complex spiritual implications. But before attacking the problem which these present, we must further explore the *eravo* to see what other kinds of spirit inmates belong there.

Hohao

Perhaps hidden and almost smothered by the skirts of the *hevehe*, or perhaps prominently displayed, we see a number of large plaques of wood, carved and painted. These are called generically *hohao*. Their proper place is on either side of the front *larava*; but when the *eravo* is full of *hevehe* they may be relegated to a dusty and rubbish-strewn corner at the rear. There may be half a dozen of them, and they mostly conform to the same general pattern, viz. that of a pointed ellipse some 4 or 5 feet high and 12 to 18 inches wide. The wood is an inch or more in thickness, and the slight convexity of the surface shows that the *hohao* have been made from old broken canoes. The carving, deeply incised, depicts a highly conventionalized human face with forehead, eyes, nose, and mouth, together with a number of decorative additions.[1] It is grotesque in the extreme, but not without its effectiveness in the total surroundings. In some rare cases a whole human figure is displayed; and in some others the flat board has developed into a figure carved in the round and bearing on the crown of its head a tousled mop of human hair.

It is averred of some *hohao* that they are merely decorative,

---

[1] The *hohao* of the Elema correspond to the *kwoi* of the Purari Delta, though they are much less numerous. See *Natives of Purari Delta*, pp. 66–7.

PLATE 19

A *Kaiavuru* of unusual type at Yogu. An *erekai akore* stands
beside it

and while here we may sometimes suspect concealment of magically important information, there is no reason to believe that this, viz. of *baupa*, or 'decoration', is not often a sufficient reason for making them. The carved and painted boards which are sometimes set horizontally above the *larava* alcoves are made for no other purpose; though these, as well as the *hohao*, are so often dirty, dust-covered, and disfigured by the peeling-off of their paint that they cannot be said to serve it very efficiently.

These merely decorative *hohao* are nameless. But others are given personal names, and whenever this is the case they are recognized as sacred objects. They may then be called *kaiavuru*, which is another of those words used in a perplexing variety of meanings. There can be little doubt that it is the same as the *Namau kaiaimunu*.[1] Among the Western Elema, however, it is applied loosely to the *hohao*, to the bull-roarer, and to the sorcerer's *marupai*; and once again it must be emphasized that identity of name need not imply identity of meaning. To avoid confusion, any further reference to the above-described plaques will be by the name *hohao*.

Fig. 6. An Orokolo *Hohao*

4 ft. 9 ins. high

As with any other of the objects connected with Elema religion, a full dissertation on the *hohao* would run to inordinate length. It is enough here to record a few particulars showing that they are regarded as representing, or housing,

[1] In *Natives of the Purari Delta* this word was spelt *kaiemunu* and derived from *kaia*, sky. But it seems that it may be derived rather from *kaia*, rear; so that the wicker-work monsters *kaiaimunu* are perhaps merely the *imunu* kept in the rear of the men's house.

various spirits of the bush (*ove-hahu* or *kora marita*). Their anthropomorphic form and the fact that they themselves bear the names of such spirits may indicate that they are to some extent images.

As already stated, there are many tales of encounters with the *ove hahu*, who are in reality the Story Folk; and the man who has been so privileged as to get into touch with one of them may thereafter make an image and set it up in the *eravo*. Two brief examples must suffice.

Iravapu once had a narrow escape from a bush-pig while hunting. That night the pig came to him in a dream and informed him that it was really Iroro, a mythical character of the *Kaia aualari*; it told him to make a *hohao*, and promised to be of assistance to him in further hunting. Iravapu (since deceased) duly made his *hohao* which is now, together with the relevant magic, in the safe-keeping of his son Oakore.

Again Maka was once fishing in Hopaiku creek and was fairly astonished at his success. Later he was visited in a dream by an *ove-hahu* who disclosed his name as Hurava and averred that it was he who had given him all the fish. Maka made his *hohao*, giving it the name Hurava, and prospered accordingly in his fishing. On his death the *hohao* passed into the hands of his son Horaki. But Horaki revealed the name and alleges that in consequence his luck has given out.

These are recent examples, and the last sentence shows that the owner likes to keep the name of his *hohao* a secret (and incidentally leads one to suspect that some of those which are dismissed as purely decorative may really have their names after all). But many of the most important *hohao* are obviously very ancient, and the fact that their names (some of them those of mythological notabilities) are known, does not mean that they are powerless or unworthy of confidence. While made originally by individuals in the interests of private magic, these ancient *hohao* have become virtually the property of the whole *eravo*; or at least their virtue is placed at the *eravo*'s disposal by the curator, in the typical case a descendant of the original owner, who has inherited his magic. In course of time the curatorship of several ancient *hohao* may come to be vested in the *eravo kariki haera*, whose responsibilities in connexion with them have been already described.

There is no question but that the principal *hohao* in any *eravo*, despite the practical neglect which they commonly suffer, are highly sacred objects. The fumigation, the re-painting, the offerings of food, are means of retaining their favour (the word *moreapaiakive*, which embraces these attentions, would seem to mean 'putting them in a good humour').[1] And they are something more than mere idols. They have their *ove*, and they can at times be very much alive. When the hunt is up and some old man sits in the *eravo* awaiting the return of the young and able-bodied, he may hear something fall to the floor behind him; the spirit of the *hohao* has thrown down a coco-nut-husk to inform him that they have caught a pig. Sometimes, it is said, the spirit leaves its straitened quarters in the wooden plaque and walks about the deserted *eravo*; in fact people have caught glimpses of strange men sitting just inside the door and gazing out into the village. And one of my best informants, Auaverare of Yogu, tells how he was once lying beside his fire, nursing an attack of fever, with but one companion in the *eravo*, when he was roused by the sound of a footfall in the *kaia larava*. Starting up he distinctly saw a big man, young and handsome, but with a withered leg, standing near the rear of the building. It was Airaka, the spirit who resides in the principal *hohao* of Yogu. But when he called on his companion to look, the figure vanished.

Such are the *hohao*, which the more ardent of Christians in Arihava and Vailala regard (with some literal justifica-tion) as 'graven images'—though, somewhat curiously, they have mostly retained them while doing away with so many other appurtenances of heathenism. It is seen that they have some real magico-religious meaning. But, lest that be over-estimated, it may be repeated that they are for the most part neglected and ignored, and there is no reason whatever to believe that this is a phase of modern indifference. Like

[1] One of my assistants, Korovahea, gave as illustration the English 'Good morning, *Taubada* (i.e. Master)!' which he always bellowed at me, at any rate with the intention referred to, when we met after breakfast.

most other aspects of Western Elema religion they are largely out of mind.

Bull-Roarers

Let us now explore the *eravo* a little further. We shall find it sadly untidy. The far corners of the *kaia larava*, which is probably more or less clear of *hevehe*, are veritable lumber-rooms, with long fish-nets propped against the wall, *haie ruru* (i.e. packets of palm-spathe containing feathers) dangling by lawyer canes from the roof, a surprisingly large stock of pots, and the remains of *eharo* masks (of which we shall have much to say later on), a mass of mangled cane and tattered bark-cloth. On the hearth-racks which at intervals line the flanks of the building, we may find blackened drums, strips of bark-cloth, and various private odds and ends, and, as evidence of a new turn in Elema economics, little heaps of copra which have been drying in the smoke. On the floor here and there are copra sacks or coco-nut-leaf bags full of the same commodity.

Among all this rubbish, so well exemplifying the alleged association of holiness and dirt, we shall come across a bulky package which might well be taken for one of the copra sacks. But not every one will lay hands on this; and when some old man (he should be one of the *amua* or the *kariki haera* at least) opens it, he does so very carefully. Several bundles of large bull-roarers are revealed totalling perhaps fifty and more. They are much like bull-roarers in other parts of the world, but big specimens and comparatively broad; and they are in many cases well decorated with incised *motifs*, human, crocodile, lizard, or snake. A peculiarity of many Western Elema bull-roarers is that the proximal end, just below the hole which takes the string, is bifurcated in a manner which recalls the Elema 'fish-mouth' drum. A number are illustrated in fig. 7.

It is not proposed to say much of the bull-roarers here as they have already been dealt with in a separate publication,[1] and we shall have to refer to them again in the next chapter.

[1] The writer's *Bull-Roarers in the Papuan Gulf*, Anthropology Report No. 17, Government Printer, Port Moresby, 1936.

It is enough to say that, like the *hohao*, they are thought to contain, or be animated by, spirits which are derived from the myths. But whereas the *hohao* are often more or less recent in origin, these bull-roarers are thought to date from the very foundation of things. Not every one in the package bears a name; in fact one general name typically covers the lot. But the name-bearing specimen can be singled out (being treated with a specially high degree of reverence though all lie together without distinction in the same package). And the name of this specimen is found to be that of some mythological forerunner of the *bira'ipi* which founded the *eravo*. We shall refer to one or two bull-roarers later on and these will provide sufficiently typical illustrations.

The Eravo-*grandmother*

So far in this chapter we have alluded to spirits for whom there is some material counterpart within the *eravo*. We now come to an individual spirit who in mystery surpasses all these others, who is represented by no sort of image, and whose precise dwelling-place is a matter of some uncertainty. This is *eravo-ve-uvari*, the '*eravo*-grandmother'. In some cases, the sex being of no real significance, it is *eravo-ve-birari*, the 'grandfather', but as these appear to be fewer we shall continue to use the feminine gender.

The grandmother lives, not in, but under, the *eravo*; some say in the dark and rather noisome forest of piles on which the building is supported; others, more specifically, in the ground beneath the *papaita* (i.e. the ladder which gives access to the front door), whence she is sometimes called *papaita ipi-ve uvari*.

Her influence, however, would seem to pervade the whole, and the *ivaiva* ceremony (to be described later) which is directed towards her more than any other power, embraces, if somewhat sketchily, every part of the building and everything within it. No man professes to have ever seen her; but if an empty pot falls off a rack, or if, more seriously, a full one topples over on its round base when set on the floor, such occurrences may be set down to her passing displeasure.

One of the reasons, again, for decorum in the *eravo* is the fear of disturbing her; so that when a man tramps too heavily down the aisle he may be reminded that the 'grandmother' dislikes noise.

Sometimes, like the spirits of the *hohao*, she is thought to influence the success of hunters: if she is not duly placated she will go before them and drive off the pigs or hide them. But it is mostly over the *eravo* as a building that her influence is exerted. Amid a great variety of building-magic it is often found that the *kariki haera* uses the name of the 'grandmother' herself as he lays the magical foundations: the pillar is *loa hau*, her 'shinbone'; the first floor-board, *kaka uki*, her 'backbone'. House-builders may dispense with magic, but I do not believe an *eravo* would be expected to stand without it; and in this procedure the building and its 'grandmother' are in a sense identified.

It may seem surprising, and yet is wholly in consonance with the principles of Elema magic, even when devoted to public service, that the name of the *eravo-ve-uvari* is completely unknown to most members of the *eravo* itself. It is in the keeping of the *kariki-haera*, and belongs to a subject which the majority simply dare not discuss. I have succeeded in unearthing the names of the 'grandmothers', or 'grandfathers', of several *eravo*. That of Hohi Ravi, for instance, is Oro Ipi Avu whom incidentally we shall meet again; that of Meouri Ravi is Bea Laivi[1] the old woman of the *Purari aualari*, identified with Lakekavu, mother of Kivavia who originated betel-nut. They would all appear to be ancient names belonging to the mythologies of the founders of those *eravo* with which they are associated; those that I know of, in fact, are plainly stated to be *lau haera* or Story Folk.

Spirits of Ancestors

The last category of spirits residing in or frequenting the *eravo* consists of the ghosts of the true ancestors, i.e. of *ou erarura haera* as distinguished from *lau haera*. It has been pointed out already that native ideas concerning the after life are not a little vague and confused, and if the notion of

---

[1] *Bea laivi* is a name for a little earthworm or grub.

even long-ago ancestors remaining in their *eravo* does not consort with other more general beliefs, then we must simply admit that the Western Elema have not fully made up their minds on their eschatology. While rival views are a good deal less numerous and complicated than Christian doctrines on the subject, the native is perhaps more prone than ourselves to hold first one and then the other of the mutually exclusive views that lie open to him. At any rate, despite a general belief that the dead withdraw to a remote home in the west, we meet the conviction that ancestors continue to haunt the *eravo* where they spent their lives. They do so in entirely disembodied form, the material objects which we have described being definitely associated with spirits of a different order. It is not necessary to dwell any further at this stage on human-ancestral spirits in the *eravo*. We shall meet them again later on when we come to discuss the differences in native theory which may underlie identical ceremonies.

IX

THE WORD *HEVEHE*

Hevehe *and Bull-Roarer*

WHEN in our exploration of an *eravo* we come upon the bundle of bull-roarers, the old man who unwraps it will probably lean back with the air of one revealing a secret, and utter the single impressive word, '*hevehe*'. This may well come as a shock since we have hitherto been using that word for something so widely different. But the fact remains that *hevehe* is also the name most commonly used for bull-roarer.

In the present book we shall have but little to say about bull-roarers since they have been dealt with at some length in the report already referred to. But it is proposed to repeat something of what was written there in order to clear up one or two essential points.

In the first place, in order to separate it from the larger matter in hand, it should be stated explicitly that the Bull-Roarer is merely one of three distinct cults known to the Western Elema, the other two being *Kovave* (which has already been sketched) and *Hevehe*, by far the greatest, to which this book is devoted.[1]

Initiations to these several cults (which are, or were, universal in the sense that all males normally passed through them) occurred separately, and did not of necessity follow any set sequence. The usual order was Bull-Roarer, *Kovave*, *Hevehe*.[2] But this could be varied. When, for instance, a *Hevehe* initiation took place (and this was comparatively a rare event), children would be put through it who had not previously been initiated to *Kovave*. It may be laid down with emphasis that the three cults are not regarded by the

---

[1] Reference will be made later to the *Hii* ceremony. But this belongs to the Berepa and Keuru tribes. See pp. 343–5.

[2] The last mentioned, as will be seen, involves two initiations, viz. to *Apa Hevehe* and *Hevehe Karawa*. The second of these was for adults only, and always came last in the individual's life.

natives themselves as parts of one great whole, nor can they possibly be treated as such by the ethnographer.

Various Meanings of the Word

But we shall have to say something more of the bull-roarer in connexion with the name '*hevehe*' which it bears in common with the tall mask. Here we encounter another, and most troublesome, example of the use of one term in a great variety of meanings which may be only remotely connected. To avoid confusion we shall restrict our use of it throughout to one meaning, or group of meanings: '*hevehe*' stands for the distinctive kind of mask, or the kind of being which it may be taken to represent; '*Hevehe*' for the cycle of ceremonies which belong to it. In other of its meanings the word will be distinguished by an appropriate prefix or suffix.

'*Hevehe*' in one form or another, e.g. *hemehe, semese, sevese*, is a word common to all the dialects of the Elema. Since masks of the same general type as those we are concerned with were formerly used down the whole coast from the Aivei to Cape Possession, it is not surprising that they should all be known by this name; though it covers some considerable differences in details of form, and some vital ones in the meaning of the associated ceremonies. But unfortunately it covers much else beside.

At the eastern end of the coast the name was commonly applied to certain wooden effigies to be found in the *eravo*. These, as their personal names clearly show, represented certain mythical characters, or Story Folk, though Chalmers seems to have regarded them all as images of one and the same being.[1] To Holmes the *semese* were 'warriors';[2] but while that meaning no doubt attached to the word in some contexts, it must have done so in the Eastern dialects only.

Among the Western Elema we meet with at least three specific kinds of *hevehe* to which we can fortunately add qualifying words. First of all there are *be'ure hevehe*, which means literally '*hevehe* from under the ground': these are the

[1] *Work and Adventure in New Guinea*, p. 138.
[2] *In Primitive New Guinea*, Seeley Service, 1924, pp. 129, 194.

bull-roarers. Secondly, there are *ma'ure hevehe*, or more often simply *ma-hevehe*, which means '*hevehe* from under the water': these are certain monsters inhabiting the sea and great rivers. Thirdly, there are *apa-hevehe*, which means 'drum-*hevehe*': these are the masks, or the beings represented by the masks, with which we are dealing and which we shall continue to refer to simply as *hevehe*. It should be noted that all three categories are commonly referred to in the same way by the native, i.e. without qualifying the word. Bull-roarers, marine monsters, and dancing-masks are all *hevehe*. This does not mean, however, that he confuses them or identifies them.

Now this muddle of meanings presents no problem to the native. When he uses the word *hevehe*, the context usually makes clear what he is talking about; and he is in no wise worried by the fact that it can mean so many different things. Nor, when this is posed as a problem, can he offer any solution. It must be pursued then—if it is worth pursuing—without his aid. Perhaps he is wise not to meddle in such questions, for the writer must confess that he is about to commit the sin of hypothetical reconstruction.

Their Derivation: Hevehe *the Snake*

An unexpected light is shed on the mystery by the fact that in the Berepa, Keuru, and Opau dialects the word '*hevehe*' is the generic name for 'snake'. There are not a few indications that the tribes in question have formed, as it were, a centre of dispersal for certain features in Elema culture at large; and I think the elementary fact referred to provides the clue which will enable us to bring the various meanings of *hevehe* somehow together.

Among the Western Elema the ordinary word for snake is *ekaroa*; but there are at least traces of the other word as a name for reptiles. Thus the expression *be'ure hevehe* is applied (and without conscious thought of the bull-roarer) to millipedes. *Hevehe* by itself is also a word for earthworm. And *hevehe harihu* are a special class of bush spirits which take the form of water snakes, eels, &c., inhabiting small creeks and

inland pools.[1] It is not possible to say whether these expressions remain as traces of a once more general use of the
word or whether they are borrowings from a neighbouring
dialect; but it seems at any rate likely that they refer to
reptilian species directly, and not through any devious cultural route. But whatever is the case in the Western Elema
dialect, it is enough to note that *hevehe* means 'snake' in the
dialects of three centrally-placed Elema tribes. This is the
first point in the argument.

The second point is that the bull-roarer may be assumed,
if only from its vastly greater distribution, to be prior to the
hevehe (i.e. more strictly the *apa hevehe*, our main subject) in
the cultural history of the Elema. Among the Western
Elema it is always thought of as such, being called *akoreapo*,
'the elder brother'; and indeed there is historical evidence
to bear the opinion out.

The third point is that in the older cult itself the bull-
roarer is most commonly represented to the uninitiated as
a snake. They hear its extraordinary voice, are duly impressed (or pretend to be), and bring offerings of food to
placate it. It is not as if they inquire too particularly as to
its nature: it is enough that they think of it as a voracious
and noisy monster which the initiated males are entertaining.
It may take the imaginary forms of a variety of creatures;
but predominant among them is that of the monstrous snake.
It may thus come about that the word for snake is applied
to the esoteric object which represents it. The bull-roarer
becomes a *hevehe*; more specifically *be'ure hevehe*, the sort that
dwells underground.

The reader need not be reminded that this is a hypothesis
and no more. But we may now proceed from the premiss,
hevehe = bull-roarer, and branch off from it in two directions.

Hevehe, which begins by being the esoteric snake, becomes
in due course an esoteric monster of any kind, crocodile,
lizard, shark, or entirely fabulous creature. And thus the

---

[1] For *harihu* see p. 127. The *hevehe harihu* are baneful, so that strangers or nursing
mothers refuse to bathe in such waters. If an eel were seen to shrivel unnaturally
on being caught it would be thrown away as a *hevehe harihu*. Double-headed or two-
tailed snakes or snakes with a head at each end are also put into this class. *Hevehe
harihu* may be employed as familiars by sorcerers.

word comes to include the special class of marine or fluvial monsters known as *ma-hevehe* or *ma'ure hevehe*. We shall have much to do with these as we proceed; but we may anticipate by pointing out that the most favoured theory of the *hevehe* masks in the *eravo* is that they are the children of the *ma-hevehe* themselves, who have come up from the sea. The *hevehe* masks are properly called *apa-*, or drum-, *hevehe*; so they are thus the sea monster's children carrying drums.

Let us now start once more from the premiss, *hevehe* = bull-roarer, and pursue another line. The bull-roarer is a slab of wood, some 18 inches or so in length, flat, narrow, and in outline roughly elliptical. The *hevehe* mask, or rather the face of it (the remaining features being regarded as adjuncts), answers to the above description with surprising exactitude, except in regard to material and size. The mask, then, does at least recall the Elema bull-roarer if we can think of the latter as magnified 150 times; and indeed its appearance is such that I can think of no other object to compare it with. It is not beyond the bounds of possibility, then, that in origin the *hevehe* masks were actually made to represent huge bull-roarers. Their wearers concealed their bodies with bast and sago-leaf mantles, took drums in their hands, and thus became *apa-hevehe*, the dancing bull-roarers armed with drums.

This explanation, it should be added, is wholly independent of any native suggestion. The resemblance on which it is based does not appear to have occurred to the native's mind, nor do I know of anything in his mythology which could be claimed to bear it out. Like the explanation previously advanced, it is no more than a hypothesis to account for the name *hevehe* as applied to both bull-roarer and mask. The hypotheses are alternative; and if neither is true, the writer can take comfort in the reflection that it does not matter.

The other meanings of the word '*hevehe*' along the coast do not concern us directly; but having proceeded so far down the broad and easy path one may go a little farther and suggest an explanation of Holmes's 'Warriors'. This, I feel convinced, is a derivative meaning and far removed

FIG. 7. Orokolo Bull-Roarers
Traced from rubbings. Longest 24¼ ins.

from the original. It is not found among the Western Elema,
though I have heard the phrase *haera hevehe* for a very muscular, athletic man;[1] and there is also a distinction sometimes
drawn between the *avai* (as the old men who sit down and

---

[1] Hau (Pl. XXI. D) and Area (Pl. XX. C) were referred to as examples.

eat) and the *hevehe haera* (the younger, more able-bodied, sort who do the 'chores'). But this, I suggest, is no more than an echo of the distinction, made much more definitely in the tribes east of Kerema, between the *bukari* (i.e. the chiefs, who controlled the bull-roarers) and the *sevese karu* or *mai karu* (who swung them). Since the *bukari* possessed some peace-making functions, it might come about that the other category of men, viz. the *sevese-karu*, should be known by contrast as the 'warriors'.

The foregoing hypotheses may be presented schematically as follows:

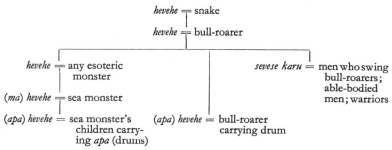

In justification of them I can hardly do better than quote from the report in which they were given somewhat fuller treatment.[1]

'The foregoing may pass as an example of that fanciful kind of reconstruction which for so many anthropologists (myself included) constitutes a pleasurable exercise. Not for one moment would I bank upon its validity; nor, granted it has any, would I be certain of its value. While it does seem to be probable that the original meaning of *hevehe* is nothing more than "snake", the attempt to trace its application to all these other, widely differing, things must be merely conjectural; and one doubts whether it serves directly any useful purpose.

'The mere fact of this multiplicity of meanings has been, however, worthy of attention. For it seems to me to illustrate very well how an element of culture (and a word, a name, is as truly an element of culture as a method of fishing or a burial rite) may pass over from one place, or from one set of circumstances, to another, and in doing so may leave its old meaning behind it and pick up a new one. It illustrates the piecemeal, haphazard manner in which cultures build themselves up, and the strange conglomeration in which this process results.'

[1] *Bull-Roarers in the Papuan Gulf*, p. 10.

X

HEVEHE OF THE SEA

Ma-hevehe

IN the waters of Orokolo Bay and in the mouths of the Purari and Vailala Rivers there dwell a number of large, powerful, and dangerous monsters, the *ma-hevehe*. They are variously conceived of as huge fish, sharks, whales, leviathans; but they also take the form of drifting tree-trunks; and two of them, at least, are thought to be concealed rocks. Ideas regarding them are somewhat vague and fluctuating, but it is agreed that they are individuals, male or female; that they are limited in number; and that, while their cruising range is more or less unbounded, they belong severally to special parts of the coast. Whether they are immortal the native refuses to say. If pressed too hard with such questions he is apt to reply, 'How on earth should I know?'

The *ma-hevehe* of Orokolo Bay and the adjacent coast are with a fair amount of agreement named as follows (though the list does not pretend to be complete):

Aivei River: Aihari, Makoko, Baitoo.
Arihava: Huhu, Ohara, Bovoiea.
Yogu: Maiavu.
Orokolo: Ohariapo, Iharuapo, Haihaiapo, Bevahapu.
Auma: Mapupu, Mahevehe,[1] Heveavu.
Vailala River: Houhekure, Koukaa, Oboharo, Yave.
Keuru: Keakea, Ira, Ope.
Kerema: Aa, Biro, Kaiapa, Lahero.

Many of these names are interpretable: some appropriately (as Baitoo, a kind of fish; Bovoiea, 'flotsam debris'; Ohariapo, 'sea foam'; Iharuapo, 'a drift log'), others less so (as Aihari, 'head-rest'; Huhu, 'plank'; Koukaa, a kind of palm; Oboharo, lit. 'eye-head', a coco-nut shell with its two 'eyes' exposed; and so on). The names no doubt have their origin somewhere in Elema mythology, but life is far too short to endeavour to trace them all. It is enough to say that they

---

[1] An individual so named.

are now fanciful appellations for supposedly real things:
Aihari does not take the form of a head-rest, nor is Ohariapo
merely sea foam: both are some sort of sea monster.

Ma-hevehe are seldom visible, though it is claimed that
fishermen have seen them lurking beneath the surface, multi-
coloured forms with wide, gaping mouths. But I have
never heard an account of any such meeting at first hand.
It is rather by superficial signs that they reveal their presence
—by *ma-ohari*, floating foam; or *ma-hapa*, the line of flotsam
that indicates the edge of a current or the margin between
the brown flood waters and the green sea. You paddle or
pole for life itself when the monster has given any such
indication of its presence.

Many encounters go to prove the power of the *ma-hevehe*.
Some of them are rather trivial, for the native easily gets the
wind up. When the woman Hariripa was fishing with her
keve net on the beach at Yogu she found some unaccount-
able difficulty in raising it. One or two tries, and she fled
screaming out of the water, leaving her *keve* net behind. It
had been dragged under by Hevehe Maiavu who is believed
to take the form of a hidden rock somewhere off Yogu.
When Korabuga of Harilareva was out shark-fishing in his
small canoe (a dozen or so of these little craft, manned by
individuals or couples, may be out together) he suddenly
felt it sinking towards the stern. He sprang forward to
redress the balance and then felt it upended in the opposite
direction. The flood waters were sweeping out of the Aivei,
and there about him was the tell-tale line of flotsam. He
was instantly sure that a *ma-hevehe* had him in its power and
shouted for help. His brother Hairi and another pluckily
paddled to the rescue, and Koraguba, weeping with fear by
the time they reached him, leapt into their canoe and left his
own to sink. The fact that it was never cast up on the shore
was sufficient verification of the theory that it was claimed
by a *ma-hevehe*.

Again, when the Yogu people were building the new
eravo, they had floated a fine hardwood log down the Aivei
for an *ive*. It was made into a raft with lighter logs alongside,
and the young men were poling it cheerfully in good weather

round the spit towards Yogu when it began to behave strangely, to wobble and to plunge. They were seized with panic and left it for another raft, whence Biravai, the leader of the party, exhorted the *ma-hevehe* to relinquish its hold. 'Hevehe Ohara, Hevehe Bovoiea . . .' (so he runs through the list of names). 'Let go the *eravo*-post. It is ours. Have pity on us.'[1] But the *ma-hevehe*, whichever it was, paid no attention, and the Yogu people watched their raft drift away. It was eventually broken up in the surf and the lighter timbers washed ashore. But the heavy hardwood *ive* was not seen again. It was taken by the *ma-hevehe* for his own submarine *eravo*.

It is not worth multiplying instances. *Ma-hevehe* can be responsible for wrecks and drownings. They are a danger which the trading canoes (*bevaia*) must brave on their voyages to and from the east,[2] and it is said they could bring disaster if they wished even to the *Papuan Chief*, that redoubtable old steamer of 150 tons which is the largest the Orokolo native ever sees. Even if the captain of the *Papuan Chief* pays small attention to them, the *bevaia haera* is fully armed with magical weapons against their attack. As master of the craft he is versed in the lore of *hahi*, or trading expeditions. He knows one or more of the tales of successful voyages undertaken by the Story Folk, and for the time being he is as one of them himself; and he has a stock of secret names to identify not only himself but his crew and his vessel with some one or other of the argonautical expeditions of Elema mythology.[3] So, for instance, he may impersonate a hero of Auma mythology, Maiaiapo (the speckled hawk), who went by sea to Kerema River and after many adventures brought home his bride, Iviri, who lived on a rock of that name. 'I am Maiaiapo', he whispers, 'You, Heveavu and Paveavu, make room between you, this is my voyage path';[4] and he is ready to throw con-

---

[1] '*Ivera paraea, Erave ive. Eraro iki heroe leiki.*'

[2] For the abandoning of a fully loaded *bevaia* when supposedly seized by a *hevehe* see 'Trading Voyages from the Papuan Gulf', *Oceania*, vol. iii, no. 2, 1932, pp. 145–6.

[3] For examples see 'Trading Voyages from the Papuan Gulf', loc. cit., pp. 157–63.

[4] '*Ara va Maiaiapo. Eva Heveavu Paveavu, haikiravi avae. Maiave arave hahive aki.*' *Haikiravi avae* = lit. 'sit apart'. Heveavu (or Hevehe Apovea) and Paveavu are stone *ma-hevehe*, two submarine Scyllas, which are particularly dangerous to *bevaia*. The one is supposed to be off Auma, the other off Kerema.

ciliatory betel and coco-nuts overboard. Or he may threaten them with his medicines: 'I have two bottles here, *Hevoho hika* and *Pairava*' (bamboo containers for magic leaves and magic barks); 'they will make you sick and sorry.' If those methods fail he can still scatter his powdered lime on the water to blind them.

While the *ma-hevehe* are responsible for some of the misadventures at sea (and the Western Elema, who are indifferent seamen, meet with an unduly large proportion of them in their few voyages) it cannot be said that they represent the sailor's bugbear. It is rather personal sorcery and the mischievous interference of the dead that he fears; so that the *ivaiva*, which precedes the voyage, is addressed to deceased *bevaia-haera* and the spirits of the dead in general, while every effort is made to ensure that the sorcerers who remain at home are not offended. Similarly the work of destruction on land, viz. the sweeping away of the beach by high tides and heavy seas, which may be attributed to the *ma-hevehe*, is more often put down to the few sorcerers, such as the *Baiu* men, Hepe and Ekavo, who specialize in those departments of magic. Altogether it may be said that although the *ma-hevehe* are generally believed to exist and to be very dangerous, they are by no means constantly, or even frequently, in the thoughts of a people who have so obvious a liking for *terra firma*.

The Tale of Oa Birukapu

In order to illustrate further the ideas regarding the *ma-hevehe*, as well as to introduce to the reader some characters whom we shall meet later on, the rest of this chapter will be devoted to an extract from the myths.

It is a widely known story belonging to both *Hurava* and *Kauri* mythologies, and I have recorded it many times at different points along the whole coast. The renderings[1] are so variable that any one seeking for an 'orthodox' version would be driven to distraction until he came to realize that there was no such thing. The diversity is characteristic; and such that at the outset one finds it necessary to select the

---

[1] One is given by Holmes, op cit., p. 189.

names of the characters from among a number of variants. In most Western Elema versions the story begins with the adventures of a man named Bitavabu (which is incidentally one of the general names for bull-roarer); in others the same man is called Birau Apo (Old Man Dracaena); in others again, Evarapo. The last mentioned was the name used by a *Hurava aualari* informant named Hapeho who gave me one of the completest renderings of the story; and since we shall meet this mythical character again as one of the *dramatis personae* in a *Hevehe* ceremony we may as well introduce him at this stage by telling the story as of him.

Evarapo lived in the west. An ugly, dirty person who never so much as combed his hair, he was despised and avoided by his neighbours. The *Hurava* girls, Iau and Havoa[1] and Urumari[2] and Harumari[3] used to laugh at him from a distance, shouting 'Stinker!', while he prowled up and down the beach. Being unable to find a mate (in some versions he is married to a sexually incomplete woman),[4] he was always on the look-out for some means of satisfying his desires; and whenever he saw a log on the beach he would leap towards it with obscene gestures mistaking it for a woman. Altogether he was a lustful and disreputable character, a figure of fun.

Evarapo's fortunes, however, were to change. At Lavao (the mouth of the St. Joseph River) there lived a very beautiful girl, Aviara. How Evarapo first got into touch with her is itself a long story and one in which informants greatly disagree. But if we adhere to Hapeho's version it appears that this girl's brothers, Lere and Pove,[5] flew to the west and told Evarapo about her; and that on their return he gave them a token, a sort of love-letter in the form of a betel-nut inscribed with certain marks, to deliver to their sister.

Not to let such a promising matter drop, Evarapo then determined to send his younger brother Iriri as an envoy. To prepare him for the long journey he made a *ruru*, or mask of bark-cloth, in the form of a little beach bird; and

---

[1] Now varieties of nipa palm.   [2] A kind of taro.
[3] A kind of tree.
[4] He is sometimes said to be married to the two *Hurava* women, Hokape and Haekape (cuscuses).   [5] Long-legged fishing birds.

when Iriri put this on he temporarily assumed the form of the bird which now bears his name. Thus equipped for flight he took off from the beach next morning and successfully skimmed over the first two breakers; but the third caught him, and he was rolled ignominiously back to Evarapo's feet. We now see Evarapo holding his little brother up by the legs, shaking him out, and drying him over the fire. But when he suggests another try, Iriri not unnaturally demurs. At his wits' end, Evarapo is guided by a dream; he must make a second *ruru*, not of bark-cloth, but of coco-nut fibre. This he does, and having persuaded Iriri to don it, sees him rise triumphant and disappear into the east.

We may pass over the adventures of the little bird in its flight and the long catalogue of geographical names which mark its stages. Iriri at last comes to rest at Lavao in the boughs of a tree under which Aviara happens to be sitting. He drops the marked betel-nut which he has brought with him, and the girl, picking it up, is thrilled to discover that it is a duplicate of the token she has previously received from her lover in the west.

That night, when Iriri doffs his mask and enters her house, she leaps to the false conclusion that he is Evarapo himself and invites him to sleep with her. But Iriri excuses himself, either (as in this version) from loyalty to his brother, or (as in others) because sexual intercourse would make him 'heavy' and possibly impede his homeward flight. Instead, he explains that he is only a proxy and puts his brother's proposal with all his eloquence, extolling the attractions of the Aivei River as a home. Aviara hesitates: she should marry one of her own people, Kave or Kive the phalangers who live in the coco-nut palms; or Harai, the morning star; or Barara, the sweet-scented tree. But at last she is persuaded, and Iriri flies back with her promise.

This time the flight is almost too much for him. Exhausted he seeks rest on two floating logs in the Gulf. But they are two *ma-hevehe*, Hariau and Mapupu, who mean to lure him to his destruction, and when he alights on them they sink. Escaping from this and similar dangers, however,

he at last reaches home, enters the *eravo* unnoticed, and
wearily crawls under a mat to sleep it off. There Evarapo
discovers him next morning; nurses him back to strength;
and hears his news.

Now reassured, the elder brother begins his preparations
in earnest. He takes his axe and fells a *meouri* tree for his
canoe, and, henceforward, Meouri is the magical name in
Hurava mythology for the *bevaia*. The blows of his axe are
peals of thunder, and, their reverberations reaching the
sensitive ears of Aviara, she understands and busies herself
with her trousseau.

At last the canoe is completed, and Evarapo launches it
for a trial. He has got together a crew of bushmen, and these
start pluckily enough. But once through the shallows and
at close quarters with the mighty breakers they are appalled.
All is confusion; some continue to paddle on; others have
turned about and are striking for the shore; Evarapo at the
stern is in a frenzy. The next breaker has caught the canoe
and overwhelmed it, and the crew, scrambling to safety,
vanish into the bush. But Evarapo is undaunted. He succeeds in engaging some of his experienced fellow villagers,
and with these at the paddles sallies forth afresh. They take
his vessel safely out into the open sea, and turn eastwards.
On and on! They have a journey of 120 miles and more
ahead of them. They begin to exclaim. 'Keep going,' says
Evarapo. 'This is my business.'

Meanwhile Aviara is on the look-out. She sees a speck
on the horizon. A floating nipa palm? No, my lover! She
returns to her preparations and, when presently the canoe
lands on the beach, she hurries down to meet it carrying with
her the pots, bags, fish-nets, &c., that a bride always brings
to her husband's home. It does not appear that she is taken
aback by her bridegroom's appearance; indeed the narrator
seems to have forgotten that unpromising introduction, and
by now Evarapo is almost a fine fellow.

Meanwhile the cause of all this precipitancy is at work in
the garden. It is Aviara's formidable father, Oa Birukapu,[1]
who has hitherto known nothing of her intentions. Twice

---

[1] Called Oa Iruapu, Oa Idiva, Oa Laia, &c., in other versions.

the brothers Lere and Pove come to tell him that his daughter
is making off, and twice he answers roughly, 'The girl is
not mad! Go back to your fishing.' But when they come
a third time his suspicions are aroused. He returns to his
house and finds it empty. Then in a mighty rage he tears it
up, sets it on his back, and plunging into the sea becomes a
ma-hevehe. The bridal pair have only just got under way and
Oa Birukapu is after them.

The story of the pursuit is always told with great gusto,
though the versions are much at variance. The terrific
episode of the house seems to be hardly understood by the
story-tellers themselves. According to Hapeho, whom we
are following in the main, Oa Birukapu soon cast it off—
because it floated and kept him on the surface—and substituted for it a huge rock; others say that he carried the house
right through; and yet others that he started with nothing
of the kind, but tore up an *eravo* as he passed Toaripi and
carried that.

By now, however, he is in close pursuit of the elopers.
Aviara is terrified.

'Beware my father!' she cries. 'He is a bad man.'

'Bad man!' answers Evarapo. 'So am I.'

'He has great power.'

'So have I,' says Evarapo. 'I am as good as he. I was not
born of woman. I was made in the beginning.' And to Oa
Birukapu he cries, 'Come on, I am your match.'

Oa Birukapu replies by charging the canoe and smashing
all the paddles on one side; but Evarapo defeats this move
by scattering powdered lime in the water to blind him, and
so they leave him astern.

As they pass Kerema a man, Laho,[1] entices them close
inshore with offers of help. He will replace the broken
paddles, he says, though his real intention is to puncture the
canoe with his claws and seize Aviara for himself. While
they are haggling, however, Oa Birukapu rises again, now
in the form of a huge tide which sweeps up and, somewhat
undiscriminatingly, demolishes Laho's house. Evarapo
scatters more lime and speeds on with what paddles he has

[1] A sea-gull.

got until at last he succeeds in beaching his canoe at the Aivei and bringing his bride ashore. So close, however, has been the father-in-law's pursuit that he is borne in on a great wave just behind them and deposited high up in the belt of brushwood lining the beach. Here he remains in hiding. His arrival has been unnoticed save by his own daughter Aviara.

There now ensues a peaceful interlude during which Aviara settles down in her new home and in due course bears a son. This promising boy, Birau Upu Make, grows up to play with his little age-mates on the beach and in the brushwood. But from time to time one or other of the little boys, to the consternation of the village, disappears. Aviara alone knows the cause of their disappearance; they are snapped up by Oa Birukapu in his hiding-place. To save her own son, however, she has made an arrangement with her father: she will hang some hollow seed rattles round the child's neck so that he may be distinguished from the others and therefore spared.

But on one occasion the children are engaged in stalking grasshoppers, and it is found that Birau Upu Make's rattle scares them away. So they bind up the seeds to silence them, and when next the little boy passes by, Oa Birukapu, not hearing the warning sound, snaps him up and devours him. It is only when his teeth close on the rattle itself that he realizes that he is eating his grandson.

At this moment Aviara, making sago with her husband in the bush, sees some drops of milk issue from her breast and knows that her son has met with disaster. Both hurry home to hear the news that the child has disappeared. Evarapo (by way of comic relief) makes a fool of himself by diving repeatedly into the streams behind the village, seizing the crocodiles under water, and looking into their mouths. But Aviara knows who has killed her son. She rouses the villagers and leads them to Oa Birukapu's hiding-place.

Arrow after arrow is discharged at him, but without the slightest effect. Hapeho tells us that the monster was lying *under* the stone and that the arrows did not enter his body; others that he was lying inside the house which he had

823155   Q brought with him; others again that he was *like* a house. But, for whatever reason, he proved invulnerable, and the villagers finally gave up.

Not, however, Aviara and Evarapo. They go into the west to seek help at the village of Aikere and Maikere.[1] Nearing it, Evarapo sends his wife ahead to parley with them while he waits on the track. But he has to wait a long time. At first she finds the village empty except for the old mother of the two men; but on the latter's advice she sounds a shell trumpet which she has found in the empty *eravo*, and presently they come in, covered with mud from crabbing in the swamps. Having insisted on intercourse with her as a price for their help, they bid her go home and prepare a feast, and on the morrow they will come. Then we see Aviara rejoin Evarapo, who appears once more in his comic role, this time as a grumpy husband who walks apart and will not speak because he has been so long kept waiting.

True to their promise Aikere and Maikere arrive next day in the midst of an *avara*, one of those dark and furious squalls that sweep down from the west. Blackened with charcoal from head to foot, and with head-dresses of cockatoo feathers and sombre cassowary plumes, they bear the forbidding appearance proper to *Hurava* cannibals. But instead of long bows and real arrows they bear miniature weapons, mere playthings fit for little boys. Thus armed, and blowing the shell trumpet, they come into the midst of the crowd which surrounds the seemingly invincible Oa Birukapu. Advancing upon him they stoop down and shoot him from beneath, transfixing him in his one vulnerable spot—the navel.[2] Oa Birukapu rolls over on his back and dies.

[1] In other versions Mikya and Kaepa. There was some difference of opinion among Orokolo savants concerning these. Some said they were the same as Aikere and Maikere under alternative names; others that Aikere and Maikere had usurped the place in the story that belonged properly to the other pair named.

[2] Informants are unable to give a really intelligible account of this episode. In some versions the two Westerners look down the interior of the house and shoot the monster inside it, the others having apparently shot at the house itself. But the navel represents the generally accepted version.

In a dramatic performance seen at Karama (in connexion with a marriage) the actor representing Oa Birukapu was finally shot in the *heel*, which is surely an astounding case of parallelism?

There follows the feast which has been got ready at their order. The pigs are eaten by the local people, for they are not cannibals. But the visitors (and it is assumed that they have brought many of their own folk with them) feast on the body of Oa Birukapu himself, his entrails being presented to their women.

It is these entrails which contain what is in some connexions the *raison d'être* of the story: that is to say, I have heard it told more often to explain the origin of the thing that was found in them than for any other reason. For the western women took the entrails home with them to the Upper Purari, washed them, cut them up, and found inside them the bull-roarer. It was in this way (according to the present myth) that the women first became acquainted with this secret object which they used thenceforward to hoax the men until the latter seized it from them and reversed the position. Some informants, in their lavish style, go on to say that the Western women discovered not only the bull-roarer but also *kovave* and *hevehe* in Oa Birukapu's entrails. But others declare emphatically that this is not the case.

We have not quite done with Oa Birukapu. Aviara was sorry for her father when she finally saw him killed, and in revenge caused a great tide to come up and destroy the village. The two *Kauri* men who came with it, Loi and Kakahu,[1] carried his bones back to the east whence he came, and there buried them; and from the place of his burial there sprang up various kinds of taitu, yams, and bananas which are consequently *Kauri aualari*.

Its Possible Relation to Ritual

Such a tale as this (and it is only one of many resounding tales in Elema mythology) will provide a fruitful field for the researcher who looks for parallels between myth and ritual. But it seems to the writer that this kind of research, fascinating as it is, and profitable as it may be, is full of pitfalls. It will be seen later on that some of the *Hevehe* ritual can be made to correspond with certain incidents in the myth of Oa Birukapu, e.g. the dramatic representations of Evarapo

[1] Ebb-tide and Half-tide.

and the two Westerners, Aikere and Maikere, at the finale
of the cycle. But although we have used these names in
narrating the story it will be recalled that we selected them
from a number of competitors; and, in fact, it is open to
question whether they should not be regarded as interpola-
tions. At any rate we shall tell, at a later stage and more
briefly, quite other stories of Evarapo and Aikere and
Maikere which correspond better with their actions in the
drama as it is presented. So that there are at least two
independent myths for one and the same piece of ritual.

There are, however, deeper-seated similarities between
the myth and the *Hevehe* cycle, e.g. the emergence of the
ma-hevehe (Oa Birukapu) from the sea and its stay in the village. But here again there are other myths which provide a
closer parallel. It is, in fact, impossible to equate the ritual
of *Hevehe* at large with this or any other myth; though it is
true that for separate incidents or elements in it a mythological counterpart can be found.

As a general observation, however, which bears, I believe,
on the question of correspondence between myth and ritual,
it should be noted that *Hevehe* ritual, which we shall be
describing in detail, would appear to be uniform throughout all the *eravo* in which it remains extant; indeed the degree
of uniformity in practice, together with the consistency of
verbal accounts from different sources, has struck the writer
as remarkable. The ritual, then, however rich, is relatively
simple and straightforward. On the other hand, the mythology which belongs at large to these *eravo* is not only complex and confused, but is virtually divided on the basis of
aualari groups into a series of different mythologies; so that
where any part of the ritual routine is found to have its
mythological counterpart, it may well prove to be one myth
for one *aualari*, and another for another. Further, by reason
of the secrecy entailed by magic, the majority of men, so far
from knowing the myths of other *aualari*, know only a
fraction of their own. Yet in spite of all this they strictly
adhere, through cycle after cycle, to the same ritual routine.

In view of these considerations, and of the sheer unwieldy
bulk of the mythological corpus in comparison with the

relatively economical and well-regulated ritual, I cannot
believe it possible, in the case of the Western Elema, that
myth and ritual could be made to strike a balance. That
every ritual element should somewhere have its mythical
parallel is a thesis which might be defended, though it would
involve an amount of research sufficient to drive any investi-
gator to madness, since the natives who practise the ritual
and possess the myths are usually unconscious of the connexion, and therefore unable to point the way. But the
converse proposition, viz. that every myth has its ritual
parallel, is one which the writer, for the reasons stated above,
feels he must dismiss as untenable.[1]

Possible Symbolism

It is worth referring in passing to a specific piece of
symbolism which may be discoverable in the myth of Oa
Birukapu. It will perhaps appear obvious to some readers
that Oa Birukapu, the *Kauri ma-hevehe*, symbolizes the *eravo*,
and his swallowing of the children, their initiation. This
is a tempting, and possibly correct, interpretation. But it
should be pointed out that I have never, despite certain
judicious leads, heard any of my informants expressly identify Oa Birukapu in the story with an *eravo*; and never have I
heard them, in commenting on the *eravo*, make any reference
to Oa Birukapu. And if, incidentally, any one were to seize
upon this myth as evidence that the *eravo* came to Orokolo
from the east, whence Oa Birukapu came, I think he would
probably be mistaken; for there is stronger presumptive
evidence indicating that it came from the opposite point of
the compass.

Again, the devouring of the small boy, which as a common
theme in many mythologies has been equated with the rites
of initiation and seclusion, is, at any rate to the modern
native, no more than an episode in the story (and it should
be noted that Birau Upu Make was not disgorged or
evacuated by the monster, but died irrevocably in his

---

[1] Cf. treatment of myths and ritual of the Bull-Roarer in *Bull-Roarers in the
Papuan Gulf*, pp. 12–15; also *infra*, pp. 341–3.

jaws).[1] The devouring is never, I believe, consciously compared with any kind of initiation, nor does the native in his wildest flights of imagination think of the *eravo* as a monster. If, then, this symbolism is really present in the myth, it is by virtue of some far-away significance that is lost on the present generation. It receives no more than a passing mention here, since it is irrelevant to the kind of treatment which is given to *Hevehe* in this book.

[1] Some one may suggest that Birau Upu Make *became* the bull-roarer. No native ever suggested this to me. It has been said on the other hand that Oa Birukapu brought it with him from the east.

XI

DURATION OF THE CYCLE

A Series of Ceremonies

THE *hevehe* masks which were briefly described at the beginning of Chapter VII were in an advanced state of preparation. In other *eravo* they may be much less so. But generally speaking it will be found that at a given time all the masks in any one *eravo* are approximately at the same stage of manufacture. Thus they may be all practically complete and only lacking the last item of full dress, viz. their mantles of dyed sago-leaf: instead of these we see only the underskirts of pale-coloured bast. In another *eravo* we may find merely frameworks covered with bark-cloth; or again, bare skeletons of rattan cane and palm-wood.

The condition of the masks indicates, obviously enough, the stage which the *Hevehe* as a whole has reached. It must be understood—and this in itself gives a hint of the magnitude of the whole affair—that it is not a matter of weeks or months, but of years. It might conceivably be compressed into the space of one year; but such haste would be economically impracticable as well as alien to the natives' wishes and intentions. For each successive stage involves the community in a very considerable effort, and together they are definitely meant to stretch over a much longer period. It will be convenient, therefore, to speak of the *Hevehe* as a 'cycle' comprising a series of ceremonies.

Never does it happen that one and the same *eravo* building sees more than a single cycle.[1] The rule is glibly said to be: One *eravo*, one *Hevehe*. 'We have got our *eravo* built,' the people are supposed to say. 'Now to fill it with *hevehe*!' Yet in point of fact I know of only one instance where the cycle was carried through from beginning to end in the original building; in most it outlasts three or four. *Eravo* are com-

---

[1] In the Purari Delta, where the corresponding cycle, called *Aiau*, or *Aiaimunu*, is much shorter, one man's house may see several complete performances.

monly built from the rear forwards. The construction of *kaia* and *aruhihi larava* having exhausted the willingness of the builders, these quarters must meet their requirements for a long time. If there is no *Hevehe* already in progress, then the cycle is probably begun as soon as these quarters are prepared; but as stage follows stage and the masks grow in size, it becomes necessary to provide them with accommodation, so the loftier *oropa larava* is added. When in due course the *eravo* has to be abandoned, the masks are transferred to the new one which takes its place.

Causes of Delay

I give in detail some examples of the long delays in the cycle which are so exasperating to an ethnographer. They are due first and foremost to the tabu following death in the community, which inhibits all activities in any way connected with the drum. Early in 1935 I was in hopes of seeing an important stage carried out at Waiea Ravi; but a wife of one of the members had died some months before, and there was the usual slowness in paying over the gifts from one *eravo* side to the other.[1] And then, when they had been paid, the deceased woman's father (one Area, who has a big reputation as a sorcerer and a bad one as an unsociable, difficult person) still refused to beat the drum and thus raise the tabu. There was no little dissatisfaction in the *eravo* on this account, but nobody had the courage to take Area to task. When, late in 1936, I was again at Orokolo, I found that this had all blown over and that preparations had been promisingly advanced for a further stage; but the recent death of the wives of both of the Drum-Leaders had held them up again. Both sides, however, seemed willing to get on with this second case of drum-beating; and, when suddenly called away for a brief period, I was so pleased at the prospect that I left a substantial present of wheatmeal for the *eravo*. On returning two months later I found nothing done. Of the two widowers, Ovehaera had been ready for the ceremony, but the other, Harupa, had failed at the last

[1] See p. 34.

moment to put in an appearance. He informed me that the wheatmeal had been eaten during his absence in the bush, and that therefore he was offended. Now he meant to wait till his new house was built. But Harupa, who was an unpopular man (I have never seen one look more dispirited in his widower's black), was having some difficulty here. Being out with his own *eravo* people he had issued an invitation to the next *eravo* (Ori Ravi) to help him in a working bee; but they had not turned up.[1] Meantime Harupa was making very slow progress at thatching his house with the assistance of one *akira* and one *ai*, the other *ai*, on whom he depended, having quarrelled with him and refused his help.[2] Needless to say, the house was still unfinished when I left six months later. But by that time Harupa's house no longer mattered, for one Laru, the *karigara amua* of Waiea Ravi, died while on a trading expedition; and, as all agreed, the death of so important a person must put off further celebrations for a very long time to come.

Sometimes the delay may be due to private quarrels and resultant threats. Meouri Ravi is at present so far gone in delapidation that it threatens to collapse; yet the masks in it are mostly in fine condition and are virtually ready for the finale of the cycle. It had been intended, in fact, to carry out an important stage quite recently, but there arose a squabble as to who should succeed one of the Drum Leaders. The rights of the case as well as the sympathy of the *eravo* favoured one of the claimants who actually lived in Orokolo. But the other who lived at Biai, some miles down the beach, brought proceedings to a standstill by threatening all with sorcery if they ventured to carry the ceremony through. Although there was some indignation in Meouri Ravi at this form of pressure, none was ready to defy it.

[1] Investigation proved that most of them knew nothing about the affair. Harupa had approached Tahia, the chief of that *eravo*, with his request, and Tahia informed me, in the non-committal and unauthoritative manner of Elema chiefs, that his men, he supposed, would help if they wanted to.

[2] At the *hehe eapoi*, in connexion with the death of Harupa's wife, this *ai* had cried out, somewhat rudely, 'Where are the coco-nuts? I want a drink.' 'You are my *ai*,' said Harupa. 'You ought to help me by getting some.' The *ai* did not respond to this suggestion, and Harupa's sister then gave him, in public, a piece of her mind. He was now paying Harupa back by refusing to help him with his new house. He explained—if it is an explanation—that he was *maioka*, 'ashamed'.

Sorcery as a Cause of Delay

Other instances are not wanting in which the threat of
sorcery is directly the cause of delay. When Miki Harapa,
one of the *amua* of Aivaroro Ravi, died, the death payments
were duly made; but certain of his distant kinsmen in the
bush villages of Pareamamu forbade any further proceedings
in connexion with the *Hevehe* under pain of sorcery. There
was no small amount of dissatisfaction in Aivaroro Ravi; so
much so that some of its members declared their intention,
in a huff, of leaving Orokolo and allowing the *hevehe* masks
and the *eravo* to rot. But happily the Pareamamu people
(who, like other bushmen, are credited with special powers
of sorcery by the coast-dwellers) relented or were bought off,
and a year or so later the cycle actually reached its conclusion.

There was no such happy ending, however, to the *Hevehe*
in Yogu. The first time the writer set eyes on a *hevehe* mask
was in 1923 when he passed through this village. The masks
were then far advanced; and, duly impressed, he copied
a number of the designs with which they were decorated.
Some years later a man of the village died, and one of his
kinsmen, Biravai, leapt to the conclusion that his death had
been caused by a fellow member of the *eravo*. Biravai, who
is a strong, energetic, and rather formidable character, took
it upon himself to barricade the front and rear doors of the
eravo with thorny sago-leaves, and issued an edict that any
man who entered would die by sorcery. No man ever did.
The *eravo* eventually fell down and was cleared away and
burnt, the masks with it. How many years they had been
preparing is not known, but they never saw the light of day.
Biravai's threat of sorcery killed that *Hevehe* cycle outright.[1]

It will be seen that sorcery may be in a very direct manner
responsible for holding up a cycle of ceremonies to which
the community as a whole has devoted itself. It may also be
said to do so in an indirect manner; for there can be no
doubt whatever that the threat of sorcery lies behind, and
gives practical effect to, the obstinacy of some men in refusing to lift the drum-tabu. One reason for giving the above

[1] A new cycle began after the new *eravo* was built in Yogu. The masks are by
no means so far advanced as those I saw in 1923.

details is, therefore, to demonstrate that sorcery, or the belief in it, while protecting some institutions may equally well run counter to others. But that is incidental. They are relevant to the matter in hand in that they help to explain the astonishing length to which the *Hevehe* cycle may be drawn out.

The Duration of the Cycle

It is possible to gather some fairly reliable data to establish this latter point more definitely. From the general testimony of Orokolo it appears that all its seven *eravo* began their last cycles (some of which are concluded while others continue) practically at the same time. The reason for this somewhat remarkable simultaneity is found in the fact that there was a general southward move on to the new shore built up by the tides south of Biha creek.[1] The Western Elema insist on living by the shore, and it is in keeping with their general desire for unanimity that they should move, building their several *eravo* on the new site, more or less together. At any rate, it is agreed that the previous cycles had all been over for some time, and that the seven *eravo* began new ones all within a few months of one another, in the order given in the list. This was from four to six years (according to various informants, none of whom, it must be confessed, are very good at counting) before the Vailala Madness. The Vailala Madness began in 1919. So it may be taken that the last *Hevehe* cycles in Orokolo Bay date from between 1913 and 1915.[2]

Meouri Ravi	began 1914 approx.	Unfinished.
Waiea Ravi	,, ,,	,,
Aivaroro Ravi	,, ,,	Concluded 1934 from 4th *eravo*.
Hohi Ravi	,, ,,	Unfinished.
Hare Eravo	,, ,,	Concluded 1920 (?) from 1st *eravo*.
Ori Ravi	,, ,,	Unfinished.
Avavu Ravi	,, ,,	Concluded 1932 from 4th *eravo*.

[1] The tides play havoc with parts of the Gulf coast, but the general tendency at the head of Orokolo Bay is to make ground.

[2] The Great War was a small event to the Western Elema in comparison with the Vailala Madness. Many of them have hardly heard of it. But some who profess to remember its beginning say that the *Hevehe* cycles started before it.

The first of them to bring its cycle to an end was Hare Eravo. It is regarded as an achievement that it did so with such speed. The date is fixed approximately by the Rice-planting Scheme which the Government was endeavouring to forward in the Gulf. All was then ready, but the finale had to be put off once because so many of the villagers were in jail for refusing to work. Shortly after, however, the ceremony was brought triumphantly to a close, and Mr. G. H. Murray, Acting Resident Magistrate of the Gulf Division, the officer in charge of the Rice Scheme, came down from Kerema expressly to see it. This makes the finale of the Hare Eravo cycle about 1921, say seven years after it commenced.

The next (Avavu Ravi) occurred in 1932, when the writer had the good fortune to be present; and the next (Aivaroro Ravi) in 1934. In the four remaining *eravo* the *hevehe* are still waiting indoors, twenty-three years after the cycle began.[1]

It may be thought that this dragging out of the cycle is the result of modern influences, as if the *Hevehe* were drawing a series of long, dying gasps. But while it seems wholly likely that such influences have extended the intervals, they have not done so to any disproportionate extent. There is ample evidence to show that formerly, as well as now, the *Hevehe* cycles occupied very long periods. An old man, Koraguba of Waiea Ravi, for instance, has seen only three final celebrations in his *eravo*. The first took place prior to the coming of Chalmers to Orokolo in 1881[2] (an event which Koraguba has special reason for remembering since, in the scramble to obtain a view of the first white man, he struck his shin against a stump and suffered long afterwards from a sore). Since that date only two cycles have been begun and ended in Waiea Ravi, the masks with which it is now crowded being those of a third. Thus Koraguba has seen his *eravo* carry out three *Hevehe*, and, if he is lucky, will survive the completion of a fourth—this in a life of perhaps sixty-five years.

---

[1] In Hohi Ravi and Ori Ravi the *hevehe* are still very backward.
[2] J. Chalmers and W. Wyatt Gill, *Work and Adventure in New Guinea*, Religious Tract Society, 1885, chapter ix.

In view of the similar testimony given by other old men, there can be no doubt that *Hevehe* was always an extremely protracted affair. It must be understood, however, that after the conclusion of a cycle some considerable time might elapse before another was commenced; so that it is impossible to strike an average duration by simple division. The cycle varied in length according to circumstances. The shortest of which I have record took six or seven years; but that is spoken of as a fortunate case, where there were few deaths and no dissensions to hold things up. Others, under the somewhat discouraging influences of modern times, remain far from completed after twenty-three years. If we say that even in the old times a *Hevehe* cycle took, from beginning to end, between ten and fifteen years, we shall still, probably, be underestimating.

Frequency of the Cycle

It is obvious that the foregoing refers to the duration of the *Hevehe* cycle as a self-contained series of events in any one *eravo*. The frequency of the cycles, if we take the whole Western Elema tribe into consideration, can hardly be determined, but *a priori* the splendid festivals which belong to them must have been of fairly common occurrence. Since the commencement of the last cycles only eight communities in the tribe have participated directly. Formerly there must have been three times that number. And if, further, we take into account the Muru, Pareamamu, Berepa, Keuru, and Uaripi tribes, all of whom practised *Hevehe* in a form similar to that of the Western Elema, it will become conceivable that major ceremonies, attracting visitors from far and wide, may have taken place every year. Even nowadays more cycles reach their brilliant conclusion than is realized by Europeans. One young man of Orokolo, for instance, who is known to the writer, has been 'initiated', in his own and other tribes, on six different occasions, definitely arguing that six cycles have been concluded within his approximately twenty-five years; and no doubt there were a number more.

But it is all too plain that in these times the successful

conclusion of a *Hevehe* cycle is a rare event. For the reasons outlined in this chapter, they must always remain more or less unpredictable; and the ethnographer who happens to be present at the grand finale must indeed count himself lucky.

The Programme of Hevehe

For purposes of reference the separate ceremonies which constitute the cycle are here set down chronologically. They will be described as we come to them except in so far as they are recurrent. It will be clear from what has gone before that the intervals separating the items are highly variable.

Programme of the Hevehe Cycle

Beginning

Cleaving the coco-nut.	200
Cutting the first cane .	207
Hevehe Karawa brings the first pair of rudimentary masks (*paiva haro*) into the *eravo* .	210 ff.
Cutting of general supplies of cane	229, 234
Making of mask frames (*paiva haro*) proceeds .	235

Stages of Construction[1]

(At long intervals)

Hevehe Karawa brings the mouths (*ape*) .	242
Hevehe Karawa brings the bark-cloth (*pura*) .	242

Covering the frames with *pura* proceeds (called *Hevehe Ohira'uve*, 'lying down', because they are laid flat); also decoration (*hohoa*) with cane strips; also construction of basket-work (*arara*).

Hevehe Karawa brings the bast (*koro*) for the undermantles .	242

The 'backs' (*avaha*) of the masks are covered with *pura*.

Hevehe Karawa brings the first sago-leaf (*mae*) for the overmantles.	264

Women proceed to manufacture *mae*.

Ceremonies of the New Door

(After a further long interval)

The *eravo* is furnished with a hinged door (*dehe*) .	271
Visit of totemic dance masks (*eharo*) in the morning .	274

---

[1] These are in some *eravo* more numerous than are shown here, and visits of *Hevehe Karawa* are accordingly more frequent.

[1] As a complex, *Hii Kairu* seems to embrace the three last items of the preceding day, viz. bathe, fire-fight, and fire-presentation. See p. 343.

XII

BEGINNING OF THE CYCLE

WHEN the long-drawn *Hevehe* cycle has at last reached its close there probably ensues a period of quiescence. The *eravo* from which the masked figures have emerged is then vacant, or at most thinly populated by mere human beings and by the spirits of bull-roarers, *hohao*, and ancestors, which take up little room. The great building, already somewhat tattered, is allowed to fall into ruin, and finally dismantled, when the men of the village will resort to the *baupa eravo* for a club-house, transferring thither the *hohao* and the bundle of bull-roarers. With their more crowded quarters they will rest content, maybe for a long time. But, granted the necessary will and sufficient supply of man-power, they will eventually set to work upon their new *eravo*. The new *eravo* is for a time open to all the males of the village; but it will not remain so for long. It is a mansion prepared for the *hevehe*; and when the first of them has crossed the threshold it will be closed to all but the initiated.

In describing the cycle I propose to start as from this point. The actual beginning of *Hevehe*—so rare a happening as it is—I have not had the luck to see; and this chapter therefore is based on verbal accounts. But the discrepancies are remarkably few and trivial, and it may be assumed that procedure, when it comes to the point, will conform fairly closely to tradition. For there is much discussion and planning, not only among the elder men of the *eravo* immediately concerned, but among the members of the *avai* from other *eravo* who enter into their informal counsels; and many old heads make a good united memory as well as a thoroughly conservative policy. Uniformity of traditional practice follows from two factors: on the one hand, a clearly stated duty to conform to the ancestral way; and, on the other, an insistent desire that all should think and act alike. As far as actual performance goes, therefore, the following account, sifted from those of many independent witnesses, may be taken to represent the routine.

The Urge to United Action

It is, of course, impossible to discover the particular seed of thought or motive that takes root in an individual's mind and finally develops into the full purpose, shared by the whole community, to carry out some great enterprise like building an *eravo* or instituting *Hevehe*. It seems that the community at large gathers force, a slowly rising urge, as it goes about its humdrum work during the periods of quiescence, until, at the original instance of some individual, its whole united mind is turned towards the performance of a further stage in the ceremony or to beginning it all again. Such common decision is undoubtedly dependent on prosperity, on increase, both in men and pigs. *Hevehe* is not undertaken in a period of weakness or want. There must be many young men, and strong ones, available for the heavy work, as well as a number of boys awaiting initiation; and, *sine qua non*, there must be a multiplying of pigs. Given these favourable circumstances, some individual sets the ball rolling, and then, what with the power of example, we may witness (or perhaps we never shall again) such a remarkable phenomenon as that of 1914, or thereabouts, when every one of the seven *eravo* of Orokolo began its *Hevehe* cycle within a few months.

That desire for unanimous thought and action which has been several times noted implies that the community will not budge until every one, at least within its own bounds, is in the mood for co-operation, so that we cannot by any means imagine *Hevehe* to be begun and carried out upon the orders of an *eravo amua*. The original suggestion may come from some quite obscure individual, perhaps from a lad who complains to his father that his mates are initiates while he is left out in the cold. The leaven spreads through the lump, and eventually the leading man of the *eravo* is nominally ordaining a process upon which his people are virtually agreed beforehand.

Eravo *Personalities*

Once affairs have reached this stage, their further conduct undoubtedly does rest largely in the hands of the leading *amua* of the *eravo*, or at least in those of its leading personality. Thus the veteran Haio of Avavu Ravi managed its *Hevehe* with a quite unusual show of authority. Yet even Haio was in no sense an autocrat; he had no individual whims, nor did he give any unacceptable orders; he was the mouthpiece of tradition and he kept things going along the lines which tradition dictated.

It seems worth while to pause for a moment to introduce some of the leading personalities of the various *eravo*. Most of them will appear more or less prominently in the description of the ceremonies.

The leaders are normally, though not always, the *eravo amua*; and of the two it is usually found that one is predominant. In Aivaroro Ravi they were Miki Harapa and Hitovakore; and of these the former, though much less imposing in appearance, was certainly the more energetic and intelligent and therefore the more important, so much so that people usually spoke of Miki Harapa's *eravo*. Now that he is dead it is spoken of as Hitovakore's. The latter is a tall, spare, dignified man, very reserved and silent. I do not think it unjust to ascribe his silence to a relative lack of ideas. Whenever I sat in Aivaroro Ravi his face was a mixture of boredom and puzzlement.

The leading *amua* of Meouri Ravi was Hiri, just such another but more so. He was the most impregnably silent man I have ever met. Despite an obviously friendly attitude and a desire to please he was never of any use as an informant because he could never induce himself to speak even on the most trivial and most straightforward subjects. Yet, while as an anthropologist I might justly have detested him, I found that as an ordinary man I rather liked him. Among his fellows he was, in his grim and silent way, rather a masterful figure, though, like his old age-mates, somewhat despondent because Meouri Ravi had been so depleted in its membership.

The other recognized *amua* was Area, a man of entirely different character. A very big, muscular man with showy manners, he was a prominent and well-known figure; but he was a good deal feared as an active sorcerer and disliked as one too ready to quarrel and inclined to bully. He later deserted Meouri Ravi as the result of a disagreement, and took up his residence at the far end of the settlement, viz. at Avavu Ravi, where he lived as turbulently as ever. Area was an agreeable man to meet, fond of his joke and voluble. But he again was a poor informant: it was difficult to get sense and consistency out of him, partly because of muddle-headedness and partly because of the cunning which was always prompting him to conceal things.

In passing one should mention another character of importance in Meouri Ravi, viz. Akeavira. He was the *kariki haera,* the custodian of *eravo* magic, and the importance of that office is shown by the fact that the *eravo* was sometimes spoken of as his, though to be sure he was the meekest and most retiring of little men. His importance certainly did not lie in his personality, but only in his magic.

The one and only chief of Hare Eravo was Heveheapo, one of the oldest men in Orokolo. Despite his age and frailness he carried himself like an athlete and was still careful of his appearance. His community was a small one—indeed in latter years they have had no *eravo* and can hardly muster man-power to attempt building one. But he was a person of renown and importance throughout the Western Elema. I think that age had begun just slightly to fuddle a remarkably good memory; but if any one ventured to question what he said he would answer in high-pitched querulous tones, and the others usually let him have his way about it. Always friendly to the European, Heveheapo had retained a rather pleasing air of being quite the European's equal; and a certain austere dignity called for a rather special show of respect. He wore a beard in perpetual memory of his son who had been killed in a quarrel. His other sons had not avenged their brother, much to the old man's disgust, and he wore the beard as evidence of implacability.

One of the parties concerned in the above-mentioned

PLATE 20

A. Hitovakore

B. Hiri

C. Area

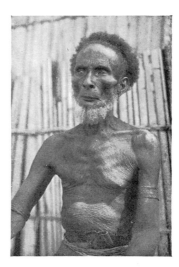

D. Heveheapo

Amua of Orokolo, I

quarrel was Havaiveakore who had fled from Hare Eravo
to Arihava to avoid the risk of vengeance. Now, years afterwards, he had come back; but his relations with his old *eravo*
were still not altogether happy and he mostly frequented
Meouri Ravi. He was another example of the more refined,
almost ascetic, type of Elema native. Credited with a good
deal of magic, he was certainly well versed in the lore of his
aualari, though whatever he told me was given out with
an almost exaggerated air of mystery. He was, however,
a highly intelligent man and could be voluble. He was
temperamental, looked as if he suffered from headaches,
and possessed a violent temper which often got him into
trouble.[1]

The other person of importance in the Hare Eravo community was Havai, the younger brother of Heveheapo. It
was well known that bad blood existed between these two
elderly brothers (a very rare situation), and I never remember seeing them together. Indeed, it is told how Heveheapo
once requested Havai to leave the *avai*, in that he was the
younger brother and therefore not entitled to sit in that
company with the elder. Havai certainly looked perpetually
sour. I do not know what was the cause of these disagreements, but suspect that Heveheapo, despite some agreeable
qualities, was a jealous and difficult old man.

Hohi Ravi was a small community of which again one
individual stood out as chief. This was Kaivipi, a man in
the early thirties and one of the most admirable specimens
of Western Elema manhood that it was my pleasure to meet.
Although the youngest of the effective *amua*, he possessed
considerable personal dignity, which he carried off by an
imperturbable manner. Yet he was capable of sudden flashes
of humour and would sometimes cast off his restraints and
indulge for a brief space in violent declamation, with all the
evidences of passion. But this sort of outburst would end
as suddenly as it began; it was a sort of oratorical device,
and when it was over he would appear as unruffled as ever.
Kaivipi, though a somewhat inscrutable character, was an

---

[1] Havaiveakore, by way of giving an example of an *aiha-haera* (see p. 112), said that
he was one himself.

excellent informant; he was fairly steeped in mythical lore, and consequently possessed a very wide reputation as a magician and sorcerer. It will be no surprise that he was not very amenable to mission teaching.

The other people of importance in Hohi Ravi were Hau and the elderly, ineffectual Hohoa. The former was not much older than Kaivipi; as a man of exceptionally fine physical development and what, I think, might be called good character, he carried a good deal of weight, being *amua* of the side opposite Kaivipi's. But he had none of the latter's finesse, and was always ready in his good-humoured way to defer to him. As for Hohoa, the only elderly man in the *eravo*, he would in the ordinary course have been its chief if only his personality had been equal to the position. But he was of a retiring nature and obviously acquiesced in the leadership of Kaivipi.

I pass briefly over Ori Ravi because I never got on intimate terms with its leading *amua* Tahia, and because I never saw this community engaged in any large social enterprise. Tahia, however, was clearly recognized as its first man, though he was dry and somewhat unsociable, not only towards the ethnographer but also towards his fellows: he rather failed in one of the chief duties of an *amua* in that he preferred his house and was not often seen in the *eravo*.

Coming to Waiea Ravi we encounter a much more lively community. The *eravo amua* were Mahevehe (on the right) and Koraguba (on the left), both really old men. The former, a very small man distinguished by a tremendous wen on his forehead, was perhaps as influential as the latter, though certainly less intelligent. He had a reputation for destructive pig magic, and this must have stood him in good stead, for I have several times seen him ranting at the village at large, and with such a reputation behind him it is certain that his words would be listened to. He was, however, a good-tempered man, anxious to please, and popular. The same may be said with more emphasis of the other *amua*, Koraguba. He showed an almost paternal affection for his *eravo*, and in his hours of leisure was constantly to be found

PLATE 21

A. Havaiveakore

B. Hohoa

C. Kaivipi

D. Hau

Amua of Orokolo, II

in it. Very thin and frail, and with one arm contorted to the point of uselessness, he was always diligent and cheerful. He was one of the best of my informants, quick in the uptake, knowledgeable and open, so that I had good reason to be grateful to him; but it was the charm of a gentle old man that I remember best, and it was this which endeared him, I think, to all.

A person of more force of character and more real power than either of these was Tahia, *eravo kariki haera*, sometimes called also *oharo kirea haera*, i.e. the person who transmits orders.[1] He was the real moving spirit of the community though without unduly pushing himself forward. He was vigorous and inclined to be bluff; incidentally a skilful craftsman who liked to stick to his job; and lastly, a man who knew his own mind very well and showed towards the European a rather agreeable independence.[2]

The seventh *eravo*, viz. Avavu Ravi, was up to 1935 under the two old men Haio and Ere. The latter was recognized not only as *amua* of the left side but as *kariki haera* for the whole *eravo*. He was consequently a person of considerable importance, though as a somewhat retiring old man, as well as a sick one, he was not a very prominent figure in the great *Hevehe* ceremony which I saw in this *eravo*. The conduct of that ceremony was largely (indeed to a greater extent than I should have thought possible from previous observations of Elema leadership) in the hands of Haio. This remarkable little man was not an *amua* in the strict sense of the word, viz. a hereditary chief of either *eravo* side or of the whole village. The *amua* on the right was one Biai, but he was so little prominent that I fail to recall him. Haio, however, gave orders in no uncertain voice; and when he scolded the village at large, as he did now and again in a veritable broadside of objurgation, men and women did not merely hear his words (which is their usual reaction to the harangue, unless they answer back), but actually bestirred themselves. This peppery little man with his dynamic energy and his

[1] See p. 91, n. 2.
[2] Laru, the *Karigara amua* of Waiea Ravi, was spoken of as a man of importance, but he was absent during some of my periods in Orokolo and at other times was so little in the picture that I cannot remember him at all.

unusual show of authority did much to keep an unwieldy ceremony on the move.

The credit for this success, however, in so far as it is due to individuals, he shared with the two Drum Leaders. It will be recalled that there are two such functionaries, one for either side, in every *eravo* where the *Hevehe* cycle is under way. In Avavu Ravi they were Duru on the right, and Aori on the left, and both in their different ways rose well to the occasion. Being a Drum Leader is a somewhat expensive and exacting honour. It means a lavish sacrifice of pigs as well as attention to many details; and Duru, a large, rather slow-moving[1] man, was too preoccupied with his duties to open his mouth. But Aori was both *horova eapapo haera*, 'a great worker', and *ape eapapo haera*, 'a man with a big mouth', that is to say one capable of strong talk. Yet it was less by words than by practical example that he gave inspiration. It would be hard to imagine any one better fitted for his office than this indefatigably willing young man.

The First Rite: Cleaving the Coco-nut

After this digression upon the personalities of some of the *eravo* leaders we may begin the *Hevehe* cycle as one or other of them would begin it. When it has been decided that the hitherto vacant *eravo* is to have its *Hevehe* there are certain preliminaries which must be performed unknown to the women. Firstly, as the initiation of certain young men is involved, their respective *aukau* must be notified or approached. They do not shirk their obligations, and soon a corresponding number of *aroa*, trimmed round the edge with dogs' teeth and hung with handsome arm-shells, pearl crescents, and *apakora*, are smuggled into the *eravo*. They are virtually on view, suspended from the rattan-cane clothes-line, though they may be covered, for at this stage a high degree of sacredness attaches to them. From the purely mundane point of view they are the gifts which the respective *aukau*, probably hailing from other communities, have prepared for their *arivu*, the prospective initiates. By the

---

[1] Duru is slightly affected on both legs with that very prevalent disease, elephantiasis.

PLATE 22

A. Koraguba

B. Mahevehe

C. Aori

D. Tahia

Amua of Orokolo, III

same token, each *arivu* (the novices are full-grown young men) must have in readiness his pig as counter-gift to the ornaments. Thirdly, as a final preliminary, word has gone forth to various other *eravo* to hold their young manhood (only those previously initiated) in readiness to play their part in the forthcoming drama, and to collect all available drums, *puva* (fusus-shell trumpets), and *harau* (hollow seed rattles) for its essential sound-effects.

Apart from these preliminaries the first ceremonial step takes place in the *eravo* itself. It consists in the simple act of splitting a coco-nut—one sudden effective stroke which marks the beginning of a cycle which is to last perhaps fifteen years and more. I have seen the same rite performed a number of times in connexion with the Bull-Roarer initiation. In the case of *Hevehe*, where, of course, I have not seen it, it is said to take place on the afternoon preceding the first cane-cutting expedition (or on the morning of the same day). A few elderly men of the *avai* alone are present. To judge from the Bull-Roarer rite, it is really a moment of some solemnity, the old men sitting in silence. But there is no rigid constraint. If one of them feels impelled to spit, or to pass the bamboo smoking-tube, he does not hesitate to do so. It cannot be said that the ceremonial drill is perfect. The *amua* who is to officiate takes the unhusked coco-nut, which has been placed ready in the centre of the *eravo*, and sets it before him in their midst. Then he chews a little *apiapi*, spits on his axe to give it power or heat, perhaps mutters a word or two, and then, with one skilful stroke, splits the coco-nut fairly down the centre. Somewhat carelessly he places it against an *eravo*-post and proceeds to ladle out the food, while the *avai* return to their betel-chewing and conversation. Next morning (or perhaps the same day) the Drum-Leaders and their young men will set out to cut the cane.

Whenever I have witnessed this rite in connexion with the Bull-Roarer the words spoken by the coco-nut-splitter have consisted at most of a barely audible monosyllable; and I have seen it done with no word at all, not so much as a movement of the lips. Yet when I have questioned the officiator afterwards (such questioning must be private), the spell appropriate to the occasion may expand to almost inordinate length.[1] So it is with this cleaving of the coco-nut for *Hevehe*. The alleged spells or utterances are not for the public ear; they are strictly secret. Therefore they are not spoken save under the breath; or maybe they are only thought; or maybe they are not even that. However, they are worth recording because, if only retrospectively, they show the theory (as far as he indulges in theory) which underlies the coco-nut-splitter's action.

Now the manual rite, as simple as any rite could be, is common to all *eravo*. But the theory of it, in so far as it is revealed by these utterances, is somewhat surprisingly vari-able. Thus Heveheapo of Hare *eravo* as he splits the coco-nut speaks as follows:

> 'Master Havae, rise up and sit here, I pray you with my lips. Your own *eravo* men, your mat, your head-rest, your sleeping-place are here. Depart not to any other *eravo*; remain here and here alone. As we are about to do this thing, do you guard us. Go not to any other place.'[2]

Heveheapo is the undisputed head of the Akai people of Hare Eravo, and Havae is their ancestor. He is a human ancestor rather than one of the Story Folk, legendary rather than mythical; for he is supposed to have led his people from Popo to Orokolo, and that migration or dispersion is by common consent long subsequent to the mythical epoch. His name embodies those of intermediate ances-tors, so this utterance of Heveheapo's well illustrates that attitude towards the departed which constitutes, so to speak, half of Western Elema religion. Heveheapo has his spells and magic and his knowledge of the myths like any other man; but in this connexion it is his reverence for and devotion to his human ancestry that are uppermost in his mind. It will be seen that he offers no explanation what-ever of the actual splitting of the coco-nut: that, he merely

PLATE 23

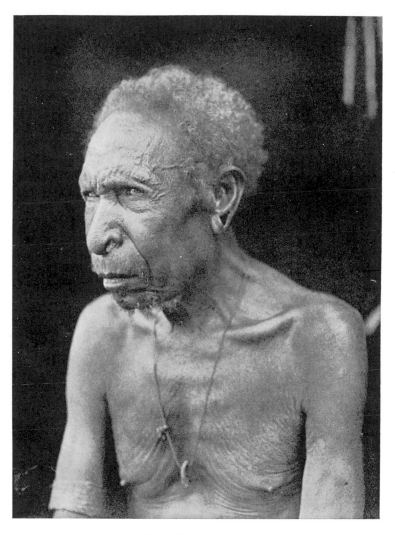

Haio of Avavu Ravi

says, is what his ancestors did, and therefore he should do the same.

Let us next consider the words of Koraguba of Waiea Ravi. Spitting on his axe he addresses it:

'If my village people are to die, then split the coco-nut badly. If they are to keep well, then split the coco-nut well.'[1]

The stroke therefore contains an omen, and the prospects, whether of dissensions, sorceries and deaths, or of good feeling and good health, with an uninterrupted course for the *Hevehe*, depend largely on the skill of Koraguba himself. The above words he might, if he wished, utter aloud for all to hear; but not so the name Uravu, which he communicates afterwards and which at the moment of striking he would at the most mutter under his breath. For the adjuration is not directed to the inanimate axe, but to Uravu,[2] viz. the bull-roarer of Waiea Ravi which lies with all the other lesser and unnamed bull-roarers in a package in the *eravo*. The old woman who lives on in the bull-roarer is very definitely one of the Story Folk. Koraguba distinguished her emphatically from his human ancestors, who are *ou-erarura haera*, people 'born from the womb'. He names his own best-remembered ancestor in that category, viz. Pekoro; but expressly dismisses him from notice in the present connexion, and makes it plain that he is asking Uravu, by implication, for protection. If he splits the coco-nut fair and square down the middle, then Uravu has heard his prayer.

As a third example I quote the formula of Kaivipi of Hohi Ravi:

'I am about to open Apu's jaws. I, Oro-Ipi-Avu, am about to pour into them pig meat and sago.'[3]

---

[1] '*Arave karigara haera apakive laraikirava, la heahari kovaira. Beveke laraikirava, la beveke kovaira.*'

[2] Uravu (sometimes called Oro Uravu), according to Koraguba's version of the story, was the old woman who, hearing two branches of an *oro* tree rub together in the wind, poured out food at the butt, thinking it was a supernatural voice. She herself, he says, made the first bull-roarer under the inspiration of the noise; but she also is the bull-roarer, and the bull-roarer is Oro Uravu.

See *Bull-Roarers in the Papuan Gulf*, p. 22, where the same name is borne by a bull-roarer in another *eravo*.

[3] '*Ara Apuve uhare hakive-leive.*
Ara, Oro-Ipi-Avu, ira poi kakaitakive-leive.'

This is a typical Elema spell, Kaivipi's secret magic for the occasion. He speaks in the first person, as Oro-Ipi-Avu herself; Apu is the bull-roarer of Hohi Ravi; and the opening of his jaws is symbolized by the splitting of the coco-nut. In Oro-Ipi-Avu[1] we meet one of those most secret and mysterious persons in the whole Elema world of spirits. She is, in fact, *eravo-ve-uvari*, the '*eravo* grandmother'. In this particular case the *uvari-apo*, or 'old grandmother', as she is sometimes called, was the very person who ministered to Apu, the present bull-roarer, when he was a man. Apu travelled from Kauri, the East, to the Purari. There he seems to have settled. But he lay for ever roaring and howling in the *kaia-larava* of his *eravo*, and it was the old woman Oro-Ipi-Avu who alone succeeded in quieting him by pouring pig meat and sago-balls down his throat. He now lives on in the slat of wood which is occasionally roused and placated in the bull-roarer ceremony; Oro-Ipi-Avu, as the mysterious and potentially mischievous old woman who lurks beneath the *eravo*.

FIG. 8. 'Apu', the chief bull-roarer of Hohi Ravi
19½ ins. long

Thus Kaivipi, like Koraguba, concerns himself with the *lau-haera* and not his flesh-and-blood ancestry,[2] and his method of approach is typical of Elema magic. It is not a prayer but rather an act of impersonation. 'I am Oro-Ipi-Avu', he says, 'and I am going to pour food into Apu's mouth as successfully as she did.' Things can hardly go wrong with such a precedent.

[1] Lit. 'Woman at the butt of the *oro* tree'. There is plainly some connexion with Oro Uravu. Elema mythology is a perfect network or tangle of cross-references.
[2] Kaivipi fully recognizes the distinction between the cult of the *lau haera* and that of the human ancestors. Asked if ever he placated the latter, he answered readily that he did so in another connexion, viz. as captain of the *bevaia*. Then he burns his medicines in the potsherd and appeals to his great-grandfather and great-grandmother, Auha and Ira, to protect him from the seas. In the *eravo*, however, he makes no such appeal to human ancestors.

As a last brief example there is the secret formula of Akeavira of Meouri Ravi:

'I am splitting open Oa Birukapu's belly.'[1]

These words have reference to the myth recounted in Chapter X, where it will be remembered the bull-roarer was discovered amid the monster's entrails. It seems as if Akeavira the *kariki haera* is conjuring it up once more for the ceremony.

Hevehe *and Bull-Roarer again*

The analysis of these formulae has but little connexion with the course of the *Hevehe* cycle, and it may seem that more than enough has been said on the brief matter of cleaving a coco-nut. But I have dwelt on it for two reasons: first, specifically, to recall the possible connexion between *Hevehe* and Bull-Roarer; and second, more generally, to show the variety of 'theory' that may accompany a uniform practice in one and the same culture.

As for the connexion between Bull-Roarer and *Hevehe* we have already, in a previous chapter, sought to explain the identity of name (*apa-hevehe* and *be'ure-hevehe*) and have drawn attention to the similarity of form. In neither respect has any native informant ever associated or compared the two things. But here in the opening act of the *Hevehe* cycle we find two men referring very plainly, and a third by implication, to bull-roarers. All of them declare indeed that the formulae or utterances which, if they do not actually speak them out, they still have in their minds, are the same whether they are splitting the coco-nut for the *Hevehe* or for the Bull-Roarer ceremony.

Now although the bull-roarer may actually be sounded on certain subsequent occasions in connexion with *Hevehe*, it must be reiterated that the two cults are at present among the Western Elema to all intents and purposes independent. On those few occasions when the bull-roarers do sound, one may perhaps accept the mundane explanation which some put forward, viz. that they are used as a sound-signal to

[1] '*Ara Oa Birukapu-ve eharau kovairave.*'

clear the women from the scene. Nothing indeed could better serve this purpose. Yet it is said by others that the bull-roarer is *karigara pupu*, 'a sacred thing of the village', always at home; whereas the *hevehe*, however long they may stay, are merely visitors; therefore the bull-roarer's voice should be heard on occasion as a prelude to this or that movement in connexion with *Hevehe*.[1]

Further we may recall the fact that bull-roarer and *hevehe* are said to stand to one another in the relation of elder brother and younger brother (*akoreapo* and *akoreheare*). The common explanation for this relationship is that initiation for the former takes place first. But since *Kovave*, the third secret ceremony, is *akore-heare hekai*, the 'little' or youngest brother, and since boys are almost invariably initiated to *Kovave* before *Hevehe*, this explanation cannot cover the whole three—a point which always reduces one's informant to a discomfited silence. If this classification of the ceremonies by seniority is worth anything at all, another interpretation (already mentioned elsewhere) leaps to the mind, viz. that of priority of origin or introduction. Although the Orokolo native usually regards all three as dating from eternity, it seems at least likely on general grounds that the Bull-Roarer is prior to the others.[2]

However interpreted, the relation of senior to junior does not in itself prove any connexion between Bull-Roarer and *Hevehe*. All that can be said is that the priority of the former is obviously necessary to the thesis (which I have no particular desire to stress) that the *hevehe* mask is actually derived from the bull-roarer.

Having pointed out this much I propose to drop the subject of bull-roarers in the present book. The original connexion between them and *Hevehe*—if any—is a matter for surmise; and at any rate it appears to have vanished from the present-day native's mind. We can afford to dismiss the

[1] In some *eravo* it is claimed that the bull-roarer is sounded whenever the *ma-hevehe* come up from the sea; but it is agreed that this feature is an introduction from the Houra Haera (Keuru and Berepa tribes). I have never actually heard it on such occasions.

[2] In the Muru tribe, a few miles inland from Orokolo Bay, this is definitely the case. I have circumstantial historical accounts of the introduction of both *Hevehe* and *Kovave* to this people, who already had the bull-roarer.

subject in an appreciation of *Hevehe*, for *Hevehe* now stands by itself.

Practice and Theory

The second reason for dwelling on the alleged utterances accompanying the coco-nut-cleaving is of more real importance. There is hardly any room for deviation in a rite so simple, but when we seek the native theory of it we find variety enough; and the further we go the greater it becomes. I have no hesitation in crediting Heveheapo, Koraguba, Kaivipi, and Akeavira with sincerity, and each gives a different explanation. Others, less educated (in a legitimate sense of the word), would be able to give none at all. For it is quite certain—and the better one comes to know the people and their culture the more obvious it grows—that a great majority of natives could give no reason for performing such a ceremony except that it had been performed by their fathers before them. However interesting or illuminating the 'theory' may be, then, it seems a fair inference that to the majority of natives it is the fixed rite that matters rather than the variable theories, known to the privileged or educated few, which may lie behind it. It is indeed likely that, as long as *Hevehe* and the Bull-Roarer remain as cults in Orokolo Bay, the coco-nuts will continue to be split in twain at the right moment, theory or no theory.

Having given the above examples for the sake of the points that can be made out of them, the writer suggests that as explanations of the actual splitting of the coco-nut they are entirely beside the mark. It seems more plausible to regard this act as some ancient rite of beginning or of opening, a clean, decisive act of inauguration.[1] The current native explanations are probably no more than accretions.

Cutting the First Cane

We may now follow the two Drum Leaders and the party of young men as they set out to cut the cane (*paiva koerapakive*). They must travel some distance, passing through

[1] Cf. the splitting of the coco-nut among the Keraki people of the Morehead District to mark the end of mourning or the beginning of freedom from mourning; also in rain-making magic. *Papuans of the Trans-Fly*.

the lands that have been in past years used for gardens, until they come to a tract of virgin forest. Here the climbing calamus or rattan (*paiva*) is found trailing its immense length from the ground to the tops of the tall forest trees, where it can find the sunshine and put forth its graceful thorny fronds. The young men explore till they have found a hanging loop that seems to promise well. Then the Drum Leader lays hold of it, cries out the name of the leading *hevehe*, and cuts it through at a stroke. The young men utter their *yakea*, the united hoot, '*Uah!*', and drag it down.

Once again the utterances appropriate to the occasion are probably compressed into the mere name or names of the *hevehe* called upon; but they are capable of expansion. Heveheapo would call, 'Kero and Marere' (two of his own *hevehe*), 'come both of you and eat of my coco-nut and sago.'[1] Koraguba cries on Miri Laru, the leading *hevehe* of Waiea Ravi; and, as in the coco-nut-cleaving, so in the dragging down of the cane, sees an omen in the way things go: 'If our village is to thrive, come down easily. If we are to have dissension and death, resist our pulling.'

Kaivipi, perhaps more thoroughly steeped in magical lore, has his own secret formula. Needless to say, he does not speak this out, but merely calls on 'Harau' and 'Hevehe Aa'. What he says to himself is, 'I am Huravakore. I am about to drag out Birukapu's entrails. I am about to drag away his tail.'[2] As a typical Elema spell this has reference to a myth, viz. the one already told in Chapter X. Huravakore means literally 'Son of the West'; it is Kaivipi's private synonym for Mikya and Kaepa,[3] the two Hurava men, or Westerners, who came and killed Oa Birukapu, the *mahevehe*, as he lay on the beach.

It is not permissible to read too much into such a spell as the last-mentioned, to regard it, for instance, as a clue to the meaning or origin of *Hevehe*. It is no more than a magico-

---

[1] '*Kero, Marere, evari'ira iki, arave la poi darive.*'
[2] '*Ara Huravakore. Ara Oa Birukapu-ve eh-ra haititavakive-leive. Areve aue hakeaviava'ukive-leive.*'
[3] Mikya and Kaepa (alias Aikere and Maikere) are names known to all. Huravakore, despite its generalized character, is a word which, in this connexion, Kaivipi keeps to himself.

metaphorical allusion which Kaivipi uses in the present connexion, feeling that it will help things to go off well. Other magic in the same connexion will refer to other myths. For other men, other spells; and for some, no spells at all. It is no doubt true, as informants say, that many Drum Leaders would cut their cane without any such spell, for the ample reason that they possessed none.

Only a small quantity of cane is cut on this first occasion, sufficient for the frameworks of the two *hevehe* masks belonging to the two Drum Leaders. The party now returns to the village; but they hide their cane in the bush at some convenient spot half a mile down the beach. There it is left in readiness for the evening's performance.

HEVEHE KARAWA

Visit of the Ma-hevehe

IT would need a very observant eye to detect anything unusual about the village in the late afternoon, when the young men have returned from their excursion into the bush. Women and children are supposed to be quite unaware of any approaching excitement, and so jealously is the secret kept from them that we may perhaps believe they are eventually taken by surprise. Maybe one or two older men from other villages are being entertained in the *eravo*; and after dark it is to be observed that the young men have gone off on some occasions of their own. But while these facts may easily pass unnoticed and should hardly rouse suspicion, it is not so easy to imagine that the women fail to notice the disappearance of certain pigs; for even if the business of throwing and binding them, always a noisy one, is conducted in the bush, there is still the highly disturbing circumstance that they do not turn up for their evening food. In fact the pigs are often trussed up quite openly in the village, and when this is the case it is certain that the women know there is something in the wind.

A moonless night has been purposely chosen, so that no parties of children will be playing on the sands; the village as usual retires early; and the only lights are those of flickering fires inside the houses. Here and there through an open door, an oblong of smoky red against the tropical blackness, you may see the inmates sitting placidly at their betel, sometimes with desultory conversation, but mostly in sociable silence.

Suddenly far down the beach there is heard a noise—a faint one because of the distance, but so meaningful as to electrify every feminine soul in the village. It is weirdly distinctive, a conglomeration of voices, which defies all description. At first the round notes of shell-trumpets seem to predominate, in strangely exciting discord; but we hear also the distant thunder of many drums; and what seems like the shriek of some tremendous, superhuman voice. The shriek gives place to, and alternates with, a deep-toned roar; and the whole volume of mixed sounds swells terrifyingly, drawing momently nearer. We may now distinguish a harsh background of noise, a kind of rhythmical yet continuous rattle; and the whole is punctuated by detonations, rapid and irregular, like rifle-fire.

At the very first note of the shell-trumpet the women have been thrown into a state of alarm—not very serious, for they have been through all this before, but sufficient to make them hurriedly extinguish their fires and shut their doors. Any one who is abroad makes haste to shelter in his house; and in a very few moments every one in the village is waiting in tense, immobile expectancy. Meanwhile, whatever is creating the noise is fast bearing down upon them, and now at close quarters it is an unearthly noise indeed, in all senses of the word. It would be hard to believe that any one could be of soul so dead as not to feel some thrill of dramatic terror at its approach, or some sense of dramatic climax in its arrival. For, wheeling in from the beach and across the village to the front of the *eravo*, it surges through the doorway, seeming to struggle in the narrow entrance, and the noise continues within, muffled by confinement but all the more impressive. Then, with a suddenness that leaves one astonished, it is simply cut off, giving place to breathless silence.

This is the *ma-hevehe* coming up from the sea. Let us go back a little and see what has been happening down the beach. Since nightfall a crowd of men, perhaps a hundred and more, and mostly youngish, have been making excited preparations. It will be recollected that the cane brought home by the Drum Leaders' party was secreted at a convenient place some half a mile distant from the village. Two lengths of it have been bent and bound into loops, roughly in the shape of *hevehe* masks, one for each Drum Leader. Bedecked with *hapa*, i.e. fresh pale-green sago-leaves, these two loops of cane represent the *raison d'être* of the ceremony, for they are no less than the first two *hevehe* destined to enter the *eravo*.

But the young men's minds are mostly occupied with more worldly matters. They have come together from various *eravo*, bringing with them every drum and shell-trumpet they can lay hands on; they have shell-rattles by the score, bunches of hollow seeds (*harau*) attached to bands which they will presently tie round their legs so that every

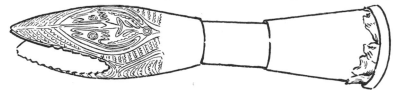

FIG. 9. An Orokolo Drum

movement is accompanied by that harsh rattling which we noted in the synthesis of noises; and many of them are armed with the midribs of coco-nut palms, which, being brought down smack on the hard sand, make a noise like a rifle-shot. The time for real noise-making, however, is not yet. In the meantime they are not particularly silent (there is no need to be at this distance), but are jesting and skylarking, all in high spirits. Many of them carry bows, arrows, and clubs, partly because this is the traditional practice in the ceremony, and partly out of mere habit, for such is the inflammability of Elema crowds that it is well to have your weapons handy. But here there is no likelihood of their use. All is good humour. Only a few older men, befeathered and armed with spears, wear a somewhat more business-like mien.

We may now see black forms moving with some purpose in the darkness. They are erecting a rough barricade of palm-leaves along the seaward side of the beach. Presently they divide themselves into two parties, one crouching behind the barricade, the other hiding in the low bushes that fringe the beach on its landward side. They take up their drums and trumpets, adjust their rattles, and all fall silent. For the hour is at hand.

These men on the beach, it must be understood, have all been initiated at some previous performance of the ceremony we are describing. It is now their turn to initiate some others, and they may be depended on to do their job thoroughly, to give the new initiates as lively a time of it as they once went through themselves. The sudden silence which we have observed is in response to a message just received from the village; and now we may see a party of seven or eight men approaching from that direction; a glowing fire-stick waved to and fro lights them on their way, and the voices of some of them are raised in rather loud conversation. They are the maternal uncles (*aukau*), or their substitutes, escorting their *arivu*, say two or three of them, to their initiation. The ostensible reason for this evening walk down the beach is of course something quite different: maybe they are going to exchange some ornaments at Lariau, and the *aukahura*, their hearts full of mischief, are discussing the prospects in a manner which is meant to put their nephews off the scent. As for these nephews, there is no reason to suppose that they have not a very good idea of what lies in store for them. It may be taken as certain that they do not anticipate meeting a *ma-hevehe*; but they are nevertheless, as some of them have admitted, not a little apprehensive. Thus, vaguely prepared, they walk into the trap.

As they draw level with the barricade there is suddenly heard the tap of a drum, and in instantaneous response a hundred throats give vent to a horrifying shriek such as must instantly shatter the initiates' remaining nerve, and a hundred black forms leap out of the darkness upon them. The first time I was present at one of these performances, merely as an onlooker hiding with the others in ambush, I was fairly staggered. The noise is cataclysmic. The drums, the shell-trumpets, the rattles, burst simultaneously into action; ear-splitting cracks come from every direction; and above all there is the concerted falsetto shriek, siren-like in its quality, which alternates with deep roars. It is a vocal and orchestral triumph, a Surprise Symphony with a vengeance.

In the midst of all this the novices—and they are adults, not boys—huddle together for protection. They are jostled right and left, and the drummers hold their instruments above them, beating them furiously as if to pour the noise out on their heads. I have seen two novices with their arms tight clasped about each other's necks and their faces buried on each other's shoulders : it was plain they were not enjoying it.

This uproar continues without lessening for some three or four minutes. Then there is a brief pause and all begin to move along the beach towards the village. But the noise is recommenced in a moment and, henceforward, continues with something of rhythm about it, the shell-trumpets blowing in dissonance together, and the wearers of the rattles leaping in time rather than merely running. The novices have now been liberated, their ordeal, not a very serious one after all, is over; and together with their escorts they speed on ahead to enter the *eravo* by the back door. (I have come upon one of them in this situation and by the light of an electric torch saw him cowering at the rear of the building, speechless and still frightened : he had obviously received a bad shaking.)

Advancing along the beach the party of noise-makers seems merely a chaotic crowd, but it really possesses some formation. At times more highly organized, the participants are said to be disposed in three or four bodies at intervals along the beach, so that they can take up the noise from one another, and thus give the impression that the *ma-hevehe* is advancing and retreating, or else rushing along at incredible speed. But I have never seen this idea put into practice. There are, however, apart from the main body, the *karawaporoi*, those men armed with the *hou* (palm midribs) who advance in scattered formation ahead of it, and the *hovori-hovori*. The latter are those older men whom we observed before, armed as if they meant business. They are *harihu-ore-haera*, the kind of sorcerers who are not only dangerous to others but themselves invincible to attack. It is their business to spy for wanderers or for lights in the houses, and to deal with them by sorcery or else directly with a spear-thrust.

The whole party, having now reached the village and swept through the gap in the fence which has been hurriedly made beforehand, is brought somewhat to a halt before the *eravo*. But the noise continues without abatement; and already, led by the *hovori-hovori* and the Drum Leaders bearing the two rudimentary *hevehe*, the party is pouring through the bottle-neck of the *eravo* door.[1] Those who have remained inside the building appear to resist them with drawn bows. Defenders and attackers surge back and forth, advancing and retreating, while the whole building shakes under their stamping feet. Then, as we saw, the uproar comes suddenly to an end. After that tempest of noise the silence creates a strange blank. A smothered cough, or the accidental tinkling of a rattle, seems only to make it tenser. So several minutes pass. Then there is a sound of banging on the *eravo* floor: one of the old men is merely hitting it with a stick. At this signal the whole party files out as rapidly and as quietly as possible, and once assembled on the ground outside bursts once more into their full hullaballoo of roaring, screeching, trumpeting, rattling, and drumming. So they begin their retreat. Out of the village they go, and once more down the beach, until the noise is heard only faintly in the distance. At last some of the trumpeters half fill their conch-shells with sea-water, and blow a few gurgling blasts as a farewell. The *ma-hevehe* has paid its visit to the *eravo* and has returned to its element.

But before the sound of its voice has quite died away an old man will issue from the *eravo*-door and, standing on the veranda, declaim a brief address. He calls on a number of *ma-hevehe* by name (for it is not given out that any particular one of them has paid this visit), and bids them stand by, or wait in the offing, for their next summons. Then the affair is over for the night; fires spring up again; and people may come and go without danger, or turn in and sleep without further disturbance.

[1] I have only once (Waiea Ravi, 1933) seen the *ma-hevehe* party actually enter the *eravo*. On most occasions it halts on the ground outside and only the leaders, *hovori-hovori*, mount the steps. However, I am assured that on this first occasion in the course of a cycle it is proper for the party to enter, and have therefore introduced that part into the present description.

It is not unlikely that the usual method, that of halting outside, is a modification of the original designed to meet the difficulty of getting the whole party through the narrow door. I can find no satisfactory rule saying when the party should enter and when not, and imagine it is an open matter.

The ceremony, however, does not reach its real conclusion until late in the following day. The *aukau* still have to invest the novices with the *aroa* of ornaments, giving them at the same time a fusus-shell from which they must produce at least one formal blast; and the novices in return have to present their pigs to the *aukau*. It is in the disposal of these pigs that most of the day is spent. They are for the men only, and consequently the affairs of the day are kept as secret from the women as were those of the preceding night.

Hevehe Karawa *as the Final Initiation*

The ceremony above described is called *Hevehe Karawa*. It is performed not once only, but again and again, perhaps a dozen times or more in the course of any one cycle; in fact such a ceremony ushers in each important stage in the progress of events, and further it may be performed without any such pretext, merely, in fact, for the purpose of putting certain candidates through their initiation.[1] I have had the good fortune to be present, either in the village or on the beach, at a number of celebrations in connexion with different cycles and different *eravo*, and am therefore able to describe the ceremony as it were from both ends. The first *Hevehe Karawa* of a cycle (which the above purports to be) I have, of course, never seen; but those at which I have been present have all adhered closely to pattern, so that the above description, as of a typical case, may be taken to show what happens.

The ceremony involves an initiation, and we noted that the candidates were not boys, but grown men. Although it has been described first, *Hevehe Karawa* provides the *second* of two distinct kinds of initiation in connexion with *Hevehe*. It reveals the important secret of the *ma-hevehe*; whereas the other, a much less thrilling experience, reveals only the secret of the masks (i.e. strictly the *apa-hevehe*). In the course of an individual's life, initiation to *apa-hevehe* comes first, when he is a boy; he goes through *Hevehe Karawa* only years later, when he is an adult and in the normal case married. In the course of any *Hevehe* cycle, on the other hand, a

---

[1] For another pretext see p. 227.

PLATE 24

An *Aukau* haranguing his *Arivu*, newly initiated to *Hevehe Karawa*. He has just presented him with the *aroa* of ornaments

number of *Hevehe Karawa* ceremonies will take place before the stage of *Apa-Hevehe* initiation is reached; so that, as we are describing the cycle, it is necessary to deal with the later initiation first.

The act of initiation is really only incidental to *Hevehe Karawa*. It is true that whenever I saw it a number of candidates came forward; but the ceremony is essential to the cycle, and it would be permissible to perform it without any such candidates. There are seldom more than three or four of them, and unlike the other kinds of initiation known to the Western Elema (viz. Bull-Roarer, *Kovave*, and *Apa-Hevehe*) *Hevehe Karawa* is passed through once and once only. The comparative frequency of its performance caters for all in due course, and accounts for the small number of the novices on each occasion.

The Name Hevehe Karawa

The fact that there are two distinct kinds of initiation in connexion with *Hevehe* will suggest at the outset that the cycle as it exists is a composite one, a fact which will claim a good deal of our attention later; and there is no doubt whatever that *Hevehe Karawa*, in its present form at any rate, is an accretion. It has been, in fact, imported, under circumstances which the old men can definitely recall, from the Houra-Haera, i.e. the people of the lower Vailala (Berepa tribe).[1] We might, therefore, look to those people for an explanation of its name. But they can give only the same unsatisfactory explanation which we hear among the Western Elema, viz. that *Karawa* is the name of that kind of small fish which, when brought ashore, inflates itself with air, and is often to be seen lying dead on the sands like a hapless little balloon. It is said that these fish precede the others, like scouts, when the tide turns and they come in looking for the scraps of food washed out of the women's pots. Another variety of the fish is called *poroi*; and the above-alleged circumstance may explain the name *Karawa-poroi* given to those members of the *ma-hevehe* party who precede the main body along the beach. It is said by others that *karawa* is a

[1] See p. 164.

name used for the sorcery of those men in the *eravo* who
make a special point of safeguarding the food (though I have
never elsewhere heard of this as a function of any particular
members). They are called, according to these informants,
harea-karawa-haera, and as such keep an observant eye on
their fellows, seeing that the food is not taken on the sly
and that it is not distributed by any save those who are
entitled to the privilege. This use of the word, however,
may be derived from the phrase *Hevehe Karawa* itself, since
the pig meat eaten after the ceremony is certainly the subject of very jealous observation. But neither of these
explanations seems particularly illuminating, and we must
be content, like the native, to take the expression simply as
it stands. An alternative name for the ceremony should be
mentioned, viz. *Ma-Kaikara*. This, which means literally
'Salt-Water', is now in very common use, but it is recognized as one of missionary coinage. I cannot say how it
arose.

The Graver Side of the Ceremony

There can be no doubt that *Hevehe Karawa*, besides possessing all the values of a tremendous rag, is also taken very
seriously. As a secret it is guarded from the uninitiated
with more strictness and severity than can be said to belong
to the other mysteries. Sometimes, it is said, elaborate
measures are taken to mislead the women: palm-branches
are dragged over the sand to serve the double purpose of
obliterating the many footprints of the participants and of
representing the track of the *ma-hevehe* dragging itself up
to the *eravo*; and a stranded nipa, encrusted with barnacles,
may be deposited by night fairly in front of the *eravo*, as
something the monster has left behind it, a souvenir of the
deep. But these are rather in the nature of jokes. More
significant is the real fear of the uninitiated, even though
they are adults, and their refusal to have anything to do, in
speech or action, with this supreme mystery. Once they
have paid their pigs and been initiated they will discuss it
freely, and like to dwell on its amusing side. But until then
they will give a wide berth to all concerned with it. Even

the morning after, when the village is cleared of women and children for the pig-killing, uninitiated men are afraid to pass by on the beach-highway opposite. Thus two young men of Arihava who came daily to work for me at Orokolo refused point-blank to pass an intervening village at this stage, and therefore took leave for the day. What they feared was, of course, the sorcery by which inquisitiveness, or even accidental observation of the secrets, would be punished. Deaths are, in fact, frequently put down to this cause, and it is one of the strongest and most stubborn arguments in the mouths of those who protest against the revival or continuance of *Hevehe*. A veiled and sinister expression is current for those who have met their death in this way: they are said to be *eravo ihauvea*, 'underneath the *eravo*'; they have been put out of the way. It is incidentally worth observing that here is another example of sorcery, or rather the belief in it, militating against a social institution.

It will be recalled that the older men who led the *ma-hevehe* party, viz. the *hovori-hovori*, were fully armed, and it is alleged that they are prepared to use their weapons against possible spies. It is, of course, alleged further, after the native fashion, that they readily did so; but, as so often happens, this sort of general statement boils down to one or two notorious occurrences. I can, in fact, discover only one as illustration in this case. It was that of Keia, a Birahiru man who happened to be in Yogu when a *Hevehe Karawa* was in progress. Various explanations are given: some say that he was making for home and anxious to get there; others that he was merely careless; others that he sauntered off in a spirit of bravado. But, whatever the case, he met the *ma-hevehe* party on the beach and was speared. His dead body was found in the morning and buried secretly; and it was given out to the women that the *ma-hevehe* itself had slain him. Three of the six *hovori-hovori* who had led that party survive to-day, Havaiveakore,[1] Marupi, and Mahevehe[2]—all of them incidentally good informants and friends of mine—but I did not discover whose spear it was that put Keia 'under the *eravo*'. It is not likely, perhaps, that such summary methods

[1] Pl. XXI, A.   [2] Pl. XXII, B.

would ever be put into force in these days of Government control; but neither is it in the least likely that any one would willingly lay himself open to them.

The Fiction of Hevehe Karawa

(a) As an Act of Initiation.

We may now discuss the fiction of *Hevehe Karawa* or, as some might prefer to say, its meaning. What can it be said to represent? It seems that we may legitimately divide the subject into two: on the one hand it is a ceremony of initiation accompanied by an exchange of gifts; on the other, irrespective of initiation, it is an integral part of the *Hevehe* cycle. We shall discuss these two aspects in turn.

Mention has several times been made of the two practical preliminaries to *Hevehe Karawa*, viz. the provision of pigs by the novices and of ornaments by their *aukau*; and the ceremony only reaches its close when these have been duly exchanged. Now this exchange is merely one of many, of almost exactly the same sort, between *arivu* and *aukau*, and it possesses no distinctive feature except that the ornaments in this particular case are always affixed to the string-bag, *aroa*.[1] To the initiated the exchange is merely the fulfilment of a regular social obligation. It is one of the functions of an *aukau* to see his *arivu* through the initiations, and each such initiation is made an opportunity for the pig–ornament exchange. The menfolk, therefore, do not require any far-fetched explanation of a straightforward business: the young fellows have to be put through it; they pay their price; and they receive their uncles' presents.

Yet the ceremony admits of another kind of explanation, and such would almost seem to be necessary if the women are to be taken in by it. They must usually see the pigs trussed up and carried into the *eravo*; but they certainly do not see the *aroa* of ornaments beforehand, since these are prepared with so much secrecy. In short, they hear the *ma-hevehe* come; in due course they see the new *aroa* come

---

[1] They are not given in this form at Bull-Roarer or *Kovave*, but they may be at other presentations in connexion with *Hevehe*. The ornaments carried by the bride to her husband's home are also affixed to an *aroa*.

out of the *eravo*; while, as for the pig, it has simply vanished. The *ma-hevehe*, then, has both brought the *aroa* and taken away the pig in payment.

I had long previously been given this explanation by some one or other, and it seemed so water-tight that I took it for granted. But quite recently I thought of verifying it, and then, much to my surprise, I could not find it put forward anywhere. As far as the pig was concerned, yes: the fiction was that the *ma-hevehe* took it. But in one *eravo* after another I received nothing but a severely rational explanation of the *aroa*: it was a present from the *aukau* to the *arivu* on the occasion of his initiation, and the women knew that the *aukau* had given it. I pointed out that, if the women believed the *ma-hevehe* had taken the pig, then it followed they must believe the *aukau* had got nothing in return for his ornaments; to which it was answered, 'Well, the women know well enough that the *aukau* eats the pig.' Finally, after the most exhaustive investigations on this particular point, without ever hearing any hint that the *ma-hevehe* was supposed to have brought the *aroa*, I felt at liberty to put the leading question. Not unexpectedly my informants endorsed the interpretation above suggested: 'Of course', they said, 'the younger women call it the *ma-hevehe*'s *aroa*.'

I cannot but believe that this was the original fiction. The apparent sacredness of the *aroa* would seem to bear it out. It is true that the secrecy involved in their preparation, the partial covering of them as they hang in the *eravo*, &c., are explained away on rational lines: these, it is said, are simply measures to secure a surprise effect upon the uninitiated. But there is a detail in the well-remembered circumstances of the introduction of *Hevehe Karawa* to the Western Elema which throws a different light on the *aroa*. One of them had been worn by a woman on her way home from the festivities, and this unwitting offence amounted then to the violation of a highly sacred tabu;[1] one feels pretty sure, without having verified the point by inquiry, that if such a thing happened to-day it would be regarded hardly less seriously. Finally,

[1] See p. 399.

to show that the fiction may still survive, I am assured that
if ever the novice's father and mother differ about the ownership of the various ornaments, the latter may bring argument
to an end by saying, 'That *aroa* was given to my son by the
ma-hevehe!'[1]

If it is true that this was the original fiction, it is equally
true that it is in process of dying out. It is to be presumed
that the pretences of secret organizations will tend in this
direction: they are revealed, gradually or suddenly, and they
are eventually dispensed with. The notion that the *ma-
hevehe* receives the pig as a sacrifice is already a little shaky;
the other notion, which would seem to be its logical comple-
ment, viz. that the monster brings up a return gift from the
sea, appears to have virtually collapsed. Be it noted, however, that initiations, together with the exchange of gifts,
continue unabated wherever *Hevehe* is practised. It seems to
follow that what may be called the religious aspect of the
exchange, i.e. the placation of the *ma-hevehe*, or the making
friends between *ma-hevehe* and novice, is not essential to its
continuance. The same fading out of religious meaning and
religious motive will be equally evident when we come to
certain other parts of the *Hevehe* cycle.

(b) As an Episode in the Cycle.

It remains to inquire what fiction, or what meaning,
attaches to *Hevehe Karawa* as an episode in the cycle. No
one ever succeeded in giving me a very satisfactory myth
of which it could be called a dramatization. Since the
relevant story was said to belong to the *Baiu aualari*, I was
recommended to old Hepe of Arihava.[2] He told of the *Ma
Marea Haera* (Sea-House People) and the *Kera Marea Haera*
(Hill-House People). The latter, as their name indicates,
lived in the hills. They possessed fine gardens, but these

---

[1] Adult members of a family own their ornaments, as well as their pigs, individually, using them to meet their several exchange obligations. But parents give
ornaments and pigs on behalf of their children, for which in due course they expect
a return. There is often some uncertainty regarding the ownership of pigs as between
husband and wife: it may be joint ownership. In such a hypothetical case as the
above the wife claims part of the ornaments given in exchange, and the husband
invokes the higher sanction in order to get them all, or the lion's share. He is 'putting one over' his wife.   [2] Pl. LXII, B.

were subject to continual depredations by the Sea People, who possessed little food of their own and would come up now and again in the form of great waves (*ma roru*) to sweep away slices of their land, gardens and all.[1] These attacks were made under cover of night, and were accompanied by the blowing of shell-trumpets and beating of drums, at the first sound of which the Hill People would hide in their houses, extinguishing the lights so as not to be seen by the marauders. It was only when the brave leader, Horova, determined to oppose the raiders alone that their depredations came to an end. He went down to the beach, and when the Sea People came up, confronted them. But they were only human after all. They put aside their weapons and fraternized with him, and he led them to his *eravo*, where they were entertained in so friendly a fashion that they decided to leave the sea and thenceforward remain ashore. Now, as land-dwellers, they constitute one portion of the *Baiu aualari* group.

It was my informant Hepe's opinion that his ancestors instituted the *Hevehe Karawa* in imitation of what actually happened according to the myth. Despite, however, the incidental resemblances between the story and the dramatic procedure (and they may very well have been put into the former for the sake of the comparison), it does not seem that the two are very closely parallel; for the visits from the sea were in the nature of raids or robberies; and when the visitors were finally met and entertained, they remained on shore. This, however, is the only story which informants can think of as appropriate to *Hevehe Karawa*, and it is the only one which I can find in a large assemblage of myths that seems to have any bearing on it.[2] It should be recalled, however, that *Hevehe Karawa* in its present form is a comparatively recent introduction, replacing what seems to have been a much simpler ceremony involving only a few performers. The

[1] This may well be a reference to the disastrous effects of big tides and heavy weather which are too often to be seen on the Gulf coast.

[2] Another version of the same story gives the name of the Sea People's leader as Baiu. (Though this was only revealed at the end; during the telling it was concealed under the harmless synonym, Ma, i.e. Water.) Baiu has many subsequent adventures. It is he who goes on foot to the Motu district where he invents the *lakatoi* and institutes the *hiri* trading expedition. (See Seligman, *Melanesians of British New Guinea*.)

significance of this fact will be dealt with later on; but in the meantime it may be noted that it is difficult to reconstruct the former ceremony, and that it may have borne a closer relation to the above story than does the modern one.

The fiction of the ceremony as a whole is soon stated. The *ma-hevehe* comes up from the sea to visit the *eravo*, and leaves there some of its daughters. The *ma-hevehe* is sometimes called in this connexion, *hevehe havahu*, i.e. 'the real *hevehe*', more often *hevehe-lau*, the 'mother *hevehe*'. Its daughters are, of course, the masks (or *apa-hevehe*); and, to carry out the idea, these are referred to as *hevehe mori*, the 'daughter *hevehe*'.[1] Not that there is any insistence on their femininity: indeed, if that point is raised it is denied, and as individually named masks they are more often masculine. Like *kora marita*, Tree Maidens, the *hevehe mori* are so called by way of a pretty figure of speech.

This is the current fiction. It is not for one moment to be imagined that any adult woman believes that the mask is really the daughter of a sea-creature. She knows very well what it is; but she joins with her husband (albeit they never, I am emphatically assured, discuss the subject together) in keeping up this charming and picturesque fancy. Whether the current explanation can be made to square with all the complex details which we shall encounter as we proceed, is another matter. I think it is really superimposed upon an older theory of the masks which has no direct connexion with the sea; but this is a matter of inference which I shall endeavour to establish later on. In the meantime it may be repeated that all nowadays agree in pretending that the *hevehe* masks are daughters of the sea-monsters.

The daughters remain in the *eravo*, but the *ma-hevehe* will visit them again and again, each time bringing them some fresh article of dress or equipment until, towards the end of the cycle, they are ready to issue forth into the village.[2]

---

[1] *Marita* is the collective form of *mori* = daughter or girl. But by some vagary of language the singular form appears to be used in this phrase: *hevehe mori*, not *hevehe marita*.

[2] Or, according to a slightly different fiction sometimes given out to the women, they bring at each successive visit more daughters, until the latter are mustered in sufficient numbers for descent.

We have witnessed the first of these visits. Now, when it is over, the two leading masks are to be seen affixed to the two central pillars inside the door. There are only two of them, and they are really no more than rough, temporary models of the masks which will take their place. But they are enough for the present to represent the flock of sea-daughters brought up from the deep for a sojourn of some fifteen years in the *eravo*. The *hevehe* have crossed the threshold, and the first major movement of the cycle is over.

XIV

THE SANCTITY OF THE *ERAVO*

Tabu

WHEN once the *hevehe* have entered it, the *eravo* acquires a new sanctity. It becomes *aiha*, or supernaturally dangerous (almost like an *aiha haera*—touchy, quick to anger); and it is now, like those temples of the Vailala Madness, though not in the same disreputable sense, an *ahea-uvi*, or 'hot-house'.[1] Previously, during that probably short interval between the completion of their quarters and the *hevehes*' arrival, the *eravo* has been accessible to all males. But from now on it may be entered only by those who know the secret of *apa-hevehe*,[2] i.e. those who realize (in a socially determined meaning of the word which is independent of common-sense observation) that they are things made by human hands. Many boys as well as adult males will know this secret. But the former, although qualified by initiation, do not frequent the *eravo* proper. For one thing their elders would not tolerate them there; and for another they have no wish to go there. They are afraid of the place. Youth is very nervous of the supernatural.

The sanctity of the *eravo* waxes and wanes, and there are times in the cycle when it is tabu to all save old men, when only the *avai* will venture beneath the *hapa*, or curtain of fretted palm-leaves that hangs over the door for a sign. It would seem that increasing age confers some immunity against the supernatural, as against measles.[3]

At all times, however, the *eravo* is in greater or less degree

---

[1] The house in which the leaders of the Vailala Madness used to commune with the dead were called *ahea uvi*, which might be translated 'power-houses', rather than 'hot-houses'. See *Vailala Madness*, pp. 21–3.

[2] The initiation referred to is, of course, not the one described in the foregoing chapter. For the distinction see p. 216; and for the initiation in question, p. 304.

[3] My Port Moresby office-boy, a young Mission-educated Orokolan, had once or twice, and quite incidentally, to handle some old skulls. He told me later that he had been compelled to fast for as much as two days after doing so, consuming nothing but tea (which, by the way, was mine). Such work, he assured me, might be undertaken well enough by an old man, but for him it was full of danger, in consideration of which he suggested a rise of 2*s*. per month.

sacred, a place of tabu; and it is not merely *pupuir'a*, tabu in the passive sense, but *aiha* and *ahea*, a place where impropriety may be visited by strange vengeance. Its atmosphere should be one of peace. Outside in the village voices are often raised in altercation—that is a thing which public opinion deprecates yet seems to suffer readily, for every one has a right to air his grievance. But the *eravo* is no place for quarrelling; not even for heavy tread on the floor-planks; and least of all for horseplay. Its sanctity, sufficiently assured by its other spirit inmates, is merely heightened by the new presence of the *hevehe*.

Hevehe Karawa *as an Instrument of Peace*

Two examples of indecorous conduct will illustrate the above and serve as well to throw a new light on *Hevehe Karawa*, revealing it as a means of enforcing, or rather restoring, peace in the community. This function, which is typical of *Hevehe Karawa* in the Uaripi tribe, belongs but rarely to the ceremony among the Western Elema, and it is obviously extraneous to their *Hevehe* cycle; but it deserves at least passing notice as an interesting method of law-enforcement.[1]

Mahia, of Arihava, discovered that his true younger brother, Kora, had helped himself to some dried sago which their father had placed on one of the hearth-racks in the *eravo*. He began to scold his brother within the sacred precincts; his brother responded; and in a few moments both had so far forgotten themselves that the quarrel turned into a stand-up go. In the thick of this scandalous brawl, Mahia (who was perhaps getting the worst of it) suddenly shouted that the *Hevehe Karawa* should come up as Kora was fighting him in the *eravo*. It came up, and each of the now penitent brothers provided a pig which was eaten within the *eravo* by their fellow villagers. The fiction, supposedly accepted by the women, is that the *ma-hevehe* comes to claim the penalty for desecration.

The second incident, which did not pass off quite so well,

---

[1] Cf. *Bull-roarers in the Papuan Gulf*, pp. 42 ff., for a similar function of the Bull-Roarer ceremony.

occurred during one of my stays in Orokolo. A young man,
Hivi of Waiea Ravi, had been much about my camp, where
he was a welcome visitor and the life of the boy-house.[1]
A very genial character with a propensity for playing the
fool, I never saw him in anything but a good temper; but
a certain emotionalism could lead him to extremes. One
afternoon he returned to his village to find that a stick of
tobacco which he had secreted somewhere or other was
gone. Hivi began to advertise his loss and his indignation
in the usual way, by a harangue in the village; then, convinced that the culprit was one of his *eravo* mates, he sprang
up the steps and began to storm and stamp in the *eravo*
itself; and finally took to slashing at the pillars of the sacred
edifice with a 16-inch trade knife. Every one was outraged,
'for the *hevehe* were in the *eravo*', and Hivi was speedily
restrained. But that night a number of men conspired to
bring up *Hevehe Karawa* to teach him a lesson. It was at
this point that the hitch occurred. It is regarded as essential that *Hevehe Karawa* should be performed only with the
unanimous consent of the whole *eravo*, and on the present
occasion, what with the hurry of preparation and the excitement that pertains to a rag, this consent had not been
obtained. Nevertheless, the business went forward, and in
due course a numerous party of young bloods swept roaring and howling up to the *eravo* door. While they were
withdrawing, however, they heard in their rear the appalling
voice of the widower Tahia, one of the chief men of Waiea
Ravi. In a rage because the drums were being sounded
while he was still in black mourning and the tabu had not as
yet been lifted, he rushed forth to disperse *Hevehe Karawa*
with drawn bow and a bunch of arrows. The army broke at
the sound of his voice, retreated in full disorder to the beach,
and fled east and west from his curses. But, although the
night's performance ended thus ignominiously, the show
took its course next morning. The volatile Hivi killed his
pig and bustled about at the work of carving and cooking,

---

[1] Hivi enjoys the distinction (alas, a posthumous one) of appearing on the nine-
penny Papuan stamp (1932 issue) as a fisherman standing with drawn bow on an
erohore (tree-stump), see Pl. VI.

with tears of shame pouring down his cheeks. He was watched with mingled emotions—some hidden amusement, some sympathetic shame, but (I was assured) no pity.[1]

The Ivaiva

Disturbances within the *eravo*, however, are very rare, and the exercise of punitive functions by *Hevehe Karawa* is hardly a regular part of Western Elema culture. We may now go on to consider a ceremony which is often performed in the *eravo* in connexion with *Hevehe* and illustrates very well the sacred character of the building and its associations. This is the *ivaiva*, one of the most interesting and impressive rites of Elema religion, the name of which has been fittingly adopted by the Mission for church service. In its purely native form it consists of what may fairly be called a prayer followed or accompanied by a food-offering. The *ivaiva* does not belong expressly to *Hevehe*, nor does it always take place in the *eravo*. It is performed during the lesser *Kovave* cycle as well; and the same ceremony may be seen in the garden or in the bush at the felling of an unusually large tree; or again on the deck of a *bevaia* on the eve of its departure on a trading voyage. I shall describe it, however, as seen in the course of *Hevehe*. It must be understood that *ivaiva* will occur from time to time throughout the cycle, as a ritual preparation, in fact, for every major expedition into the bush which *Hevehe* calls for.

In the last chapter we saw how the first cane, viz. that for the two leading masks, was carried up to the *eravo* at night by *Hevehe Karawa*. The cane for all the other masks has yet to be cut; and for this purpose the whole *eravo* will shortly afterwards make a combined expedition. This expedition is preceded by the first *ivaiva* of the cycle.

Various old men of different *eravo* have been invited to

---

[1] There is a well-known historic case in which *Hevehe Karawa* was invoked to restore peace. A *mare*, or intervillage battle, developed between Yogu and part of Arihava as the result of a murder in revenge for supposed sorcery. It had continued for some days, with a number of casualties, when one of the *eravo* participating thought of calling on the Houra Haera to bring *Hevehe Karawa*. The party came, leaving by night on the beach a number of broken weapons as a sign that hostilities should cease. Both sides were ready to obey. It is said that they would have feared to do otherwise as they would have been punished by the old men's sorcery.

attend, and they are now, in the almost completely informal manner of such ceremonies, sitting about in the *oropa larava*. The women have been cooking before their houses during the afternoon, and it is about 5 o'clock when their menfolk begin to carry in the pots of steaming *papaa*. These are ranged, forty or more of them, in two parallel rows, one on each side of the central passage according as they are furnished by this or that *eravo*-side; and supplies of fresh coco-nuts, betel-nut, crabs, and baked fish are added until the materials of a very respectable feast are on hand.

Now an axe, a trade knife, and an *ea* (palmwood fighting-stick) are brought and placed in the centre; and silence falls as an old man rises with a rough half coco-nut shell in his hand to perform the ceremony. He dips it at random into three or four of the bowls of *papaa*, some on either side. Then he retires to the far end of the *eravo*, and, as he returns, passes the coco-nut shell round the central pillars, changing it from one hand to the other. He turns aside to pass it briefly over one or two of the hearth-racks and thus comes finally to the weapons and implements lying on the floor. He sweeps his coco-nut shell over these and next turns to pass it round the heads of one or two of the *avai*. Having completed the circuit he goes to the front door, squats there for a moment with his back to the audience, mutters a few inaudible words, and finally, with averted head, pitches the coco-nut shell and its contents to the ground, where they are swooped upon by hungry village dogs. Conversation is now resumed, and the food, ladled out into shallow dishes, is speedily and noisily disposed of.

When, at later stages of the cycle, there are numerous *hevehe* masks hanging in the *eravo*, the officiator will pass the coco-nut shell round the projecting jaws of a few of them, or underneath their bast mantles. If the *ivaiva* precedes a sago-making expedition, a sago-scraper will be included among the implements on the floor. If there is a group of newly initiated boys in the *eravo* the coco-nut bowl will be passed round the heads of one or two of them, and if some old, feeble man dozes alone in the *kaia larava*, he will not be neglected. Although performed rather perfunctorily, it is

PLATE 25

An *Ivaiva* on a trading vessel (*Bevaia*). The officiator is about to throw
the bowl of food on to the beach

an all-inclusive rite: the officiator takes samples, so to speak, of everything and every one concerned.

The Meaning of the Ivaiva

The writer has seen a number of *ivaiva* on different occasions and all conformed to pattern. The general intention also is consistent; it is to safeguard the members of the expedition, whether for hunting, sago-making, cane-cutting, or what not, from misadventure in the bush. But the theory underlying the manual rite is found once more to be highly variable.

It was observed that the officiator may utter some words while performing his round and in the moment before casting out the food. During the first part of the performance he may indeed be quite vociferous, though in most cases the human audience hears precisely nothing; when he comes to squat over the *papaita* they do not even see his mumbling lips. What he is heard to say, if anything, is something as follows: 'Do not be angry with us. We are going forth to cut the cane. Guard us from hurt—from bite of snake, from sting of wasp and centipede, from sago-thorns, from falling tree, from accident with knife or hatchet. Be kind to us.'

Now this, from the officiator's point of view, is all very non-committal. He lets out no magical secrets. The audience, the passive participants in the rite, are in most cases ignorant of whom he is talking to, and he intends they shall remain ignorant. For the performance of *ivaiva* is a function of the *eravo kariki haera* or some other individual to whom it appertains as a duty or privilege; and such individual is able to perform the rite by virtue of his own private magic, which magic he will in due course hand on to his son, and which in the meantime he guards jealously as a secret.

It is true that the layman may know in general terms to whom the prayer is addressed; and it appears that some do know the actual names which it is not their proper right to know in this connexion. But it is certain that these latter are very anxious to disclaim such knowledge, or very nervous and secretive in the matter of admitting it; and it is equally certain that to a great number, probably the great majority, the names remain unknown. It is not their business to know; they take the *ivaiva* on trust.

The views of the laity, positive or negative, should be not less significant than those of the magical priesthood to a general appreciation of the rite. Apart, then, from those who declare blankly that they know nothing about it, some believe it is addressed to the real human ancestors, others to the spirits of the *hohao*, and yet others to the *eravo-ve-uvari*, the grandmother of the men's house, who dwells at the foot of the *papaita*. Consultation with actual officiators who are ready to reveal their secrets shows that each of these interpretations may be right in its own circumstances.

Thus Heveheapo, whose concern for his ancestors we saw in connexion with the rite of cleaving the coco-nut, repeats here his prayer to Havae to remain with his own people; and as he throws out the coco-nut bowl, he adds:

'Havae, here is your stew, which I throw out lest you be hungry. Look upon us as we are about to do this thing, we pray you.'[1]

I do not think that there is any secrecy at all in this appeal to the human-born ancestry. The idea of placating them would appear to be often present either side by side with, or in lieu of, the appeal to the far more distant and wholly supernatural *lau-haera*. It is generally known that magic, which derives from the *lau-haera*, is very unequally distributed, and that rites, as well as the business of ordinary life, may be performed with or without it. Heveheapo denies the knowledge of any *maho* for the *ivaiva*, so he falls back on his *birari havahu*, his real historic ancestor.

So Hitovakore of Meouri Ravi, in an *ivaiva* preparatory to hunting, appeals to his two real ancestors as he does his round of the *eravo*-posts:

'Arirape and Merava, do you two accompany my little boys lest the pig should kill them. Let your eyes watch over them.'[2]

In this there is no secrecy, because no *maho*. But when he

---

[1] 'Havae, ave papaa ma, ara kiparaeakive leive, a eroa hariave. Ava eraro obohae eavaki, era ma eharu leiki-leiro, aro-lairave ape veravera leiro.'

[2] 'Arirape Merava, evarira arave mekehaku-ra laiai, erero-ra ira hariave. Obohae auhohi eavaki.' (*Mekehahu*, lit. 'small boys', means his young men, the hunters.)

comes to throwing out his coco-nut shell he is appealing to a different order of beings:

> 'Loua and Piku, you two stand one on either side as I throw out the stew, for we are going forth to hunt.'[1]

Loua and Piku are his own particular *maho haera* for this purpose, and we are here dealing with *lau-haera*, the mainspring of true magic, so that we shall not expect him to utter their names aloud.

As a third example let us hear Akeavira, the *eravo kariki haera* of Meouri Ravi. He is the curator of two *hohao*, not merely decorative plaques as some are, but true *kaiavuru* who go by the names Koivi and Airaka. It is on them that he calls as he does his preliminary circuit. This is a matter of semi-public magic, for the *lau haera* in question have been set up as images and their names are known. Nevertheless, the layman displays some reluctance in uttering the names of such *hohao* and often tries to put one off by declaring that they have none; at any rate, he has no direct dealings with them and would not dare infringe the prerogative of their curator: what spells or further secret names the latter may have for them is no matter for inquisitiveness. When, however, Akeavira comes to cast out the bowl of food he uses a name which is wholly hidden from the majority of the *eravo* members and one which even the older, and presumably better informed, will not confess to knowing.

> 'Bea Laivi,' he says, 'there is your stew. I have thrown it out. Eat it.'[2]

Bea Laivi is no other than the *eravo-ve-wari*, or *papaita-ipive-wari*, 'the old lady under the stairs'.

The fact that the *papaa* is thrown to the ground beside the *papaita*,[3] just where the *eravo-ve-wari* is usually said to take up her abode, inclines one to believe that in the original form of the ceremony the offering must have been meant for her.

---

[1] '*Loua Piku, evarira haera eva ukaiepavaki, papaa leikiparaive; era dakea leikive-leiro.*' (Hitovakore knows nothing, or professes to know nothing, of the myth of Loua and Piku. It may be one of those numerous cases where the names alone suffice, the magician being ignorant of their story.)

[2] '*Bea Laivi, ave papaa la. Ara leikiparaive. Ava arero dari.*' Bea Laivi is a little earthworm or grub; in mythology, she is identified with the *Purari* woman Lakekavu, mother of the hero Kivavia who brought betel-nut to the Elema.

[3] Possibly *papaa-ita*, lit. the place of the *papaa*.

But we have seen that the theory underlying the rite has departed from this interpretation—if it really was the original—and has taken on a variety of new colours; and further than this, to no small proportion of the people affected, the theory is more or less remote from knowledge or interest. They display no curiosity about it. It might be, conceivably, that they are hiding a curiosity which they really feel; but mostly, I think, the explanation is simpler: they feel none.

It is to be noted that there are two stages in the ceremony: first, passing the bowl round the posts, &c.; second, casting it out on the ground. Now the intention of the second part is hardly open to question: it is a food-offering. But that of the first is not so clear. Is it also a food-offering? Is the passing of the bowl round the posts, over the hearths, and so on, a symbolic way of offering food to the spirit inmates of the *eravo*? Or is it perhaps a means of embracing them all in the category of suppliants before making the final offering?

I cannot but believe that both ideas are present and not deliberately distinguished. When, as sometimes happens, the bowl is passed round the heads of certain distinguished and magically powerful old men among the visitors, it is then expressly an act of conciliation. But when, on the other hand, it is passed over the knife and the axe, or (as I have seen at a later stage of the cycle) round the heads of certain small novices, it is patently not conciliation, but rather a gesture of inclusion. In short, the *ivaiva* seems to cover both a wide field of suppliants and a mixed body of powers. The powers are those vaguely conceived spirits which share the men's house with all its human occupants; so the officiator is virtually appealing for the *eravo* to the *eravo*.

The reader may be reminded that the *ivaiva*, as we have described it, purports to be the first to take place in the cycle. Once it is over, the men set out for the bush to collect their rattan cane. As they did with the cane used for the two leading *hevehe*, they dump it on their return in some place of concealment near the village. Thence it is brought into the *eravo* under cover of night, and thereafter the owners proceed in their own time to the making of the individual masks.

XV

THE MASKS

THE rudimentary masks such as were brought up by the *ma-hevehe* are called *paiva-haro*, i.e. 'cane-heads'. Individuals now set to work making similar structures for themselves, or causing them to be made, until there may be 100 or more *paiva-haro* in the *eravo* which, by very slow degrees, will eventually turn into as many complete *hevehe*.

Ownership of Hevehe

Any *eravo*-member will probably have the right to make several such masks (though he usually contents himself with making only one or two); and it is necessary to understand the system of ownership and bequest which governs this right.

In the first place, each *hevehe* represented by a mask is an individual with a personal name; and each is affiliated to one or other of the *aualari* groups, so that it is spoken of as a *Kaia hevehe*, *Ahea hevehe*, *Hurava hevehe*, or what not. Further, it has an indefinitely long life, indeed a theoretical immortality, being re-created in one cycle after another. As far as human memory can ensure, it appears on each fresh occasion in precisely the same guise. But it does not necessarily appear in every cycle. There are, in fact, far more *hevehe* in the abstract, so to speak, than ever appear at any one time in the form of masks. They may miss one cycle or more, and there is no doubt that a great many, having thus been missed, are forgotten and simply drop out of existence.

Now the ownership of *hevehe* in the abstract, which carries the right to make the corresponding masks, is personal, and is passed on by inheritance or bequest. Sons naturally inherit from their fathers; a family of brothers will all have a right to each of their father's *hevehe*, though in practice the different *hevehe* come to be divided among them. But women also own *hevehe*; so that we find daughters inheriting from their fathers, and mothers bequeathing to their children.

Further, *hevehe* may be inherited or received by gift from other relatives, e.g. the *aukau*, though this is not so usual.

Ownership of *hevehe* by women, which must seem out of keeping with what is virtually a male monopoly, requires some explanation. The woman, of course, is supposed to know nothing about the actual making of the mask by hand —though, as we have seen in other connexions, there is no reason in common sense to suppose that she is so entirely unobservant. What she is alleged to say to her husband after the initial *Hevehe Karawa* is something as follows: 'Will you give the name of my *hevehe* to one of those in the *eravo*?' The mask will then be made as for her. Possibly the matter is one of more straightforward arrangement between them; but the fiction is preserved to all outward seeming. As for bequest by a woman owner, this should receive the sanction of her brothers: if one of them wishes to claim the *hevehe* on her death he may do so, but in most cases he surrenders it to her children.

Since inheritance is from both the father's and the mother's side it comes about that an individual may own several *hevehe* which are of *aualari* different from that to which he himself belongs (descent being purely patrilineal). To take a concrete example:

```
   HOKO    m.   IROVO              |
 (Purari)   |   (Nabo)     ┌───────┴───────┐
            |              |               |
            |              |               |
         MAHIRO    m.    Orilau        MAHEVEHE
        (Purari)    |    (Ahea)         (Ahea)
                    |
                    |
              KARAVEHAPE
               (Purari)
```

Karavehape owns the following *hevehe*:

'Hevaire' (*Purari*) inherited from MAHIRO.

'Mori Herarave' (*Auma*) inherited from MAHIRO (originally from HOKO's mother).

'Ave Herarave' (*Auma*) inherited from MAHIRO (originally from HOKO's mother).

'Kavapu' (*Ahea*) inherited from Orilau.

'Lakekawari' (*Nabo*) given by MAHEVEHE.

Of Karavehape's five *hevehe*, it will be noted, only one belongs to *Purari*, his own *aualari*.

Another concrete example will illustrate the method of inheritance and show, incidentally, that it is not exactly cut and dried.

| TAHIA | *m.* | Hariripe |
| (*Purari*) | | (*Kauri*) |

| KIKI | AVEA | EREVU | NAVA |
| (*Purari*) | (*Purari*) | (*Purari*) | (*Purari*) |

Tahia owns four *Purari hevehe* and one *Ahea*; Hariripe, two *Kauri hevehe*. Now I consulted Tahia on the question of how the seven *hevehe* available would be distributed among the four children, and made a full note of his answer. Some year or so after—long enough for him to forget what he had said—I asked him again. Without giving the details it is enough to say that when I came to compare my notes I found his two answers hopelessly contradictory. Hoping to clear the matter up I asked him a third time, and he then said that, when he died, his eldest son Kiki would make the distribution. This indeed seems to be the typical arrangement. The ownership of the *hevehe* is not decided by definite bequest, as if a man were making a will. It is vested in the family, and as in the case of land-ownership, the eldest is really the controller. He does not make any formal distribution: the ownership of the seven *hevehe* in the above case will sort itself out by more or less friendly agreement, Kiki having the main voice.

Thus every *hevehe*—and in the abstract there are hosts of them—has its recognized owner or owners; and, though an individual who boasts half a dozen of them will perhaps make masks for only one or two in a cycle, he will not suffer the appearance of any of the others without his authority.

Personnel Associated with the Mask

So much for ownership of the *hevehe* as abstract beings. Let us now consider those which appear concretely as masks in any one cycle. There are several persons closely concerned with each.

Firstly, the man who makes the mask, or causes it to be made, is *hevehe-oa*, the 'father' of the *hevehe*. Normally the mask will represent one of his own *hevehe*; but, even if the right to make it has been granted to him by another, he is still, for the term of the cycle, the *hevehe*'s 'father'.

His wife is the *hevehe-lau*, i.e. 'Mother' of the *hevehe*.[1] If he is a widower, then the duties of *hevehe-lau* may be carried out by his daughter or son's wife. They consist particularly in food-getting and cooking; but she also contributes her share towards the actual making of the mask by preparing its *mae*, or sago-leaf draperies.

Thirdly, each *hevehe* mask has its *harehare-akore*, i.e. the person—boy, youth, or man—for whom it is expressly made. He will undergo the rite of initiation, and will wear the mask personally on its first formal appearance.

And fourthly, there is the *aukau* of the *harehare-akore*—either his *aukau havahu* (i.e. real *aukau*) or the person who has assumed the obligation. He has certain ceremonial duties to perform from time to time during the cycle; and he makes these an occasion for giving shell ornaments to his *arivu*. In return for them he receives pigs, from the *harehare-akore*'s parents if the latter be a child, from the *harehare-akore* himself if he be an adult.

We shall see these in their various relations as we proceed. In the meantime it must be said of the *harehare-akore* that they are called candidates for initiation in a somewhat loose sense of the word if it implies admission to a secret. For an individual may be 'initiated' on a number of occasions in different cycles, and the whole secret (in so far as it is a secret at all) is divulged on the first. Subsequent initiations are in the nature of honours; and for each of them the subject receives the right to wear an additional hornbill feather in his hair. It is true that many, even among the old, are entitled to wear one feather only; but two or three are common; and I know of one young man, Hoko of Avavu Ravi, who flaunts no

---

[1] The same expression is used in a different connexion for 'Mother-*hevehe*', i.e. the sea-monster, *ma-hevehe*. See p. 224.

less than six such trophies gathered in different *eravo*,[1] outstanding proof that he and his kin are people of enterprise
and wealth. These are, of course, initiations to *apa-hevehe*,
the mask. The distinction between this kind of initiation,
which has yet to be described, and the initiation to *ma-hevehe*
(Chapter XIII) has, it is hoped, been made sufficiently clear.

The *hevehe-oa*, when he undertakes the making of a mask
and all the business associated with it, does so expressly on
account of some *harehare-akore*,[2] e.g. his own son, his younger
brother, or his brother's son. The commonest situation is
the first-mentioned. But by way of mutual service or com-
pliment, brothers often see to the initiation of one another's
sons, e.g.:

AUAVERARE   HEVEAPO

HURAVARI   OA-APO

hevehe, 'Hapekavu': *Hevehe-oa*, AUAVERARE; *Harehare-akore*, OA-APO.
hevehe, 'Hiriavu': *Hevehe-oa*, HEVEAPO; *Harehare-akore*, HURAVARI.

Another very common situation is shown by the following
example:

KAVO   OVAKERE

AVU

hevehe, 'Lahero': *Hevehe-oa*, KAVO; *Harehare-akore*, OVAKERE.
hevehe, 'Aruai': *Hevehe-oa*, OVAKERE; *Harehare-akore*, AVU.

It is not for the *hevehe-oa* to supply the pigs on behalf of the
harehare-akore, unless, of course, the latter is his own son.
This, however, is very commonly the case; and over and
above the pigs which he must then provide in this connexion

[1] The places were: (1) Avavu Ravi (previous cycle); (2) Koialahu; (3) Berepa;
(4) Aripi (in Arihava); (5) Yogu; (6) Avavu Ravi (cycle ended 1932). The man
appeared to be under thirty. Two other cycles (Hare Eravo and Pareamamu) had
been concluded during this time; which means that within easy reach of Orokolo
at least eight cycles had been concluded in less than thirty years.

[2] In the event of the death of either *hevehe-oa* or *harehare-akore* his place is usually
taken by another; but the mask may sometimes be allowed to go out of action and
will eventually be burnt without ever appearing in the open.

the *hevehe-oa* will certainly be giving some to his own *auka-hura*, since ceremonies in connexion with *Hevehe*, *Kovave*, &c., are made occasions for the settlement of debts on all sides. Needless to say, they are accompanied by return payments of ornaments.

The Making of the Masks

Every *hevehe-oa* is competent to make his own mask, and he probably does the greater part of the work with his own hands. It is of necessity a long, slow business, for in the limited space available within the *eravo* only a few masks can be under construction at any one time. It is, therefore, put aside for long intervals, and from beginning to end the making of the mask lasts nearly as long as the cycle itself. In the course of so many years it probably needs more than one repairing, and parts of it may have to be scrapped and remade.

While the *hevehe-oa* is responsible for the whole, he may seek assistance from his *okeahi*[1] or his *aukau*; when the mask is for his own son as *harehare-akore*, then it is usually the latter's *aukau* who will be asked to help. A small feast is provided in the *eravo* at the end of a day's sociable labour to which the *aukau* (or *okeahi*) and some of his people, also visitors, have at least contributed something. I have witnessed a pleasant little scene where the *aukau* in the case was one Berarikere. A garrulous, doddering old man, he did not do a hand's turn himself; but there were plenty of willing workers, and a good deal of progress was made with the mask. For any one, kinsman or no, will lend a hand, and there are some, those known as *evera haera* because of their skill as general craftsmen, who positively like the work. Old men, without actually handling the mask, may play an essential part by dictating, from their remarkable memories, the special forms of decoration which it should traditionally bear.

The building up of the mask follows a series of well-defined stages.

1. *Paiva-haro.* The loop of cane, rounded above and

---

[1] See p. 73.

coming to a point below, provides the foundation. The longest such loop I have measured was 13 ft. 6 in.; the shortest 6 ft. The average would be 9 or 10 ft.

2. *Muruvu.* Thin slats of palm-wood, affixed transversely at close intervals and projecting beyond the sides of the *paiva-haro*.

3. *Ape.* The mouths, projecting and furnished with teeth of palm-wood. At the same time such masks as traditionally possess them are given *avako*, ears.

4. *Pura.* Coarse bark-cloth, stretched over the face of the *paiva-haro*; applied wet, it dries taut and is sewn along the edges. Often a raised rib (*overa*=nose) runs down the centre beneath the bark-cloth, terminating in a bulge called *hevere*, the 'forehead'.

5. *Hohoa.* The face of the mask receives its decoration (*hohoa*) with traditional designs; embroidered on with thin strips of split cane; roughly painted.

6. *Hara.* A sago midrib affixed behind the mask. This projects above in the form of a long spike, enveloped in *pura* (the longest measured was 7 ft. 6 in.); below, it projects a distance of about 2 ft., reaching down between the wearer's thighs so that he is better enabled to balance the mask.

FIG. 10. Front and Rear of *Hevehe* Mask

a. *hara* (sago midrib)   e. *obohae* (eye)
b. *overa* (nose)   f. *ape* (mouth)
c. *hevere* (forehead)   g. *avaha* (back)
d. *avako* (ear)   h. *arara* (wicker frame)
j. *muruvu* (cross-strips)

7. *Arara.* Framework of open wicker in rear of mask.

This is semi-cylindrical in form at the base, fitting over the wearer's head. The wicker-work provides attachment for the mantles of *koro* and *mae*.

8. *Koro*. Strips of white bast hanging loose from *arara* so as to cover the reverse side of the mask and the body of the wearer down to the knees. This is the mask's under-mantle.

9. *Avaha*. The 'back'. The upper third of the obverse is neatly covered with *pura* which, like the face, is decorated with *hohoa*.

10. *Mae*. The frayed sago-leaf forming the overmantle; covers reverse side of mask and completely hides body of wearer except for forearms and calves.[1]

11. *Hoaukuwe*. Painting; and *Love*, sprigs of feathers decorating centre and edges of mask-face.

The stages in the building up of the mask are correlated with stages in the progress of the cycle; for each major step is ceremonially preceded by a performance of *Hevehe Karawa*. The *ma-hevehe* is supposed to bring up the materials: first the *paiva haro*, then the *ape*, then the *pura*, and so on; and thereafter the *eravo* members may—in fact should—proceed with the work indicated. This explains why in any *eravo* we are likely to find all the masks at much the same stage of development. It is true that a good many individuals lag behind, but none may press on ahead. Reference to the programme of the cycle (p. 190) will show the correlation.

---

[1] *Hopa*, broad belts of cane passing round the chest, are worn underneath the mask. These are hung with *koro* so as to conceal the body of the wearer still further.

XVI

ART OF THE *HEVEHE*

THE full-fledged *hevehe* is an outlandish figure, like
nothing on earth, and, with its voluminous mantle, a
somewhat ungainly one. But its ungainliness is largely re-
deemed by the surprising grace and agility of the wearer, and
in full career it is so imposing that one ventures to use the
word majestic. Whatever our opinion of the *tout ensemble*,
however, the colouring and the decorative detail of the
masks are altogether charming, and each represents a very
large amount of work and skill; so that we may properly
devote some attention to the *hevehe* in respect of art and
craftsmanship alone.

The work varies in quality, as it must, since individual
natives vary in manual skill. But it is always painstaking,
and by that much-abused word the writer intends high
praise. He has examined many scores of *hevehe* masks, and
familiarity has bred more and more admiration. Amid much
that is shoddy and untidy in the village or the *eravo*, the care
lavished upon the *hevehe* mask and the general excellence of
the workmanship are matters for satisfaction and mild surprise. They show what the Orokolo native can do.

Technique and Material

We shall concern ourselves here with the decoration of
the mask-face in which the rich variety of design is mainly
evident.[1] The *ape*, or mouth, has been made separately and
already affixed. It usually takes the distinctive form shown
in the illustrations, and is armed with fifty or sixty sharp
teeth (*kau*), slivers of wood from the particular kind of palm
known from this circumstance as *hevehe-kau*. But a few odd
forms are seen—a real hornbill beak or a well-modelled
dog's head, for instance—in keeping with the special character of some particular masks. The *ape* is very skilfully
constructed and constitutes the most difficult part of the

---

[1] A few masks have projecting features such as grotesque head, arms, and
shoulders, affixed to the upper part of the face.

mask-maker's work; so much so that it is often saved from the ceremonial flames and put aside for use in the next cycle.

The work of embroidering the face proceeds of necessity very slowly, for it must be done inside an *eravo* already crowded. There is room at the most for two or three masks at a time at the front and rear ends of the passage; in its middle reaches the light is too dim even for native eyesight. But there are years in store, and therefore no hurry. In all my time at Orokolo I only twice came upon men embroidering a mask.

The structure, already faced with tightly stretched *pura*, or bark-cloth, is laid flat upon low trestles—the *aihari* or 'head-rests' of the *hevehe*. Two or three helpers could be engaged on either side if there were a rush, but the work is mostly quiet and deliberate. The technique is best described as 'braiding'. The braid consists of thin strips of *merove* cane, split and scraped. It is bent into the required form and affixed to the *pura* with stitches about 1 in. apart. The thread is a finer strip of the same *merove* cane or else of the white bast of the *oro*-tree. The proper needle (*karahe*) is a bone from the wing of a flying-fox with a hole drilled through one side at the butt; but there are various modern substitutes, favourite among them a short section from the spoke of a trade umbrella. Trade umbrellas fall easily to pieces and their bones make admirable needles, for each has a ready-made eye.

The designs are worked straight on to the material without preparatory marking. The *hevehe-oa*, or the expert who knows the required pattern, will direct his assistants, and if they go too fast and make mistakes the work can be easily undone and re-done. But neither he nor his assistants are always so scrupulous. As there is a marked desire for symmetry and a very fair achievement of it, any error over-looked on one side will be reproduced on the other; and thus the design will depart in some degree from its traditional form. Although it is maintained that the same *hevehe* reappearing in a succession of cycles always does so in exactly the same form, it is, of course, impossible that this should be strictly so.

PLATE 26

Sewing the patterns on a *Hevehe* mask

Mouth-piece of a *Hevehe* mask. This is a *Miri aualari* mask: the dentates represent ripples on the sand

PLATE 27

Detail of another *Vailala* mask. The motif is *arohae*, tendril of the gourd vine

Lower portion and mouth of *Vailala* mask

The braiding completed, the responsible artist roughly paints in the designs and the background, perhaps merely with a series of daubs to show how the colours should be eventually applied. For the full painting will take place long hence on a special day shortly before the emergence, so as to ensure a good stage appearance. A final touch, subsequent to the painting, is the attachment of feather tufts round the edge and down the centre of the mask. But this last, brilliant and effective as it is, must be called rather an embellishment than the completion of a set design.

The painting, however, is very definitely part of the design which consists of a series of coloured patterns, neatly outlined by the cane braiding, against a white background. The pigments are as follows:

White: *Oro*, lime (manufactured by burning shells).
Black: *Aro*, charcoal (by plunging the red-hot brands of certain timbers into water).
Red: *Mou*, a pink ochre obtained by trade from the Kairuku district; *Haira*, a redder ochre from Upper Vailala.
Yellow: *Bea*, a clay obtained from the hills a few miles inland.
Grey: *Uruvita*, a kind of soapstone obtained from the rocks at Auma and Kerema.

All these are applied as water-paints, readily absorbed by the porous bark-cloth. The surface of the lime is inclined to flake amid the buffetings that the *hevehe* will receive during the masquerade; but the colours themselves seem to be absolutely permanent. There can be no question but that they blend very happily together, delicate hues all with a pleasing matt surface.

Mou varies about rose pink; *haira* about Indian red; *bea* is a fine pale yellow that does not clash with the other colours; and *uruvita* provides a delightful range of soft greys, some inclining slightly to green and others towards a much diluted indigo. One may occasionally see the use of bright red European paint (mixed with water) and, rather regrettably, that of Reckitt's blue. This must horrify those who are horrified by every touch of modernity in native art; but in the writer's judgement the former can be used with very good effect, and even the latter, an entirely new note, need not always be out of tune.

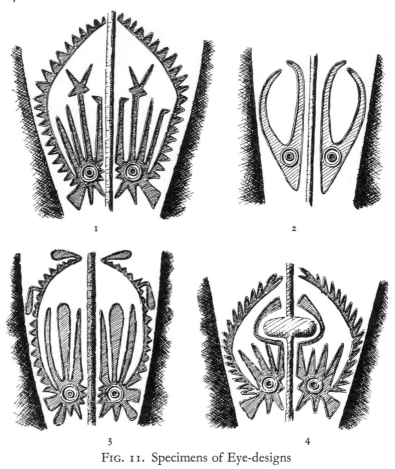

FIG. 11. Specimens of Eye-designs

| 1. *Kauri* | 2. *Baiu* |
| 3. *Ahea* | 4. *Purari* |

1. *Maria aue*, tail of *maria* fish. 2. *Yarape, lakatoi* sail. 3. *Korope* leaf.
4. *Love*, amaranth leaf.

The Aualari *Designs*

The designs on the mask-face consist of (1) symmetrical eye-designs, sometimes highly ornate; (2) a narrow border, filled mostly with common dentates; and (3) the highly characteristic formal designs that occupy the central space.

PLATE 28

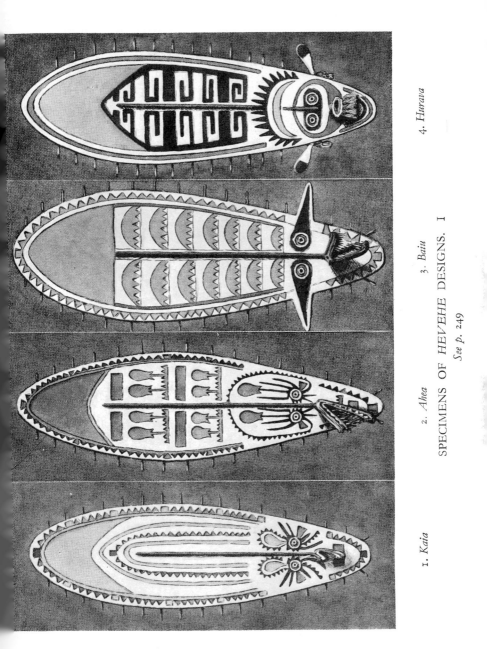

1. *Kaia* 2. *Ahea* 3. *Baiu* 4. *Hurava*

SPECIMENS OF *HEVEHE* DESIGNS. I

See p. 249

After a little experience it is possible in most cases to tell at a glance the *aualari* group to which any *hevehe* belongs. For the designs are conventional, and each *aualari* group has a fund of them to draw upon; further, allowing for a few cases where the same design is used (under different names) by different *aualari*, they are severally distinctive. The eye-designs and the borders are not so easily sorted out, but the simple themes of the centre will nearly always enable one to recognize whether the *hevehe* is *Kaia*, *Ahea*, *Kauri*, or any other of the ten *aualari* groups.[1]

While the stock of conventional designs is limited it provides scope for considerable variety. The illustrations are merely samples and by no means cover the whole field.

The Origin of the Designs

While every *hevehe* belongs definitely to one *aualari* or another and is usually to be recognized for what it is, there is, nevertheless, some uncertainty regarding some of the designs. Not every man can name them or ascribe them to their proper *aualari*; for it is evident that among these natives, as among ourselves, some are interested in art while others remain more or less blind to it; indeed, the inequality of such interest is as striking as that of craftsmanship and taste. But even among those who are plainly interested in the *hevehe* designs, one discovers a good deal of disagreement in identifying them. Where this is due to malobservation it is soon corrected by discussion. But the disagreement is not always a matter of error.

The present is not a dissertation on native art in general, but it is worth noting how this point, the disagreement referred to, may bear on the origin of decorative design. For while most of the designs are prerogatives of the *aualari*, and are distinctive in name and character, others may have alternative names, and furthermore may be held in common

[1] Some few masks are half and half, the two sides of the face bearing different *aualari* designs. E.g. 'Pekeaupe', the leading *hevehe* on the left in Avavu Ravi, was half *Nabo*, half *Purari*. It is fortunate from the aesthetic point of view that these are exceptional.

Some masks are distinguished as '*Muru hevehe*'; but *Muru* does not fall into line with the *aualari* groups. See pp. 41-2.

by two or more *aualari* groups, in which case they are almost invariably found to be named differently.

Thus the spiral illustrated on Fig. 12 as the *Vailala* design

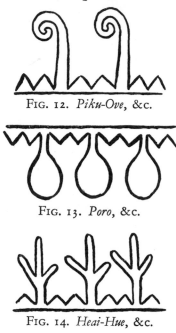

FIG. 12. *Piku-Ove*, &c.

FIG. 13. *Poro*, &c.

FIG. 14. *Heai-Hue*, &c.

'*Piku-Ove*', the caterpillar, is sometimes also called '*Hivivi Huka*', the tendril of a certain creeper (another *Vailala aualari*). Further, it may appear on *Nabo* masks, in which case it is called '*Pipi Hehe*', the spiral antenna of a butterfly; and on *Auma* masks, where it is called '*Marivi*', a kind of cane, the reference being to the spiral tip of its leaf. Again, the simple design shown in Fig. 13 is on *Ahea* masks called '*Poro*', the broad leaf of the convolvulus-like plant of that name which grows on the beach; on *Kauri* masks, '*Beve*', the mango. And as a third example there is the three-pronged design seen on some of the masks belonging to the so-called *Muru aualari*: it is here called either '*Heai-Hue*', a shrimp's claw, or '*Haihiava*', a kind of three-pointed croton leaf; whereas on *Vailala* masks it is *Iva-loa-haro*, the three-toed foot of the cassowary.

It is plain that the alternative names are used by different *aualari* groups because they belong to certain of its *aualari* in the sense of totems. But—if we assume that such designs were originally pictorial—the question arises, which of the objects named provided the model? The possibility that all of them did so independently, and that the designs reached identity by a sort of convergent evolution, may perhaps be dismissed. If one of them did, then we are certainly unable to tell which it was, nor can the native help us, for each backs his own *aualari*. But there is a third possibility, viz. that none of them did. It is conceivable that the designs may

PLATE 29

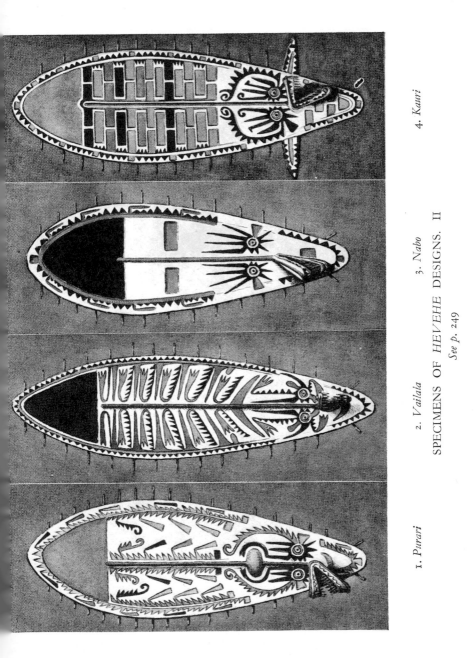

1. *Purari*   2. *Vailala*   3. *Nabo*   4. *Kauri*

SPECIMENS OF *HEVEHE* DESIGNS. II

See p. 249

PLATE 30

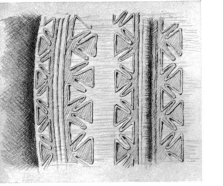

1. *Kaia*

2. *Kauri*

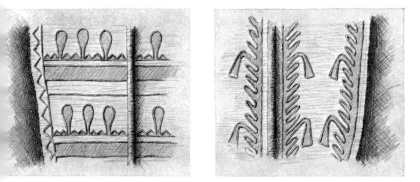

3. *Ahea*

4. *Purari*

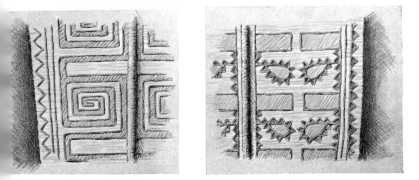

5. *Hurava*

6. *Kauri*

Specimens of *Hevehe* designs, III

have arisen from an almost mechanical manipulation of the *merove* cane in the hands of a fancy-free artist; and that they were named subsequently, either by the artist himself or by those who came after him, because of their chance resemblance to some familiar object.

But it is not with the origin of these designs that we are concerned. Nor is it with their social implications. The close correlation between the decorative art of the *hevehe* and the social groups to which they severally belong has been shown in passing; but this, from our present point of view, is of small importance. The purpose of this description is to show the beauty, such as it is, of the *hevehe* designs and the high finish of the artists' workmanship. The designs must speak for themselves. The illustrations are admittedly selected, but if any one suspects that the sketches have been unduly idealized he should consult Plate XXVII.

NOTE ON ILLUSTRATIONS

PLATE XXVIII

1. *Kaia.* The long grey strips in the centre represent the python, *biai*; the upper part of the eye-design, *hia-koro*, the leaf of the *okari* tree.
2. *Ahea.* The central *motif* (in yellow or grey) is *poro*, leaf of the beach convolvulus.
3. *Baiu.* The half-moon with dentates is *ahiru*, yellow foam, suds on the beach.
4. *Hurava.* The black design is *arakaita-hohoa*, i.e. the carving along the edge of the Namau dugout (*arakaita*).

PLATE XXIX

1. *Purari.* The uppermost 'leaves' (appearing also in the eye-design) with dentates and spiral end are *love*, the amaranth; the plain, wedge-shaped ones are *aikaupe*, a kind of lily.
2. *Vailala.* The three-pronged 'leaves' are *erere-koro*, croton; the black dentates, *popoka*, bracken-leaf.
3. *Nabo.* The red 'leaves' in the border design are *ahehe*, an orchid.
4. *Kauri.* The central oblongs are *huhu*, stratus clouds. The spiral appearing twice in the eye-design is *kave-aue*, phalanger's tail.

PLATE XXX

1. *Kaia.* The cockle-shell (*aihau*).
2. *Kauri.* The yam-leaf (*mapore-koro*).
3. *Ahea.* Cumulus clouds (*bea uru*) piled in tall columns on the horizon.
4. *Purari.* Lily-leaves (*aikaupe*), see Pl. XXIX, 1.
5. *Hurava.* Arakaita-hohoa, cf. Pl. XXVIII, 4.
6. *Kauri.* Coleus-leaf (*buroburo*).

XVII

NAMES OF THE *HEVEHE*

IT has been noted that each one of the *hevehe* masks bears
an individual name. It is that of the real *hevehe*—whatever that may be—of which the mask is only a representation; and this *hevehe* may reappear in cycle after cycle. The
mask is created, destroyed, and re-created. The being which
it represents is an old friend who pays repeated visits to the
eravo always under the same name and in the same form.

Interpretation

The writer has recorded the names of many scores of
hevehe (122 in Avavu Ravi alone), and has sought diligently
for an explanation of each. This laborious business was
undertaken in the hope of discovering what the individual
masks were really supposed to represent; and while the
method was not unprofitable, it should be stated at the outset that to a large proportion of the people concerned with
them the names are merely names. Not a few of them defy
interpretation; and even in those cases where they can be
given a meaning, its relevancy often remains quite unexplained.

In most cases, however, the names are, at any rate, interpretable, and they are found to be taken from a variety of
spheres, but predominantly from the bush. The vegetable
kingdom supplies the largest quota. A number of random
examples are given.

Plants, &c. Mapore and Kaurara (both *Nabo*), varieties of
yam; Muru Haihiava (*Auma*), Kero (*Ahea*), Marere (*Ahea*),
varieties of croton; Ari (*Nabo*), Havoa (*Purari*), varieties of
sugar-cane; Havara and Poro (both *Ahea*), beach flowering
plants; Ahehe (*Nabo*), an orchid; Biau and Havare (both
Kauri), varieties of banana; Ehere-haro (*Ahea*), a betel
husk; Kakape (*Kaia*), sago midrib; Kida (*Kauri*), a kind
of taitu; Havuhu (*Baiu*), casuarina tree; Keroro-Hakaia
(*Nabo*), splinter of *keroro* wood; Hekaiape (*Purari*), inner

spathe of areca palm; Kekeri (*Nabo*), a kind of bread-fruit; &c.

Birds. Perea and Ahirape (both *Vailala*); Lakekawari (*Nabo*); Baiva Haruapo (*Nabo*), 'One Hornbill'; Airape (*Nabo*), 'Flock of Birds'; Kera-ve-Ori (*Nabo*), 'Mountain Bird'; &c.

Fish (sea or river). Kava-Apo (*Ahea*); Maria (*Kauri*); Kaiakaia (*Nabo*); Lahekaa (*Purari*); Koraia (*Kaia*); Loukai (*Auma*).

Reptiles. Bivira (*Purari*), a kind of snake; Keroro Maiaku (*Kaia*), a snake; Hahepa (*Vailala*), a kind of lizard; Eho (*Vailala*), a leech.

Animals. Haua (*Nabo*), a bandicoot; Hepe (*Purari*), small brown bat; Bereri (*Purari*), small black bat; Behoa (*Vailala*), a dog.

Miscellaneous. Maura (*Baiu*), S.E. wind; Apuviri (*Nabo*) and Kerorai (*Purari*), names of songs; Herere (*Nabo*), northerly breeze from mountains; Nabo Aidava (*Nabo*), Mt. Aidava; Orereu (*Auma*), a rock at Auma; Dorevari (*Kauri*), a rock at Bie, The Bluff; Kekea (*Baiu*), sago-frond tabu sign; Mairau ve Hore (*Purari*), Mairau's cassowary-plumes; Kora-uku (*Hurava*), drifting log; &c.

The Story behind the Name

These things are *aualari* in the vague sense of totems. We have seen that the *aualari* come into being, or are claimed as belonging to the several groups, by virtue of their mytho-logical associations; and so it is to be expected that each such *hevehe* name will have a story behind it. Apart from some which would appear to be named in a purely fanciful way, I believe that this is typically the case. The *hevehe* name is a reference, however indirect or allusive, to Elema mythology.

The following few examples are taken at random from among *hevehe* masks in Avavu Ravi.

'Poro' is one of the two beach maidens who were be-trothed by their parents to Berare (the river bird) from the west. But the two girls were carried off by Iviki and Kaivoko (sea birds) to an island, and so Berari was left lamenting. Poro is now a heliotrope convolvulus; her sister Havara-havara, another kind of flowering plant which grows beside it on the beach. Both are joint *aualari* of *Miri* and *Ahea*.

'Hariha' and his younger brother Kere lived, as young men, on an island. They fished continually, but, having no fire to roast their food, had to be content with exposing it to the sun. Then Hariha made a model of a garfish, bound up his hair tightly, and, clasping the model to his breast, dived into the sea and swam to the mainland. He encountered there the two girls, Aro and Poro (frigate birds), and after further adventures obtained fire from them and carried it, concealed in his bunch of hair, safely back to his younger brother. Hariha and Kere are now varieties of garfish.

'Orereu' and the friend, Harakape, with whom her name is always coupled, were two girls of Auma. They were among the numerous wives whom the hero Epe picked up on his wide travels; but their own brothers Evoa (the mangrove-tree *ova*) and Mauri (the *pira*-tree) were ill disposed to Epe and got rid of him by inducing him to sit on an ill-constructed platform on the shore, whence the waves, having demolished the platform, carried him out to sea. Thereupon Orereu and Harakape turned into the two rocks of that name at Auma (or, according to another version, into two species of small crabs).

'Lapelavu' and Hapekavu were the two foster-mothers of Iko, joined back to back like Siamese twins. Iko, when he grew up, paid them for their kindness by cutting them apart. They both survived this operation and play no further part in Iko's history, except that the rhythm which he beats on his mysterious drum is 'Lapelavu-lapelavu, Hapekavu-hapekavu'. It appears that these twin women are never identified with any natural species or object. Like Iko himself, they are merely mythico-human.

The names of the *hevehe* thus call up literally hundreds of episodes from the myths. The episodes, however, are not to be discovered without some research. In the first place, it is a distracting business trying to record them, since one's informant, being unable to confine himself to a few relevant points, is prone to embark on the whole weary length of the myth concerned.

In the second place, one often encounters a reluctance to tell the story at all because of its magical implications; and this may amount to a politely stubborn refusal. Thus an otherwise open-handed informant named Kavakore declined to tell me the tale of two of his *hevehe* because it would bring on, of all things, a plague of mosquitoes. (His real concern was, I believe, to keep his magic dark; the mosquitoes, over which his magic gave him control, were merely a subsidiary risk to which, however, the mere telling of the story might lay us open.)

In the third place, and most significantly, many men simply do not know the stories. The *hevehe-oa* himself is often as ignorant as others; and it is by no means to be thought that he is merely feigning ignorance, for if he is one of the open and obliging sort he will appeal to some one more versed in mythology to help him out. The right to make the mask having been inherited from long ago, it is perfectly plain that in a large proportion of cases the meaning of the name, together with its associations, has faded out of memory.

In the face of this very common ignorance we can hardly avoid the conclusion that to most people the mask does not represent anything specifically. Both its form and its name are merely traditional. However disappointing, this in itself is a most important conclusion: the whole ceremony can continue and the many *hevehe* go on living although the individual participants are largely ignorant of their specific meaning and indifferent to it.

New Hevehe

There remains, however, one promising line of inquiry. Whereas the vast majority of *hevehe* are *overa*, or ancient, there are some admitted to be *are*, i.e. new inventions. In fact any man is at liberty to make his own new *hevehe* and give it a name. It seems likely that such newly created examples may give us a clue to what the *hevehe* really mean.

It is interesting, as a commentary on primitive logic, to

note the sequence of question and answer on this head. In the first place, your informants will agree emphatically in declaring that the *hevehe* are all old, so old that the question of who originated them is dismissed as unanswerable. This is merely a thoughtless generalization; for by careful questioning (in pursuance of a clue you have already raised elsewhere) you will ascertain that some of the *hevehe* in the *eravo* date back only a generation or two, and perhaps that some of them have been invented by men living to-day. Having thus established the fact that there really are some new *hevehe*, you go on to ask if these inventions occur often.

'Oh, there are lots of them!' they say.

'Would you, then, name a few others?'

They are dumbfounded; and you will be lucky if you succeed in raking up another case in point. It is true that there is some reason, as we shall find, for secrecy concerning new *hevehe*, but that does not exonerate our natives from the error of facile generalization.

The way in which the invention of new *hevehe* occurs is allegedly as follows. A man has some dream experience, or perhaps loses his way and spends a lonely night in the bush. In one or the other he comes face to face with one of the forest-people, the *kora marita*. He observes its appearance and learns its name, perhaps engaging in further conversation and receiving the promise of patronage, help in fishing, hunting, &c. Subsequently he makes a *hevehe* mask to represent his spirit friend, and if the decoration which purports to represent something distinctive in its appearance goes awry, a second visitation will correct it.

Now this is precisely the way in which new *kovave* and *hohao* are created, and in their cases, particularly that of the former, examples are not in the least hard to come by. With *hevehe*, however, while we may accept the explanation offered, the examples are comparatively rare; though this is no doubt due simply to the fact that *Hevehe* is performed so much less often.

When we come to examine concrete cases it is found that some of them are ostensibly independent of any such magico-religious background. Thus Havai, a *Hurava* man of Waiea

Ravi, observed that among the many masks made and decorated in the *eravo* there were none belonging to his *Hurava aualari*. So he made one and called it 'Arakaita-kikiri' (which in the Namau language means 'Carving on the Canoe'), devising decorations out of his head which were declared, somewhat unconvincingly, to resemble the patterns carved along the edge of the Namau dugout.

Again Yave, the owner of 'Avirape' (which is the name of a kind of shrimp), avers that his mother once caught some of these creatures—which are certainly highly decorative—and that his father, now deceased, had admired them so much that he made an *Ahea hevehe* of the name. This simple explanation, which my informant first gave me in 1932, he repeated in 1937. It is possible that it contains the whole truth.

For another example of the same sort, Karavehape (a Purari man) visited the Delta to exchange armshells for tobacco with the labourers at the Saw Mill. On his journey he was impressed by certain insects, *hevaire*. Sitting lazily in a canoe while others paddled, he watched them darting back and forth over the smooth water, amused and fascinated. Later he made a new *hevehe* and called it 'Hevaire'.

Further parallel examples are not wanting; so that some, at any rate, of the new *hevehe* may perhaps be made as the result of a mere whim or flight of fancy. There is, it would seem, no hidden meaning in them, nor any spiritual experience, true or alleged, behind them. Inventions of this sort are not out of keeping with that state of ignorance and indifference regarding the underlying meaning of the *hevehe* masks which is so common among those who make and wear them.

But Karavehape is the inventor of two other *hevehe* which, he assures me, he calls simply 'Ave', 'Dogs'; and these prove to have some real significance. Telling me of them, he pointed to a deep scar on his leg as evidence of veracity. He had been making a canoe in the bush, doing the rough preliminary work of hollowing it, when his axe slipped and inflicted a terrible gash on his leg. Through shock or loss of blood or whatever it was, Karavehape sank to the ground, closed his eyes, and died. But then, as in a dream, he saw two dogs come out of the bush and stand before him. He opened his eyes again (his purely material eyes) and the dogs

Fig. 15. Dog's Head *Ape* of *Hevehe* Mask

vanished. Karavehape recovered from his injury and made two *hevehe* (with model dog's heads for *ape*) calling them simply, 'Ave', 'Dogs'. This is in keeping with the traditional method of inventing or creating new *hevehe*. To fill the bill completely, the dogs, as spirits of the bush, should have revealed their names to Karavehape and he would then have given them secretly, if not openly, to his masks. Without thinking that Karavehape's spirit experience actually included any such intimate revelation by the dogs, I strongly suspect that he has some more specific names for his masks which he did not care to reveal.

While some new *hevehe* may actually arise from dreams or similar experiences, it would be credulity to think that this explanation, when given, is necessarily true. An old man told me how he had travelled in company with some others to Opau. Spending the night there he had been con-

fronted in a dream by two girls who had risen out of the
River Karavure, upon whose banks the village is built. They
gave their names as Lariri and Lapari, and he later made two
hevehe masks to represent them.[1] He seemed to be quite at
a loss as to their antecedents, but admitted that he used their
names in a formula for building the *huita*, or hide for shooting birds in trees. As he fixes the beams on which the structure is to rest he calls them 'Lariri and Lapari's shin-bones'.
This magic he professes to have learnt subsequently from
another who informed him that the young women's names
could be used for this purpose. Although, therefore, my
informant professed to have made his new *hevehe* as the result of a dream, it seems not unlikely that he made them to
represent two magical names which he had learnt from some
other source, and that the dream was subsequent and a
fabrication. His explanation may well have gone down
with his fellow villagers, but there seems no very compelling
reason why it should do so with us.

Magic in the Name

This instance, whatever the fact may be, serves to introduce the subject of magic in connexion with the *hevehe*
names. One highly provocative point about these new
hevehe is the secretiveness of their owners or inventors in the
matter of naming them. In some cases the new mask has no
name, and the owner refuses to give it one, at any rate until
after the final descent. Thus, when listing the masks inside
the *eravo*, I was in certain cases put off. The cases proved to
be those of new *hevehe*, and some of the owners were ob-
durate: they said, 'Not yet!' What they meant was that
they had the names up their sleeves, but did not see fit to
reveal them. Again, certain of the traditional, long-established *hevehe* are found to have false names for general use,
the real one being the owner's secret. And further, some of
the names are allusive rather than definite, baffling synonyms
or periphrases for something more real that lies behind
them.

[1] He hivered and havered as to whether the girls were *kora marita* or *ma-hevehe*,
but finally veered towards the latter explanation on the grounds that they had come
out of a river.

All this points to magic, and there is a general impression that certain *hevehe* do have magic connected with them. This on deeper inquiry proves to be the case; though it remains clear that the great majority are, now at any rate, devoid of such association. The most intensive search for concrete evidence, among informants who were willing to reveal their magic in other matters, resulted in only very few admissions of magic in the *hevehe* names; and even then it seems sometimes highly remote or indirect.

To take an example: Ira, a *Nabo* man, has invented two masks, the names of which, 'Lapopo' and 'Kiraea', not hitherto made public, he revealed to me as a favour. They prove to belong to a formula which, as captain of a *bevaia*, or trading vessel, he uses in passing a certain sandbank west of Kerema River; for they are now *ma-hevehe* who haunt that spot, and if he failed to call upon them they might wreck his voyage.

> Kiraea, stand clear and watch Evoa's vessel pass: Master Lapopo, let Mauri's canoe go by.[1]

Needless to say, this is a private formula. It remains a question, which neither Ira nor any one else was able to answer, why he should conceal the names now if he intends eventually to publish them when the *hevehe* masks descend. But he declares that, even when he does make the names known, their true significance will pass over the heads of others.

As an example of a false or substitute name there is 'Kerave-Ori', 'Mountain Bird', given out for his *hevehe* by one Maverare. It is a synonym for Irava, the *Nabo* hero who is identified with the hornbill. The owner of the mask happens to possess magic for certain very specific operations, viz. those of closing the *eravo* door upon the secluded boys and

---

[1]   'Kiraea, Evoa-ve pasi maia eavi-lapaivira;
            Lapopo Vira, Mauri Vira-ve sariva maia eavi-lapaivira.'

The speaker is impersonating the mythical voyagers Evoa and Mauri who sailed up the Kerema River to bring back the *Nabo* woman Iviri. The words *pasi* (*hahi*) and *sariva* are Toaripi dialect, showing that Ira has got his formula from some distant source.

Kiraea and Lapopo were men of the upper Vailala who, after killing Ira Karaita, entered the sea and became *ma-hevehe*.

opening it before their formal emergence. As he sets up the coco-nut-leaf mat he whispers:

'I, Irava, put up my shelter. Your pile of excrement is within.'[1]

Or again, there is 'Love Kavape', 'Plucked Amaranth', which stands, inexplicably, as a pseudonym for Akaiapo. The owner here, Mekavakore, is an *eravo kariki haera* whose duty or privilege it is to fumigate the hunters' arrows before the *hohao*, and to sweep the *eravo* when they have gone forth on their expedition. Akaiapo is the secret magical name which he gives to the potsherd in which he burns his scented barks, for Akaiapo was a mythical *Purari* hunter of pigs. He was married to Puri, whose name is given to the *kariki haera*'s broom.[2]

A more straightforward instance of magic inherent in the name of a *hevehe* is that supplied by Koraguba. He has two masks named 'Miri Laru' and 'Laru Miri'. The relevant episode in the myths tells how Miri Laru, the elder brother, appealed to Laru Miri, the younger, to help him build a hide in a tree where the hornbills had been stealing fruit. The younger brother, however, is huffed because he remains unmarried, his father having so far declined to pay his betrothal price; so Miri Laru builds his hide and waits for the hornbills by himself. All day he waits without success until at evening a very fine bird alights on the tree. As he shoots it he is horrified to hear it exclaim, 'Oh, my brother!' It is none other than the jealous Laru Miri, who, thinking to play a trick on his brother, has built himself a *ruru* and, in the form of a hornbill, come to steal the fruit. Knowing this story and the names of the principal actors, Koraguba is, therefore, in possession of magic for shooting hornbills (though he is too old to climb trees and has long ceased using it himself). His simple formula, or perhaps rather what he

---

[1] '*Ara, Irava, kavukavu aipave; ave eh-kari koetavalaia.*'
The reference is said to be to the *Nabo* hero Kauaru when he shut his child in the *eravo*. The pile of excrement refers, metaphorically, to the rubbish which the boys will leave about in their seclusion. There may be a further reference to the strange habit of the hornbill in walling up its nesting mate in a hole in a tree. *Oa Irava!* is the *Nabo maea-ihura* (see p. 132).

[2] The informant was obviously rather hazy about the names, though he stuck to it that 'Love Kavape' was to be identified with Akaiapo the potsherd; it occurs to the writer that as a piece of imagery it would go better with Puri, the broom.

would think as he took aim from his concealment, is, 'I am Miri Laru. I am about to shoot Laru Miri.'

It would appear, then, that a certain proportion of *hevehe* masks are bound up through their names, whether public or secret, with magic. There remains the important question of what purpose, in connexion with the magic concerned, could be served by the actual making of a mask. No present-day informant, as far as I can discover, is able to answer this question satisfactorily. To pursue the above examples a little further: Ira does not believe that the existence of his *hevehe* masks, 'Lapopo' and 'Kiraea', assists him to clear the dangers of the sand-bank where the *ma-hevehe* of those names lie in waiting; nor does Maverare think that the mask 'Kera-ve-Ori' (alias Irava) enables him to perform any better his ceremonial task of closing the *eravo* on the secluded boys; nor Mekavakore, that 'Love Kavape' (alias Akaiapo) helps him fumigate the arrows. There is even some doubt in their minds as to whether the beings represented by the masks, the *hevehe* in abstract, have any existence at all. It seems to the writer that the Western Elema, like most other natives in his experience, range in their philosophy between an awestruck belief in the existence of a spirit world, on the one hand, and a thorough-going materialism on the other. Mood and circumstance will determine which attitude is in the ascendant. Thus Koraguba, who at other times is ready to expound the theory of the *lau-haera*, or Story Folk, and of their continued existence in the form of *kora marita* and spirits of the bush, is caught in a rationalistic frame of mind when we discuss his *hevehe*, 'Miri Laru' and 'Laru Miri'. They *were* Story Folk, it is true; but no such people exist at present, not in the bush or anywhere else, neither they nor their spirits. And he expressly denies that the making of the masks of those names ever helped out his magic for shooting hornbills.

In the face of such candid denials—and they are obviously such, since having gone so far as to reveal his magic the owner of the *hevehe* would not baulk at this point—it is difficult to imagine that the mask is made in the interests of the magic, as if to strengthen it. It would appear that, in so far as magic supplies any present motive for making the mask, it is by way of a semi-veiled boast. The existence of the mask is presumptive evidence that its owner possesses magic. And it is assumed that the mask will make reference, through its name and its more or less distinctive pattern, to some kind or department of magic in which the owner specializes. Thus Koraguba alleges that his ancestor first made 'Miri Laru' and 'Laru Miri' *because* he knew the magic for shooting hornbills; and Maverare says he must have some knowledge of *Nabo* magic before he can presume to make *Nabo hevehe* masks.

What would seem an obscure motive for inventing new masks and concealing the names thereof has been mentioned independently by a number of witnesses. A man who is huffed because his brothers have not given him an opportunity of making one of the *hevehe* they have together inherited may devise one of his own and keep them guessing as to its name and magical meaning. The name, if he did reveal it, would probably be found to allude to magic which he and his brothers possessed in common, and such revelation would incur their severe disapproval.[1] But once all the masks have come into the open at the final descent he can name his own if he pleases. It has done its work in showing that he is not devoid of magic, and he has at any rate defied his dog-in-the-manger brothers. When visitors at the finale of the cycle see this mask for the first time and perhaps recognize their own *aualari* symbols on it, they may exclaim, 'And what right have you to make a new *hevehe*? Have you any magic to back it up with?' It is then that the owner and inventor will reveal the name if it suits him to do so.

There are no doubt less complicated motives than the above, and we have seen that new *hevehe* may perhaps be made merely in fulfilment of a happy idea. But there is at least the presumption that such *hevehe* should have some magical support.

Original Significance of the Masks: a Surmise

The subject of magic in connexion with *hevehe* names has been given this amount of attention because of its intrinsic

[1] And, it is said, even the destruction of the mask. But I have no case in point and do not believe it.

interest and its possible significance. But it may be dismissed nevertheless as not really essential, because, as already stated, the majority of *hevehe* have no explicit magical associations whatever. Their names are handed down from generation to generation without understanding and without question, traditional names of traditional masks. The modern mask may imply the existence of magic, but it really needs none and very likely possesses none: it is an end in itself.

The general significance of the magic which does in fact belong to some of them lies in the theory to which this association might point, viz. that originally all the masks owned magic. This is obviously a hypothetical reconstruction, and it is presented here merely for what it is worth as such. But it may be that each mask in bygone times was made to represent one of the 'magic people', or *maho haera*, of its owner, i.e. one of the Story Folk whose name he adopted or employed for this or that magical purpose. What may have been the intention in creating material representations of such *maho haera* is wholly a matter of conjecture. It may perhaps be surmised that it provided a means of maintaining contact with them, or even of impersonating them dramatically, as if in pursuance of that idea of impersonation which is so characteristic of Elema magic.[1]

It is not proposed, however, to dwell further upon this theory. If it was ever the case that each mask represented a *maho haera* and was made in the interests of magic, then it can only be said that the idea has faded into disuse, until now only a proportion retain this significance and new *hevehe* can apparently be created without it. But, apart from magic, the general consideration of the *hevehe* names to which this chapter has been devoted does seem to indicate that the masks at large represent, or at least represented, the *aualari*, the Story Folk, the spirits or beings of the forest, the sea, and the air. And the *Hevehe* cycles are those periodic sojourns during which they feast, dance, and rejoice in the company of human beings.

As a final observation one may draw attention again to the great predominance, as indicated by the names and their

[1] See p. 136.

associations, of *bush* spirits among the *aualari* with which the
hevehe are identified. And we must contrast the theory of the
individual masks, as treated in this chapter, with the theory
of the masks *en masse* as revealed in the chapter on *Hevehe
Karawa*. The one is hazy and sometimes obscured by
secrecy; the other is delightfully clear. The one takes a broad
sweep of the whole environment, but lays all the emphasis
on the bush; the other points directly to the sea. In fact
you cannot square the two.

XVIII

THE TOTEMIC DANCE-MASKS

Sago-leaf Mantles and the New Door

WE may assume that the *hevehe* masks have passed the several intermediate stages of construction, each ushered in by a *Hevehe Karawa*, until they are now clothed with their *koro* under-mantles. The next item of their attire is the frayed sago-leaf (*mae*), the preparation of which, in the usual desultory manner, is likely to occupy at least a further year or so. The *mae*-making itself is inaugurated by a visit of the *ma-hevehe*, which brings up a wisp of the material as if from the sea and deposits it in the *eravo* at night. Next morning it is displayed, stuck in a split pole, in front of the building as a public intimation that the *mae*-making is to begin.

Mae[1] is the material of the women's skirts and the manufacture of it is women's business. It is their contribution—quite a considerable one—to the make-up of the mask, and the fact that they prepare it with their own hands is enough to dispose of the idea, if it could be entertained at all, that the uninitiated believe the *hevehe* to be other than they are. But the fiction is nevertheless preserved: the *mae* is supposed to be merely an extra gift to the *hevehe* from its *lau*, or mother in the sense of proprietress.

As it is made it is stored away in the houses of the *hevehe-oa* in readiness for the highly spectacular ceremonies which are described in the present chapter. These ceremonies surround two particular events: (1) the making of a door (*dehe*) for the *eravo*, (2) binding the *mae* and affixing it to the masks, the latter being introduced by yet another *Hevehe Karawa*. I shall describe them as witnessed at Aivaroro Ravi in 1931. It is to be understood that when this important stage has been consummated the *hevehe* are virtually in condition to

---

[1] It is made from the central shoot of the sago-palm of which the leaves have not yet unwrapped themselves. It is a soft, pliant material, and, when freshly dyed, a very beautiful one.

PLATE 31

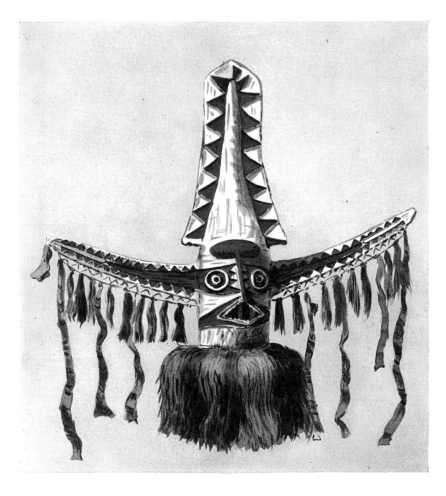

EHARO MASK

One of the plain variety, i.e. without totemic model. For the dance it is
trimmed round the edges with feathers.

emerge. It only remains to add certain finishing touches. Yet these in themselves will involve a good deal of work; and there is no hurry. The final preparations and the actual emergence did not take place in the present instance till three years later.

Before any major ceremony the whole community gives itself to amassing food. Men and women are busy for a month ahead making sago; and it is to be noted that the women do so with as good a will as the men, for they look forward to such festivities with probably greater pleasure. The food is for the entertainment of the many hundreds of guests who have already been invited from all Orokolo Bay and its near hinterland. And various villages will honour the occasion by organizing dances. For here, as very commonly throughout Papua, it is the guests who dance; the home villagers (except for their women-folk) act merely as spectators and hosts.

The Eharo *Mask*

If we entered any one of the *eravo* of Orokolo or the other villages of the Bay we should probably find some men busy at work fashioning masks of a kind not hitherto mentioned. These are the *eharo* which are to appear in numbers at the forthcoming festivities.

The Western Elema have three kinds of mask. *Kovave* and *hevehe* have been already described. They conform very closely to their respective types. The third category, that of *eharo*, is extremely variable. Like the other masks, the *eharo* is constructed of cane with a covering of bark-cloth; but it may assume the most fanciful forms. Some, like the *love hae*, are more or less conventional, resembling *kovave* in their general form but much more ornate and lavishly decorated with *love*, i.e. sprigs or tufts of feathers.[1] Others are mere grotesque head-pieces, the wearer's body being clothed in a suit of bark-cloth something like an engineer's overalls, perhaps dyed brilliant yellow. But the typical

---

[1] Informants are unable to etymologize *love hae*. *Love* means either the amaranth or a sprig of feathers. For *hae* see p. 126. The expression *love hae*, like the mask itself, is said to come from the Houra Haera (Berepa).

eharo bear on their heads, so to speak, the effigies of all manner of totemic creatures, or *aualari*. There are birds, fish, insects, reptiles, dogs, trees, even mushrooms and jelly-fish. The Elema possess no small skill in modelling with cane and bark-cloth, and these figures possess not only the virtues of realism and artistry, but often succeed in being really comic. Both makers and wearers give full rein to their humour and the *eharo* on parade have the amusing and exhilarating effect of the grotesque figures at a carnival. Some of them, a special class which we shall deal with individually at a later stage, represent well-known mythological characters; while others are improvised and purely fanciful.

Rehearsals

With the excitement of the coming event to spur them on the workers soon have these masks completed. They have been made under cover, and during the day you may hear the sound of drums inside the *eravo* as the young men, with the *eharo* on their heads, practise the appropriate steps. Sometimes a *hirita*, a high palisade of palm-leaves, encloses a space of about 12 square yards abutting on the front of the *eravo*, and in the cool of the late afternoon a number of young men wearing their masks come out to rehearse, all the rest crowding on the veranda to watch and criticize. First—to describe a scene witnessed at Meouri Ravi—there come two *love hae* (*eharo* are usually in pairs). They shuffle down the ramp (specially provided in lieu of the ordinary ladder-steps) and peer comically round to get their bearings, for they can see only through the fabric of the bark-cloth. Each carries a drum, and now they begin to beat the time, performing a sort of stationary goose-step. The rhythm quickens and the great grotesque figures begin to circle round, each on his own spot and in opposite directions, to the huge amusement of the old man, Berarikere, almost in his dotage, who tells them to kick out better, and shows them from the veranda how to do it. While these are still practising, out come a pair of *birarihu*[1] clad in handsome

[1] This presumably means 'ancestors' (*birari*) either in the sense of human ancestors or *lau haera*.

PLATE 32

A pair of *Love Hae* on their way to the dance. The boy is adjusting the *harau* rattles for one of them

A pair of comical *Eharo*. The tall one represents a secluded boy with a large mop of hair; the other is a bald-headed old man about to comb it

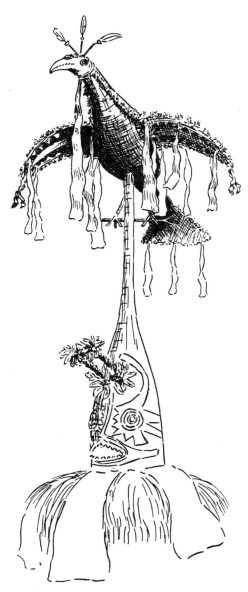

FIG. 16. A Hornbill *Eharo*

new raiment of *mae*, vertically striped in red, yellow, and cream. These have to master a more complicated series of

FIG. 17. Model Human Head on Bird *Eharo*

movements, advancing side by side first forwards and then backwards and beating their drums alternately—a trick which they find very difficult. When one of them holds his drum too high, Area the *amua* leaps off the veranda and good-humouredly but rather violently knocks it down.

Meanwhile, the father of one is giving a spirited performance by way of demonstration, though it is certain that the men in the masks cannot see him. Next comes *pipi* (the butter-fly), which is like a bird except for its long spiral antennae; then a pair of *leraita* birds with wide gaping mouths which give them the appearance of gasping for breath; and, finally, an imposing pair of *baiva* (hornbills) with real beaks for *ape* and wide spread of wings. These last are astonishingly realistic, like two birds flying side by side, their great wings flapping regularly with each step.

Such rehearsals go on for perhaps a week in advance of the festival. Their purpose is partly to try on the masks and effect adjustments in fitting, balance, &c., and partly to school the performers in the particular steps and drum-rhythms which the *eharo* may own as distinctive possessions.

Eharo are not made in the home *eravo* (where the cere-monies are to be held), but are brought there by the guests as an accompaniment to their dances. Each, however, is made at the express invitation of some one in the home *eravo*. An *arivu* asks his *aukau*, or an *okeahi* his reciprocal *okeahi*, to honour him in this way, and on the occasion we are describing there must have been nearly forty *eharo* made in response. Many of them simply go and return with the dancers, but a number enter the home *eravo* and remain. These have been previously bespoken by the *arivu* or *okeahi* concerned. Each of them will leap over a live pig, laid out bound before it, and then enter the *eravo* by the back door. The pig is given by the *arivu* to his *aukau*, who carries it home with him; and the *eharo*, with all its *mae*, its highly valued feather decorations, and the shell ornaments which hang on its breast, belongs to the *arivu*. He will strip off and appropriate all these valuables, while the bare body of the mask is merely stuck up out of the way in the rear of the *eravo*.

Poilati

We may assume now that all is in readiness for the great day. The principal materials for the new door—stout bam-boos and bundles of cane—are assembled, and prodigious quantities of food have been got together to feed the visitors. Every house in the community has its own display; and verandas are loaded and decorated, like stalls at a fair, with sago, bananas, coco-nuts, taro, and bunches of yellow areca-nut; while numerous pigs, already trussed to poles, lie in the shade beneath. On the morrow the ceremonies will begin.

Before sunrise in the morning I was awakened by the noise of *harau* rattles on the beach and hurried out to see the first forerunners of the invasion of guests. They were a pair of *poilati*, extraordinary figures clothed from head to foot in sago-leaf, newly and brilliantly dyed in red and yellow, and with their faces concealed behind small masks. The masks, one of them yellow with black spots, the other black with coloured spots, were made hideous with staring eyes and crooked mouths, and each figure, loaded at wrist, knee, and ankle with jangling *harau*, carried full-sized bow and arrows. The *poilati* were a pair of gorgeously arrayed clowns, and as they shuffled noisily along they were accompanied by a crowd of highly appreciative adults and youngsters. In the lead was Horevuhu, the chief of Hohoro, one of the most influential chiefs and sorcerers of Orokolo Bay, who was solemnly conducting the party from his village, some miles down the beach. Now the *poilati* paused to rehearse their dance. First they revolved together face to face; then quickly turned and revolved back to back, all the time leaning to one side as if about to topple over. Having done this once or twice very skilfully, they sharply twanged their bows and set off again at a jog trot.

Once opposite the home *eravo* they turned in and clambered over the fence, and in doing so one of them nearly lost his footing. There was a sympathetic gasp from the crowd of followers, for it would bring discredit on them all if their man came to grief. But he recovered himself, and the pair made straight for Aivaroro Ravi, in front of which they performed their dance very well. Then they went off together and repeated it before one house after another, escorted now by a large, admiring crowd of local children, who clustered round them while they danced and scattered like a flock of birds as soon as they turned towards the next house. It was a very pretty scene, somehow reminiscent of Christmas carollers in broad daylight.

Three other pairs of *poilati* had by now arrived from other *eravo*, and when all had completed their round they assembled in front of Aivaroro Ravi, where offerings of food, brought from every house visited, were set out in four heaps. These were picked up by their followers, and with them the *poilati* shuffled off home again.

The above is a traditional performance in connexion with the *dehe* day and one of which informants can give no explanation. It is the function of the *poilati* to collect food in advance for the guests, for some of them may have come from a distance and will be camped near by under the coconut-palms awaiting the moment for entry, and they must be fed in the meantime. It was suggested that the word derives from *poi*, 'sago' (though nobody could interpret the second syllable);[1] and it may well enough stand for 'sago-fetchers'. For the rest, it is pointed out that this observance is an introduction from the Houra Haera and thus really an accretion on *Hevehe*, so that it is probably beside the mark to look for any deep-lying explanation.

Making the Door

Before the *poilati* had disappeared the men of Aivaroro Ravi were at work on the scaffolding which had been erected against the doorway. Numbers of *hara*, or mats of plaited coco-nut-leaf, were being brought as gifts by *aukau* of other *eravo* to their *arivu* in the home *eravo*, and the framework of the *dehe* was gradually covered with these, working from top to bottom, the old doorway being dismantled at the same speed as the new one replaced it. Hitovakore, one of the two *eravo amua*, himself began at the top and worked there for some time, pausing at one stage to harangue the village. He wanted the mat-bringers to hurry, as he did not intend to stay up there all day, but was only showing the younger men how to go about things. He soon gave up, but work continued till well into the afternoon when, with

[1] One man, anxious to help, said that it meant 'stone'. But it proved that his thoughts had skidded into the Motuan language: he was thinking of *nadi* (Motuan for 'stone'), which he pronounced *lati*.

the sun shining full on the face of the building, it must have been extremely hot. Once finished the new *dehe* was decorated with many sprigs of croton, with single leaves stuck into the meshes of the mats, and with numerous *hapa*, i.e. horizontal midribs of young sago with the pale green leaves hanging like a curtain. The door was hinged down one side by a series of cane loops, so that when the time should come—at the very climax of the *Hevehe* cycle—it might be drawn open from the outside. In the meantime it was lashed securely against the front wall of the *eravo* and was to remain closed, as it proved, for the ensuing three years.

Introduction to the Avai

This, when the new *dehe* has been completed, is one of those times when the *eravo* is in special degree tabu. One of the above-described *hapa* actually hangs over the low entrance at the base of the door, and none but an old man, tacitly recognized as a member of the *avai*, would dare to part it and enter. This, however, was a privilege always readily accorded to me despite my lack of qualifications, and I had the good fortune to see a somewhat rare observance inside the *eravo* on this particular afternoon. It was the presentation of a young man, the son of the *eravo amua* Miki Harapa, to the members of the *avai*. They were present to the number of a dozen or so, having come from various villages of the Bay and its hinterland, and were now sitting or sprawling at their ease in the dark, cool interior. The young man, Hauhakore, was led in by his *aukau* and accompanied by his father. He carried in his hand a *hapa* from which were hanging a number of small neat rolls of cooked pork, the tastiest morsels of the pig which his father had specially provided for this introduction. The *aukau* now took the *hapa* and, laying it down before one of the old men, turned to give his nephew the customary talking-to. He had brought him into the *eravo*, he said, to show him the *avai*. Henceforward he should leave all stealing of pigs, women, and garden property; and he should show himself hospitable to visitors, giving them food and inviting them to sleep in the *eravo*. It was the usual somewhat platitudinous address of the *aukau*, and in this case it was a little short and lame. Miki Harapa, the father, briefly told his son to listen to his uncle's admonitions; and, finally, the oldest man present, Kaeva of Yogu, uttered a gruff word or two. The young man looked abashed, as well he might, and the old ones did nothing to make him welcome or dispel his nervousness. After a moment's pause he sheepishly retired, without having uttered a word.

This kind of presentation to the *avai*, of which I have recorded very few instances, is said to be in the nature of a public initiation, since the candidate goes up to the *eravo* in full sight of the women. The young man so privileged is shown the real recipients of the pigs ostensibly given to the *ma-hevehe*: for the old men are the pig-eaters *in excelsis*, and even for the privilege of seeing them in the *eravo* while it is under tabu the initiate (or his father for him) must provide yet another pig of which they will get the pickings. But, whatever the explanation, it has seemed worth while describing this episode if only to show the deference in which the *avai* are held by their juniors.

Visitors

The remainder of the day passed quietly in the village and the only episode of the night was a visit from a party of *kavo*, or 'flying foxes', who come, like the *poilati*, to collect a tribute of food. In keeping with their name they come under cover of darkness and indulge in what is meant to be a realistic squealing, while some of them with glowing fire-sticks in their hands flap their arms wildly, like the bats flapping their wings.

This party was sent by a detachment of visitors from Vailala who had arrived at sundown on a large double canoe under sail. Since they camped in a large shelter next the rest-house, which I then occupied, I saw almost more than enough of their preparations for the morrow. The scene was one of crowded confusion, with costumes and masks stuck up everywhere on poles, feather head-dresses, brightly painted bark-cloth, weapons, songs, incessant chatter, and betel-nut. This seemed to continue throughout the night and to be redoubled in the morning; for then they were engaged in painting and dressing themselves for the first entry into the village.

The visitors make two such entries. The first occurs in the morning. It is by way of showing the *eharo* which they have brought with them, though some of these even then enter the *eravo* and remain. The majority, however, after their initial parade, return to the various *eravo* or the temporary camps of the visitors, there to remain until in the late afternoon they re-enter the village, this time in company with the dancers.

Both occasions are so packed with detail that there is danger of going to too great a length in describing them. In order to spare the reader I shall pass quickly over the first of these two entries. The procedure was much the same as that of the afternoon though on a somewhat smaller scale, and of course stopping short of the dance by which the latter was followed.

First Entry into the Village

The visitors participating had formed themselves into four composite bodies. The first of these, recruited from all the various off-shoot villages of Orokolo as far as Biai, had mustered at Herekera Creek before sunrise, under the leadership of Horevuhu. This man made the nearest approach to an officer leading his forces that I have ever seen under purely native conditions among these people; though the impression was mainly due to his tall figure and commanding air. Had he given any orders they would have been drowned in the din of rattles and drums, for the massed *eharo* were now advancing along the beach in the midst of a dense crowd of supporters, of both sexes and all ages, with a broad, mobile fringe of excited children.

A far more numerous band made up by the Western communities of Orokolo together with those of Yogu and Arihava was already in position opposite Aivaroro Ravi, and, as these led the van, we may watch their entry into the village. A wide section of the fence has been demolished to clear the way; but as they advance a line of determined women rushes out as if to resist them. Each carries a stick which she brings down on the sands with a loud report, and then scatters handfuls of scraped coco-nut over the approaching *eharo*. It resembles nothing so much as snow-flakes or confetti, but is really magical shrapnel; and, what with fierce looks and loud yells, the women's onslaught seems like a heroic defence of their village against the invading host. The women of the visitors, similarly armed, rush forward to meet them, and there is a moment's lively skirmish; but the main body, now irresistibly in motion, sweeps on and envelops them.

These defenders are women of the home *eravo* scattering magical medicines over the visitors for the express purpose of neutralizing their effect upon the local girls. For a man in an *eharo* may be expected to exercise a fatal attraction over the female heart, and there is a chance, which must be averted if possible, that the visitors may eventually seduce away the girls of Aivaroro Ravi. It is this same danger in particular, as well as the risk of more generalized magic, that makes certain men, themselves recognized magicians, post themselves in the forefront between the two opposing forces. Each is uttering his private spells and wafting them over the multitude by gentle movements of his cassowary-plume switch, something like a feather duster. A line of four or five such men stands in open order before the *eravo* as its protectors; and an advance guard of the same precedes the visitors. It is the special business of the last-mentioned to make magic so that their *eharo* will not be brought to shame by stumbling, falling, or coming to pieces.

But these individuals like the women before them are simply engulfed by the onrush of a body a good many hundreds strong. With the queer figures of the *eharo* riding high in their midst they sweep across the open space to the front of the *eravo*. The village is filled as if by magic with a dense throng, pouring in from the beach and reinforced from every house, and the only quiet spot left in it is the *eravo*-veranda, where four or five old fellows sit at their ease and unperturbed. The *eharo* congregate at the very foot of this Royal Box of the *avai*, pause there a moment, and then break off, right or left, to career up and down the village.

The second party, from Hohoro, the third, from Vailala, and the fourth, from Pareamamu, bore down in succession on the village, adding their bands of *eharo*; and these broke up to dance, singly or in couples, each surrounded by its escort of adoring women and girls—mothers, wives, or sisters of the wearers. It was a marvel that collisions were so few; but, seeing only through the meshes of their head-pieces, the wearers yet managed to steer a course, and, if some were jostled, none disgraced their village by falling over.

Among them were various figures of fun, the kind of *eharo* that wear bark-cloth suits and trousers and are called *oa heaha*, 'bad old men'. Their role was purely comic; but there was at least one side-show which could not escape the charge of obscenity. It was provided by two men of Arihava, Loavira and Kuru. The former, his body powdered from head to foot with light red ochre, wore a veil of black cassowary feathers over his face. He was the male. His companion, a sturdy little man hardly more than a dwarf in size, was the female, clad in a skirt with a cape of bark-cloth hanging from the crown of her head after the manner of the Kukukuku bush people. These danced back and forth amid the throng, pausing a dozen times to imitate the act of copulation *a posteriori*. This performance was so completely irrelevant to the main proceedings that it is happily un-necessary to mention its amazingly indecent details. It is worth saying, however, that they were not in the least offensive to those who saw them; the two performers were, on the contrary, greeted by men, women, and children with shouts of laughter and applause.

Meanwhile dozens of youngsters were skipping about the village in masks of quite a distinctive kind. Made of coco-nut fibre, these rose to a peak at the rear, and with their round eyeholes gave the boys the appearance of Klu Klux Klans-men, very juvenile and mischievous, and with their legs swathed in banana-leaves. These figures, known as *Kokopi*, or 'little lizards', were wholly delightful. They flashed

PLATE 33

A. Dancers and *Eharo* massed on the beach opposite the *Eravo*

B. The line of women standing ready to defend their village

C. The skirmish

The approach of the dancers

about the village at great speed, each armed with his toy bow and handful of arrows with which he transfixed bunches of bananas or lumps of sago on the house-verandas. I saw half a dozen of them swarming about one man's house, and his vegetables were fairly bristling with their shafts. Meantime some adult members of the party, disguised as old women, the 'mothers of the *kokopi*', and bearing bags on their backs, followed to collect the spoils. For whatever the boys succeed in shooting is willingly given up. The very imps of mischief, they darted in and out among the crowd, in striking contrast to the ponderously-moving *eharo*, and finally formed themselves up in single file before the *eravo*, danced a few steps forward, twanging their small bow-strings, and then dispersed. The whole manœuvre was performed at speed, and they seemed to vanish in the crowd. The contribution of the *kokopi* was one of the most spirited of all, and they had good reason to be proud of it as well as satisfied with its material results, which were carried off to feed the visitors.

The various parties now gradually dispersed and, taking their *eharo* with them (except for those which had already entered the *eravo*), returned to their villages or camps to prepare for the much more pretentious display of the afternoon.

The Dances

Two separate dances had been prepared: the beach villages of the Bay were combining to give '*Apuwiri*', the bush tribes of Pareamamu and Berepa to give '*Yahe*'. There are a number of different dances known to the Western Elema, distinguished by the songs which accompany them and by costume-characters of their own, and it would be more than tedious to describe even these two in full. As a more or less typical example, however, it may be said of *Yahe* that it has at least seven sets of performers, exclusive of the numerous band of women and girls who surround it. There are first the *Apa-eravarava*, or special drum-beaters, of whom I counted four, two being completely blackened, two completely covered with dry mud, and all with their faces veiled by cassowary plumes. They contrive to make themselves very picturesque but farcical figures with skirts of banana leaf and torn husks of coco-nut hanging over their backs to represent shell ornaments. Then there are the *Yahe-morita*, two youths disguised very convincingly as girls, with pointed half-coco-nut shells for breasts, their bodies oiled and reddened, and wearing the skirts, necklets, ear-rings, &c., appropriate to the other sex. Further characters are *Kara* (the Mangroves), whose head-pieces are stuck like pin-cushions with long tubular mangrove fruits; *Kako* and *Pora* (two birds) bearing miniature bows and sheets of bark-cloth hanging from their backs with pictures of the birds in question; and several pairs of fully-arrayed *eharo—Hahepa* and *Pau* (the Frilled Lizards), *Biai* (the Pythons), &c. The real dancers (*idihi vira*) are called *poekoro haera*, or wearers of head-dresses; and of these there were perhaps a score, almost hidden from sight beneath their finery and the wide-spreading frames on which their feathers were displayed. And lastly there are the small boys, known as *Hohoro*, or Fireflies, who are to circle round and round the whole party as it moves.

The songs which accompany *Yahe*, *Apuviri*, and such dances are mythical ballads consisting of an inexhaustible number of stanzas, each of which is first sung by a precentor who knows all in their sequence, and then taken up by the chorus which clusters round him. There is no doubt that the special costume characters represent various of the persons referred to in the ballad; but such is the variety in the renderings of the songs, and such their length, that a clear correlation is out of the question.

In order to dispose of our description of the dance it may be said in advance that it will eventually arrange itself in a circular formation when once it has reached the village. In the very centre stand the drum-beaters and singers (*hivi haera*), clustering together as if to hear one another's voices better; and round them move the gorgeous figures of the *idihi vira*, in a ceaseless slow circle; while on the outskirts the women and girls form a dense crowd of stationary dancers swinging their skirts in time to the drums. By the time the dance has thus settled down to its real business the

PLATE 34

Dancers and *Eharo* sweeping into the village

various costume characters will have taken themselves off and changed.

Second Entry

So far, however, the dancers have not even entered the village. We must imagine that they have now completed their preparations—and the toilet of a *poekoro haera,* down to the painting of his face in minute patterns, is not of a sort that can be scamped—and amid excited, piecemeal rehearsals of individuals and groups, have at last mustered themselves on the beach. Here the women and girls, who have waited long, advance jubilantly to meet them and the whole throng moves forward. In the centre are the *eharo,* among which we can distinguish two great *berare* birds, *biai* (a python), four *larovea* fish, four *aitari* (sharks), two *makoura* (mushrooms), two *huva* pigeons, three *pipi* (butterflies), and two *hepe lahoha* trees—tall masks surmounted by branches from which flutter innumerable bark-cloth streamers. As well as these there are *eharo* of the more conventional kind, *love-hae* and *birarihu* and *oa haeha,* and prominently in the forefront the two grotesque frilled lizards *hahepa* and *pau,* who menace every one with their long spears. There is very little order about it all. The disreputable *apa-eravarava* dance about each other in almost frenzied circles, and dozens of little boys dart in and out amid the moving crowd or rush on ahead to climb on the stranded logs for a better view.

The *Apuviri* dancers are already in position opposite Aivaroro Ravi and have settled into some order, awaiting the arrival of the second party. From time to time their drums beat and the whole mass breaks into a stationary dance. The women and girls, their breasts and shoulders reddened with ochre, their round heads freshly barbered in pretty patterns, and their necks and arms bedecked with every piece of jewellery—shells, beads, or dogs' teeth—that they possess, are ranged in masses around the dancers. Every one of them has her head turned in the same direction, down the beach toward the second party; but as their own drums strike up afresh they turn inwards in a flash and begin, as if automatically, to dance.

Suddenly—with that remarkable unanimity which seems to dispense with any necessity for orders—the *Apuviri* party is on the move. There is a rush of unattached, beweaponed men to line the way for a better view; there is the same patrolling of the entrance by magicians with their cassowary-switches; and the same fierce attack and counter-attack of the women. But the dance party, three times as great as those of the morning, sweeps irresistibly on. Clouds of dust and sand fill the air, through which the afternoon sun shines on the tall brave front of Aivaroro Ravi. Above the tumult we may distinguish two great hornbill masks with necks outstretched and regularly flapping wings; behind them two tall 'trees', swaying unsteadily and trailing long ribbons of fluttering bark-cloth. So they advance to the *eravo*, where once again we see the old men, undecorated and unmoved, chewing their betel on the veranda.

When in a few moments the second party enters the village in rear of the first there must be a press of several thousand people. The house-verandas are crowded with onlookers, and many more are standing about or moving up and down the village after the *eharo*, who have broken off to perform their separate dances. Every female, old or young, has attached herself to some *eharo* or other and is dancing to the sound of its drum. Now one catches sight of a dog hurtling through the air. Its owner has caught it unawares by the hind legs and with one fatal swing dashed its body on the ground: it is an impromptu present to some *eharo*-maker, and next we see the portentous masked figure leap over it, perform one or two departing capers, and then make off to the rear of the *eravo*. Many bound pigs have been laid in the path of other *eharo*, and these, accepted in the same dramatic way, are speedily picked up and carried off by the *aukahura* or *okeahi* concerned, while the wearer of the mask disappears into the *eravo* to relieve himself of his burden.

It is noteworthy that a large proportion of men are armed with bows and arrows, clubs, waddies, axes, or trade knives, for there is always the possibility of a flare-up when different villages come together in a crowd. But all is good humour. A few succeed in making their voices heard in public

PLATE 35

Three *Idihi-Vira*, or dancers in costume

Three *Apa-Eravarava*, or drummers

PLATE 24

announcements. Old Mahevehe of Waiea Ravi, one of the
visitors, is apologizing for his *eravo*'s contribution: he declares that sorcerers have been killing off his people, hence
the comparative smallness of their dance. Another of the
visitors, however, an old woman hideously got-up in black
and yellow and fairly covered in dust and sweat, is not so
apologetic. 'What do you think of yourselves in comparison
with us?' she cries. 'See the dance we have put on for you.'
'All right,' answers a voice from the crowd; 'you have come
to a fine village. This is no little island. There are plenty of
us, and when the time comes we will do as good a dance for
you.' Another visitor is shouting that his young men intend
to captivate the girls of Aivaroro Ravi. But there is of
course some possibility that the opposite may happen, since
the visitors have brought their girls with them, and an old
man answers at the top of his voice, 'We will see whose
young men are the hotter, yours or ours.'[1] At that moment
one of the *oa heaha* who has been giving a very spirited performance as a clown runs blindly against a spear which
some one has left stuck in the ground and is nearly thrown
off his balance. This brings the house down in favour of
the old man: 'There you are!' he cries. 'Your *eharo* cannot
keep their feet!'

As in the morning there are diversions and side-shows.
The most effective is provided by a small party which makes
a belated entry from the bush—two amazingly realistic
cassowaries which seem to be pursued by an old woman
covered in mud. Their long necks and sharp beaks get in
everybody's road, but all make way good-humouredly and
this strange procession soon loses itself in the throng.
Another diversion is provided by the pair of 'singers', the
Birava-Hivi, who, coming as characters in the *Apuviri* dance,
now detach themselves and stroll off to visit the houses on
the outskirts, singing before each as if they meant to beg for
money. Thus, chanting loudly and dismally, they disappear
towards the deserted end of the village. They represent, I

[1] i.e. which of them have more *ahea*, in the sense of power, particularly magical
power. The boast refers to marriage, not to any possibility of licence during the
festivities. The village is not concerned about the virtue of its girls but about the
likelihood of losing them to another village in marriage (see pp. 54, 275).

am told, the man who tracked Apuviri from Kerema to the
Aivei by her footprints, and they are still looking for her.[1]

By now it is almost sundown. Those *eharo* that have not
been bought with pigs are returning to their villages, and
men of the home-*eravo* are carrying hither and thither the
pots of food which their womenfolk have cooked during
the day. There is a general lull for rest and refreshment, but
the two dances, *Apuviri* and *Yahe*, still go on. They may
now be seen clearly, forming two many-coloured circles
in the open space before the *eravo*. In the centre of each is a
high stack of fresh coco-nuts which will be used to slake
the performers' thirst throughout the night.

The Coming of Ma-Hevehe

In the cool of the evening the dance gets into its full
swing. The scene is now lit by fires, and sometimes by
torches of dry coco-nut leaves held aloft by the hosts, and
these uncertain means of illumination make it the more
fascinating. The magnificently befeathered *idihi-vira* troop
round in an endless circle, holding themselves upright and
stiff for fear their head-dresses might come to some harm;
and the singers and drummers in the centre, first listening
to the precentor's cracked tenor while he gives them a
stanza of the ballad, burst into full chorus when he has
finished. The women and girls have flocked to the scene
in still greater numbers. Whenever there is a pause they
chatter and giggle amongst themselves, but no sooner do
the drums strike up again than they turn, as unanimous
as a shoal of fish, to renew their dancing, facing inwards
towards the centre and with occasional downward glances
of approval at their own swinging skirts. It is, indeed, a
festive scene, and none are enjoying themselves as much
as they.

So the dance goes on, with only brief pauses for rest, till
at about 9 p.m. there are heard from down the beach the
distant blasts of the shell-trumpet and those other unmistak-

---

[1] Apuviri is said to be another name of Lavari Avu in this story. *Bira-hivi*, or
bira-ve-hivi, which means literally 'singing man', is also an expression used for 'flash
bachelor'.

PLATE 36

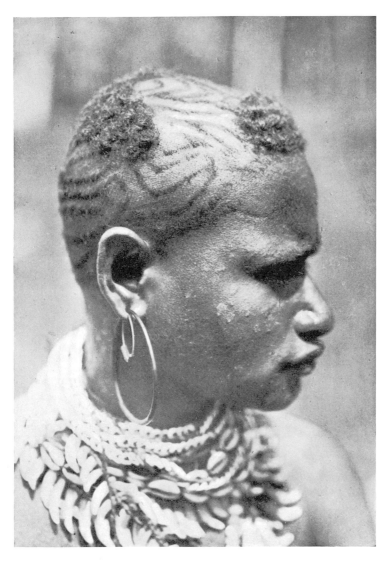

A Western Elema girl with her hair shaved in patterns. Necklaces of shell and dogs' teeth; ear-rings of flying-fox bone and cassowary quill

able sounds that prelude the coming of *ma-hevehe*. There are excited shouts of warning; the drums cease; and the formation of the dance dissolves. Fires are extinguished, and in a trice the village square is practically deserted. The women have all taken to the houses in a hurry while the men, somewhat more leisurely, withdrew to the outlying parts of the village on either side.

There is not long to wait for the *Hevehe Karawa* party to arrive. Swelled by the co-operation of many initiated visitors, it is especially large, and the onrush of this black mass of men, together with the terrifying sounds they produce, provides a stirring climax to the events of the day. They do not enter the *eravo*, but halt before it with that sudden cessation of noise which we have noticed as so dramatic. Then after a moment is heard the signal for departure, and the *ma-hevehe* retreats, the babel of sound growing rapidly fainter. Before it has quite died away, however, the voice of Hitovakore is heard from the *eravo*-veranda. He first calls on certain *ma-hevehe* by name, asking them not to go too far away but to abide the summons which they will presently hear from Meouri Ravi. Then, descending the steps as he does so and walking off in the darkness towards his house, he gives the village a brief harangue which none can fail to hear: they are to show some energy with preparing the *mae*, and the feathers too, so that they can get the *Hevehe* over. Let them all agree. It is no good one man saying this and another that; he wants a village where all say the same.

I do not know that Hitovakore had any specific complaint in mind, but what he said so well fits in with the desire for unanimity which characterizes this society, that we need not suppose he had any at all. He had hardly finished speaking when the sound of drums was heard from another quarter. The *idihi-vira* were streaming back to renew their dance: the women reappeared; the fires flared up; and the dance went on till morning.

Shell Ornaments and Pigs

Early next day the guests departed. Palm-leaf barriers were set up on the east and west boundaries of Aivaroro

Ravi community, and its women and children were told to absent themselves during daylight hours for the next two days. The reason was that these were to be occupied with the presentation of ornaments, the killing and eating of pigs, and the binding of *mae* for the *hevehe* masks, none of which proceedings must be seen by uninitiated eyes. It is true the barriers are very flimsy and perfunctory, and I myself observed a small boy stray through one of them on to the forbidden side. But his cries soon after informed me that he was being punished, and there is at least strong insistence on the form of concealing the goings-on at the *eravo*. As we have seen, the beach opposite is closed to traffic, and this in itself must amount to a considerable inconvenience.

The novices in this case were eight in number, all fully grown young men; and on the following morning each of them received at the hands of his *aukau* an *aroa* of ornaments. There is little ostentation about this gift-making, for the village now holds only its own male inhabitants and the parties of *aukahura* and *aiapi* immediately concerned. It takes place on the ground before the *eravo*. The *aukau*, having placed the *aroa* on his nephew's shoulder, usually stands off and addresses him, perhaps bestowing some praise, perhaps giving him a thorough slating, perhaps airing some personal matter with which the young man has no connexion. As he receives the *aroa* the initiate is handed a shell-trumpet to blow.[1] Then he is led up the steps into the *eravo*, where the old men are sitting about. He blows the shell again as he enters, and taking the *aroa* from his shoulder hangs it up. It is to remain in the *eravo* for perhaps a week, during which time the initiate must sleep there rather than at home: he is ostensibly 'guarding' his *aroa*. At the end of that time he makes a further small feast in honour of his *aukau*, and is then at liberty to take the *aroa* home and stow its contents in his box.[2] They constitute a valuable gift:

[1] It is only those who have blown the *puwa* on this ceremonial occasion that are entitled to blow it as prelude to a harangue (i.e. when they want to attract the village's attention to some private grievance).

[2] If the pig has been supplied, e.g., by the initiate's father rather than by himself, then the *aroa* is appropriated by the former. I saw one father, a visitor from Arihava, take it off his son's shoulder in a very abrupt fashion. He carried it home the same day. Initiates do not necessarily belong to the *eravo* celebrating *Hevehe Karawa*.

PLATE 37

Dancers and *Eharo* before the *Eravo*. Members of the *Avai* may be seen on the veranda

a European trader who examined one of the *aroa* in my company told me that at current rates £10 would not buy the ornaments which hung on it.

The pigs provided for this occasion are eaten solely by initiated males. They fall into three categories. First, there are the very large specimens, two or more, which must be provided by the Drum Leaders for every celebration of *Hevehe Karawa*: these are for the *eravo*-members at large and any others who give their help, and they are killed and eaten on the day following the ceremony.[1] Second, there are the pigs provided for the *aukau* of the new initiates to *Hevehe Karawa*. Third, there are those given to the *aukau* of various *harehare-akore* or *hevehe-oa* in acknowledgement of the work they do in binding the *mae*, i.e. the further phase in the construction of the masks which the latest *Hevehe Karawa* has inaugurated. The pigs of the second and third category are given in exchange for ornaments (the nominal work being, so to speak, thrown in), and, if the *aukau* concerned belong to other *eravo*, will be carried off alive. They are, however, to be eaten *in* those *eravo*, by men only, and they must be carried off secretly, either by a detour through the bush or under cover of night. Woe betide any uninitiated person who sets eyes on such a pig in transit: he or she will die by sorcery, will be put 'under the *eravo*'. For ostensibly the pigs are all gifts to the *ma-hevehe* and have been taken off to sea, and the form of that pretence must be preserved. Hence the reluctance of unauthorized persons to go near the scene during these two days.

Since many of the *aukau*, however, belong to the *eravo* in which the ceremonies have taken place, there is a sufficiently large slaughter of pigs on the spot. While the younger men do the carving and cooking, using the pots which we saw stored in the back of the *eravo*, the old men have no other duty than that of blowing the shell-trumpets and beating the drums, and even this they do rather casually. The conventional movement consists of two blasts, three tattoos,

---

[1] In the corresponding ceremony, *Erimunu*, in the Purari Delta, the pig or pigs so provided are actually done to death by the party as it enters the men's house—speared, hacked with knives, and trampled on.

two blasts, three tattoes, two blasts; it is repeated at desultory intervals which grow longer as the day advances. The chief blower in this case was the aged Heveheapo, not because it was any special office of his, but because he was anxious to do things according to form and rather fancied his skill. He kept the others at it for a time, but by and by the instruments were laid aside altogether, and the orchestra gave itself up to betel, tobacco, conversation, silence, and sleep. During the afternoon I saw the two *amua*, Miki Harapa and Hitova-kore, bring into the *eravo* various select portions of pork on improvised platters of areca-spathe—small junks of the tongue and liver. Each of the *avai*, who were then sitting in the cool interior, received (in characteristically ungracious manner) a raw tit-bit in his hand; and while some put their shares aside, others poked the hearth-fires into a blaze and proceeded forthwith to grill each his own tender morsel. There is no question that the *avai* are, as they claim to be, the 'eaters'.

The binding of the *mae* was begun on the morning following *Hevehe Karawa*. The *hevehe-oa* brings masses of it from his house where he has kept it in storage, and the *aukau* proceeds to bind it on to a cord in much the same manner as a woman binds it on to the cord which encircles her waist. Various measurements of the mask are taken, and for this purpose it will be unhooked and laid on the *eravo*-floor, or even taken out into the open—a procedure which does not matter, since there are only a few people present to see it, all of them long since initiated. It is only in some cases that the binding of the *mae* is performed by the *aukau*, and he may be *aukau* of the *harehare-akore* or of the *hevehe-oa* himself: it is one of those services (and perfunctory ones at that) which are made pretexts for the pig–ornament exchange. If then there is a suitable pig on hand the *aukau* may be called in. But the *mae*-binding, like all other handiwork in connexion with the mask, is the responsibility of the *hevehe-oa*, and in most cases he does it himself, probably assisted gratuitously by other members of the *eravo*. With a hundred and more *hevehe* awaiting attention it is a long business, likely to stretch over many months at least. As each set of *mae* is finished it is rolled up and put away. The *hevehe* are not yet to receive the rich, many-coloured raiment which will do so much to set off their charms. For the present they continue to wear their rather shabby under-mantles of *koro*. But a further stage has been accomplished. They now await only the painting and befeathering of their faces.

Hypothetical Meaning of Eharo

Much of this already long chapter has been devoted to the *eharo*, and it seems worth while to spend some further time in trying to discover what they mean. Although the *eharo* in general may be distinguished from the other kinds of mask, *kovave* and *hevehe*, they do not represent a separate, self-contained cult. They appear almost solely in connexion with the *Hevehe* cycle. It is true the writer saw a number accompanying a dance which had only an indirect bearing on *Hevehe*,[1] and it is at least alleged by some that they may be prepared for dances which have no bearing on *Hevehe* at all. But nearly all dances prove to be part of the *Hevehe* cycle; and it is agreed that there are two special occasions for the *eharo*, both of which are very definite episodes of that cycle, viz. (1) the making of the new door or *dehe*, and (2) the dance preceding the final descent. At the former, which we have described, they are very numerous and heterogeneous; at the latter they are fewer and adopt specific forms. It is said that they may appear at earlier stages in the cycle also if the home *eravo* invites others to bring them. But the above-named are the two recognized occasions for their appearance. It is very often stated by informants that *eharo* belong to *Hevehe* and *Hevehe* alone, and while they may possibly appear at other times it seems that this is in general practice the case. They claim that *Eharo* is part of *Hevehe*.

It is also claimed by the oldest of living informants that the *Hevehe* cycle has always had its *eharo* (especially for the occasion of the *dehe*), though it is agreed among them that certain of the specific *eharo*, whom we shall meet later in the festivities preceding descent, are comparatively recent

---

[1] Viz. a dance brought by two other *eravo* to celebrate the extension of Hohi Ravi.

introductions from the Houra Haera of the Vailala River. It may probably be accepted as true that the *eharo* (apart from these novelties and from random appearances elsewhere) have from the beginning formed an integral factor in the *Hevehe* cycle.

The writer for a long time exercised his mind to discover their general meaning. What did they represent as a whole, and how did they fit into *Hevehe*? It is sufficiently plain that as individuals they represent various mythical objects or creatures, *aualari*. A mask surmounted by the effigy of a great bird and called *Berare* obviously represents the totemic bird of that name. Further it is found that, as with *hevehe* and *kovave*, new *eharo* may be created from time to time as the result of contact, through dreams, &c., with spiritual beings of the environment. Thus, to give a single example, a man Maii created a regular band of grasshopper *eharo* because he had been visited by four 'grasshopper men' who told him that he would fish successfully in a certain creek to which they belonged, or which belonged to them. It is true that the making of new *eharo* gives a great deal of play to creative imagination, and many are probably expressions in the main of Elema humour.[1] But individually the *eharo* seem to follow the lines of *hevehe* (and *kovave*) in representing spirits of the environment, viz. mythical characters, or *aualari*. Indeed, they do so rather more obviously in that they often carry a model of the thing represented on their heads.

There are, however, differences between the *hevehe* and the *eharo* masks more significant than those of mere form. *Hevehe* is a cult with an esoteric meaning, however confused and uncertain; *Eharo* would appear, now at any rate, to be merely an ornamental adjunct to it.

The writer pestered informants for an interpretation of the word. As usual they mostly failed to realize the intention of the question and would reiterate almost angrily that it was the name of a mask. One or two bethought themselves of another kind of *eharo*, viz. the long-legged insect that

---

[1] One of the most ingenious seen by the writer was the 'cutter' in full sail made by a man of Uaripi.

skims over the surface of stagnant pools; and this gave rise
to some extempore interpretations of the masks as a whole.
The *eharo*, it was suggested, came down in the heavy rains,
walked about on the water, and then somehow got into the
eravo whence they emerged in the form of gorgeous masks
to mystify the women. But this was plainly fanciful and
ad hoc. The derivation of the word, which is clear enough,
dawned finally on some brighter intellect. It is *e*, 'dance',
and *haro* 'head'; so that *eharo* means simply 'dance-head-
piece' or 'dance-mask'.[1]

The significant differences between *hevehe* and *eharo* masks
may be summarized as follows: (1) *Eharo* involve no initiation. Any one may make such a mask and may wear it without having paid a pig for the privilege. (2) *Eharo* involve
no pretence. The women know they are made by men;
they know that they have men inside them; and they know
who those men are. And they do not have to pretend
ignorance of these things.[2] (3) There is no ceremonial
beginning and ending of the *eharo*'s life. They are made
speedily to serve a brief moment. There is no smuggling of
the materials into the *eravo*, and when they have served their
turn the completed masks are allowed to rot. In short they
are what every one, in a bald phrase, says they are—*erau-
eharu*,[3] 'play-things'. They are *aiha-va-ka*, 'not sacred', and
are thus devoid of the danger which belongs implicitly to
sacredness. They are *maea morava eharu*, 'things of gladness'.

But while modern informants are emphatic in dismissing
the *eharo* as figures of fun, there yet remain some hints of a
deeper meaning which may serve to bring them into intelligible relationship with the *Hevehe* cycle. Thus, although
secrecy is disclaimed, there are some suggestions of it in
that the masks must be made inside the *eravo*, and their

[1] *e* is the word for dance in the sense of a massed performance. The verb is *e'idihikive*, to perform such a dance, the dancers being *idihi-vira* (dancing males).
[2] A very good description of the *Eharo* festival at Kerema is given by W. R. Humphries in *Papua, Ann. Report*, 1925–6, pp. 16–18. It is denied by Orokolo informants that women there speak to the *eharo* as Mr. Humphries describes their doing at Kerema. But a woman may publicly exclaim, as the *eharo* issues from its *eravo*, 'Here comes my brother', &c.
[3] *eharu* (distinguished from *eharo*) is the common word for 'thing'; sometimes more specifically for 'property', in especial shell ornament.

rehearsals conducted in concealment. Even in their home village the women must not see them till they emerge, full-fledged, on the eve or the day of the dance. Again, although there is no ceremonial farewell to the *eharo*, those that enter the *eravo* (having been bought with pigs) stay there and cannot be brought out again. It is true that, stripped of their valuables, they are treated like so much lumber in the *kaia larava*; but there they remain, taking up space, until with the final burning of the *hevehe* masks they are thrown with them into the flames. So that it appears there is at least a suggestion of ceremonial about the making and the disposal of these lesser masks.

The significant fact is that some of them, having been presented with a pig, enter the *eravo*; and that, as far as the village at large is concerned, those *eharo* are never seen again —or never again in the same form.

As a result of these considerations it occurs to the writer that the *eharo* may deserve a deeper interpretation than is given them by the modern native. The suggestion—which, as far as he is aware, has no support in native theory, since he has never submitted it to any native for his opinion—is as follows: that the part nowadays played by the *eharo* in the *Hevehe* cycle has degenerated from a much more significant one which they played in the past; that the festival in which they make their main appearance once constituted an integral factor in the cycle instead of being, what it nowadays amounts to, a merely decorative, frivolous by-play; that the *eharo* themselves were the representations of *aualari*, of mythical spirits of bush, river, air, and sea, who paid a visit to the village in order to leave some of their number in the *eravo*; and that these remained in the *eravo* until they eventually issued in the less graphic but more imposing form of *hevehe* masks.

Hevehe *as a Composite Cycle*

As with the one or two other hypothetical reconstructions in this book, the writer does not pin any faith to a theory that can but little affect the present meaning of the ceremonies we are dealing with. But it may serve to explain away one or two difficulties. In the first place, there is this minor question: What is supposed to happen to the *eharo* that enter the *eravo*? They are seen to enter it; they are never seen to leave it; and finally their remains are burnt with those of the *hevehe*. Presuming they really belong, as informants mostly agree in saying they do, to the *Hevehe* cycle, then it seems a possible assumption that they are in some way identified with the *hevehe* masks themselves.

But there is a much more serious difficulty which the *eharo* may help us to resolve. It has already been hinted that the whole *Hevehe* cycle as it stands to-day is a composite one, and the farther we go the more obvious that conclusion will seem. There is, on the one hand, *Hevehe Karawa* with its own initiation, and, on the other, there are the *hevehe* (i.e. *apa-hevehe*) with their initiation. It is the writer's opinion that the former represents an accretion upon the latter, the incorporation of a sea-cult with an earlier land-cult. What I presume to be the newer cult has imposed its interpretation upon the *hevehe* masks *en masse*: they are the daughters of the sea-monsters. But the results of our examination of the individual masks, their names and associations, point in the opposite direction—to the bush. This might be enough to indicate the mixed character of the whole cycle. But in order to clinch the argument that it is a blend of sea-cult and land-cult, we may reveal in anticipation the fact that when it comes to the final disposal of the *hevehe* they are actually bidden farewell, in two separate ceremonies, one for each direction—first to the bush, and then to the sea.

As for the question of priority, there is, in the first place, positive evidence that *Hevehe Karawa* in its present form is a relatively late introduction; and there is presumptive evidence, in the second place, that the actual masks, i.e. *apa-hevehe*, once belonged to a cycle of ceremonies concerned with the bush alone.[1] It is, therefore, I believe, a reasonable

---

[1] In the Purari Delta *Aiaimunu*, the counterpart of *apa-hevehe*, appears to have been a 'bush' cult only. *Erimunu*, the counterpart of *Hevehe Karawa*, is recognized there as a recent introduction. It has not reached Iari, the large tribe of the Purari Delta which lies a little farther inland. Here *Aiaimunu* continues to be a purely 'bush' cult. The masks *aiaimunu* (lit. 'drum-*imunu*') represent *irimunu*, i.e. supernatural creatures of the trees (*iri*).

assumption that the bush element in the *Hevehe* cycle is the earlier; and it is to this presumably earlier stratum that the *eharo* appear to belong.

If, then, the *hevehe* formerly represented bush spirits rather than sea spirits, what was the fiction by which they were introduced into the *eravo*? It is conjectured that it may have been carried out by means of the *eharo*, which would thus have played a part of real significance in the cycle.

But once more, right or wrong, it does not matter. So long as *Hevehe* continues, and perhaps long after the cycle as a whole has died its death—if that must happen—the Orokolo natives will continue to make these *eharo*, without worrying their heads concerning their significance. They will continue to make them as *erau-eharu*, their playthings; and let us hope they will continue to feel *maea-morava* in doing so.

XIX

PRELIMINARY DESCENTS

NOW that the door has been made and the binding of the *mae* is under way, the *hevehe* are almost ready for their public appearance. But it remains to repair, paint, and befeather them, and each of these operations is made the occasion of a great united effort, a working-bee which involves all those immediately concerned as well as many visitors. Since there is no room for all to work inside, the masks are on each occasion brought out into the open, the uninitiated being of course warned to absent themselves. There are thus three preliminary descents:

1. *Avaha Haipuravakive*, 'Stretching the Backs'.
2. *Biai Huaukive*, 'Rainbow Painting'.
3. *Orikoro Huhakive*, 'Binding on the Feathers'.

These are described as they were seen at Avavu Ravi. The first took place on 17 December 1931; the second and third on 7 and 8 February 1932, being quickly followed (10 February) by the full ceremonial emergence.

The Hevehe *Stretch their Backs* (*First Descent*)

The phrase *Avaha Haipuravakive* is a fanciful one serving to disguise the practical nature of the proceedings, or at least to maintain a suitable pretence before the womenfolk. They are to suppose that the *hevehe*, cramped with sitting so long in the *eravo*, have now come out to straighten or stretch their backs. The women of course are under no misapprehension. They have gone off early in the morning to fish or make sago, or have merely moved a hundred yards away to pass the time with their neighbours of Ovarova. These latter might easily, if they wished, see through the newly erected screens of coco-nut fronds which, thrown across either end of the village, are meant in a perfunctory way to hide the mysteries; but when I drew attention to this circumstance the men treated it as a joke. All that need be said is that the women, if they still feel any curiosity, are very careful not to show it.

Rows of bamboo poles (*keko*) have been set upright in the ground before the *eravo*, each with a small branch left near the tip to serve as a hook; and now by 7.30 all the masks needing attention (and there are few exceptions) have been brought outside. No ceremony is observed except that a group of old men, sitting on the ground, beat drums and blow the shell-trumpet from time to time: the women in the distance are to understand that the *hevehe* are taking their exercise, beating their own drums as they do so. Thus one after another the masks are brought out horizontally through the small doorway, up-ended, and attached to the hooks on the *keko*.

Reduplicate Initiations

Before the actual work is commenced there are a number of 'initiations' to perform.[1] The 'candidates' are the *harehare-akore* of various masks now hanging on the *keko*; but in each case the person concerned has been through it all before. It has been pointed out that an individual may pass through several cycles as *harehare-akore*, but on each occasion he goes through the form of initiation afresh.[2] On the *Avaha* day, then, the initiations are all second-hand and involve no surprises for the candidates. There are many other *harehare-akore* who have not yet been initiated; but their time is to come, and to-day they are not present.

The form of initiation consists in placing the mask on the candidate's head; and this serves also the practical purpose of a trial or fitting. The young men are first girdled about with their *hopa*, which constitutes their underwear so to speak, and then the great structure of the mask is hoisted up and lowered on to their shoulders. Some old man (an elderly kinsman of the candidate's *aukau*, if not the *aukau* himself) stands by till the youth has gained his balance and settled

---

[1] Initiation to *Apa-hevehe* has been distinguished from initiation to *Hevehe Karawa*, see p. 216.

[2] Some of these reduplicate initiations take place independently inside the *eravo* at an earlier date, the *aukau* of the *harehare-akore* being invited to a small feast. Some of them will take place later, on the Painting and Feather Days.

himself comfortably, which he does very soon with an expert shuffle or two, as if eager to be off; whereupon the old man beats out the particular rhythm which belongs to that *hevehe* and hands over the drum. Then, beating time for himself, the *harehare-akore* dances for the first time in his mask. He has already had some private schooling in his part, and he manages with surprising skill (at least it came as a surprise to the writer, who had never seen a *hevehe* actually worn until this moment). Making use of the lower projection, viz. the *hara*, which, although not seen, reaches between his thighs, he can fully control the heavy super-structure, and that with small appearance of effort. His body has disappeared beneath the mantle of bast-strips; only his muscular forearms and calves are visible, the former vigo-rously at work on the drum, the latter nimbly skipping and stamping under a gigantic figure perhaps 20 feet tall—truly a portentous sight! The largest of all the masks were on this occasion balanced by long ribbons of bast, held, like streamers from a may-pole, by four watchful attendants. But such precautions were not necessary later on, when the *hevehe* were really out and about; and although I have some-times seen the tall masks stagger alarmingly, I have never seen one fall.

The *harehare-akore* is meanwhile dancing to a perfect orchestra of declamation—mostly abusive—on the part of the *aukahura* and any others who care to join in. We shall meet with some further examples of the maternal uncle's harangue later on. It is enough at this moment to note one or two typical incidents. Thus I noticed particularly a man named Tahia whose performance was greeted with shouts of applause from his fellow villagers of Yogu. But these were by way of counterblast to the recriminations heaped upon him by his kinsmen of Orokolo, where he originally belonged; they were calling him a slacker and a deserter. The old man Mahevehe, who led the attack, finally appealed to the other side to abate their praises, or Tahia under his mask would grow bashful; and this piece of good-natured satire brought the dancer's ordeal to a close. Shortly after-wards Mahevehe, who had got his blood up, delivered a violent speech, an interlude in the proceedings, which received more attention than is usually given to such outbursts. The people round about, he declared, had been stealing his pigs, and so he had none ready to kill for this occasion. But when it was all over they would see his retaliation: he would sorcerize everybody's pigs and they would die as if stricken by the plague. Such a threat as this might well have provoked consternation, but none seemed to take it in full seriousness, and in a moment all were busy again with the matter in hand, a number of initiations proceeding simultaneously.

These done with, the masks were taken down from the *keko* and laid out on improvised tables, about waist-high, and the work of the day commenced. Ostensibly it should consist only in the making and embroidering of the *avaha*;[1] but some required the wicker framework, *arara*; and many had rents on their *pura* to be mended. The general object of the working-bee is to bring all the masks up to scratch for the next stage, that of painting. And even this may be anticipated: Horevuhu was exhorting the workers to get on with the painting now, so as not to be rushed at the last moment.[2]

In the meantime pigs had been killed to feast the guests, and the usual two, provided by the Drum-Leaders, were formally put aside for the *avai*. Not that these pampered old men are capable of eating two whole pigs between them; they merely get the best, and as much as they want. It is good policy to send your elderly guests away in a state of repletion, and on this particular afternoon I met Heveheapo on his way home in that condition. He was a lean old man and not always very cordial; but now he patted a stomach visibly distended and, in high good humour, addressed me in the following cryptic words: 'The sea has no mouth; the birds have no mouth; nothing else has a mouth—only the old men!' I did not think it the right moment to press for explication, but he later revealed his meaning as follows: 'It was nonsense to say that the pigs were given to the

---

[1] See p. 242.

[2] These final stages, viz. making the backs, painting, and befeathering, are not introduced by *Hevehe Karawa* and so may be done in advance.

PLATE 38

A *Harehare-Akore* dancing in his mask on the *Avaha* day

The mask is an *Ahea* specimen, especially large. It is not yet painted or
furnished with *mae*

hevehe, or that they were eaten by birds or crocodiles or any other creatures. It was the old men who ate them.'

But while the *avai* were taking their ease in the *eravo* all the others had been busy on the masks, and by four in the afternoon the last of them had been carried in again. The *keko* were uprooted, the holes trampled over, and the rubbish hastily cleared away. Then the women began to return to the village and set to work on cooking for the feast which was to follow the presentation of Ginger Leaf and Coco-nut Spoons.

Ginger Leaf and Coco-nut Spoons

It is almost sundown before the pots are ready. Men carry them from their houses, piping hot (with wrappers of green leaf to protect their arms), and set them down in an orderly row before the *eravo*. Behind them at intervals a number of sticks have been planted in the ground, and to each of these is attached a bundle of coco-nut spoons and ginger leaves. The spoons (*arita*) are those smoothly polished and often well-carved little implements of coco-nut shell with which the Elema native ladles his food into his mouth; and each of those now provided has attached to it a loop of plaited sago-leaf, dyed red, as well as a few roots and green leaves of ginger (*upi*). They make very pretty little favours which are now to be bestowed on the *harehare-akore* by their *aukau*. Every *harehare-akore*, whether previously initiated or not, should be present to receive his gift.

Quite a throng of people have assembled to witness this simple rite, and the *harehare-akore* fall into some sort of line facing the pots. There are a few blasts on the shell-trumpet, and the *aukau* proceed to their business. Each slips the loop over his *arivu*'s head, or, if it is too tight a fit, simply gives the spoon into his hand; then, if the spirit moves him, he utters the usual avuncular warnings. The *harehare-akore* range from married men down to children of three. One elderly man may be heard shouting into the uncomprehending ears of such a little boy: 'Don't eat coco-nut; don't eat meat; chew this ginger; and by and by you will shoot many birds and pigs.' And then the same old man turns to address the *harehare-akore* at large: they must forgo all intercourse with women, not even touch them or look at their bodies (by the last he means that they should avoid temptation); and he goes on shouting other instructions, his voice little heeded amid the general conversation.

The bestowal of *upi* and *arita* is the finale of the day. It is the beginning of a lenten period for all the *harehare-akore*; for henceforward they are to eat neither coco-nut, fish, nor meat, but only *mahea* (boiled sago), bananas, taro, and sweet potato; and they may neither associate with women nor wash themselves with water. The purpose of these tabus is twofold: first, it is to make the initiates 'light', so that they may wear their masks well; and second (somewhat obscurely), it is to ensure that the precious feathers, which are now to be got ready for the *hevehe*, will remain in good preservation. The *harehare-akore* are given the spoons for their exclusive use since their diet is now to be mainly *uahea*, and it is risky to use another's (which is the friendly fashion of the Elema) because it may be contaminated by the forbidden foods. Their *upi* will serve to neutralize the weakening effects of fasting and, more positively, to make them 'hot' and strong. As for the tabus on intercourse and the use of water, these are to prevent the 'heaviness' which may result from either kind of indulgence.[1]

All these restrictions are to help the *harehare-akore* get themselves in training for the ceremonial emergence. How they are expected to preserve the feathers from insects or other agents of harm is far from clear; but it is certain that the minds of all are much exercised on this point, and the two *harehare-akore* of the leading *hevehe* go into a kind of seclusion for the express purpose, as if to give them an example of immobility. For the next six weeks or so they should remain largely in the *eravo*, resting as much as possible so that the feathers may not be disturbed.

The Song Adidiavu

The work of binding these feathers in tufts, &c., for attachment to the masks will only begin on the day following

[1] Though other reasons are also given—they may lead to sores or ill success in pig-hunting.

PLATE 39

Duru, one of the Drum-Leaders, at work on his mask, *Avaha* day. The picture illustrates the *arara* and the under-mantle of bast (*koro*)

the *upi* presentation, and almost the whole intervening night is spent in singing the song *Adidiavu*. It is one of those which belong traditionally to *Hevehe*, so that it may be perhaps regarded as part of the cycle. But it may be said in advance that, except in its few opening words, it has defied all my attempts to find in it any relevance to the main proceedings. The following, therefore, is admittedly an excursion: *Adidiavu* is treated as a typical example of Elema song.

The leader, or *hivi-haro-haera*, was in this case Idave of Hohoro. He was the only man available who knew the song well enough, and even he was confessedly ignorant of the meaning of much of what he sang; for *Adidiavu* belongs to the Houra Haera, and is in a dialect different from that of Orokolo. Idave had picked it up at a village in the Vailala bush, viz. that of his *aukau*, having learnt it by constant practice in the *eravo*. The old man who taught him had told him to take it to his village, and Idave had answered timidly that if he were 'hard' inside he would forget. But happily he proved 'soft', and on a subsequent occasion in Orokolo was able to assist and even correct a singer who had been imported for the occasion from the Vailala hinterland. Since that time his reputation had been assured. The significant point is that *Adidiavu*, which belongs to the *Hevehe* cycle of the Western Elema in that it is traditionally sung at this stage (and the following one, of painting), is yet in a foreign dialect. It is the common practice to invite bush people to lead the singing as *hivi-haro-haera*, and the local chorus has only a vague idea of what the words mean.

Adidiavu is sung inside the *eravo*, sitting, and without the drum. Like other such songs it is divided into an endless number of stanzas which are first sung by the precentor and then repeated by the chorus who sit round him. As we saw with *Yahe*, the content of the whole song is a myth, or series of myths, which together attain to epic length, since the singing goes on intermittently till morning.

The first few stanzas do seem to have some connexion with the matter in hand, viz. that of binding the feathers into sprigs, or *love*. They refer to some tale of Laia, daughter of Obo, the python; and my informants, struggling with the strange, and probably archaic, words, discovered references to red *love*, yellow *love*, combing the hair, fitting the hornbill feather on its prong, whittling down the quill to make it flutter, and so on; and there is some figurative description of birds flocking about a tree which is understood to refer to the women who later on will flock as dancers round the *eravo*.

But there the connexion seems to end. The song goes on (at any rate according to Idave's version) to tell the tale of Aruaru and Lauape, elder brother and younger, the latter of whom had married the two girls Dive and Lauve. Aruaru, jealous of his younger brother, induces him to climb a certain tree, and then by magic makes it grow so tall that he is unable to descend. Thus having got rid of him he is in a position to appropriate his wives. But the girls are led to the tree by Lauape's faithful dog, Behoa (to whose neck they have attached a long string), and seeing their husband, already almost starved, in the top of it, they turn themselves into two tall trailing palms and thus climb up to him. Lauape is brought safely down and nursed to recovery, but all the time kept hidden from his brother. At last he has regained sufficient strength to shoot an arrow through the trunk of a banana (this by way of testing himself), and so lays a plot with the girls for his revenge. They are to invite Aruaru to submit to a lousing. He falls into the trap; and while he sits with bent head, enjoying the sensation of the girls' fingers searching for parasites in his hair, the younger brother steals on him unawares and shoots him through. The story ends with Lauape weeping over the death of the man he has murdered.

This is merely a chapter in a highly disjointed saga. Other stories follow with complete change of scene and characters; and though I have pursued them at some length I can discover no connexion between them nor any relevance to *Hevehe* as a whole.

After the night's singing the binding of the feathers begins. As highly valued material they have been stored in the *haie ruru*, envelopes of palm spathe, against the ravages of insects. Now they are brought out and tied onto small

PLATE 40

Idave, the Song-Leader

prongs so as to form the *love*, pretty tufts of cockatoo and parrot feathers which will be attached as fringes to the masks. The binding is a long, slow business, and once again the work is nominally done by the *aukau* of the *harehare-akore*. As they are finished the *love* will be tied in bundles and put aside against the day when they will all be affixed to the masks.

The Painting Day (*Second Descent*)

The ensuing seven weeks were spent in busy preparation —mainly food-getting—for the series of ceremonies which constitute the climax of the cycle. When all was ready the masks made their second preliminary descent, this time for the Painting, *Biai Huaukuve*, which may be translated 'Rainbow-Painting'.[1]

Once more the women left the village, all going off in a body to the Aivei with their triangular fish-nets. The *keko* poles were erected and barricades of palm-leaf again hid Harelareva from the next *karigara*.

On this occasion the masks descended somewhat more ceremoniously. At about 7 a.m. a man took his stand in the centre of the open space before the *eravo* and swung a bull-roarer—and this was the only occasion on which I ever heard the sound of that instrument in connexion with the cycle. Its possible bearing on the significance of *Hevehe* has already been discussed;[2] but the insignificance of the part which it plays in the cycle is enough to show that, now at any rate, the two cults are mutually independent. We may perhaps be satisfied with the practical explanation which is offered by the men—the awful voice of the *be'ure hevehe* is merely intended to frighten the uninitiated out of sight and hearing. The fiction which, in typical fashion, is superimposed on this, as on other actions in the cycle, may or may not throw light on its original meaning, but it has no

---

[1] This interpretation is my own. *Huaukuve* means to lay on paint with a brush, and *biai* means rainbow (also a mythological name for a great snake). But no natives, despite my repeated inquiries, could think of a meaning for the expression *biai-huaukuve*. They seem to have one-track minds when it comes to a question of derivations: if asked for the meaning of a word, a name, or an expression, they find it difficult to go beyond the immediate context.   [2] See pp. 205–6.

intelligible bearing on the theory of *Hevehe* as it now stands. This fiction, which the women and children are supposed to accept, is that the bull-roarer, *be'ure hevehe*, is now calling on its 'younger brothers', i.e. the masks, or *apa-hevehe*, to come forth into the open.

The sound of the bull-roarer was accompanied by a rattle of drums, beaten by the old men sitting inside the *eravo*, and now the masks began to come out horizontally, one after another. The biggest of them, the *Ahea hevehe* named Kawabu, was borne by four men and hoisted upright only with difficulty, while a fifth had to climb the *keko* in order to hook it on to the projecting branch at the top. Yet this apparently unmanageable structure was to be carried by one dancer, and in the vertical position he would somehow contrive to balance it. Another of the masks fell to the ground as its owner was struggling to hook it on to the *keko*, a mishap which drew cries of consternation from all sides. But as they were accompanied by so much laughter it was plain that the consternation was only affected.

Soon all were at work on painting the masks, laid out on improvised branches, a score or so at a time. They had long since been smeared roughly with paint, showing how the maker wished it applied. Now they were completely repainted in fresh colours and hung up to dry as they were finished. It was a busy, quiet morning, relieved now and again by jokes and banter. The sun grew fiercely hot, and shelters of palm-leaf had to be run up to shield the workers. But they stuck to their task (for this was the last opportunity of getting it done), holding their rough coco-nut-shell palettes in one hand and wielding in the other the tiny brushes of areca husk, crushed and frayed at the ends.

The deserted *eravo* was strangely empty. Innumerable long rattan canes dangled from the roof, each with its hook at the end for suspending a *hevehe*. It was as if the great gloomy space were filled with giant cobwebs; and everywhere, to increase the untidiness, there lay to-morrow's feathers, in bundles, rolls, or tied to long strips of cane. One lonely *hevehe* remained amid this scene of desolation while all its fellows were being bedizened for the forth-

PLATE 41

Members of the *Avai* drumming while the painting is in progress

The masks laid out for painting

coming gaieties. It was that of a man named Hapeha who had died four years previously. Some other might have taken it over as *hevehe-oa*, but Hapeha had no brothers; and to make matters worse the *harehare-akore* for whom it was made had also died, so that the mask, doubly bereaved, remained without a claimant. It was said to be 'dead'. Thus the 123rd *hevehe* never saw the light of day until, at the end of the cycle, it was taken out with its fellows to be burnt.

Meantime the work went steadily on, each mask, finished and dried, being carried in and hung up without ceremony. By five o'clock the village was clear; the *keko* were once more removed and word was sent to the women that they might return.

There were no further special activities during the evening and night. Avavu Ravi was very quiet. When I visited it at about nine in the evening I found the old man Haio sitting in a corner of the *oropa larava* busily engaged by the dim light of a trade hurricane lamp in sewing dogs' teeth onto an *erekai* belt: he was preparing a ceremonial gift for a kinsman. Two other old men were talking over a fire in the rear. But otherwise the building was silent and in darkness. When I remembered its vacancy in the morning, it was a wonderful revelation to shoot the beam of an electric torch into its upper regions. The apparently empty blackness was suddenly thronged with the faces of *hevehe*: long white ovals, patterned in colour, with their great round eyes and gaping jaws, they hung in dense array, crowding the building. Outside, in a dark night, the *eravo* towered enormous among the coco-nut palms. One or two fires threw their flickering light on its tall façade, but the village was mostly dark and probably asleep. Only from Waiea Ravi and Ori Ravi in the distance came the hoarse voices of those who were singing *Adidiavu* and intended to make a night of it.

The Feather Day (Third Descent)

The following morning there was a slight threat of rain and nobody seemed in a hurry to begin work. But presently a few masks made their appearance, and it was then that I first saw Haio in one of his angry moods. It appeared that they had been carried down prematurely, without the appropriate drum-beating, and the old man opened out in full volume on the offenders. Drums were speedily procured and the remainder of the *hevehe* were carried down in proper style.

It is worth noting a small inconsistency in the use of drums at these preliminary descents. As we have observed, it is part of the pretence that the *hevehe*, during these descents, beat their own drums; and yet they are supposed to have none. We shall see later that the drum is the last item in the equipment which they receive by a series of gifts from the *ma-hevehe*, and the time for this ultimate gift is not yet. But this is a minor point, and on the whole it may be claimed that the inconsistencies in the cycle are remarkably few.

The business of the day is the attachment of the feathers, mainly in the form of *love*, or sprigs, to the masks. The full decorative splendour of the *hevehe* is not achieved until this last moment when it is bordered and lined down the centre with these white or multi-coloured feathers of cockatoo, parrot, and hawk; and it is only now that the brilliant mantles of sago-leaf are brought out of their wrappings and draped upon the frameworks. When at about 3 p.m. the work was over and the *hevehe* replaced in the *eravo* they were ready in all their finery for the ceremonial emergence.

Initiation of Novices

There now followed the real initiation to *apa hevehe* which we have had occasion to mention several times in advance. The performance described on p. 294 was really no more than a perfunctory repetition: the *harehare-akore* who then donned the masks already knew the secret. Now it was intended to initiate a number of boys who had never been through the ceremony before and who believed, ostensibly, that the *hevehe* were living creatures.

The characteristic cheering or hooting known as *yakea* announced the approach of the novices and their escorts of *aukahura* from the eastern end, and several masks were hurriedly carried towards the palm-leaf barrier to be hidden behind the houses near by. The remainder still hung on the *keko*, and the approaching party must have been able to see them pretty obviously through the palm-leaves. (Secrecy and surprise effect are not managed so carefully here as in the initiation to *Kovave*.)[1]

Every one flocked to meet the novices, and when their escorts, tearing down the palm-leaves, burst their way through the barrier, the boys had to run the gauntlet of a large crowd. The men who had brought forward the few light masks to be used for the purpose sprang out of their hiding and clapped them roughly and clumsily on the heads of two or three of the *harehare-akore*; and many of the by-standers who had armed themselves with light sticks gave the boys some fairly harmless and good-humoured strokes as they passed through. All were jostled along at speed, the bigger lads unperturbed or actually enjoying it; the smaller ones quite overwhelmed by the uproar, some of them in tears; and the smallest, riding on their *aukaus'* shoulders, wondering with wide eyes what it was all about. Each initiate carried a *hapa* in his hand with junks of cooked pork as a present to the *aukau* who had led him to the scene; but before they had time to hand them over, the cheers of the party approaching from the opposite direction drew the crowd to the barrier on that side.[2] Here the second band of novices met with the same rowdy welcome, and then without further delay all those concerned gave themselves to the business of trying on the masks.

The first to be brought forward was 'Pekeaupe', that of Aori the Drum-Leader on the left (or Vailala) side. The *harehare-akore* was his true younger brother Hareho. The pair of them stepped into the centre, but in answer to shouts from the crowd moved back to a more formal position, just in front of the *eravo* on the left side. Hareho put on his own *hopa* underskirt, and then Aori (the *hevehe-oa*) assisted him, not without a good deal of effort on the part of both, to get the mask on to his head. Having got his balance, the

---

[1] See p. 142.
[2] The initiates enter the village from east or west according as their masks belong to the Vailala or Aivei sides of the *eravo*.

harehare-akore was handed a drum by the *hevehe-oa*, and immediately began to beat the appropriate rhythm and to dance.

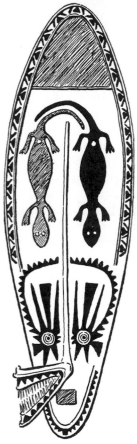

FIG. 18. 'Koraia', Duru's Mask

(black and yellow lizards, *Kaia aualari*)

Since Pekeaupe was one of those divided *hevehe*, with *Purari* designs on one side and *Nabo* on the other, Hareho beat the appropriate rhythms in turn.

The next mask was that of Duru, the Drum-Leader on the right side. The *harehare-akore* in this case was his own young son, who danced bravely while the mask was supported on either side, his small legs moving briskly to the *Kaia* rhythm beaten by his *aukau*.

Both these initiations had been watched by a wide circle—publicity or attention is the Drum-Leader's reward; but as soon as they were finished the onlookers broke up into a number of small groups each surrounding a novice and his mask. The open space was soon filled with *hevehe* careering in all directions, with narrowly averted collisions. The young wearers had some difficulty in balancing the masks, but by dint of swift turns in the direction of fall they somehow managed to do so; and if any seemed to be toppling the bystanders rushed to their assistance. The smallest of the novices made no attempt to dance. They merely stood beneath the folds of the *mae* mantles while these were trimmed, the mask being worn meanwhile by an adult.

The Maternal Uncle's Harangue

All this activity was accompanied by a babel of praise and blame—the harangues of the *aukau* and of any others who

PLATE 42

Entry of the novices

felt inspired to vent their feelings. I always made a point of noting down what I could of such harangues while they were in progress and of getting the speakers to amplify them later: they throw some interesting sidelights on the Elema idea of what's what.

Now, for instance, we hear Duru singing the praises of an adult dancer from Arihava: he is always ready to help; he has worked hard in the building of Avavu Ravi, fetched timber, lent his canoe, and so on. He compares well, says Duru, with some other Arihava men, who are happy to see a *Hevehe* in Orokolo and take the chance of getting their sons initiated, but themselves do nothing to help. (Thus in the midst of praising the dancer Duru contrives to let some of the visitors know what he thinks of them.)

Another is praising Aori.[1] He is a strong man; all the others are lazy in comparison. He, and his wife too, they have fed the *eravo* men till their bellies were full. Look, see how he can dance! A strong man, that! (Although so highly laudatory, this speech is given in the violent manner favoured by Elema orators, accompanied by furious, threatening gestures, and driven home with the actions of a bowman shooting his victim through and through.)

Here a *hevehe-oa* is addressing his younger brother in the mask. 'Dance well!' he cries; and, pointing to the *eravo*, 'This is our *eravo*; mine and yours; our *ive* posts, our work. These others' (referring to the visitors) 'are strangers. The credit is ours. Dance well!' (This theme was touched on by a number of the haranguers, viz. that of pride in achievement and reflection on those other villages which, having thrown away both *Hevehe* and *eravo*, were glad enough to see the festival in Orokolo.)

More usually, however, the addresses tend towards invective, not by any means savage, but none the less intended to take effect. So we hear a man upbraiding his *arivu*, a mere lad, calling him a lazy boy, always lying down, and a sponge. 'When your mother scolds you, you come running to me,

---

[1] A man may be *hevehe-oa* to one mask and *harehare-akore* to another. In this connexion Aori is dancing as a *harehare-akore*.

your *aukau*, and eat my food. When I mention work, you run back to your mother and eat hers.'

Another is fulminating against a fellow member of Avavu Ravi. He is not seen often enough in the *eravo*, and he is a shirker. Whenever there is work on hand he fades from view, goes and sleeps in his house. But now that the *hevehe* are coming down he is making merry with those who have borne the burden. Another is abusing a youth from Vailala: 'When we pass your village you do nothing to entertain us; you slip off and leave it to others, and you never think of lending us a canoe to cross the river.'

So the chorus of reproach swells louder as the number of dancers increases. It is in truth doubtful whether many of these sarcastic arrows penetrate the covering of the *hevehe* mask; the wearer is probably so busy in keeping it upright and remembering his steps that he hardly hears what is said. I heard two men roundly abusing a young fellow, by name Horeakore. Again the charge was laziness and absence from the *eravo*. He had gone off to live in one of the hamlets. He was always to be seen on the beach, but in the men's house never. Was he a strong man? Yes, at sexual intercourse no doubt, but not when it came to work! Meanwhile Horeakore was dancing in the most spirited fashion, managing his mask and drum with great skill. I marked particularly the liveliness with which he moved, as if the *hevehe* itself were something animated and irrepressible; and later one of my boys told me he had heard the two haranguers say jokingly to their victim, 'Well, did you hear what we said about you?'; to which he had answered, 'I took no notice of you. The *hevehe* heard all that. I heard nothing'. But whether the harangues find effect upon the *harehare-akore* or not, they at least provide a salutary means of airing personal opinions. Such occasions as these are the safety-valves through which the Elema let off their superfluous steam of feelings.

Having finished his dance each *harehare-akore* had his mantle of *mae* trimmed to suitable length. Most stood on improvised mats of plaited coco-nut leaf so that the remnants (*edoroba*) could more easily be gathered up; for no traces of base human handiwork should be left for the

PLATE 43

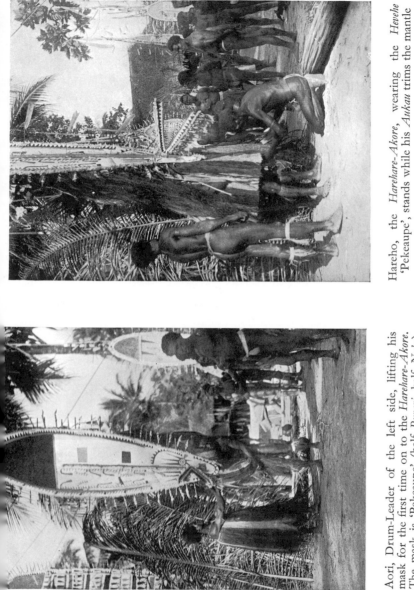

Aori, Drum-Leader of the left side, lifting his mask for the first time on to the *Harehare-Akore*. The mask is 'Pekeaupe' (half *Purari*, half *Nabo*). Note the *hopa*, or underskirt of sago-leaf

Hareho, the *Harehare-Akore*, wearing the *Hevehe* 'Pekeaupe', stands while his *Aukau* trims the mantle

women to see. Some of the boys took handfuls themselves as material for the armlets and leglets which they were to wear on a state appearance the following day; the remainder, a considerable mass, was collected and stowed in the *eravo*, where it was to remain until at the end of the cycle it should be ceremonially disposed of. Finally, as each mask was finished it was carried back to the *eravo*, where a long queue of them had mounted up, all waiting their turn to enter the little door.

Bathe of the Harehare-akore

It was nearly sundown by the time the village was clear and the women permitted to return, but there was no rest for the *harehare-akore*. Their next duty was to cross the creek and bring in the great logs and other timbers which had been made ready and left at some distance in the bush. These were the materials of the *papaita* or ramp, some 8 feet broad and 20 feet long, which leads obliquely from the *eravo*-veranda to the ground.[1] It is to be covered with transverse flooring of palm-wood, and will furnish a broad highway for the *hevehe*. Solidly made but pleasantly springy, it must stand some rough usage; and its construction calls for the magical supervision of the *kariki haera*, or *eravo* architect. In this case, since Ere was ill, his younger son Morea deputized for him. Far more experienced hands were responsible for the actual work, but Morea had his essential part to play in laying the first and bottom-most of the transverse boards. I never asked him for his magic and, knowing him, feel fairly sure he would not have told me if I had. But it probably had to do with the *papaita-ipive-uvari*, the 'Old Lady under the Stairs'.

While this work was going forward by the light of lamps and torches something much more exciting had attracted the attention of the village. No sooner had the *harehare-akore*, arriving in a body before the *eravo*, dropped the timbers from their shoulders, than with one mind and one voice, raised in a resounding cheer, they raced down and plunged

---

[1] The ordinary *papaita* is a mere ladder. For *Hevehe* (in the *eravo* proper) and for *Kovave* (in *baupa eravo*) this is replaced by a ramp by which the masked men come and go.

into the sea. Well might they cheer, for this was the first time they had entered the water, or even allowed water to touch their bodies, since they received the ginger and coconut spoons seven weeks before! The girls had been drawn up waiting for them, and now, adding their shrill, delighted shouts to the uproar, they entered the water at the same moment. All that could be seen from the shore was a closely packed mass, a dark patch which seemed to float, not without a great deal of splashing, on the calm surface of the water. Then the shouts and shrieks of laughter began to give place to those concerted cries, *yakea*, in which the Elema excel. Perhaps 300 voices were raised in a long-drawn musical cry, bell-like and of great volume. One after another these cries rose and died away, immensely magnified examples of the sort of noise a crowd of Elema natives make when they are raising an *eravo*-post or hauling a dugout through the forest.

Now the bathers were making for the shore, chattering, laughing, and shouting. The men were working on the *papaita* with what seemed like feverish speed, while some one led a group of singers in *Hurava Hakare*, for the moment to sing this song, which belongs to the later stages of the cycle, had now arrived. It was a more than usually solemn performance, delivered with fine sonority and almost declamatory in places, but dying away to a melancholy close as if the singers were ready to weep their eyes out. It would be hard to imagine a grosser *mésalliance* between words and music than that which joined this impressive chant to its ribald and highly obscene subject-matter.[1]

The Fire-Fight

The bathers, men, boys, and girls, were seen gathering for a moment about the bright fires by which the scene was illuminated. They seemed to be drying themselves, and as they did so they joined spontaneously in the chorus which rose to tremendous power. But they had something else in view, and this was merely an interlude. All were arming

[1] See p. 338.

PLATE 44

General scene: the novices trying on their masks

themselves with bunches of dry, inflammable coco-nut leaves, one in each hand, in readiness for the Fire-Fight.

Now they divided themselves into two parties according as they were associated with the east and west sides of the *eravo*, and faced each other across the fifty yards open space directly in front of it. Across this space a rough hurdle of bamboo poles had been hastily run up while the bathe was still in progress, and it now stood as a very flimsy frontier between the two forces.

Suddenly on the east side all the torches seem to flare up simultaneously, and a moment later those on the west also, making perhaps 200 in all. The foremost on either side dash forward and shatter their torches on the hurdle, so that they seem to burst in a shower of sparks. Reinforcements charge in regardless. In a moment the barrier is broken down and the two sides mingle in a welter of flames and flying sparks. They pursue one another round and about with screams of laughter, striking, dodging, and clashing their weapons together, while lighted torches, flung spear-fashion from the hand, travel through the darkness in blazing arcs, like meteors. For a few minutes the battle rages in the village, and then with one consent the combatants turn on to the broader spaces of the beach and the black distance is soon alive with darting and circling points of fire. Meanwhile the village constables have been blowing their whistles in a well-meant effort to restore order, though happily they are completely disregarded and their shrill blasts only succeed in adding a frolicsome tribute to the revels. But in a few minutes more the thing is all over. The remaining torches are dashed out on the sands, and all return to the village.

The Presentation of Fire

This delightfully spontaneous display of fireworks is known as *A-mare*, *Puo-mare*, 'Fire-fight, Sparks-fight'; and it is possibly to be viewed as a last ritual licence in the use of this dangerous element. For now the participants, or some of them, were to receive at the hands of their *aukau* a formal gift of fire together with appropriate warnings as to its use. All the *harehare-akore* in fact who had not under-gone the rite previously were to line up for the presenta-tion now.

It took place in front of the *eravo* amid a large throng of people. The candidates came forward in fairly rapid succes-sion, a number being dealt with simultaneously at different centres in the crowd. In most cases a *hara*, or rough screen of coco-nut leaf, was held over the boy's head so as to shield him. His *aukau* struck the edge of the *hara* with a burning coco-nut-leaf torch, and thus the candidate received a very light dose of sparks, though enough in one or two cases to make him flinch. Others had to do without the protection of the mat: the *aukau* passed the torch over his nephew as he stood, and then, by striking him on the crown, caused the sparks to fall in a shower on the farther side. But all came off very lightly. In some cases the torch was merely passed round them, from one hand to the other.

Having in this perfunctory manner inflicted a little pain on his *arivu* in order to show him what fire feels like (though having just passed through the *a-mare*, *puo-mare* he should know well enough), the *aukau* hands him a burning brand, makes him a present of a shell ornament, and reads him a brief lecture. The gift is not a large one: it may be a single pearl-shell crescent or armshell, but on this occasion it conventionally takes the form of a multiple shell wristlet (*maipairi*). This may be an effective ornament; but since it is made of fragments or of small shells, valueless in them-selves, it is not held in high esteem.[1] Needless to say it is recompensed with a gift of pork, though this payment is deferred until the following day when the pigs are to be killed.

The lecture is in most cases as perfunctory as the ordeal of sparks; but if we construct a composite record from the many that were noted down as heard on this occasion, its terms are something as follows—and not wholly relevant to the matter of fire: 'Steal no woman belonging to another man; do not kill another man's pig; do not steal the belong-

[1] It is interesting to note its resemblance to a bow-bracer, from which it may well be derived.

ings he has left in the *eravo*; do not take the food from his garden. Be good to the aged and the infirm in the *eravo*; never abuse them; when you bring in coco-nuts and betel, give them some.' Then, adverting more closely to the

Fig. 19. *Maipairi*, Multiple shell wristlets

matter in hand, 'Take care lest you set fire to another man's garden. And when you go into the *eravo*, bring your own firestick. Don't take it from another man's hearth, but from your own house. If you are accused of stealing fire, mention my name; say, "My *aukau* gave me fire; I have no need to steal it." Or if another steals fire from your hearth, say to him, "Did your *aukau* never give you fire, that you come thieving from me?" '

The general purpose of this whole episode may be to instil into the young a salutary notion of the power and danger of fire. Considering the combustible nature of the village some training of the sort is assuredly necessary, and it may be assumed that Elema children are brought up from their earliest years to treat fire with a proper respect. Indeed it is something to marvel at that, what with south-east gales, inflammable thatch, and open hearths, the whole village does not go up in flames. This ceremony of bestowing fire, then, is only an episode in a long training, and possibly has little effect in itself.

As for the origin of the ceremony and of the *a-mare, puo-mare* which precedes it, we must, I believe, look once more to the Houra Haera of the Vailala River for a clue. Together they certainly form an integral part of the *Hevehe* cycle as it stands, but it is very difficult to find a place for this pyrotechnic interlude in the scheme of the cycle, and it is the writer's belief that we are once again dealing with a cultural interpolation. We shall return to this question at the end of Chapter XXI.

XX

THE YELLOW BARK-CLOTH BOYS

THE next day and night are crowded with incidents—festivities, spectacles, ceremonies—which are to reach their climax only at the following dawn. Business begins early. By sunrise the young men are already at work on the *kora papaita*, a kind of scaffolding some 10 to 12 feet high which is to be erected immediately in front of the *eravo*-verandas on right and left, while a forward extension will flank both sides of the broad *papaita*, or ramp. As will be seen from the diagram (Fig. 20) the scaffolding provides two sides for each of a pair of rectangles in front of the *eravo*. The remaining sides will be set up only with the approach of night, when the two rectangles, thoroughly walled up with mats of coco-nut leaf, will serve a particular purpose. In the meantime the men press forward with the *papaita kora* which is merely a framework of mangrove poles set horizontally on stout uprights.

Presentations to Women

But while this work is in progress a crowd is collecting for quite another purpose. At about 6 o'clock the first of the women steps forward to receive her gift of ornaments. It is the regular course in connexion with both *Hevehe* and *Kovave* to make the presentations to women and girls in the morning, and those to men and boys in the afternoon, though no one was able or ever thought it necessary to advance a reason for this convention. Now, however, the various women who have been associated with the masks are to receive their recognition. The recipients are typically the *hevehe-lau*[1] (mostly wives or daughters of the *hevehe-oa*), who have had much to do—if only in cooking, food-getting, and manufacturing *mae*—with the success of the cycle. The donors are, in the case of married women, their brothers; in the case of girls, their *aukau*. But such an occasion is seized

[1] See p. 238.

upon to satisfy many and various gift-obligations, and we shall see little girls receive ornaments who have never done a stroke of work in their lives; and some few presentations will have nothing to do with *Hevehe* at all. The great majority, however, are definitely connected with the present cycle. The reason for making the others at this moment is merely that the presence of a crowd ensures publicity.

The presentations were very numerous, running on well into the forenoon, and one or two examples must suffice. (They will incidentally provide a brief exercise in kinship.)

The first recipient to come forward was Maero, a pretty and dignified girl of about 16 years. She was the sister of several brothers who formed a strong group on the left side of Avavu Ravi, among them being Aori, the Drum-Leader. As usual the actual investiture was performed by one of her

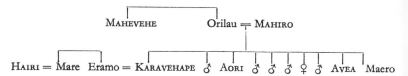

own sex. A middle-aged woman named Mare, who was accompanied by her husband Hairi, hung a very handsome *aroa* of ornaments over the girl's back, tied a freshly dyed skirt of *mae* about her waist, and knelt to trim it. Maero was an unmarried girl and so the proper donor should be her *aukau*, and in point of fact Hairi had stood towards her in that capacity from her infancy. She had been adopted by Eramo, the wife of her eldest brother who happened to be childless. The girl's real mother, Orilau, who boasted more children than can be named in the table, had readily passed one over to her son; while Mahevehe, the genealogical *aukau*, having his hands more than full with existent nephews, was equally glad to surrender his function of gift-giving to a volunteer. So Maero's *aukau-havahu*[1] happened to be, not her real mother's brother, but her adoptive mother's sister's husband. The circuitousness of this relationship did not,

[1] See p. 61. Maero ordinarily called Hairi *uvari*, as the husband of her (adoptive) mother's elder sister (also called *uvari*, 'grandmother').

PLATE 45

Carrying away the meat (see p. 320). These are visitors
from Arihava

Iva being presented with a new skirt by
her grandmother

however, affect the issue; in kinship it was fictitious; but it was real enough on what mattered—shell ornaments and pigs.

Now Hairi, an ugly and disreputable-looking old man, was giving a harangue. He wore a fringe of dark cassowary feathers (an ornament affected by none but old men) and carried a long fish-spear, the point of which he plunged into the ground now and again to give emphasis to his words. These were not meant expressly for his pretty *arivu*, but for the public at large and her brothers in particular. He was complaining that on the death of Eramo there had been no *haro eharu* paid over to her sister.[1] All she had got was a miserable fish-net. Now, he cried sarcastically, he was paying for that fish-net.

The brothers were too busy working on the *kora papaita* to give him a very good hearing. But they were not wholly inattentive, for one of them, Avea, suddenly shouted that there was no *apakora* among the ornaments. No, answered Hairi, and there was not going to be. But then the brothers, whose attention had been aroused, reminded him that he was getting a very large pig; and at that the old man, who was really in a good humour, appeared to relent somewhat. He fumbled in the string bag under his arm, and, producing a very fine *huaiea*, slipped it on to the girl's arm.

Meanwhile the energetic Aori was clambering down from the *kora papaita* and, as soon as he reached the ground, launched forth into a speech (some bystanders assured me that he wanted to encourage the girl, who was by this time beginning to feel shy at so much publicity). It was quite right, he said, that she should stand there having her skirt trimmed, with the remnants falling on the ground. For she was a girl who knew her duty; she was always diligent at sweeping the village, and no one would mind if she made it untidy now. But let no other women come forward to strew the ground with their rubbish when they never did a hand's turn towards cleaning it up at other times. Needless to say this was all taken in good part. The other women

---

[1] See p. 63. Eramo being brotherless, the *haro eharo* should have been paid to the sister, i.e. Hairi's wife.

did not hesitate to come forward in their turn; and the present episode was closed when Aori and another of his brothers brought a very large pig on a pole and set it down beside the girl, to be carried off immediately by Hairi's people.

The next presentation was to Aori's young wife, the *hevehe-lau* of 'Pekeaupe', and the donors were her own brothers, though the investiture was once again performed by a woman, the wife of one of them. This was a typical case and many of the same sort followed.

Most of the gifts were given in silence, for women are largely spared the ordeal of listening to a harangue; but there was some banter now and again to enliven the proceedings. One very bashful little girl, Iva, was receiving a present from an elderly woman, Uravu. The donors, her

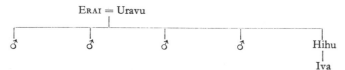

mother's brothers, were all at work on the *kora papaita*, and they had entrusted the business of presentation to the old grandmother, who carried it off very pleasantly. While she was doing so her husband Erai, a bluff old man, roared out for the shell-trumpeters (who had been slacking) to do their stuff, and amid much laughter they gave him blast upon blast. Soon after this, Erai, who was in an expansive mood, was to be heard joking an elderly woman. 'How is it you are not getting an *aroa* of ornaments to-day?' 'I am an old woman,' she answers; 'I have had many an *aroa* in my day. Now is the time for my daughters and the wives of my sons.'

Every one was in a good humour except perhaps Haio, who was very busy and no doubt harassed by his cares. Now in the midst of some work he found time to pour an angry broadside into the women at large. They were a lazy lot and had never kept the *eravo* properly fed. Now, to be sure, they were getting plenty of presents, but they had done nothing to deserve them. And a moment later he gave them a violent scolding for not keeping the ground swept—

to which incidentally they responded at once, for this vitriolic little man came nearer to getting his orders obeyed than any one in Orokolo.

The Pigs

Sometimes the presents to *aukahura* consist of whole pigs which are carried off alive; but more often, since various obligations have to be met at the same time, they consist of parts only, forequarters, substantial legs, and so on. Now, therefore, before the presentations were concluded, the pigs were already being killed, scores of them in different parts of the village. The air was soon filled with their squealing— an appalling noise of which happily one's ears soon grow tolerant. Pigs are not very easy animals to kill, but they are dispatched as quickly as a native knows how. There is no thought of torturing them or provoking their squeals, but, through lack of efficient means, their death may be rather a lingering one. Whereas in *Kovave* the pigs must be shot with bow and arrow, they must be killed in *Hevehe* by a thrust, either with a cassowary dagger or a knife or an arrow- point. The killer drives for the heart (the animal being of course safely trussed up), putting his whole weight into the movement; then he joggles the weapon or moves it rapidly up and down, like a man pumping a tire, until the pig appears to have expired, when he hastily withdraws it and plugs the wound with some kind of stopper to prevent the blood from escaping. In a few minutes the pig is singed and then in some shady place the work of dismemberment begins. Large quantities of meat are given away during the forenoon: it has already been paid for, so to speak, by the ornaments given to the women. But the majority remains either attached to poles and cross-pieces on either side of the *papaita kora* or else ranged on the house-verandas like so many butchers' stalls. There is assuredly a fine display of scarlet meat such as might shock the weak fastidiousness of Europeans but is a cheerful sight indeed to the Elema. It is mostly for distribution in connexion with the presentations to men which are to take place later in the day; some of it will be cooked for the guests, of whom there will be many hundreds to feed; and some of it, otherwise undisposed of, will be actually sold for ornaments during the evening and night.

It should be noted that all this meat is for general consumption, by women as well as men, in Orokolo or elsewhere. It is sometimes averred by those who declaim against *Hevehe* without knowing much about it that the pigs are eaten by men alone, the poor deluded women being put upon. It is only of the pigs for *Hevehe Karawa*, which are killed and eaten in secret, that this is true; and these form only a small proportion of the number killed for the cycle as a whole. The general slaughter which we see to-day will benefit the women as much as the men.

But even on this occasion there are a few pigs set aside. They lie hidden beneath the *eravo* at the rear in readiness for the *ma-hevehe* which is to visit the village again during the night. Two exceptionally fine ones are reserved for the crowd of important old men who are to be present as guests: they will be killed after dark and cooked and eaten in secret. The others will in due course be carried off under cover of darkness as presents to the *aukahura* of certain young men who are presently to undergo their initiation to *Hevehe Karawa*.

Toilet of the Yellow Bark-Cloth Boys

Innumerable pots were by now cooking before the houses, set in rows on the fires and stirred by perspiring but cheerful women. As they did not seem to require any watching I left the scene of operations at this stage to see to my own lunch.

When I returned at about 2 p.m. the village was almost empty of males. Only the women remained toiling over their pots, and I concluded that, since this was a housewives' responsibility, the men had all seized the opportunity for a siesta. The front door of the *eravo* had been closed soon after midday by a *hapa*, which meant that none but privileged old men might pass through; but I was led round to the rear and climbed up the back stairs.

One always endeavours to get some advance account of

PLATE 46

Killing a pig with a cassowary-bone dagger

Carving the pigs. A freshly singed pig seen on the right

what is to happen, but on this occasion I was taken very much by surprise. The great building, which looked from the outside so completely quiet and unmoved, was thronged to its utmost capacity with men and boys of every age, all intent on their work and speaking only in lowered voices. Every one of the *harehare-akore* was there and I know not how many others, for each seemed to have a circle of assistants. These were engaged in decorating them for the public appearance which was to take place that afternoon; and, since their highly distinctive and striking costume consisted of yellow bark-cloth, the *harehare-akore* were called for the occasion by another name, viz. *Hii-Kairu-Akore*, which means 'The Yellow Bark-Cloth Boys'.

Each one of them was clad in a sort of tunic (*karea*) of this material, the fairly coarse variety of it known as *pura*.[1] It takes the form of a broad sheet, with a hole for the head, doubled over and sewn down the sides under the arms. It thus resembles a sleeveless shirt, hanging down to thigh-level and gathered in at the waist by a belt of the same material. The head-gear (*haro-pura*) consists of a long broad strip drawn tight over the pate, wound round the temples, and falling to the level of the waist behind. It might be compared to a probationer's cap, or perhaps more appropriately to a piratical-looking kerchief. Both this and the tunic are freshly dyed in the bright pure yellow of *kairu*, or turmeric. Broad ruffs of frayed sago-leaf, stained russet-colour, are worn at elbows, wrists, knees, and ankles; and the visible parts of the limbs are painted with oil and red ochre, while the face is carefully decorated with patterns in red and black. For a final touch each individual wears stuck in his head-dress a composite plume—four *love* of cockatoo feathers, white and yellow, surrounding one or more large white tail-feathers of *baiva*, the hornbill. One such hornbill-feather indicates that the *harehare-akore* is passing through his first *Hevehe*; more than one, that he has passed through it before —as many times as he now sports *baiva-koro*.

So crowded was the *eravo*, down the central passage and in every corner, men even crouching under the mantles of

[1] Only the finer variety, such as is used for the perineal band, is properly called *hii*.

the hanging *hevehe*, that the very atmosphere seemed yellow. Many miniature windows had been broken in the thatch of the wall and the face-painters worked intently in the beams of dusty light that shone through them. Little boys, trussed in their costumes, held up faces pop-eyed with excitement while their elders described the careful lines of red and black upon them. All had been very subdued, but now in the *oropa larava* a large group of men surrounding a song-expert from Pareamamu struck up '*Hurava Hakare*', and the work went on to the full-voiced accompaniment of this song, rendered more impressively than ever.

The Invitation

We may now leave the *hii-kairu-akore* in the *eravo* and see what is going on outside. The cooking is completed and the pots of stew stand simmering over the ashes, most of them covered with lesser pots by way of lids. The women are sitting about in the shade with the air of pleasant expectancy which they wear on such occasions; they have done their part of the work and now are ready to enjoy the spectacle. The girls, with their patterned scalps, bright new skirts, and jewellery of shells and dogs' teeth, show their excitement more plainly, for they are looking forward to active participation in the afternoon's festivities.

Now a diversion is provided by a band of Avavu Ravi women. Some fifteen of them have decorated themselves with full head-dresses, such as are worn by male dancers, and have equipped themselves with spears, drums, rattles, and palm-midribs. They appear from nowhere in the form of a band and sally forth to pay calls on the various neighbouring *eravo*. They are known as *beiu-uva* (which appears to mean no more than 'invitation-women'), and it is their business, now that everything is ready, to summon the dancers. They proceed by a detour, through the edge of the bush outside the village fence, to the first *eravo*, Waiea Ravi, and then suddenly breaking into shouts and screams invade the village, thrusting at nothing with their spears and making as much play as possible with their various sound-producing instruments. They meet with a spirited

PLATE 47

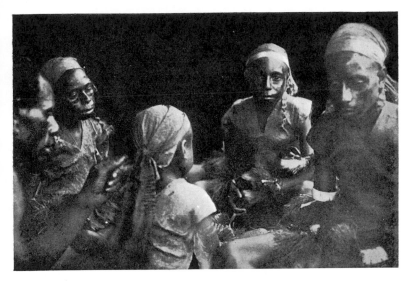

Toilet of the yellow bark-cloth boys in the *Eravo*

The invitation. A band of women go to summon the dancers

counter-attack from the local women, but these mean no more than to add their squeals to those of the visitors. Having performed a brief dance before Waiea Ravi the latter pass on to surprise Ori Ravi and Hohe Ravi, on both occasions taking the trouble to perform another detour through the bush. Then having completed their circuit they return laughing and singing along the beach.

The whole brief performance was highly amusing, a pleasant piece of feminine horse-play. No one could give me any 'meaning' for it, but it is worth noting as one of the many indexes of the women's attitude towards *Hevehe*. It is sometimes advanced as an argument by modern opponents of this cult that it involves the victimization of women. But we shall see more evidence of their delight at the prospect of seeing the masks; and, indeed, their growing excitement will come near to culminating in a riot. In fact I have never seen anything to support the above-mentioned argument, but a very great deal to the contrary.

Approach of the Dancers

It must be understood that the *eravo* visited by the *beiu-uwa*, as well as others too far away to visit, have got ready dances similar to those described in connexion with the New Door.[1] As a matter of fact the present dances are on an even larger scale, though the *eharo* masks are not so numerous. Now that the summons has been received the bands of dancers, *eharo*, and followers gather together in their respective villages, issue out on to the beach, and advance slowly from east and west until they will eventually coalesce in one great mass before Avavu Ravi.

The principal *eharo* on this final occasion play certain conventional roles, and now we may see one of them in the character of Evarapo. A grotesque and obscene figure, he shambles aimlessly along the beach far in advance of the approaching dancers. He is clad in a suit of dark-coloured bark-cloth, for he is one of the ugly *eharo*, an *oa heaha*; he carries a string bag, a lime pot, and a stone axe in its primitive hafting; and he is furnished with mock genitals of

---

[1] See Chapter XVIII.

exaggerated size. Now and again he sees some imaginary obstacle or enemy on the sands. He leaps about, strikes at it with his axe, retreats in terror; then noisily helps himself to lime and betel, brandishes his mock penis, and moves on again.

Not many people were watching Evarapo's act at this stage except for a crowd of small boys who, though highly appreciating its comic features, kept their distance and scattered in flight at each of his sallies. But an old man of Vailala, whose pupil he was, went to meet him, substituted the proper kind of croton for some which he was wearing by mistake, and gave him some verbal coaching in the further part he had to play. But now the dancers were converging from either side, and Evarapo and his instructor became lost in their midst as they joined in one great mass, palpitating in time to the drums, on the beach before the *eravo*.

Emergence of the Yellow Bark-Cloth Boys

Meantime the Yellow Bark-Cloth Boys had finished their toilet. Their helpers had unobtrusively left by the back door and were once more about the village, while the Boys themselves had crowded towards the front of the building. A great many of them, it appears, had packed themselves on the veranda which had been previously walled in by coconut-leaf mats. But these last movements were, of course, unseen from the outside: the *eravo*, despite the seething life within it, looked as undisturbed as ever.

The reader will understand that all was now in readiness for some spectacular development—the massed cohorts of dancers on the one side, and the *eravo* charged to bursting-point on the other. Some individual was to strike the blow which should set these forces in action, but no one seemed able to tell me who it would be. It seemed that old Biai, who was named as the senior *amua*, should have been entitled to the privilege; but Biai, a retiring person at all times, was not to be seen. Others mentioned Duru, but uncertainly. In the event it proved to be Haio—and who else, indeed, should it have been?

The old men were now seen emerging from the front door. Some of them paused on the *papaita* and clustered together, bending towards the door and chanting, in voices louder and more resonant than ever, the stately *Hurava Hakare*. Meanwhile Haio and some others descended the ramp and dispersed nonchalantly to their houses. Haio took from his veranda a trade axe, then turned suddenly and at top speed, brandishing this weapon above his head, rushed back towards the *eravo*. It was, indeed, an astonishing sight to see this little old man, so insignificant in stature, but with such fiery purpose on his countenance, scampering alone across the open ground between the besiegers and the citadel. He turned swiftly at the foot of the *papaita* and bounded up it, shouting as he went the strange words proper to the occasion: 'Who has stolen the bark-cloth of my grandsons?'[1] As he reached the top he smote the door with his axe and then simply disappeared from view under an avalanche of Yellow Bark-Cloth Boys.

I cannot pretend to describe how it was all done. But instantaneously the barriers were torn down from within and all the *harehare-akore* leapt forward to scale the *kora papaita*. In the bare space of a minute it was manned from top to bottom, the bigger boys and men climbing with reckless agility to the uppermost timbers, the little ones swarming on to the lower. The whole structure became a living wall of brilliant yellow, set off with points of red and black. Once in position, shoulder to shoulder, every man and boy stood motionless except that he waved slowly before him a graceful panache of cassowary plumes tipped with white cockatoo feathers. After the whole had so swiftly settled into order it was this rhythmical movement which seemed to endue it with continued vitality.

Two or three Europeans of the district had come besides myself to witness this spectacle, and it made on all of us the same impression of delighted surprise. Theatrically its success was beyond question; and the special charm of the whole conception lay in its simplicity. It seemed to me that

[1] No one could give me any explanation of this formula. It has no relation to the mythical story with which this ceremony may be correlated.

one of those fortunate Europeans said the right thing when she compared the *hii-kairu-akore* to a show of yellow flowers.

Entry of the Dancers

But the *Hii Kairu*—as this display is called for short—was not the only thing to claim attention. Even while the Yellow Bark-Cloth Boys—to change the metaphor rather drastically, they had seemed to me like a tribe of yellow monkeys —were swarming into their places, the massed body of visitors was bearing down upon the *eravo*, carrying in its midst the befeathered dancers and the tall figures of the *eharo*. The fence had been demolished to let them in, and sweeping through the wide avenue formed by the spectators they overbore the magical outposts—a line of three or four old crones waving their switches—while out of their midst, as they advanced, sped arrow after arrow, to pass over the heads of the Yellow Bark-Cloth Boys and sink into the face of the *eravo*. More than one of them flew so low as to fill me, at least, with horror and draw exclamations of concern from all around; and it is admitted they sometimes cause casualties, so that the men on the topmost rungs of the *kora papaita* carried rods of light sago-midrib to ward them off.[1]

Some informants suggested that the reason for this shooting (the arrows are supposedly aimed at the *dehe*) was to apprise the women that to-morrow the *hevehe* would break through it. But most were content to dispense with symbolism and admit the shooting to be no more than a display of high spirits. Any one among the visitors who felt so inclined might let fly and, as a great number were armed, the *eravo*-front was stuck in many places, while one or two shafts missed altogether and sailed into the bush.

The approach of the dancers and *eharo* has already been described in connexion with the ceremony of the New Door. Here once again on reaching the front of the *eravo* the whole body broke up into a series of smaller parts, the

---

[1] Such a casualty occurred at *Hii Kairu* in the previous cycle at Avavu Ravi, when Baiapuo, a youth of Arihava, took an arrow in the thigh. He was helped down and borne off to the creek near by where the arrow was extracted and the wound washed. Baiapuo is said to have taken it all very well.

PLATE 49

Display on the *Papaita*. The costumes are of brilliant yellow

dancers forming circles and the *eharo* dispersing to right and left. While they careered back and forth amid the confused and brilliant scene outside, the *eravo* remained absolutely deserted. When once it had disgorged its Yellow Bark-Cloth Boys, a *hapa* was placed over the entrance and not even an old man might pass beneath it. Informants speak with something like awe of the state of tabu which then falls like a cloud upon their men's house, though I never succeeded in discovering why this brief maximum of sanctity should occur just at this moment. Whatever the reason, it is not disturbed till two of the *eharo*, Aikere and Maikere, enter by the front door and pass down to the rear.

The Special Eharo

Among the *eharo* there were many gorgeously arrayed examples of the kind known as *love hae*,[1] but none of that kind which are surmounted by totemic effigies. These, it would seem, are restricted to the Ceremony of the New Door. Instead of them there were a number of special *eharo* which are said to appear and act their part invariably on the occasion of *Hii Kairu*. They are Hura and Kapo; Ira and Ope; and a group consisting of Evarapo, Aikere and Maikere, and the old woman Haihau'uva. It will be enough in the present chapter to describe what they did. Their significance (or lack of it) will be dealt with in the next.

The parts of Hura and Kapu as well as those of Ira and Ope were enacted by several pairs furnished independently by different *eravo*. They are *eharo* of the ugly sort, clad in black bark-cloth. The former are furnished with enormous mock genitals with which they make obscene gestures at each other, dancing clumsily around and alternately beating their drums, the one over the head of the other. They are plainly meant for figures of comedy.

Ira and Ope are more agreeable to look at. They have very fine head-pieces with huge flopping ears, and each carries a spear and a large string bag. Dancing towards each other they plunge the spears into the ground, then

[1] See p. 265.

F f

retreat, dance forward, pluck them out, and begin all over again.

The performance of both these pairs went on incessantly, their ponderous figures seeming to charge their way through the crowd. But the other *eharo* had a more interesting part to play. Aikere and Maikere appeared as two stalwart men, magnificently attired as dancers in full feather head-dress and, as is always the case with *idihi vira*, wearing heavy veils of cassowary feathers to conceal their features. Each carried a shell-trumpet, and each was armed for the fray. But their weapons were miniatures—toy bows and arrows and half-size *korepaka*, or shields. Haihau'uva, their opponent, was a disagreeable old hag (impersonated of course by a man) whose dingy costume, with a long hood of bark-cloth, marked her as a woman of the Kukukuku. She carried a stone club on her shoulder and, like Aikere and Maikere, was armed with a *korepaka*.

Such was the press and the number of other attractions that I failed to see the little drama which these three enacted. But it appears that Haihau'uva has been pursuing the young men, or perhaps that they have been leading her on in pursuit; and her *korepaka*, an oblong of tough palm-spathe, is a very necessary protection, for they continually discharge their arrows into it, sharply pointed midribs of palm-leaf such as little boys use with so much skill in their play. Advancing and retreating, this trio of *eharo* finally reach the front of the *eravo*, where Aikere and Maikere now leave their enemy and enter the building by its front door. (Although so youthful in appearance they are really, beneath their feathers, two senior men who are fitted by their age to be the first to pass the *hapa* which has placed the front door under tabu.) Once inside, they go down to the *kaia larava* and there deposit their shell-trumpets, after which they divest themselves of their finery and withdraw from the play.

Haihau'uva has meanwhile gone into hiding under a great heap of old coco-nut leaves ready prepared near the front of the *eravo* but a little to one side. It was here, as I had previously been told, that Evarapo, the fourth party,

was to find her. We have already observed him on the
beach, and presently, behaving in the same aimless manner,
he appeared near the *eravo*. He was apparently in search of
the woman, and various men would take him by the arm
and purposely misdirect him, though no doubt he knew
exactly where to go. At last he came upon the pile of coco-
nut leaves beneath which Haihau'uva was lying, only her
doubled-up knees being visible. Very timidly he stole up
to investigate, but again and again at the slightest alarm
sprang back, lifting his axe to strike. But his passions were
aroused, as he showed by his gestures, and now he began
cautiously to remove the uppermost fronds. Then suddenly
Haihau'uva came to life. There was an upheaval of palm-
leaves, and the old woman leapt out of their midst to assail
Evarapo with her club. The actor of Evarapo's part, evidently putting his soul into his work, almost jumped out of
his suit of bark-cloth. He took to his heels with Haihau'uva
in close pursuit and swerved off towards the rear of the *eravo*
intending to break through a barrier of palm-leaves and take
refuge in the building. But not seeing very well through
his mask he came into collision with a spear which somebody
had stuck in the ground as a fence-post, so to speak, for the
barrier. This brought him heavily down with Haihau'uva
sprawled on top of him. They both sprang up, Evarapo in
his genuine excitement aiming a blow at his pursuer's head-
piece which seemed to miss it by a hair's breadth, and then,
with Haihau'uva pushing him from behind, broke through
the barrier at another point and disappeared.

The encounter of Evarapo and Haihau'uva was merely
a hilarious incident or side-show in the afternoon's performance, and it was not honoured by a very large audience;
but it was a piece of excellent acting and a good illustration
of *Hevehe* in its humorous aspect. If not often revealed so
obviously, that aspect is never to be lost sight of. All the
eharo, even the true *hevehe* masks, have their comic appeal,
and the whole cycle, whatever its origins and despite its
solemn moments, seems to have developed strongly on its
lighter side. The dominant spirit throughout is one of
carnival.

Presentations to Men

When the last of the *love-hae* had leapt over its pig and entered the *eravo* the attention of all was turned to the presentation of gifts to the men. In some respects this is the most serious and important moment in the whole cycle, for, as we have often remarked, nothing reaches more deeply into the soul of an Elema native than does the traffic in ornaments and pigs. But the reader need not be wearied with a description of it. Suffice it to say that the gifts were more numerous and the throng of critical spectators far greater than at the morning presentation to women.

We may leave the scene as the sun goes down upon it. The tumult has died away, but a thousand people remain in the village; some are coming and going; many are sitting down to eat; many cluster round the two dense nuclei of dancers; but most are watching the presentations. Out of their midst we can hear the hoarse harangues of the donors and the repeated blasts of shell-trumpets as each recipient, in token of acceptance, places to his lips one or other of the instruments brought by Aikere and Maikere.

XXI

RITUAL AND MYTH

IN the present chapter we shall take leave of the action of the ceremonies—there is much more of it to come—and discuss some of the episodes that have been already described. We may begin with the acts of the special *eharo* and then pass on to an interpretation of the episode of the Yellow Bark-Cloth Boys as a whole.

Hura and Kapo

Hura and Kapo, of whom there were several pairs furnished by different guest communities, provide, as it seems, a good example of interpolation. Their performance has no relevance to the meaning of the ceremonies as a whole; it is obviously by-play and nothing more. They are said to represent historic characters, ancestors of the Berepa tribe, or Houra Haera, and so once more we see an example of the contribution of the Vailala bush-folk to the *Hevehe* cycle as practised by the Western Elema. They are said to have been two old men named Aukapa and Haive, both of them crippled and one of them further disabled by elephantiasis of the scrotum. Some suggest that the *eharo* were made in mockery of them, the highly personal nature of the joke being toned down by giving them the pseudonyms of Hura and Kapo.[1] A more explicit version, though still perhaps a garbled one, is that the dance was first performed, in a spirit of senile ribaldry, by the two old men themselves. To greet a party of returning hunters they divested themselves of their perineal bands and danced before them, beating their drums over each other in turn; and their fellow villagers were so tickled by their performance that they immortalized it in the traditional act of two *eharo*. Whether this story be strictly true or not is of little consequence. It seems probable that Hura and Kapo had their origin in some historical

---

[1] Hura is the name of a kind of jelly-fish; Kapo remained untranslated. Both are no doubt Houra Haera words which have been mangled in transit. Elema natives are not good elocutionists.

incident or circumstance, and, further, it is plain that their part, although now embodied in the *Hevehe* ceremonies, is entirely extrinsic to their main theme.

Ira and Ope

The same could be said of Ira and Ope, though for the originals of these characters we should have to go much farther back into the genuine Story Time. I have recorded a number of versions of the myths in which they appear. Kaivipi[1] (who had more than once acted one of the parts with Hau as his opposite number) spoke of them merely as *ma-hevehe*, the sons of Baiu, living in the Aivei River.[2] But there are various myths lying much deeper than this, showing, in fact, how they became *ma-hevehe*.

Ope is sometimes identified with the *Nabo aualari*, Biro (the parrot). To cut down a long story, he and his mother are the sole survivors of a series of raids on their village by Hehevari (the death-adder); Biro grows up to take an indirect revenge by assuming the form of a hawk (*a'u*) and tearing out the eyes of the people of the Kavo Nabora Mountains (arguing that since his own village is depleted it is unfair that another village should be well populated); but then he incurs the anger of the Kavo Nabora man Hekeke (another kind of hawk) who enlists the aid of certain sea-people against him; finally, having established himself in the cave known as 'Biro's *Eravo*' at Bie, the Bluff, he is swept away by the sea-people and becomes a *ma-hevehe*. Since then he has gone by the name of Ope, and continues to haunt the coast from Bie to Keuru in the shape of a sea-monster which, I am assured, is pink.

Ira joined him later. There is a legend, rather than a myth, of the journey eastwards of a group of migrants from Muro to Opau, and beyond Opau to Karama. On the way they were entertained by the people of Keuru; and here, in their anxiety to get on, they left behind for safe-keeping a very

---

[1] See p. 197.

[2] They wrecked a *lakatoi* (trading vessel) and thereby incurred their father's displeasure, for he was the founder of the *lakatoi* trade. The name Ira (pig) is said to have been given to the son of Baiu because Baiu sometimes assumed the form of a pig. *Ope* is, or happens to be, the pole stuck in the mud or sand to moor a canoe.

PLATE 50

Ira and Ope, two special *Eharo*

Evarapo receives some coaching from an experienced performer (see p. 324)

old man, Ira, who was delaying them because he could not walk.[1] When in due course they returned and fetched him in a canoe, they encountered rough weather in crossing Keuru bar and, according to one version, Ira was swept off accidentally by the waves. According to another, the ugly and useless old man was cast overboard like Jonah, but rose for a moment from the deep to bid his countrymen a magnanimous farewell, telling them not to worry, he would be well off where he was. At any rate, he was welcomed in the waters of Keuru by *Hevehe* Ope, and himself became a *mahevehe*. The two of them are always spoken of together.

The above are some of the mythological or legendary details about Ira and Ope, but it will be seen that they have no very obvious significance in the present connexion. Indeed, they give us proof—if that is necessary—that delving into mythology, which is as fascinating as the search for gold, may be sometimes as unprofitable. Any one of the *eharo*, *hevehe*, *kovave*, *hohao*, bull-roarers, *eravo*—in fact any ceremonial object which bears a personal name—would, if we followed the clue which that name supplies, lead us into a trackless maze of mythology, and it is certain that the vast bulk of the mythological matter which we discovered would be quite beside the mark.

In the case of Ira and Ope informants are more than usually muddled and hazy, for it is recognized that these mythical characters belong more particularly to the tribes lying to the east. Once more it is evident that we are dealing with an introduction, with something that has been merely added to *Hevehe*.

The circumstances of their origin, qua *eharo*, is, however, of some significance, and, as with Hura and Kapo, there is at least a legendary account of them. A man of Keuru named Ehevoa (alias A'iava, alias Makamaka) was fishing (in one version with a line and tortoise-shell hook, in others with bow and arrows from an *erohore*) when he espied under the water the forms of two *ma-hevehe*, Ira and Ope. Ehevoa fled for his life, and that night, in the usual sequence, had a

---

[1] Another account says that Ira belonged to the original people of Keuru, who were pushed farther east by the immigrants.

confirmatory dream. Ira and Ope appeared before him dressed in the distinctive manner which is now adopted by the two *eharo*, and danced and plunged their long spears into the ground just as they do to-day. Ehevoa, in fact, invented the *eharo* (and no doubt incidentally he learnt some magic from his dream visitors).[1] Why they should have become permanently attached to *Hevehe*, appearing as a regular feature at this stage, remains a mystery. Western Elema informants are content to say that they are an introduction from the east and to leave it at that.

The point which I desire to make in relation to both Hura and Kapo and Ira and Ope is that they are inessential to the main theme. That they have their intrinsic values and attractions is, of course, not to be questioned; but it cannot, in my view, be maintained that they are an integral part of the *Hevehe* cycle. If on any occasion they were dropped out of it, then the cycle would obviously be so much the poorer. But the loss would be one of plain subtraction: it would involve no disorganization.

Evarapo

When we come to the third group of *eharo* we find the mythological connexions rather more helpful, though even so it will be seen that they are involved in no little confusion. Evarapo, Aikere, and Maikere have already made their appearance as mythical characters in Chapter X, but it was observed that they were only alternative names, in that connexion, and it now appears that they may figure in other stories as well.

Evarapo is most often represented as a very primitive person who lived on the beach all by himself. Apart from the story of his voyage to the east which has already been narrated, he appears in at least three other stories which are given here synoptically.

In one of them he comes into conflict with the two women Oerapo and Aroeapo, who dwell on another part of the beach. A creek near their house has been dammed up by

---

[1] I was recommended for this magic to Area, but did not find time to pursue it. At any rate, I should not have got much out of this informant.

the sands, and they set to work to dig a way down to the sea; but, as often as they begin, Evarapo comes by night and fills up the channel (he does not wish to see his familiar beach interfered with). At length, lying in wait, they discover him at his work, chase him away, and threaten to kill him if he returns. The story goes on to tell how the women travel to the east, bring back a bagful of *maria* fish, and empty it into the creek, which thereupon breaks through to the sea. Evarapo has meanwhile faded from the scene.

In another he appears as the ravisher of Lavara, the *Vailala aualari* woman who comes down the river in her canoe and drifts off to the Aivei. In yet another he makes himself the bigamous husband of Lakekavu and Moro (mother and daughter) who have come down the Purari River.

In all of these he appears in the same character, lonely, disreputable, and obscene; but except that his general behaviour and manners as an *eharo* are in keeping with his character, the stories throw no light on his part in the little mime enacted before the *eravo*. It is true that I have heard informants bring him into the story of Aikere, Maikere, and Haihau'uva, but this, one suspects, may be an ingenious effort to make things square; he does not ordinarily appear in that story when told independently.

Aikere, Maikere, and Haihau'uva

Haihau'uva is identified with the *Purari* woman Ape[1] who lived somewhere near the mouth of the great river. She sustains a particularly villainous character in a long story which begins with the slaying of More's son Ehirira. Actuated by jealousy of the boy's mother More, Ape assumes the form of a bush-pig and succeeds in wounding him. Then, under pretence of doctoring him, she cuts off his limbs one by one and eats him piecemeal. And then she pursues the mother, who has fled for safety. But More takes refuge with some sky-people in a tall tree; and when Ape is climbing up to it by means of a liana, capsizes a pot of boiling water in

---

[1] Haihau'uva is the Houra Haera name for Ape. It is always used for her as an *eharo*, which confirms the natives' statement that this also is an introduction from that tribe. *Ape* means 'mouth', which informants interpret as referring to the mouth of the river. She is sometimes called Uvape (Uva-Ape, the Woman Ape).

her face and cuts the liana away. Falling to the ground Ape is embedded and lost to sight in the mud; but, by dint of magic, causes the river to rise in flood and bear her down to its mouth, where she remains for the time being buried under a sand-bar with only her woolly hair showing above the surface.

Now there appear on the scene Aikere and Maikere who come from the Hurava, or Purari Delta, side. It is their favourite pastime to patrol the beach, trying their marksmanship on stranded nipa palms and other targets, one going east and the other west. One day Maikere loses an arrow, and that night reports his loss to Aikere, the elder brother. Aikere dreams, and is thereby enabled to find the spot next morning. They discover the arrow implanted in Ape's (i.e. Haihau'uva's) hair, and dig her up. Once free, she turns on Aikere and chases him, Maikere shooting at her as she does so. Then she chases Maikere, and Aikere shoots her. Thus they lead the old woman on to their *eravo*, where by shooting her in the foot they manage to kill her. Having done so they drag her body into the *eravo* where it is cut up and cooked. Many pigs and dogs are killed as well, and guests are invited. Those from Muro and the Western Elema eat only the animals; but Aikere, Maikere, and the people of the Delta feast on the corpse of Haihau'uva, whence they become and remain man-eaters.

The latter part of Ape or Haihau'uva's story is obviously the one dramatized in *Hevehe*, though it stops short of the cannibal feast. Evarapo bears no part in it as ordinarily told, and it seems not unlikely that we are dealing with a case of syncretism. It may well be that Evarapo as a well-known mythical character was originally an independent *eharo*, and that somebody saw the possibility of bringing him into relation with the old woman Haihau'uva, who presented him with just the sort of quarry he was always seeking on the beach. It is noteworthy that she is found lying in concealment at the end of the chase rather than its beginning, which in itself indicates that the story has been freely adapted.

As for Aikere and Maikere, we have seen them, here and in Chapter X, under very different roles. Whether their

significance is confined to the simple part they play in pink-
ing Haihau'uva with arrows, or whether it may contain
some symbolism as suggested in connexion with the tale
of Oa Birukapu, is a question which I feel quite unable to
answer. But it may be that they do play an integral, if unimportant, part in the general proceedings, for, as we have
noted, they enter the *eravo* through the front door at the end
of their act and deposit there the shell-trumpets. It is, at
least nominally, these trumpets which are blown at the ensuing presentation of ornaments.

But questions of symbolism, however intriguing, are no
more than academic. To the present-day native, immersed
in the performance of *Hevehe*, they hardly occur at all. It is
the commonest experience, in asking a native about Ira and
Ope, Aikere and Maikere, and the rest of them, to hear him
answer, 'Yes, I have often seen them, but I do not know
their story.' This is unquestionably true in many cases, if
not in most; and, if the native does not even know the story
of the *eharo* concerned, he cannot be expected to have any
interest in their symbolic meaning. Further than this, even
those who are familiar with the stories of such actors are
quite unable, despite their desire to be informative, to explain why they act.

The conclusion seems obvious that in many cases the
mythology which surrounds them is in large part irrelevant
to the ceremony in which they appear. Any one who has
read the foregoing pages of this chapter should understand
that, however boring he may have found them, he has been
let down very lightly. He has not had to engorge a fiftieth
part of what might have been written of the myths conjured
up by these names. It is certain, on the one hand, that there
is much of Elema ritual for which the mythological counterpart (assuming it existed) is lost beyond recovery; and certain,
on the other hand, that there is a vast body of myth for which
there is no ritual counterpart at all.

The Song Hurava Hakare

Although our research into mythology in relation to the
ceremonies has hitherto been somewhat disappointing, that

is not to say that it need always be so. We shall go on to
review the episode of the Yellow Bark-Cloth Boys, and we
shall find incidentally that it provides, at any rate, one tolerably plain example of a parallel between ritual and myth.
Our subject in particular is the song *Hurava Hakare* which is
always sung in conjunction with that episode.

We have heard *Hurava Hakare* sung publicly on two occasions: first, while the Ceremonial Bathe was in progress;
second, just prior to the emergence of the Yellow Bark-
Cloth Boys. It is highly significant that when this song is
to be sung in the beach villages of the Western Elema some
expert must be brought for the purpose from the inland
people; for it is in an archaic form of their dialect, and they
alone profess to know it. On the occasions when I have
heard the song it was led by a *hivi-ore-haera* from the Pareamamu tribe; and it was only from Pareamamu informants
that I was able to get anything like an intelligible account of
its meaning.

The opening words in which the old men raise their
voices with such religious fervour were paraphrased something as follows: 'I, the girl—to descend by the *eravo*'s
vagina or by its anus, by the front door or the rear?'[1] But
this translation was offered very hesitatingly. The outstanding words are certainly not in modern use. Like so
many others in the songs they are said to belong to the
vocabulary of forefathers. It may be taken as certain that
the great majority of those who sing *Hurava Hakare* and
other songs do so with very little thought of their meaning;
and we may perhaps absolve the singers from any charge of
conscious obscenity when they utter these opening words.

I gave up the attempt to secure a literal translation of *Hurava
Hakare*, but the story which provides its main theme was
given me on several occasions, most successfully by a number
of visitors from Pareamamu led by an old man named Kea.

---

[1] Comparison with other stanzas makes it reasonably certain that the words *Mori
ara* (I, the girl) with which they begin refer to Lauara (*vide infra*). Presumably she
(speaking in the first person) is here wondering by which door the Yellow Bark-
Cloth Boys (i.e. Hurava and his brothers) are to appear. Yet a young informant
suggested that the words were to be put into the mouths of the *hevehe*, as 'daughters'
of the sea-monster.

Hurava lived with his brothers in a *hakare*-tree somewhere in the hills called Apura, behind Hepere; Lauara and her sisters in a village not far distant. On her way home from work Lauara used to sit at the butt of the *hakare*-tree to rest and as she did so Hurava, not revealing himself, would copulate with her through a hole in the hollow tree until in course of time she was pregnant, a condition which caused much mystification among her sisters.

The girls used to go sago-making. They would fell the palms during the day and leave them overnight with the intention of splitting and scraping them on the morrow. But when they returned to the scene they would find the palms standing again as if they had never been touched. This was the work of Hurava and his brothers. As often as the girls cut down a palm it would be mysteriously reconstructed.

Thoroughly puzzled, they left the youngest of their number as a spy, hidden under the fronds which they had lopped off; and, when in due course Hurava came by night and began to pick them up and piece them together, the girl slashed at him with her axe and cut his hand. Next morning she and her sisters were able to trace him by means of the drops of blood to the *hakare*-tree where he lived.

They immediately set to work to cut it down. They made some good progress with their stone axes during the first day. But when, after a night's rest, they returned to continue their work they found every chip back in its place and the *hakare*-tree apparently unscathed. Again and again they tried, but every morning the same thing had happened.

So they went to the east and enlisted the aid of the two Kauri girls, Ovaro and Mairo.[1] These came with their two axes Eke (vagina) and Auri (clitoris), and with these implements set to work on the following morning. Hurava and his brethren now knew their time had come. They began to decorate themselves while the girls were still at work, and when the tree fell and split open they issued forth in all their glory. Each of the sisters seized one of them by the wrist, exclaiming, 'This is my man!'; but Hurava himself

[1] Identified with two kinds of taro.

was nowhere to be seen. He was hiding in a branch which had been torn off by a liana as the tree crashed down, and it was not till this branch fell to the ground that he was discovered.[1] Then Lauara laid hold of him, crying, 'This is the man I was looking for!'

The girls married their men and all lived happily in the village. Lauara, already pregnant, was the first to bear a son and his name was called Hoaro. But while he was still a baby his father and mother quarrelled. During the women's absence on a day's fishing Hurava had baked some sago and given it to his son. The mother, however, had put this sago by for keeping, and when she found what Hurava had done she began to abuse him. At this Hurava and all his brothers went up into the *eravo* (they had built a real one), taking the little boy with them, and there they sulked. They refused the food which their women brought them and they refused to come down.

Now the men set up the *Hurava* song inside the building. Their wives gathered before it crying, 'Give us the boy!', but they went on singing. Presently they came out in a body, descended the *papaita*, pushed their way through the crowd of women, and disappeared into the ground, saying as they went, 'Our place is in the ground or in holes in the trees.'[2]

The men became *hurava* and *hoaro*, larger and smaller varieties of burrowing lizard with prettily marked skins. Lauara herself became *ao*, the woody ants' nest found in trees; and her sisters, various kinds of trees, birds, rats, lizards, snakes, and frogs.

Kea and his company of informants considered that this myth was to be correlated with the ceremony of *Hii Kairu*. Hurava and his brethren appeared in the form of the *hii-kairu-akore*, and their *hakare* tree as the *eravo*; while Lauara and her sisters chopping at the butt of the tree were represented by Haio beating with his axe on the door.

This was as far as they would go. Obviously they saw no further correspondence between the details of the story and

[1] Such details as this are meant merely to prolong the interest. Elema myths, like many others, are much padded.

[2] In another version Hoaro is represented as Hurava's younger brother, and on emerging from their *eravo* they go to live as men in a village nearer the coast.

the episodes of the ceremony. If we carry the correlation a little farther we must do so without the support of any native ethnographer (though they would all doubtless agree if the thing were put to them!). But some readers at least may feel tempted to follow the scent. If we interpret the emergence of the Yellow Bark-Cloth Boys as the first emergence of Hurava and his brothers from the tree, then there still remains the further part of the story, viz. the shutting up of the men and the little boy in the *eravo* and their second emergence. One might correlate this with the emergence of the actual *hevehe* masks which is very soon to take place. We shall see that the women clamour for them to descend, and that when they have done so and finished their time of dancing they do (at least in one aspect of the cycle) return to the bush. But all this is vague in the extreme. On either side, in the myth and in the ceremony, there remain episodes unaccounted for in such a correlation. We should perhaps rest content with admitting that in a broad sense it exists, and not attempt the impossible task of establishing connexions in detail.

Ritual and Myth

The foregoing discussions will show something of the relation between ritual and myth as illustrated by *Hevehe*. It may actually be the case that any ritual detail taken out of the whole cycle would have somewhere or other its mythical counterpart—unless the latter has been forgotten altogether and thus dropped out of existence (for, just as a myth might outlast the ritual that happened to be connected with it, so a ritual might outlast its myth). But while it is a possible assumption that ritual always has, or had, such mythical counterpart, it is another matter finding it. And in what is often a mythical wild-goose chase the native to whom both ritual and myth belong is not a very keen participant. The plain fact, so often verified by ethnological inquiries elsewhere, is that once the ritual has got going he is content to observe it in more or less faithful perpetuity, while the mythical counterpart first loses his interest and finally drops out of his ken.

The fact that myth may give rise to ritual is obviously exemplified by the *eharo* in general. While some of them are no more than fanciful, the majority represent *aualari* in some form or other and are known by definite names; and where this is the case they may be said to derive from the myths. For any man who, by dream or otherwise, is led to create a new *eharo* (except those purely fanciful ones) is drawing on some myth that is known to him. Any distinctive feature in the *eharo* mask itself, or anything distinctive in its conduct, its dancing, &c., is so to speak a mythical reminiscence.

The same thing is true of *hevehe* and *kovave*. And when it is remembered that every individual mask seems, as an original creation, to have had some secret magic connected with it, the question of their origin seems finally settled. For Elema magic in its distinctive form is a product of Elema myth; it relies on mythical precedents, re-enacts mythical episodes, and impersonates mythical characters.

The masks—*hevehe*, *kovave*, and *eharo*—always appearing in the same guise and always doing the same things, embody ritual in themselves, and it is clear enough that this ritual at any rate is derived from myth. Since, therefore, new ones can be, and are, created from time to time, it is seen that the already existing body of Elema myth is an inexhaustible reservoir for ritual of this kind.

The masks, however, are merely component parts or puppets in a greater ritual; and while it may seem equally likely that this ritual at large is a dramatization of myth, this is not so easily proved. Since complete correlations are nowhere to be found, I shall not attempt to prove it, but shall love it and leave it as an hypothesis.

While in our present studies we have found something to support it, it must be recognized that, supposing the hypothesis is sound, Elema ritual, all in all, represents a very casual and wholly incomplete rendering of the mythical material. However theyc ame into being, I cannot but think that the vast conglomeration of stories exists independently, and that current ritual, like current magic, has just picked here and there from the mass.

As for the converse derivation of myth from ritual, no

one need deny its possibility in given cases; but I can see nothing in the Elema material to support it as a general thesis. All the evidence seems to point the other way about. Indeed the sheer disparity in bulk between their respective contents make it inconceivable that Elema mythology at large should have had its rise in Elema ritual.

The Episode of the Yellow Bark-Cloth Boys

In discussing *Hurava Hakare* we saw the possibility of applying it as an interpretation to *Mairava* (the actual descent or Revelation of the *hevehe* masks) as well as to *Hii Kairu*, the episode of the Yellow Bark-Cloth Boys. This may seem at best a rather faint possibility, and there is an argument against it in the doubt as to whether *Mairava* and *Hii Kairu* really belong together. In other words the question is whether *Hii Kairu* is an integral, essential part of the *Hevehe* cycle, or whether it was originally a separate element which has somehow been incorporated into it. The discussion of this question will occupy the remainder of the chapter.

There would seem to be no essential link between the display of the Yellow Bark-Cloth Boys described in the last chapter and the episodes of Bathe, Fire-Fight, and Presentation of Fire described in the one preceding. Yet comparison with a ceremonial cycle belonging to a neighbouring tribe will suggest that they are all parts of a single complex. The cycle of ceremonies with which they are to be compared is called simply *Hii*, or Bark-Cloth, and is to be seen among the Berepa tribe, or Houra Haera.[1] It should be noted that *Hii* is there practised side by side with, but quite independently of, *Hevehe*, which appears among the Berepa tribe in a form practically identical with that of the Western Elema. A brief description will suffice to show the striking similarity between the *Hii* of Berepa and the series of episodes culminating in the *Hii Kairu* of Orokolo.

The *Hii* costumes consist of bark-cloth, though, while

---

[1] I have seen only the preparations for *Hii*, though it still takes place from time to time. It is practised also by the Keuru tribe where it has been introduced from the Berepa.

these are mostly dyed yellow as at Orokolo, they are finely painted in various *aualari* patterns, a kind of decoration in which the Berepa people excel. Their preparation takes some considerable time and the strips are to be seen hanging from 'clothes-lines' in the *eravo* long before the festivities are due. When all is in readiness guests come from far and near to perform their dances in the village, and at the end of the first day there takes place the ceremony of fire-giving. The novices stand under a mat while their maternal uncles besprinkle them with fire; and then they listen to a brief homily—'Thou shalt not steal', &c., and 'Receive this brand from the hand of your uncle, and if anyone questions your right to fire, say that your uncle has given it.'

On the second day all the novices gather in the *eravo* to be dressed. Their costume is much more elaborate than its Orokolo counterpart, what with the painting and the be-feathered head-pieces which they wear in place of the plain kerchiefs. But the suits are cut and fitted in the same manner, and on arms and legs the novices wear ruffs of sago-leaf.[1] When their toilet is completed the old men begin to sing and the novices issue forth from the *eravo* in all their finery to parade through the village in file. The procession is formed by some who are actually novices supported by others, similarly dressed, who have passed through *Hii* on a previous occasion or occasions. Having done the round of the village they draw up before the *eravo* to receive the ornaments from their maternal uncles, the latter of course receiving pigs in return.

The third day begins with a ceremonial bathe in which the novices are joined by the women and children; and on emerging from the water men and boys must leap to and fro across a number of bonfires which have been set going in the village. It is said that this is a very lively performance, the fires being fed with internodes of green bamboo which explode like giant crackers, so that we may have enough evidence to justify comparing this scene with the Orokolo

---

[1] I even noted (on a man dressed up, so to speak, for my information) a composite shell cuff, a detail which may be of some significance, since that type of ornament is given specially on the corresponding occasion by the Western Elema. See p. 312.

Fire-Fight.[1] By this time the guests have dispersed and the novices are free to stroll about for some time afterwards in their finery. The cycle (a very short-lived one in comparison with *Hevehe*) concludes, as all ceremonies must, with a successful hunt for a bush-pig, and after that the head-pieces are ceremonially burnt.

Allowing for some differences (e.g. the parade rather than the tableau of novices) and the obvious changes in sequence, no one could fail to mark the correspondence between this ceremonial cycle of the Berepa people and the several episodes which appear as mere incidents in *Hevehe*. From the beginning I was troubled by the apparent inconsistency of the *Hii Kairu* and related incidents in the *Hevehe* cycle. It seemed impossible to find any essential place for them in the scheme as a whole, so that I was compelled to regard them as constituting some kind of foreign body which the cycle had absorbed into its system. Consideration of the so closely corresponding ceremonies which in a neighbouring tribe form an independent, self-contained cycle serves, I think, to give colour to this view. My own conclusion is that we are dealing once more with a case of syncretism. The *Hii* cycle, or something which corresponded to it, has become incorporated into the larger mass wherein it now appears as *Hii Kairu*.

It does not seem justifiable in this case, however, to regard *Hii Kairu* as a recent introduction. The oldest surviving informants persist that the display of Yellow Bark-Cloth Boys was always in their memory a part of *Hevehe*; and it is not impossible that it may even represent a culture element, of earlier date. But the probabilities seem in favour of separate origins for the two; and, if this is the case, then we have yet further proof that *Hevehe* as it stands to-day is composite in its construction.

---

[1] At Berepa this leaping over the fire was acknowledged to be a purification. There was no such idea at Orokolo; in fact none at all except that of play.

XXII

MAIRAVA, THE REVELATION

THE present chapter will describe the events which
culminate in the formal emergence of the *hevehe*. This
last is called *Mairava*,[1] a word which may be translated
Revelation or Disclosure. The masks have made several
descents already, but only as a matter of convenience and
only before the eyes of the initiated. Now they are to be
revealed to the women who have waited so long. *Mairava*
is the climax, though not yet the end, of the cycle.

Scene in the Hirita

To return, then, to the scene of operations we find the
gift-giving over and darkness already setting in. The men
are hastily constructing the two *hirita*, or square enclosures,
immediately in front of the *eravo* and on either side of the
papaita, lining their walls with palm-fronds. For the time
has come to kill the two great pigs which have been set
aside for the older men (who are present in full force). It is
sometimes said that these pigs should be killed, cooked, and
eaten in the *kaia larava*; but it appears that the first two of
these operations at any rate always take place in the *hirita*,
which provide more space and are still sufficiently private.
There is no reason to suppose that the women are ignorant
of what is going on and there is no very strict secrecy, in
fact I saw several large pots and—modern touch—a kero-
sene-tin being carried into the *hirita* quite openly. All that
is necessary at present is that the uninitiated should keep
their distance.

The sloping *papaita* provides a station from which one
may look down into the *hirita* on either side. It is a fascinating and somewhat infernal scene. The giant pigs have
already been killed and some old men are deep in the bloody
business of dismemberment. The fires are crackling and the
pots already on the boil. Younger men are chopping wood

---

[1] The verb is *mairavakive*. I have never heard it except in this specific connexion.

and fetching water, older ones poking the fires into a blaze, sawing at the carcass with bamboo knives (time-honoured implements of the native butcher which steel cannot supplant), or merely squatting on their haunches, grim old figures not altogether unlike vultures. One or two hurricane lanterns are held aloft, but the workers depend on the firelight, which blazes redly through clouds of smoke. Prominent among those in the right *hirita*, where the work is more advanced than on the left, can be seen the small figure of Haio, busy here as everywhere. He seems to be directing the affairs of the kitchen in no uncertain manner, plays the part of host, handing out raw tit-bits to the old men, and stands with his back to the fire.

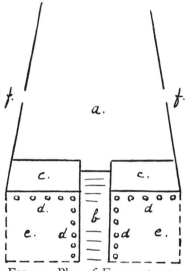

Fig. 20. Plan of *Eravo*-entrance for *Mairava*

a. Interior of *eravo*
b. *Papaita* (ramp)
c. *Mairai* (veranda)
d. *Kora-papaita* (scaffolding)
e. *Hirita* (enclosures for cooking)
f. *Harihu-ura*

Looking down the *papaita*, which forms a passage-way between the two *hirita*, one may see the *idihi-vira*, now at the very top of their form. Occasional flares of dry coco-nut leaf illuminate the scene and show them slowly revolving in their magnificent head-dresses amid the dense throng of girls and women, who very literally dance attendance upon them. And all these activities, before the *eravo* and in the open village, are accompanied by the thunder of drums and the ceaseless antiphony of song-leader and chorus.

This high pressure of conviviality was to continue far into the night, when, all being fed to repletion and a little tired, it would slacken, though only to develop into a still higher pressure of excitement with the approach of dawn.

As an observer of it I am firmly of the opinion that this is a scene of what may be called innocent enjoyment. It seems worth making this observation just here, for many who read accounts of native feasts and dances seem to expect that they are, essentially or incidentally, orgies. It will be enough to say that as far as I could detect (and I watched these people all night) there was nothing of the kind in this festival at Orokolo. That 'glad eyes' were exchanged, one need not doubt; and who knows but that the seeds of future philandering were scattered broadcast? But one cannot see these seeds in the air, and, even if they take root, they do not develop overnight. There is no slipping away of girls to misconduct themselves with visitors in the bush. Informants treat the suggestion as rubbish, and it is to be observed that the whole conduct of the night's proceedings is against the possibility. The girls stick together, and the men are perhaps too interested in their own concerns to think much about them.

The Meat-Stalls

While the cooking in the *hirita* is still in progress and the dance continues, a strange traffic in pig-flesh is going on near by. We have noted the surplus meat hung up on the poles of the *kora papaita* or on the neighbouring housefronts. This is called *huhu ipi-ve ira*, which means 'pig at the base of the boards', the word *huhu* (board) apparently referring to the planks of the *papaita*. It is to be disposed of during the night to any who care to bargain for it. The deal should be opened in a gentlemanly manner: I am told that the butcher, so to speak, remarks that he wants some betel or tobacco, and this is taken as a hint that he is ready to sell some of his meat. Some intermediary finds him a customer, and the bargain is then concluded between the two principals.

I saw several such sales effected in the darkness, not always without haggling. A village constable from Muru was engaged in a long confabulation with the owner of a fine quarter of pork which lay between them on the *papaita*. It seemed that the two could not reach agreement; the constable offered money but the owner wanted shell ornaments. Finally the constable left, disappeared in the crowd, and returned jingling a pair of arm-shells in his hand. But after further low-voiced conversation he left again, and the meat was put back. That particular deal had fallen through.

One man, Ohaka, whom I knew well, had actually erected a small roofed platform near the *eravo* and stood guard over the meat which he had displayed upon it. A small lantern, its light hardly visible within the sooty lamp-glass, hung over his stall, and when I asked if I might take it down to see what I was writing in my note-book, he objected that it was there to show up his wares, lest they disappear in the darkness. Later I saw Ohaka hoist himself onto his own platform and sit there amid the meat, while numbers of men came at intervals to do business.

Ma-Hevehe *brings the Drums*

But this, of the *huhu ipi-ve ira*, is entirely incidental to the course of *Hevehe*. It is a side-show, a stop-gap helping to pass the time before the next movement can occur.

It will be recalled that, among all the confusing variety of things known as *hevehe*, the tall masks in the *eravo* are distinguished as *apa-hevehe* because they carry *apa*, or drums. Now the hour had come to present them with this last distinctive item of their equipment. Some time during the night the *ma-hevehe*, or sea-monster, would pay yet another visit to the *eravo* bringing the drums with it.

It is on this occasion only, amid a succession of visits, that the *ma-hevehe* is actually called up by signal from the sea; and it was now necessary that the cooking in the *hirita* should be finished before the party arrived. Quite early in the evening there was a false alarm. At some fancied noise from down the beach the women scattered and made for the shelter of their houses; but they were called back and the dance resumed. Hours went by, the *idihi vira*, the singers, the drummers, and the dancing women still in action, though now not without an occasional breathing-space.

It was approaching 2 a.m. when the shell-trumpet sounded first from within the *eravo*. The dancers and singers paid no attention, and the *puva* must have sounded fully ten times before the answering voice of the *ma-hevehe* was heard from far down the beach. This was a longer delay than had been expected, but it was not due to any hitch in the proceedings. The *Hevehe Karawa* party had its preliminary work to do, that of initiating several young men, and perhaps this was so far away as to be inaudible while the dance continued in the village. Meanwhile the throng of women had dissolved soon after the first blasts of the *puva*, and as soon as the *ma-hevehe* was heard the dance itself broke up and left the village clear. One or two stray voices, thoughtlessly breaking the silence, were subdued by angry hisses.

Once heard from the village the weird voice of the *ma-hevehe* seemed to develop in an amazing crescendo. I was informed that the *Hevehe Karawa* men had employed the device, previously described, of posting several minor parties at intervals down the beach, each one of them taking up the noise in turn until it reached the main body which was assembled quite near the village. This relaying of sound gives the impression that the monster is advancing with supernatural swiftness, and on this supreme occasion its approach surpassed in impressiveness any I had heard before.

There are several alternative viewpoints from which to observe *Hevehe Karawa*, and this time I took up a fortunate position inside the *eravo*. (In the midst of all their bustle these people could treat an inquisitive foreigner with courtesy, and they made no demur in allowing me an old man's privilege.) I found myself in company with a large number of elderly men, who had assembled there for the express purpose of awaiting the *ma-hevehe*.

Next moment the monster, or rather its blood-curdling voice (for of course from our viewpoint it was invisible), was sweeping in from the beach. Drawing up at the foot of the *papaita* the party fell suddenly silent; but their leaders, a number of men bearing drums, advanced up the *papaita* itself and sought entry at the *eravo*-door. Here their way seemed to be contested by certain older men, but finally they broke in. It was impossible to see much of what happened in the darkness, but it appears that they handed over their drums to those inside. One of them mysteriously delivered a bag of something to Haio, who took it as if it might bite him; but this proved to be nothing more than a bagful of *harau* rattles, and Haio's gingerly manner was explained by his fear of jangling them when all should be silent.

While these movements were taking place, cautiously and silently, in the *eravo*, the *ma-hevehe* party had taken up its noise again and was retreating to the beach; and, as soon as they had left, a screen of palm-fronds was hastily thrown up in the darkness so as to connect the two front walls of the *hirita* and thus hide the *papaita* from outside view.

The large party of elderly men already congregated in the *eravo* had armed themselves with every drum that could be collected in the neighbourhood, while their elderly arms and legs were encircled with bands of hollow *harau*-seeds tied in clusters. Now they stole down the *papaita* so as to line it two-deep from top to bottom, while those who could find no place there crowded about the door of the *eravo* itself. Each held his drum in readiness, and each moved with comical stealth for fear his rattles might emit a premature tinkle.

All this had occupied only two or three minutes, and now every man was in position, while within and without the building there reigned utter silence. Suddenly Haio uttered a shout and banged his stick on the floor-boards. Instantaneously there arose a deafening din of drums. There were possibly not more than fifty of them, but within the confined space the noise they made was veritable thunder, and every man as he beat the drum stamped with his rattle-bound feet on the *papaita* till its heavy timbers vibrated underfoot like a swing bridge. It was no rhythmical drum-beat. Every man belaboured his instrument furiously and independently, so that the noise was nothing but a continuous roar.

The drummers had hardly been three minutes at work when Haio came down the *papaita*, shouldering his way between them. He was shouting and gesticulating as if in great anger, and I judged there must be something wrong and that he was telling them to stop. But they seemed only to redouble their efforts. He was, I was told, merely complaining at their laziness: 'They were not making any noise at all; he couldn't hear them!'

Heard from outside the thunder of the drums was, of

course, less overwhelming but peculiarly impressive. It seemed as if the noise were bottled up in the *eravo*, and the absence of any rhythm (if by chance it should develop it is deliberately broken again) gave the impression that the drums were far more numerous than they were in reality.

Any one who heard this noise might well be astonished at its volume; but far more astonishing was the fact that it continued without pause and with hardly any perceptible abatement for over two hours. It was plainly exhausting work, but individuals might rest without any appreciable effect on the sum total, and there were always reliefs at hand to take over the drums. In theory the drummers are so busy that the food offered them in refreshment has to be put into their mouths. It is averred that they either swallow the gobbets of pork while they beat, or let them fall from their lips into bags hanging open on their chests. This is of course picturesque exaggeration; but now and again one or other of the Avavu Ravi hosts would come down amongst them, sometimes with little bits of cooked pork, sometimes with the bamboo smoking-tube, and sometimes with coconuts to drink. Thus refreshed, the weary drummers (they were all senior men but mostly not old) would change stance or grip so as to bring some other muscles into play, and set to again with a stamp and a shout. It was assuredly a great feat of endurance.

A few of the very oldest of the visitors were taking their ease inside the *eravo*. I doubt whether they could have refrained altogether, at any rate in the earlier stages; but now they declared they were too old for such exercise. With them were the elders of Avavu Ravi itself; for it is the visitors only who act as drummers, the men of the home *eravo* plying them with food and drink. In the *kaia larava* there was one solitary individual, Ere, the aged *amua* of the left side. He was the father of the *eravo* in that he was its oldest man and, as *kariki haera*, custodian of the magic that held it together. But he was old and ailing and no doubt tired. And so, while the building reverberated to the noise of drumming and trembled with the shock of feet on its *papaita*, he lay stretched out by his fire, fast asleep.

The reason for this drum-beating, or, as one may say, the fiction of it, will no doubt have been obvious to the reader. The *hevehe* in the *eravo* have been waiting these many years for their drums. Now their mother, the *ma-hevehe*, has brought them up from the sea, and the daughters, wild with joy, are beating them. They are in truth making a welter of it.

While the unseen drummers were doing their utmost behind the palm-leaf wall, the *idihi vira* reassembled outside and began their dance again. But it did not last long. *Maruru*, the bitter little land breeze, had sprung up, and after a few pauses and renewals the women made off to the warmth of their houses and the men stood huddled about the fires outside. But every household was wide awake. Many were eating a midnight supper of *papaa*, and the *harehare-akore*, still wearing their yellow costumes, showed signs of restlessness. Nevertheless, time passed slowly during the next hour or so. All were waiting impatiently for dawn and not a few asked the time by my watch (which incidentally I had left at home, so that the hours given are only approximate).

The Women's Demonstration

Some time before 4 a.m., while the hidden drummers were still tirelessly at work, a number of women came out and, taking their stand before the *hirita*, began to address the *hevehe*. At first they were only a few, the wives of Duru and Aori, the two Drum-Leaders, being in the lead, and these threw themselves into a kind of spontaneous dance in which the feeling of jubilation was unmistakable. As they danced they raised their somewhat harsh voices in cries to the *hevehe*, who were ostensibly beating their drums behind the scenes. 'Come forth! It is time; the dawn is drawing near!' is the gist of what they say.

But now other women come flocking to join them and all sorts of excited cries go up. 'Come out, I want to see you. I have worked for you. In rain and heat I have made sago; I have carried food from the gardens; I have paddled up the rivers; I have shivered in the water catching fish; I have

burnt my hand cooking! All for you! I want to see you
and to touch you. Come out!'

Some address the *hevehe* by conventional *aualari* names—
Purari women call on Akeàve and Paikare (a pair of fish);
Vailala women, on Meke and Karai (another pair of fish);
Nabo, on Kerehere and Biro (parrots); *Kauri*, on Baiva and
Harova (the hornbill and some other bird, unidentified);
and so on for the other *aualari*. These are said to be traditional forms of address used inclusively for all the *hevehe* on
this occasion. The women are not particularizing. They
will recognize their own *hevehe* when they come out, but
what they want now is to see them all, for the reward of
their labours is at hand. With the emergence of the *hevehe*
the women's fun begins.

The swarm of women rapidly increased and soon the
demonstration became an uproar. Duru's wife at any rate—
and there may have been others—was armed with full-sized
bow and arrows, and twanged the string as an orator does
in giving a harangue. Others brandished sticks, and not a
few cut the air with 16-inch trade knives. But this was all
merely for emphasis. Elema women, like their husbands,
seem to like holding weapons when they are talking hard.

Now some of them were to be seen bringing forward pots
of water, and those in the front ranks of the crowd began to
ladle it out with coco-nut bowls and send it—sometimes
coco-nut and all—in showers over the barrier. Several were
filling long bamboos with water and by an overhand motion
managed to project the contents far up the *papaita*. At each
successful throw the elderly drummers, stimulated by a
shower of chilly drops, would burst into a falsetto shriek
and belabour their drums with greater fury than ever, and
from within could be heard their voices (it is the only occasion when *hevehe* ever open their mouths) crying, '*Ma! Ma!*',
'Water, water!' They were asking for more. And they
got it, again and again. The women, full of sympathy for
the *hevehe* in their exertions, were doing their best to keep
them cool!

In the midst of this excitement there now appeared
before the *hirita* a man carrying a lantern. It was difficult

to see exactly what happened, but two young men were brought up behind him, closely held by a number of others. While the women still continued their dancing and shouting, the man with the lantern broke a way through the palm-leaf barrier at the foot of the *papaita*, without really opening it, and as he stood aside the two young men were bundled crashing through, with their attendants on top of them. There followed a fearful burst of drumming, accompanied by the same sort of inhuman shrieks which characterize the *ma-hevehe*; and then, after this final climax of noise, the drums suddenly ceased.

It appears that the entry of these young men was no regular part of the ceremony. While four youths had been initiated to *Hevehe Karawa* on the beach earlier in the night, two, intentionally or otherwise, had failed to present themselves; and this introduction to the old men on the *papaita* was said to stand in lieu of the more usual form of initiation.[1]

Now, however, all the *harehare-akore* were to enter the building. The screen across the foot of the *papaita* was torn down and they began to stream up the gangway. With the cessation of drumming the clamour of the women had seemed to increase, or perhaps it was merely that one heard more of it. They were pushing and shoving in a perfect fury of joy and excitement, and the massed body of *harehare-akore*, pressing through towards the entrance, seemed almost to be involved in a struggle with them. The women desired nothing more than to see the *hevehe* emerge, but in the meantime they were surely making things difficult. No football crowd was ever more unruly at the gates. But in the end the last of the *harehare-akore* had disappeared into the *eravo*, and something like a lull ensued.

The Emergence of the Hevehe

Up till this point it had been dark, and the confused movements here described could be seen only by the light

---

[1] I omitted to clear up this point fully. The above was the explanation given me after the event, but it will be noted that the *ma-hevehe* is in theory not present at all, having returned to the sea after bringing up the drums. It is of course only *apahevehe* who are making the noise in the *eravo* at this moment.

of fires and the occasional flare of torches. But now the dawn was breaking. Despite the apparent confusion it seemed that the action, no doubt as the result of many previous experiences, had been nicely timed. The *harehare-akore* had some 20 minutes in which to prepare before it would be light enough for the emergence; and it is surprising to think that in the dark and crowded interior of the *eravo* they accomplished their preparations in the time. But every man and boy would be counted on to know his post—beside his own *hevehe*.

It was still dusk, nearly an hour before sunrise, and the tall front of Avavu Ravi hardly more than a black outline against the sky, when they began to open the door. But in the course of years the *eravo* had canted to the right, so that it had been necessary to prop it with heavy posts on one side and guy it with lawyer-vines on the other. The 30-foot door had consequently jammed, and, though the lashings had been severed, there was now some difficulty in opening it. A number of men standing on the ground to the left front of the building hauled on the lawyer-vines attached to the farther edge of the door, but, while it began to come clear at the bottom, it still stuck at the top corner. The women's cries had died away and a hush of expectancy had fallen over the crowd of watchers. They had no misgivings about the door: it was only a momentary hitch, and perhaps the delay added to the tenseness of the drama. Several men sprang up the scaffolding of the *kora papaita* for a better purchase: in the dim light there seemed something almost diabolic in movements so swift, silent, and purposeful. One of the climbers, a splendid, powerful figure, reached the topmost rung and in that precarious position threw his whole weight onto the line. At that, with a rending of wood and bamboo, the topmost corner was released and the *eravo* door swung open. Even as it did so the first of the *hevehe* was standing on the threshold.

There are many dramatic situations in the cycle, but none can compare with this supreme moment when the *hevehe*, after wellnigh twenty years of confinement, issue forth to commence the brief fulfilment of their existence. In the grey light of early morning the first of them, 'Koraia', stood framed against the blackness of the open door—a tall fantastic figure, silvery white, its coloured patterns in the atmosphere of dawn appearing pale and very delicate. The garishness, the grotesquerie, that full daylight and a near view might discover were now blurred; they faded into something fairy-like. One of the spirits—of forest, sea, or air—one of the Magic People, one of the Immortal Story Folk, was about to lead its companions out of their long immurement to dance and make merry in the village. A strange, other-worldly figure, and a heathenish one, no doubt; but none who saw it poised on that dark threshold could have failed to call it beautiful.

For a brief moment 'Koraia' stood there, the great crowd of spectators gazing in silence. Then, with a thump of the drum and a prodigious rattling of *harau*, it started down the gangway. Immediately behind it came 'Pekeaupe';[1] and after that, in crowded succession, 120 others.

As each, descending in the same stately fashion, reached the foot of the *papaita* it bore off at unexpected speed, beating its drum and dancing the measure appropriate to its *aualari*. Some turned to left or right, but most made straight for the beach, advancing through a broad avenue of spectators.

But the *hevehe* were not dancing alone. The women who had been so clamorous an hour ago had quietened down for the opening of the door; but now they gave rein to their feelings again, though in a somewhat more chastened manner. They were watching the procession intently in order to recognize their own *hevehe*, that is to say, those of their fathers or brothers, and as each set foot on the ground a little band would detach itself from the crowd to dance attendance on it. If they did not recognize their own immediately their menfolk were present to identify them, and thus each *hevehe* was joyously received. Every woman and girl, from old crone to little child, attached herself to one or the other, while infants too young to look after themselves

---

[1] The *hevehe-oa* of 'Koraia' was Duru; that of 'Pekeaupe', Aori. These were the two *apa-haro-haera*, or Drum-Leaders, of Avavu Ravi.

rode on the dancing shoulders of their mothers. The girls had armed themselves with green twigs of their several *aualari* trees,[1] and with these they lightly flicked the legs of the mask-wearers, dancing round and about them as they moved. It was a charming scene indeed. Intent on their own movements and those of their gigantic leaders, the dancers uttered no sound, but their faces wore smiles of unaffected delight. The women had come into their own at last; they were in a state of infatuation already.

Some of the mask-wearers did not see very well at first— the eyeholes in the head-piece afford only a limited field of vision—and there was some swerving and staggering and a few collisions. But in some marvellous way the bands of girls managed to dodge each other and, without dropping a step, to follow their *hevehe* in its most erratic moments until it gained the beach and could manœuvre freely.

The sun was near rising before the last of the *hevehe* had emerged from the *eravo*-door, and by this time some of the first to descend were already on their way back. It will be borne in mind that on this their first appearance the masks should be worn by their own *harehare-akore*; and, since some of these are mere boys, they cannot sustain the weight for long.[2] So these might be seen crossing with the still-descending *hevehe* midway on the broad *papaita*. At the end of half an hour the last of the 122 must have emerged; but by that time some of the earlier masks, worn by adults eager for a trial, were ready to come down a second time. And thus the process continued, the *eravo* pouring forth a ceaseless stream.

We may leave this scene of pageantry while the sun is still low in the heavens. Colour, light, and shadow are all intensified under its early rays, and the *hevehe*, fresh and untarnished, appear in their full glory. *Mairava*, the Revelation, is over, and it has been a worthy consummation.

It is a marvel that after a day and night of work and excitement men should have the energy to wear the masks

---

[1] *Kaia—Laura* and *Haravea*; *Ahea—Korope* and *Ova*; *Purari—Oro, Kaupe,* and *Haihiava*; *Kauri—Beve, Laiara*; &c.

[2] Where the *harehare-akore* is altogether too small the mask is worn on this first occasion by a substitute.

PLATE 51

A *Nabo Hevehe* dancing on the beach with its escort, called 'A Flock of Mountain Birds'

and women still be ready to dance. Yet the coming and going of *hevehe* will continue well on into the forenoon. In the meantime, however, the crowd is dispersing. The majority, with the ethnographer foremost among them, have their minds set on nothing but sleep.

XXIII

THE MONTH OF MASQUERADE

Dancing of the Hevehe

THE dancing of the *hevehe* lasted one month. The weather was calm and rainless, as it always is at this time of the year, and it was a month of general happiness; for the girls and women, one of bliss.

Morning and afternoon, even sometimes in the heat of midday, the mask-wearers come and go, the *papaita* a busy scene of two-way traffic. After perhaps fifteen minutes' exercise each will return to doff his mask and attach it to its hook and rattan, unless some other man is ready waiting to take it over. Streaming with perspiration, the last wearer sits down to cool off; but presently will be seen fitting some other mask over his head, shuffling a little to get it balanced to his satisfaction, and then making his way towards the door, fully prepared for a further tour. Any man, in fact, may wear any mask with its owner's permission; nor is the owner likely to refuse it, since he is flattered to see his *hevehe* in frequent use.

Outside, under the shade of the coco-nuts, sit the girls, prettily dressed and freshly oiled. Their eyes are fixed on the *eravo* entrance, and whenever a mask makes its appearance some of them rise to form its escort. Indeed they are much more on their feet than resting, and they turn with fickle favour from one to another; for, whereas at the first emergence they attached themselves to the masks of their fathers and brothers, they may now follow any they please.

We may picture a scene in the early afternoon. There has been a lull during the hottest hours and now a group of some twenty-five girls, having returned from a meal or a siesta, are sitting in the shade, gossiping and giggling and waiting for the first *hevehe*. Presently a pair of fine *Baiu* masks appear in the doorway, one behind the other; they are distinguished by the predominance of yellow in their decorations, and, in pursuance of the scheme, their mantles

PLATE 52

A *Purari* and a *Vailala Hevehe* dancing together in the village

are dyed, not red, but a rich golden brown. After a few preliminary beats of their drums they make their imposing way down the *papaita*. The twenty-five girls are up in a flash and as soon as the *hevehe* have reached the ground are dancing about them.

It is a pretty, bright-coloured picture, the charm of which is not lost in repetition. And somehow it is an amusing one, so that it is hard to watch it without a smile on one's face. In the centre are the portentous figures of the *hevehe*, with their staring eyes and their fierce jaws abristle with teeth, their mantles rising and falling, and their human arms and legs vigorously belabouring the drums and kicking up the dust. Though they are 20 feet high and more they dance, not lightly (that would be a sheer impossibility) but with amazing animation. The wearers' legs, bound at calf and ankle with ruffs of *mae* and clusters of seed rattles, have something of the appearance of the shaggy extremities of a Clydesdale—a very frisky specimen of the breed.

In contrast to the ponderous style of the *hevehe* the movements of the girls are light and graceful. They respond, as dancers should, to every movement of their gigantic partner, and, as they have no loads to carry, they easily tire him out. The *Baiu* masks which we have been observing are large and heavy and their wearers have had enough of it at the end of five minutes. But as they are trudging up the *papaita*, a lighter *Nabo hevehe* is on the way down. The band of girls immediately transfer their affections to the new-comer, adopting quite a different style, for each of the *aualari* has its own. Now they dance with their arms held lightly in the air : aptly and poetically the escort of a *Nabo hevehe* is referred to as a flock of mountain birds.

The next to come down is one of the *Vailala* masks which are the most beautifully decorated of all, and the *Nabo hevehe* immediately loses three-quarters of his attendants. But more and more are issuing for the afternoon parade, and, though women and girls are flocking to the scene, each will have to be content with a smaller circle of admirers.

The *hevehe* dance for the most part singly or in pairs. But sometimes in the cool of the late afternoon they will be seen in groups. I have counted one of seventeen advancing along the beach amid a swarm of adoring females, its outermost fringes consisting of tiny girls copying with ardour the movements of their elder sisters. And sometimes individual *hevehe* which have special songs associated with them will perform a sort of stationary dance in the village while the song is rendered by a group of men. When they do so other *hevehe*, of any and every *aualari*, will cluster round. I have counted twenty-one in such a group surrounding a certain tall *hevehe* called 'Mare'.

It has been remarked that the *aualari* have their distinctive drum-rhythms. They are worth noting if only because of their poetic names. *Kaia* has *kaia kukururu*, 'Sky Thunder', a series of heavy beats followed by a rumbling; *Ahea*, *Auma*, and *Miri* have *ma roru*, 'Sea Waves'—two heavy beats, followed by a series growing faster and fainter, which represent the combers turning slowly over and crumbling as they advance up the beach; *Hurava* has *arakaita kukururu*, 'Thunder of the Dugout Canoe', i.e. the inspiring noise of the paddles striking against the hollow dugout when a full crew is in action; *Kauri* has *kora haiave*, 'Chopping of Wood'; *Vailala* and *Purari* have *ma laroa*, 'The Whirlpool' (the *hevehe* revolves first in one direction and then in the other); and *Baiu* has *ma aua araive*, 'Tide Rushing Up-stream'.[1]

Dancers' Magic

As for so many other operations, there is magic for the wearing of masks. It seems to serve two special purposes, first to make them light and manageable, so that the dancer will give a creditable performance, and second to draw as many as possible of the girls and women round him.

One of the reasons for the semi-fasting of the *harehare-akore*—it seems curiously wide of the mark—was to make them 'light' and thus capable of dancing well at the first emergence; and later on each man, as he dons the mask, will

---

[1] A variant for *Baiu* is *Bevaia Herei*, said to be an imitation of the bamboo drumming practised on the *lakatoi* (i.e. *bevaia*). This recalls the traditional connexion between *Baiu aualari* and the *hiri* trade. See p. 223, footnote.

PLATE 53

Two *Kaia Hevehe*

A group of *Hevehe*. From left to right: (1) *Kauri*, (2) *Baiu-Kauri*, (3) *Ahea*,
(4) *Kauri*

utter a spell (if he knows one) for the same reason. Needless to say these are highly private, for some dance better than others and, as there is a certain amount of competition in it, a man will not give away the secret of his lightfootedness. I succeeded in recording only one such, and that seems obscure and somewhat atypical. In lifting any heavy mask to put over his head Havaiveakore would say, *Laivari Kaiavari paiheiava!* which means 'Raingirl, Skygirl, take it and sit!' He belongs to the *Kaia aualari* and he is apparently addressing the two *Kaia* maidens directly: they are to take the weight, to sit airily on his shoulders as if they were the mask itself.

But competition is evinced more clearly in attracting the females (though no doubt it is much the same thing, for they respond to good dancing), and there are plenty of spells for this purpose. An *Ahea aualari* example is as follows:

'I, Kari, am about to descend. Ivioro and Hovoho, rise and gather round me.'[1]

'I, Hare and Papare, am lifting the mask. Ovaro, Mairo, Biau, and Havare, gather about me.'[2]

A *Baiu* example:

'I am Baiu. I am placing the *hevehe* on my head. Laiva, Paiva, Hauka, and Kirara, rise and throng about me only.'[3]

Preparations for the Feast

Thus, with magic and enthusiasm to sustain them the dancers went on from day to day, though it cannot be denied that the enthusiasm, at any rate, seemed gradually to wane. After the first week the masks were not descending in such numbers, and towards the end of the month the

---

[1] '*Ara, Kari, ohaukive-leive; Ivioro Hovoho urai araro koarakive.*' Kari is the Ahea hero and traveller. Ivioro and Hovoho are girls identified with shrimps.

[2] '*Ara, Hare Papare, ruru kaivakive-leive; Ovaro, Mairo, Biau, Havare, araro koarakive.*' Hare and Papare are Sun and Moon, though my informant said he was really speaking as Harai, the Morning Star. (In repeating spells false names are often substituted for the real, more secret ones.) The girls Ovaro, Mairo, Biau, and Havari are identified with kinds of taro.

[3] '*Baiu, hevehe huhakive leive. Laiva, Paiva, Hauka, Kirara, urai ara hiki karukaiaki.*' The informant said: 'I put away my own name as I don the mask and take that of Baiu.' The four girls mentioned are identified with species of crabs.

parades were mostly limited to early morning and the after-noons from four o'clock onwards. And by this time, also, the masks were showing some signs of wear: structurally they remained quite sound, but the paint and feathers had lost something of their freshness.

The reason for the apparent falling-off in enthusiasm was, however, largely a practical one. The guests had, of course, dispersed, and the villagers were largely occupied with pre-parations for a further feast. It will be readily understood that these festivities entail a great deal of labour, and the business of food-getting took men and women away from the village for some part of each day; though it was marvel-lous to see how the girls, returning from a day's arduous sago-making, would change into their best and be all eagerness for the dance. Meanwhile the *harehare-akore*, still wearing their yellow bark-cloth, somewhat begrimed, were mostly loitering about the village. They had to sleep in the *eravo* by night; while by day the little ones, too small to wear the masks, would gather together on the *eravo*-veranda, singing a song of their own at the head of the *papaita*, some-times holding up a mat of plaited palm-leaf, ostensibly to hide the entrance. It was just another perfunctory form of concealment: the women must not look in and see the masks hanging there like empty shells. But it was only once in a while that the door was thus closed, and at other times the women saw quite enough to dispel their curiosity.

The Last Emergence

The Revelation had taken place on the morning of 10 February. On 9 March everything was in readiness for the ceremony known as *Laraa*, the Procession. This was to wind up the Month of Masquerade, and once again a great number of people from all parts of the Bay had assembled to see it.

All the *hevehe* were to come down, and by eight o'clock they were on the beach.[1] As they descended there had been many demonstrations of feeling on the part of the women. They had gathered in a crowd about the front of the *eravo*,

---

[1] Two or three remained in the *eravo*. The reason was, I understand, that drums could not be found for them.

PLATE 54

A *Hevehe* surrendering its drum

Demonstrations of grief by the women when a *Hevehe* comes down for its last dance

and as various *hevehe* reached the ground they were met with exhibitions of tenderness and of real grief at this their last appearance. Women would run forward to embrace their projecting jaws and kiss their faces, while not a few were shedding tears. I noted one elderly woman dancing behind her *hevehe* as it made out to the beach, her arms stretched out before her, limp at the wrists, and her head sunk on her breast—the very picture of despair. As she passed close to me I could actually see the tears rolling down her cheeks. Another woman, young, brawny, and obviously pregnant, with a baby perched on her shoulders, danced backwards in front of her *hevehe*. Her movements were positively wild—the baby had a rough ride indeed—and she was brandishing a stick. Bystanders suggested that she meant to use it on any one who attempted to take the *hevehe*'s drum, but she had no such violent intention. The women were resigned to the parting, but such demonstrations as these showed that they were genuinely affected.

Meanwhile the *hevehe* were streaming onto the beach, some to the west and some to the east according as they belonged to one *eravo*-side or the other; and they were now enjoying their last dance. An amusing diversion, not entirely devoid of pathos, was provided by a middle-aged couple named Aori and Koru. Koru had attached herself to the *hevehe* worn by her son. But this was plainly wrong, in her husband's opinion: her allegiance was due to his own *hevehe*, which descended later, worn by some other person. When this second *hevehe* came down it was for the moment without attendants, and Aori was insulted and cut to the quick. Armed with a long trade-knife he followed his faithless spouse down the beach, found her dancing to the drum of the wrong *hevehe*, and knocked her over. The last I saw of him, he was driving his wife back towards the *eravo*, shouting, in contradictory but characteristic mood, that he did not want her to dance with his *hevehe* at all.

Laraa, *the Procession*

But the others took no notice of this little incident. The beach was swarming with groups, *hevehe* and their escorts, more numerous than at any stage before. They were making the most of their last few minutes. But now, one after another and independently, the *hevehe* began to give up their drums. This was done informally: it appears that any one might take over the drum, and in most cases it was no doubt the owner himself, who was anxious not to lose track of it. (It is said that the transfer must not take place too far away, for without drumming and dancing the mask would grow so 'heavy' that its wearer might not make the distance back to the *eravo*.) In each case the man who took over the drum began to beat it himself and to dance, but the *hevehe* had danced for the last time. It was led off, trudging along to the sound of its rattles, to join the procession.

All the *hevehe* were now forming single file on the beach, one line on the east and one on the west. Each mask-wearer held in his hand a wisp of the mantle of the *hevehe* in front of him, so that, to use a very foreign simile, they were like a string of camels, tied nose to tail. Thus very slowly the two lines advanced to meet one another, while the crowds of spectators on either flank, having taken over the drums, continued to dance.

When finally the heads of the processions met they turned inwards and the *hevehe* moved towards the *eravo* two by two. (The Old Testament allusion is quite irresistible.) Never had they appeared so impressive as at this moment when they formed themselves in massed array, their tall spikes bristling like gigantic spears. Thus they advanced straight to the foot of the *papaita* and began to file up. It is worth remarking that this whole movement was extremely well organized; and considering the congestion the masked men disappeared into the interior of the building at a surprising speed. The retreat of the *hevehe* was conducted with an orderliness that did credit to what was on the whole a solemn occasion.

Cutting off the Last *Hevehe*

All the women had crowded about the front of the *eravo* to watch them disappear, the men standing back, partly out of consideration no doubt, since the women were the principal mourners, but mainly in order to allow them full play for the incident known as *Koerapakive*, 'The Cutting-off'. It had been arranged among the men that the rear of the procession should be formed by a number of comparatively small, light masks, the wearers of which had been selected for their strength and good training. When all but eight had passed or were passing up the gangway, these remaining few suddenly found their way barred by a number of women. Next moment they were circled about by a score of robust females clasping one another's hands. Almost immediately the circle broke up into two, one for either *eravo*-side and each imprisoning four *hevehe*.

Now there ensues a rollicking kind of 'Bull in the Ring'. The *hevehe* try again and again to burst through the circle. They turn side on and hurl themselves on the outstretched arms of the women. But the women are strong, and they are reinforced by others, standing outside the ring, who clamp their hands together. They easily hold their own and send the *hevehe* staggering back into the centre; but after repeated charges the wall begins to break and one after another the prisoners escape. Some of them are fairly tottering with fatigue, and there is no question but that the women agree to let them out. I heard one of the wearers, a young man, telling afterwards how he had said to his sister in the ring, 'Isn't it time you let me go?'; and at the next assault he was free.

Some informants, thinking rather exclusively of their own part in it, interpret the *Koerapakive* as a 'trial of strength' between *hevehe* and women. For them perhaps it means no more; and even for the women it seems to have turned into a game which is worth playing for its own sake. But the purport of the ceremony as such is obviously something other. It represents the women's last effort to prevent the *hevehe* from leaving them; it is kidnap motivated by affection.

When the last of the eight—and this was the last of all the *hevehe*—got clear and made its way up the gangway, the women turned with one accord towards the *eravo*, raised their arms above their heads with palms forward, and burst into a united chant. There were 200 and more of them closely packed together, and the sudden roar of their voices coupled with this unexpected action, so spontaneous and yet so well concerted, had a profound impressiveness. A number of men with the *hevehes'* drums had at the last moment sprung up on to the *papaita*, and the noise of the chorus was doubled by the sound of their drumming and stamping. Suddenly several men rushed forward towards the women, telling them by their gestures to make an end, and with strange abruptness their voices were silenced.

The drums also ceased. They would not sound again until the ceremony of purification at the end of the cycle. The great doorway, which had stood open for the past month, was closed again; while the low entrance at its base was covered over with mats. For this was one of those periods when the *eravo* is under special tabu. The *hevehe* had retired into it again and they should have it to themselves.

Chance Appearance of a Ma-Hevehe

I cannot forbear to describe at some length a chance incident which occurred at this juncture with what seemed like amazing aptness. The noise of singing and drumming had only just ceased and the crowd had not yet dissolved when it appeared that there was some excitement on the beach immediately opposite the *eravo*. Children were running in that direction and adults began to follow them. The attraction was a large sea-creature in the shallow water some 30 yards from the shore. The sea was flat calm and the monster was apparently enjoying itself, wallowing lazily and swishing its tail. It was between 15 and 20 feet long. I had never seen anything quite like it before, and my knowledge of marine zoology hardly allows me to guess what it was. Small whales, however, are sometimes stranded on Papuan beaches, and it was possibly one of these.

That, however, is immaterial. To the natives, or to some of them at any rate, it was a *hevehe havahu*, a 'real *hevehe*'. No one, as far as I could gather, had previously seen its like and there was some discussion. Haio said it was Oa Birukapu[1]

[1] See Chapter X. This is a well-known *hevehe* name and it was as good as any other to Haio. The fact that Oa Birukapu was killed in the story does not prevent his still existing as a *ma-hevehe*.

PLATE 56

The *Hevehe* filing into the *Eravo*. This shows the decorated 'backs' (*avaha*)

from Kauri, the East, and he claimed (being an opportunist) that it had come up at his summons. Others, however, suggested other names.

There was certainly some excitement at the appearance of this creature, but I must confess I felt a shade of disappointment in the popular reaction. It was freely said that it had come up at this moment to see its daughters; but what seemed to me a marvellous coincidence was on the whole accepted rather coolly. (Perhaps the edge was taken off it by the fact, which I ascertained later, that the monster had been seen at other parts of the coast during the week.) There could be no doubt that a great many took a rational view. While it is probably true that every native in Orokolo Bay believes that *ma-hevehe* exist in the sea, they remain as unseen objects of the imagination. When you can see anything as plainly as this, at 30 yards distance, then—as plainly as you see it—it is just a big fish. There was nothing, therefore, like a demonstration, and no sign of fear. In fact the crowd at the water's edge amused itself by pelting the *ma-hevehe* with stranded nipa nuts and other missiles. The monster, incidentally, appeared to take this in very good part and was in no hurry to move.

When it first appeared some young men had asked a local trader, Mr. F. W. Burke, to shoot it (*ma-hevehe* or no, these young irresponsibles desired nothing more than to see a successful shot), and he was already standing on a log with his rifle. But then it appeared that the older men objected, and happily he allowed himself to be dissuaded. There were good practical reasons against shooting it: for all their common-sense attitude, the natives declared emphatically that they would not risk eating it, and, therefore, a pestilential carcass would have been thrown up on the beach. But the objections of the old men were apparently of a different kind. Haio himself declared that, if it were killed, all the people would be angry with him and he would die; and it was Haio who went to Mr. Burke and finally succeeded in persuading him to put away his rifle.

Five years after this occurrence Mr. Burke told me how the argument had gone. While he was still standing on the log, undecided whether to oblige the younger fry by shooting, the old man came running from the *eravo*. He stood before him trembling with agitation, pouring forth a stream of words which Mr. Burke could not understand, and holding up between thumb and finger, as if it would explain everything, a tiny yellow feather from the crest of a cockatoo.

The redoubtable old man had been translated to another sphere when I heard this tale, so the clue could not be followed up. But it would be interesting to know what he meant by his yellow feather.

PLATE 57

Cutting off the last *Hevehe*: two *Nabo* masks left in the ring

'Feast of the Birds': laying out the food (p. 372)

XXIV

PASSING OF THE *HEVEHE*

THE *hevehe* having withdrawn and the sea-monster departed, the excitement died quickly away. It was now about 10.30 a.m., and while the men dispersed, the women set to work energetically on their cooking.

Feast of the Birds

The feast for which they were preparing, the most ostentatious in the whole cycle, is called *Ori-ve Eapoi* or *Mahea Eapoi*. The first expression means 'Feast of the Birds', the metaphor covering all those visitors who have attended during the previous month to dance in or around the masks. The second might be translated 'Feast of the Swaying Skirts', for the word *mahea*[1] stands for the characteristic movement of the dancing woman, a swaying of the hips which causes her skirt to swish rhythmically from side to side. Both men and women were now to be repaid for their efforts, though they might assuredly have said that the pleasure was theirs.

By about three o'clock the cooking was done. The verandas were thick with girls and women, lolling, laughing, and gossiping, and the *baupa-eravo* (there were at that time three of them attached to Avavu Ravi) full of men. I happened to be in one of these when Haio entered with Duru at his heels. It often fell to him to keep things on the move, and now he had to deal with a company that was rather drowsy. He departed, uttering loud sharp exclamations of indignation and disgust, to stir up the next *baupa-eravo*, and a number of men went off at his bidding to cut fresh coconut fronds.

These were to be laid on the ground for the setting-out of the feast, but there ensued a friendly dispute of unconscionable length regarding their arrangement. Some preferred

---

[1] A different word from *mahea*, boiled sago (*ma-ahea*), though hardly distinguishable in pronunciation. Another near-homophone.

the idea of erecting temporary racks of bamboo, but after long and vociferous dispute these seemed to be overruled, and there was a general movement to procure more sago branches. But still they argued, while men stood round with pots in their arms waiting to put them down. If only one could have taken command it would have been settled in a moment, but it seemed as if they would never reach a decision. Finally some one's voice prevailed, and then, in less than no time, they had the sago-fronds laid out to every one's satisfaction in a wide arc facing the *eravo*-front.

Even then there was further disputation regarding the number and sequence of the heaps of food—one for every community, far or near, which had honoured Avavu Ravi by its presence. But at last some forty piles were ranged in the right order, each consisting of roast sago in wrappings of palm-leaf, pots of stew (set upright in little circular holes ground out by a twist of the heel), piles of fresh coco-nuts, green and yellow bunches of areca-nut, red boiled crabs, and hunks of pork.

There was little formality about the distribution, and the young women, representing their communities as the cheerful beasts of burden, came forward to pick up the first shares almost before the last had been laid out. These women were to carry away the great bulk of the food, but they were anxious to dispose of their part of the hot stew before they had to leave, so there now ensued a rather hurried eating.

Slaying of the Hevehe

Some were already leaving, but many were still sitting about the pots, when the *eravo*-door opened—for the last time—and there emerged four *hevehe*, 'Koraia', 'Pekeaupe', and two others, each carrying its pandanus sleeping-mat and head-rest. They descended the *papaita* and ranged themselves abreast before the *eravo*, facing towards the sea. A youth took his stand before them armed with bow and arrows. It was Morea, the younger son and chosen representative of Ere, the old *amua* and *kariki haera* of Avavu Ravi. Perhaps Ere would have performed the rite himself

PLATE 58

Slaying the *Hevehe*

had he been fit to do so; but that very morning, while standing on a crowded house-veranda to watch the *Laraa* approaching the *eravo*, the old man had made a false step and
fallen. He was now actually dying, but his mantle of magic
had fallen on the shoulders of this young stripling.

The women were already scurrying from the village, not
without looking over their shoulders, when Morea took his
stand before 'Pekeaupe', fitted an arrow to the string, and
took deliberate aim. The arrow pierced the face of the mask,
and very realistically, as if mortally wounded, the *hevehe*
staggered and fell. As it did so the women who had remained to see its dispatch raised a great cry—ostensibly, and
no doubt in reality also, one of sorrow—and fled from the
village. They did not witness the death of the remaining
three. These were not shot with arrows, but they also fell,
one after another; though, since the women were no longer
staying to see, their wearers did not trouble to make them
collapse so theatrically. Instead they remained standing,
lifted the masks from their shoulders, and allowed them to
topple slowly over.

This is *Hevehe Harive*, 'The Slaying of the *Hevehe*', the
rite being performed representatively on the leader, or
leaders, alone.[1] It is enough for the women to see the first
of their darlings brought down: they fly from the scene
thinking (supposedly) that all the others are to suffer the
same fate.

Why the *hevehe* should be killed at all is a question which
no native was ever able to answer. Why should the spirit
visitors be ceremonially done to death, only to be re-created
in the next cycle, when they might pass from one into the
other as if living throughout?[2] They are tacitly recognized
as immortal, so the repeated act of killing them might well
be called otiose. But any primordial significance in this
'slaying of the god' I shall leave to those whose comparative
studies entitle them to explain it. The native, to repeat,
cannot do so; nor does he feel it necessary to try. All I
succeeded in getting out of him was the plain statement—

[1] I was assured that in strict form both of the *oropa hevehe* should have been shot.
[2] It is to be noted that there is no killing of the *kovave*.

given with a touch of exasperation at my stupidity—that it was *birari mai*, a custom of his forefathers.[1]

It is worth pausing, however, to mention the magic associated with the shooting of the *hevehe*, though once more it is found to vary and throws no clear light on the problem. I missed my opportunity of questioning Morea himself; but three other *kariki haera* were coaxed to reveal their formulae.

Auaverare averred that his was precisely the same as he used when drawing his bow at a bush-pig:

'I, Apu-akore, stand here and am about to kill you. I am taking all you possess. Come hither to me.'[2]

Probably this is no more than a spell for straight shooting.

Akeavira says simply,

'I am shooting Oa Birukapu.'

And it may be remembered that he referred to the same mythical character in splitting the coco-nut at the very beginning of the cycle.[3]

Kaivipi's formula looks at first sight more significant:

'I am about to break the bones of my mother and father.'[4]

When I heard this formula I received something of a shock, for it seemed to suggest that the *hevehe* might represent the spirits of Kaivipi's dead rather than any independent spirits of the environment, and up to that point I had met with no hint of any such significance in the whole cycle. But my misgivings disappeared when he went on (like Auaverare above) to state that this was merely his hunting spell, breathed on his arrow as he was waiting for the pig. He expressly denied that the *hevehe* were in any way identified

---

[1] Farther down the coast, in the Karama tribe, the *hevehe* (which obviously correspond to the Western Elema *hevehe*) represent, not independent spirits, but those of the tribal dead (see *Vailala Madness*, pp. 46, 47). It is not wholly impossible that this may stand as an earlier basis of the cult. Where such an interpretation existed it is conceivable that the spirits of the dead, having consorted awhile with their surviving relatives and friends, should be finally dispatched, sent off for good. This is merely a suggestion and cannot be substantiated. The Orokolo and Karama forms of *Hevehe* must have derived from the same source; but there is no saying which has diverged more widely from the original. There seems to be no evidence that the Orokolo cult had a mortuary significance.

[2] '*Arava, Apu-akore laipaivira, aro harive leive. Ave haruku ara avi-laipaivira. Ava arakae ekekia.*' Apu-akore ('Blood-Child') was born from a swelling in the thigh of Oa Iruapu, the *Kauri* man. He shot a great number of the people of Vailala East for maltreating his father.

[3] See p. 205.   [4] '*Oave lauwe uki koekakive leive.*'

PLATE 59

Dismantling the masks

with his parents or ancestors when, with some anxiety in my heart, I put that question; and further than this, he admitted that the words 'my father' and 'my mother' were merely blinds. They covered the real identity of some *maho haera* which Kaivipi refused point-blank to divulge. They had been given him by his father, he said, and his father had told him never to part with the secret.

If there be any justification for this little digression it is that it shows once more a point worth emphasizing, viz. that the native can perform even such an impressive rite as shooting the leader of the *hevehe* without any idea of why he does so.

The Burning

With the fall of the four *hevehe* and the exodus of the women there began a scene of deliberate destruction. Masks, no longer worn but carried, came pouring out of the door to be propped against house-walls or thrown carelessly on the ground. Without the slightest trace of reverence or regret their owners proceeded to strip them of their *mae* mantles and their feathers. In some cases the *ape*, or snout, was detached for use in a further cycle; and in three or four the cane framework (the decorated *pura* having been mercilessly stripped away) was carried off to Waiea Ravi to be used in the current cycle there—though this last was resented by some as an informality. Most, however, were far too busy with the work of demolition to care or notice. Rolls of feathers and bundles of *mae*[1] were hastily being stowed away in the *eravo*—for no such traces must be left outside—and already the much-battered masks were being borne off to the creek some distance in the rear. Here they were flung down unceremoniously in three piles, two on the near side and one on the farther, but all on the very edge of the bank whence the remains would be swept away by the tide. They were heaped up in three places instead of one merely to prevent the bonfire from being too big and possibly dangerous.

[1] For the feathers see pp. 298, 300; the *mae* is eventually given to the women who have made it. It was their gift to the *hevehe* and it is now returned.

It seemed as if the masks were to be disposed of without any touch of ceremony whatever, so keen was every one on the practical side of the business. But presently Haio came down with a dry coco-nut leaf and a smouldering husk in his hand. He applied one to the other and blew them into a flame, and then, uttering a few brief words in a slightly raised voice, thrust his torch into the first heap. Dry as tinder, the tangled mass of old cane and bark-cloth burst into flames and in a moment became a raging furnace, from the heat of which it was necessary to stand far back and shelter one's face. The second and third heaps were lit in quick succession and the flames of all three shot up to the sky together, the fronds of the tall coco-nuts swaying in the ascending currents as if they were tormented by a gale of wind. Thus the products of years of industry and art perished in a few fiery moments.

But there was no awe-struck watching of the flames—unless on the part of the ethnographer. The destruction of the *hevehe* masks is as informal and matter-of-fact as that of the *kovave*: so much rubbish has to be got out of the way. Long, therefore, before the fires had burnt themselves out the men were back in the village, and very soon their women returned also. The latter were not in strictness supposed to know that the masks had been burnt; but the men admitted laughingly that they did; and, at any rate, they had not gone so far away that they could fail to observe that column of smoke.

The words which Haio uttered at the first pile were something as follows (if we may trust his retrospective version—I do not think he said quite so much):

'Now I am about to burn you. Look kindly on the men of my *eravo*. When they hunt let not the arrow stick in the ground, but in the eye of the pig.

'I do no harm to you. Constantly, from long ago I have fed and fostered you. Do not be angry with us';

and at the second pile:[1]

'Look kindly on the men of my *eravo*. Do them no harm. Guard them when they are at work from accident with knife or hatchet.'

[1] I did not see who lit the third pile. It was probably lit from one of the others by no one in particular.

PLATE 60

Haio sets fire to the pile of masks

Consultation with other old men who have at different times performed the rite of burning throws little more light on the subject than does the utterance of Haio. They all appear to dwell on the fact that they have fed the *hevehe* well, adding that in the future those, their children, who are in a position to do so will call them up again; and some of them go on to pray that their people may be spared from accident in the bush.

Thus Kaivipi:

'I have called you up because of my pigs and sago. I have fed you constantly. In the future some other strong men will call you. Do not be angry.'[1]

(It is interesting to note that Kaivipi has also his special hidden magic for the occasion. The words first quoted, or their equivalent, are for public utterance; not so, however, the following:

'I am stripping off the skin of Obo and Youpa.'[2]

It is not at all improbable that others have their true magic also which they keep to themselves. But it is not easy to understand its function in such circumstances, and it is equally probable that some of the old men who burn the masks do entirely without it.)

The most illuminating among a number of utterances was that given me by Mahevehe and Koraguba in collaboration. The burner first cries out:

'The man of pigs, the man of dogs, calls you. But now I burn you.'[3]

Then he goes on to use the extremely secret names of two *Kaia*, or Sky, men.

'Ivo and Leravea; our women, girls, and little boys—suffer no centipedes to sting them, no thorns to pierce them, no snakes or sharks to bite them. Guard them well.'[4]

---

[1] '*Ara aro itavape yereva ira poi. Aro avikialaive ape. Aidake horova haera aro ava itavakirai. Ava hihiriva ka.*' *Horova haera* (lit. workman) is 'one who breeds and feeds many pigs and always gives food to visitors', thus getting for himself and his *eravo* a good name.

[2] '*Obo Youpa-ve ruru haiperohavakive.*' Obo is identified with the python; Youpa, his son, with a green snake. Obo is elsewhere called Biai.

[3] '*Irakore Ave'akore itavake aroava. Mahau mave avearo.*' *Irakore* = *ira-akore*, 'pig-son', or 'man of many pigs'.

[4] '*Ivo Lerevea, erave uavire morita mekehaku—eapea kavuramaruea karahe kahuaruea, ekaroa kavuramaruea, aitara kavuramaruea. Beveke hiki-leikia.*' Ivo and Lerevae are credited in *Kaia* mythology with the invention of *Hevehe*.

In this typical mixture of utterances (and if the true *maho* could be given in all cases the mixture would be much greater) there is no actual mention of the destruction of the *hevehe*; and when, in the present connexion, I have asked where they go, my informants have answered plainly that they do not know.

Yet the fact that the ceremony of burning takes place on the edge of the bush, together with the references to hunting in one of the utterances and to knives and axes, thorns, centipedes, and snakes in others, would seem to make it plain that the *hevehe* are here thought of as returning to the bush. Like the *aiaimunu* of the Delta (which are called *irimunu* or Tree-Spirits) and like the *kovave* of Orokolo Bay itself (which are plainly identified with '*kora marita*', 'Tree Maidens') it seems that the *hevehe* return to the forest side of the Elema environment—if not exclusively, at least predominantly. This is thoroughly in keeping with the results of our earlier investigation into the names and associations of the individual *hevehe*: they are spirits of the environment at large, but by far the greatest proportion have their habitat in the bush.

Descent of the Hevehes' *Spirits*

It would be asking too much to expect complete consistency in a complex so large as that of *Hevehe*; and the major rift is apparent in what follows. For, after being consumed with flames in the bush, the *hevehe* have still to go down to the sea.

During the evening of the same day there occurred the *Hevehe Ove Dehoai*, 'Descent of the *Hevehes*' Spirits'. One may be permitted to doubt whether the word *ove* would have come to be used at all were it not that the masks have already been killed and destroyed. According to the currently accepted theory, viz. that the *hevehe* have been brought up by their mother from the sea, their sojourn in the village would seem to find its natural end in a return to the sea, and might be called simply *Hevehe Dehoai*. But, the ceremonies of killing and burning having intervened, it is necessary to cover the discrepancy by pretending that it is only their spirits which go down to the water.

At about 8 p.m. a score or so of men with drums, rattles, and shell-trumpets were collecting in a whispering crowd at the foot of the *papaita*. They filed up as quietly as possible, but not without an occasional inadvertent tinkle of the rattles. Once inside they crouched down, some on either side of the *eravo*. Two kerosene lamps were lit, but they did little to dispel the cavernous darkness of the great building, which was now, of course, empty of *hevehe*. A man, Karave-hape, was going round whispering instructions. It appeared that two young men were to be initiated.[1] After they had arrived a bull-roarer would sound outside; then the floor of the *kaia larava* would be struck with a stick; and then the drums and rattles were to come into action. At this juncture Haio entered and pointed out, with every sign of irritation, that the men should have prepared their ambush in the *kaia larava*. But it was now too late to make any change, and in another moment the initiates were led in.

The bull-roarer proved a blank. The small party advanced hesitantly and stood waiting in the centre of the *eravo*. Then there came a sound of beating on the floor, but without response. The beating was repeated, and some one started up with his rattle; and at that the storm of noise broke over the initiates. It cannot be denied that the opening drill was very indifferent; but it may be remembered that this, unlike the ordinary *Hevehe Karawa*, is a rare occasion, and rehearsal is out of the question.

When the novices had been given an adequate dose of it the noise ceased. But after a moment's pause it began again, now with the addition of *puva* blasts, and all began to troop out of the *eravo*, drumming and rattling as they went. Thus crossing the village they descended to the beach and, turning towards the west, proceeded without any slackening of noise for a full half-mile. Nearing Yogu they suddenly ceased, and I noticed that some of the party entered the shallow water. The *puva* sounded again; there was a prolonged burst of drumming and rattling, and then silence;

[1] This is equivalent to initiation to *Hevehe Karawa* on the beach.

whereupon the party made its way home, doing its utmost to muffle the rattles.[1]

Ma-Hevehe *takes the Remnants*

The *hevehe* had been destroyed and their spirits had departed, but they had left behind them certain material traces —their sleeping-mats, their head-rests, quantities of *koro*, and sundry remnants of *mae*. The last-mentioned, called *edoroba*, or rubbish, consisted mainly of the snippings—a considerable quantity—left over at the trimming of the mantles.[2] These had been stored in the *eravo* ever since, and had incidentally provided some comfortable bedding for the *harehare-akore* who had been sleeping there.

All these things had now to be disposed of, and at about 2.30 p.m. on the following day they were brought out to be cast into the sea: they were to be taken away by the *ma-hevehe* itself. Each *harehare-akore* carried something—a pandanus-leaf mat, a bundle of *mae*, or one of the low trestles used in decorating the mask and called its 'pillow'—and all formed themselves into a single-file procession as they issued from the *eravo*. They were supported by the owners of the masks, i.e. the *hevehe-oa*, and apparently by others also, so that the procession must have numbered nearly 300. The *harehare-akore* were still dressed in their yellow costumes, now much the worse for wear and dirt, and sported the hornbill feathers to which initiation had entitled them. Nearly every one, except for the little boys, carried also his bow and arrows. At their head went the youth Morea, walking slowly and carrying in shoulder-arms fashion the *hohao* named 'Kevaro', which belonged to the left side of the *eravo*. It had been decorated with scarlet hibiscus blooms, and Morea, a slim, good-looking young man with an unusually well-grown mop of hair, made a very striking figure. He was obviously full of his new dignity. Farther back came a second *hohao*, 'Mariere', from the right side.

Leaving the *eravo* the procession turned left and filed

---

[1] It will be noted that there is a further slight inconsistency in this ceremony, the *hevehe* having given up their drums at the *Laraa* that morning. But perhaps their *ove* may be permitted drums at a stretch.　　　　[2] See pp. 308, 309.

through the village; then out on to the broad low-tide beach, where it turned back to the right. Coming level with Avavu, Ravi the leader halted, and the rear, already straggling to a great length, closed up. All turned to face the sea. Their bows and arrows they stuck upright in the sand as if stacking arms, and the fluttering hornbill feathers were removed and tied to them for safety. Then every one, gazing intently out to sea, stood waiting.

Before the procession had come to a halt four old men had posted themselves at intervals along the water's edge. They now stood in front like so many aged officers before the troops— Mahevehe on the extreme left, Haio and Erai in the centre, and Aravaia of Yogu on the right. Each of them held a *hore*, or switch of cassowary plumes, which he waved constantly before him just as the captain of a *bevaia* does when he wants to waft his spells over the ocean. And now each began in a loud voice to call on the *ma-hevehe*.

Fig. 21. 'Kevaro', a *Hohao* of Avavu Ravi. (3 ft. 6 in. approx.)

They called in turn, not interrupting one another, and each on a different set of *ma-hevehe*: Aravaia on Owouka, Birouku, Baitoo, and Maiavu; Erai on Haihaiapo, Lahero, Iharuapo, Ira, and Ope; and so on. The wind had got up a little overnight and it was a rather stirring spectacle, these old men shouting hoarsely into it, while behind them the full male strength of the village, drawn up in one serried rank, gazed on the waters for a sign. Meanwhile on either flank stood two bodies of women and girls ready and eager to respond to the signal.

The summoning of the *ma-hevehe* went on and on. 'Hevehe Maiavu! You have eaten our pigs and sago. Arise! Hevehe Owouka! Hevehe Baitoo!' and so on, each man going deliberately through his list. Haio's voice began to give out. From where I stood at the end of the line I saw him advance, stoop, and apparently drink. I thought it was some further rite, but he was merely gargling salt water. From then on, however, he reduced his list to the two names Ohariapo and Bovoiea.

For fully twenty minutes the calling continued without any sign of impatience or misgiving on the part of those who silently waited. It was (as I ascertained later) when Erai was in action and when he was uttering the name of Hevehe Ope that a young man, Youpa, caught sight of a large black fin and saw in a rising wave beneath it the dark shape of a *ma-hevehe*. He raised a shout, and instantaneously the whole line was off the mark. In one tumultuous charge men, boys, and little boys raced down the beach and flung themselves into the water, while the excited females of the right and left wings were hardly a second behind them.

Wooden head-rests, mats, armfuls of *mae*—all leavings of the *hevehe*—were tossed into the water to be thrown hither and thither by the youngsters in the shallows. Meanwhile the stronger swimmers had struck out for the deeper water and for some ten minutes, amid shouting and laughter, the bathe continued. Meanwhile the rising tide, which has a strong westward set, was already carrying off the *edoroba*. The *ma-hevehe*, presumably Ope, had risen in response to the summons and was taking it away.

It will have been noted that ideas about the *ma-hevehe*, their character, names, and number, are somewhat mixed. It even seems doubtful at times whether they are seriously thought to exist at all. On the whole it would appear that, just as other semi-educated people believe in ghosts at one

PLATE 61

A. The procession, Morea leading with the *Hohao* 'Kevaro'

B. Summoning the *Ma-Hevehe*. The man on the right is Aravaia

C. The dash into the sea when the *Ma-Hevehe* is sighted

Ma-Hevehe takes the remnants

time and do not believe in them at another, so the Western Elema native sometimes thinks the *ma-hevehe* exist and sometimes merely pretends they do. It is largely a question of moods and the intellectual attitudes that accompany them. But it is also evident that there are grades of sophistication among the Elema public: the ignorant masses no doubt believe at all times in the sea-monsters, but there are others who take a shrewder view.

I spent some time in trying to account for the unexpected appearance of the *hohao* in the ceremony just described, and the results of my inquiries will serve to illustrate this difference in attitudes. The readiest explanation and the one that satisfies most is merely that the parading of the *hohao* is *overa-mai* or *birari-mai*, an ancient or ancestral custom. But there is also a quite widely accepted theory that the decorated plaque is an attraction to the real *hevehe*, a temptation to it to rise and satisfy its curiosity by a closer inspection. This at least implies a recognition that the *ma-hevehe* exists. A third kind of theory, however, would seem to dispense with any such recognition. It may perhaps be called the real theory, though it should be remembered that it is not shared by, or even known to, the bulk of people. It is that the *hohao*, a genuine *kaiavuru*,[1] itself provides the apparition of a *ma-hevehe* which must be seen before the *edoroba* can be thrown into the sea. The *kariki-haera* who bears it will address it with the appropriate magic, and at last its *ove*, or immanent spirit, will slip away and presently appear in the sea, in the temporary guise of a *ma-hevehe*.

This explanation was amply verified by consultation with the best heads in several different *eravo*. It is the explanation given by those who are really in the know. There is no question that the spirit of the *hohao* is believed to exist: it is an old-established lodger in the *eravo* and has a much deeper place in the *eravo*'s religious system. But as for the *ma-hevehe* —to these more sophisticated minds its appearance was nothing but a sham. But for the *hohao* and its obliging spiritualistic fake they might have been kept waiting on the beach for ever.

[1] See p. 155.

Purification

The bathe over, most of the participants dispersed to their houses; but the younger *harehare-akore*, those who had worn masks for the first time in the present cycle, attended in the *eravo* for *Eharau Buahorive*, 'The Fumigation of Stomachs'. A feast had been prepared and certain pots of stew doctored with various herbs and leaves known collectively as *pairava*. The scented steam from these is considered to possess some purificatory value. So now the smaller boys were to be seen bending over to inhale it; then turning their heads, first to one side then to the other, to allow it to penetrate their ears; and, finally, straddling the pots on hands and knees while the lustral vapours played upon their stomachs.

It is of greater importance for the smaller boys than for the adults to undergo this rite, for it is said that without it they would fail to grow satisfactorily. But to-morrow and the next day it is to be repeated, and then the older *harehare-akore* will take their turn also. There can be no doubt that in *Hevehe*, as in *Kovave*, contact with the masks, as symbols or representations of supernatural beings, is thought to involve some danger; and now that the dance is over the wearers' bodies must be purged of it.

It seems probable that the bathe has a further significance unconnected with the disposal of the *edoroba*. For, apart from the bathe preceding the Fire-Fight, this is the first time the *harehare-akore* have entered the water since they received their ginger-leaf and began their semi-fasting.[1] It marks the end of those avoidances which they have undergone partly in order to make them light dancers under the masks and partly for the oft-repeated reason of conserving the feathers. After this they return to ordinary diet.

It is a fact to be remarked that there have been two communal bathes. It is only the second that brings the avoidances to a close; the earlier one, which took place more than a month ago, was, so to speak, thrown in. It has already been suggested that the previous bathe belonged expressly to the complex of the *Hii-Kairu*; and now the fact that the period

[1] See p. 298.

of avoidances runs right on to the second bathe makes it appear more than ever likely that the first, together with the other features constituting the *Hii-Kairu* complex, is a cultural interpolation.

For some reason, which I never succeeded in elucidating, the ceremony of the casting away of *edoroba* is always repeated at the Aivei River, some miles to the west. On the next day, therefore, certain rubbish which has been previously overlooked is carried there, though it appears that on this occasion only the men and bigger boys enter the water. It is on reaching home that they in their turn undergo the rite of purification.

Hunt for the Bush-Pig

The second purification over, they proceed with preparations for the pig-hunt which is an essential feature of the winding-up of *Hevehe*. In the late afternoon there is an *ivaiva* (and it was on this occasion that I noticed the food-offering being passed round the heads of the juvenile *hare-hare-akore* as if they were somehow to be included among those for whom intercession was made). The *kariki-haera* has already collected his barks and leaves, and they may now be seen smouldering in the blackened potsherds before the principal *hohao*, while their fragrant smoke wreathes round the numerous bows and arrows leaning against the alcove partitions. In his capacity of community hunting-magician he is imbuing them with the power and accuracy that belonged to some mythical hunter whose name he keeps a secret.

At dawn of the following day the party set forth; and although hunting is a rare and chancy undertaking they succeeded in their first attempt, returning at noon with a fine pig. I missed seeing their entry into the village, and, as I was at this stage making preparations to leave Orokolo, failed also to see the ceremonies attending the subsequent hunts. But it is said that the pig is first laid in the centre of the *eravo* 'so as to be seen by the *hohao*' before it is singed, cut up, and distributed among all the *hevehe-oa*, whether of Avavu Ravi or neighbouring communities, who have played a part in the cycle. The *eravo*-front is decorated with croton (*haihiava*), and all the men join in singing a song *Kairi* (which admittedly belongs to the Namau people and is in their dialect), while the women give expression to their feelings in the dance called *Avava*.[1]

Most of the women are content to look on, and they do so with evident amusement. But the men's sisters, and any others who are sufficiently carried away to join them, adopt perineal bands, veil their faces and breasts with *mae*, and brandish miniature bows and arrows. When first I saw this amazonian get-up[2] I imagined that the women were impersonating men; but it appears that the perineal bands are merely worn in imitation of the women of the Purari Delta, whence the dance no doubt comes and where this is the ordinary female dress. The weapons, however, have some relevance to the pig-hunt: the women are boasting of their brothers' prowess.

Stowing away of Feathers

When once the hunters had killed one pig the *eravo* was at liberty to burn the remaining *edoroba*. But, flushed with their initial success, the men determined to hunt again, and indeed they made a number of expeditions and brought home at least two supererogatory pigs before this final clearing-away was accomplished.

In the meantime, after the second successful hunt they proceeded to the rite of *Love Aivakive*, 'The Stowing away of Feathers'. I was not present at the *ivaiva* which preceded it, but I was informed that Haio, who officiated, passed the bowl round the *edoroba* of the four leading *hevehe* as well as the posts, hearths, &c., which are invariably included in the circuit. Just as he would have dealt with the living *hevehe* (or a representative selection of them) when the *eravo* was full, so now he dealt with the rubbish they had left behind

---

[1] Distinguished from the usual stationary dance called *mahea*. It is performed by women only. The 'dance' of *hohoro*, the fire-flies, is also called *avava*. It is an omen of success in hunting, a forecast of the real dance to be performed by the women when the pig is brought home.

[2] In connexion with *Kovave*, where the same dance is performed.

them. It was a substitute for the spirits which had departed to their homes.

After the *ivaiva*, the feathers, which had been detached from the masks before burning, were packed away in pots, bamboos, trade boxes, and palm-spathe envelopes. For they are among the most treasured personal possessions of the Elema—second only to shell ornaments—and as they are so perishable the greatest care is taken to protect them. It does not appear, however, that the *ivaiva* in this case had any special bearing upon the Stowing away of Feathers. It was probably no more than the usual precaution against the risks of the further hunt which was to take place next day.

Sweeping the Eravo

It was while the men were absent on this expedition that the young man Morea performed one of the special functions of the *kariki-haera*: together with one or two assistants he was giving the vacant *eravo* what was perhaps the first spring-cleaning it had ever received. Much of the *edoroba* had already been thrown into the sea, but there remained a good quantity of fine sweepings as well as heaps of the bast under-mantles (*koro*) which had not been destroyed; and all this was now collected for the burning. It seems strange that such severely practical work should be the prerogative of a ceremonial functionary, yet the *kariki-haera* is the *eravo* care-taker and factotum; and for this, as for so many other tasks where it would seem unnecessary, there exists the appropriate magic.[1] On examination, however, it is found to bear on the success of the hunt rather than that of the tidying-up. As for the latter, it can be granted that the *kariki-haera* made some noticeable impression on the place, but his work was sadly perfunctory and stopped far short of the promised redecoration of the *hohao*.

Burning the Last Remnants

The actual burning of the *edoroba* took place some days after I had left Orokolo. To judge from verbal accounts and from the parallel rite which I have seen at the end of a

[1] See, e.g., p. 259.

Kovave cycle it is done after dark behind the *eravo*, but with few precautions. The women may see the last leavings of the *hevehe* thrown on to the bonfire. But they watch, if at all, from a distance, and they are supposedly misled by the name of the ceremony. For it is called *Pairava Hakaitapakive*, 'Casting out the *Pairava*', and they are meant to think that the materials of a very considerable conflagration are merely the old leaves and barks that have been used to purify the *harehare-akore*.

Whether the *eravo* members hunted again after this ceremony I did not ascertain. But as they had already caught three pigs they had amply fulfilled the preliminary conditions. As with *Kovave*, the slaying of a bush-pig is imperative before the cycle can be concluded, and sometimes the hunters must go out again and again until they almost despair of success.[1] If they burnt the leavings, or, as the phrase goes, 'threw out the *pairava*', without first killing a pig they would be the laughing-stock of the whole coast. Yet no one could tell me why. To draw them out I suggested that under such circumstances a village pig might fill the bill; but I was made to feel that my suggestion was ridiculous.

Answers to the question at issue, then, are either simply 'Because our fathers did so', or 'So that we may throw out the *pairava*', or 'So that others will not laugh at us'. If we require any deeper explanation we must supply it ourselves.

It may be that the animal is a final sacrifice. But this does nothing to explain the emphatic necessity for a *bush*-pig, even though one of the village breed might be larger and fatter and therefore more acceptable. I think, therefore, that the reason for the hunt is not to be found in the idea of sacrifice, but possibly in that of requital—on the part of the *hevehe*. They are predominantly bush spirits (at least in what I take to be their more fundamental aspect) and as such they have a determining influence on the success of hunters. They have been entertained and feasted in the village: now

---

[1] If another *eravo* taunts them with failure the matter will take a competitive turn. When they eventually succeed they will send this *eravo* a *hapa* with portions of the pig and decorations of croton. This is a challenge. The *eravo* in question must catch a bush-pig in order to return the present and make things square.

is the time for them to show their gratitude. The *eravo* will not rest content till they have done so. The bush-pig is proof, and three bush-pigs are threefold proof, that the *hevehe* have not been placated for nothing. Perhaps then the theory of the thing, apparently unrecognized as it is, may be contained in the valedictory words of Haio, 'Let not the arrow stick in the ground, but in the eye of the pig.'

The Final Rite

The very last act of the cycle, viz. 'Plucking out the Hornbill Feathers', was performed some time after my departure. The *harehare-akore* had continued wearing them on and off; but after a large dance provided by Avavu Ravi at the invitation of the next-door community, Waiea Ravi, they were finally put away.[1]

I was assured that *Baiva Hareavakive*, 'Plucking out the Feathers', was performed without further ceremony next morning, the dance being the only necessary preliminary. But it is plain that this dance is no more than a watery substitute for the last rite of the cycle in pre-European days. Then, it is said, the *eravo* first hunted for pigs and in due course 'threw out the *pairava*'; but after that they went hunting for a man, nor were they at liberty to stow away their hornbill feathers till they had slain one.[2] Informants, not so aged, can still recall the final scene and give the names and addresses of the victims, from Muru or Keuru, as well as those of the *kiriki-haera* who won fame by killing them.

Accounts of the ceremonies which followed the successful raid are severely garbled. But it appears that they served three purposes: they were included partly to ensure success in future expeditions; partly to purify the man-slayers; and partly to drive away the vengeful spirits of the victims. They reached their climax in a night-long session within the *eravo*, when the spirits gave evidence of their presence by perching on a long *hapa* held by the man-slayers, causing it

[1] Individuals may continue to wear their feather, or feathers, if they wish and provided they are qualified; but nowadays few do so, the mop of hair having mostly given place to the short clip. It is only the older men who adhere to the older fashion.
[2] It appears that man-killing expeditions also took place on the completion of new *eravo*.

to shake or move about against their will,[1] and thereby giving oracular answers to questions regarding the next raid.

But the time comes at last for the spirits to be ejected. Three effigies have been made of *hara*, or plaited coco-nut leaf, and they are called *Iko*, after the hero of that name who died three times. They have heads and limbs,[2] but are light, flimsy structures that can be easily thrown about; and now with the approach of dawn this is just what the men in the *eravo* are doing with them. The first of the effigies is tossed ignominiously from one man to another and then thrust through the door where a waiting crowd, largely composed of women, receive it joyously and, having made sport with it in the same contemptuous fashion, trample it on the ground. Then comes the turn of the second effigy; and, finally, the third and largest is cast out to be flung hither and thither, kicked, beaten, and trodden on, from the *eravo*-door down to the edge of the sea. Thus the victim's spirit is thrice cast out: it is gone, as Iko went, never to return.

It was, in the old days, only after this strangely macabre performance that they put away the hornbill feathers and thus brought the cycle finally to a close. It is perhaps some artistic loss to *Hevehe* that it should be clipped of this last theatrical scene; but the cycle as a whole seems to have survived pretty well without it, and if the coming of peace has deprived Iko of his role there cannot be many who will regret it.

The Empty Eravo

The long story of the *Hevehe* cycle has now been told. The *eravo* stands empty except for its human occupants and those other spirit inmates who, unlike the *hevehe*, abide with them always. Gradually the great grey building falls into decay; the floor-boards rot; thatching, ripped off by the wind, goes unrepaired; and rain falls miserably upon de-

---

[1] One of a good many manifestations of 'automatic movement' among the Elema. Cf. *supra*, p. 108; also *Vailala Madness*, pp. 33–6. The same was common among the Namau; see *Natives of the Purari Delta*, pp. 148–50, 157, 159, 160.

[2] I imagine they must have resembled the *Gopi* of the Namau. See *Natives of the Purari Delta*, pp. 171 ff.

serted hearth-sides. One by one the members seek other sleeping-quarters, and at last the *eravo* is a ruin. Then, when it threatens collapse—unless it has collapsed already—the community will make a-strenuous effort and demolish it. For some years, perhaps, they will content themselves with humbler lodgings; but at last, if spirit is willing and flesh is strong, they will set to and build themselves another *eravo*, and with that the long *Hevehe* cycle will start all over again.

It remains to be seen whether the Western Elema of modern times have got it in them.

PART III

THE CRITIQUE

XXV

THE EVOLUTION OF *HEVEHE*

The Mask-making Habit

THE origin and provenance of *Hevehe* are questions
which seem unlikely ever to be answered with cer-
tainty; and since, from the point of view adopted in this
book, they are matters of no great consequence, we have
additional reason for treating them lightly.

One source of inspiration in such a quest is provided by
the myths, and several are accordingly noted; though they
will be recognized as unsteady grounds for inference.

One story (associated with the *Kaia aualari*) is that *Hevehe*
was first instituted by Ivo, the chief man of that mythical
moiety of the *Kaia aualari* group known as the *Ipi-Haera*, or
Lower People. They, it is claimed by those who tell the
story, were the first human inhabitants of Orokolo Bay, and
they owed almost everything (even, in some versions, their
own creation) to the other moiety, viz. the *Akea-Haera*, or
Upper People, who lived in the sky. According to some it
was the chief man of the latter, named Lerevea, who taught
Ivo how to make the masks and how to carry out the ritual;
but another version has it that *Hevehe*, together with some
other features of Western Elema culture, was an independent invention of the Lower People and was retained by
them in defiance of Lerevea's disapproval and warnings.[1]
It is obvious that this myth, whichever version we adopt,
cannot help us in a serious search for origins: either the cult
was a spontaneous growth in Orokolo Bay, or it descended
there from out of the sky.

A second myth has already been noted.[2] It is that of the
sea-monster for whom, from a number of alternatives, we

[1] See *infra*, p. 437.   [2] See pp. 172 ff.

chose the name Oa Birukapu. It will be recollected that, when he was cut up and eaten, his entrails were given to the visiting womenfolk who carried them to some inland region on the Purari River and there, on washing them out, found them to contain *hevehe*, *kovave*, and bull-roarer. The *hevehe* masks were first worn by the women who had discovered them (a familiar notion in regard to mysteries which belong to the male half of society); but in due course the men, who used to be driven away from their food by these alarming figures, found out the secret and turned the tables. This myth at least gives us some geographical hints, though it is to be noted that Oa Birukapu came from *Kauri*, the east, whereas the *hevehe* were only discovered when his entrails were cut up in the north-west. It might seem unfair, on the mere strength of this story, to favour the latter as the provenance of the *Hevehe* cult; but it appears utterly improbable that it could have come from Oa Birukapu's acknowledged home in the east, viz. Lavao, near Yule Island; while, on the other hand, there are actually some further hints that its place of origin was, in native belief, the Purari.[1]

Perhaps the most generally accepted account of the origin of *Hevehe* is found in the myth of Kari, the hero of the *Ahea aualari*. In one version of this tale, which is highly involved and almost interminable, the hero is introduced as inhabiting Ere Ravi, a submarine men's-house somewhere in Orokolo Bay. Here he grew dissatisfied with the primitive kind of *hevehe* which had been in vogue up to his time (made of a thin slat, or slats, of wood, supported in the wearer's belt and tied about his neck so as to cover the front of his body). He evolved from his own mind the idea of the true mask made of cane and bark-cloth, and then set forth on a long pilgrimage, boldly destroying the old wooden masks in one place after another and earning the gratitude of their inhabitants by teaching them the true fashion. According to this version he began his journeyings by entering the Vailala

[1] According to an Iari story the first *aiaimunu* was fished out of the Purari River in one of its upper reaches by a woman named Oie. The women wore the masks until they were stolen from them by a man named Kaiva who introduced them into the *ravi* through the hole in the floor at the rear. The men wore them thenceforwards, giving out that they were tree-spirits.

River, and the first place where he introduced the *hevehe* proper was Hiraki's village, some distance up-stream.[1] (This last detail is incidentally in keeping with the claim of the Vailala bush-people, or Houra-Haera, that they are the true originators of the cult.) Thence he proceeded to the Aivei; and then, turning back, went right along the Elema coast to its eastern extremity. But the informant who gave me the fullest narrative (he was Horevuhu, renowned as a master of *Ahea* magic) began by saying that Kari came, not from the sea, but from the mountains. He descended the Purari to the coast and then, travelling under the sea, came to *Ahea-Hiru* (Sea Island) somewhere about the mouth of the Aivei. His subsequent peregrinations are described in great and somewhat confusing detail. It appears in this version that he first introduced *Hevehe* in the village of Berare-Kiwai, who is a Purari Delta character, and thence proceeded eastwards, destroying the old masks and building new ones as far as the Biaru River.

If such a story has any historical significance at all, it may make it appear that *Hevehe*, or some mask-cult corresponding to it, came originally down the Purari. But notwithstanding this and the similar hint in the previous story it must be said that there seems to exist no trace whatever at the present day of any such cult on the middle reaches of that stream.

It is not proposed to pursue this subject in any further detail. As far as concerns the Elema people at large it seems certain that the cult has made its way among them from west to east; but whence it came in the first place is a question which must remain unanswered. It has its obvious parallels in widely distant parts of the western Pacific, and it may be pointed out that the mask-making habit, merely as such, is a cultural link which associates the Elema and other peoples of the Papuan Gulf with those of the Sepik, New Ireland, and the New Hebrides.

Not only the details of structure and appearance, but also the meaning of the masks and the ritual that belongs to them,

[1] Identified roughly by informants with the villages of Keke, Pako, and Havaia, about 7° 30′ latitude. It is to be noted that the courses of the Vailala and Purari Rivers converge above this point to within 8 miles.

are matters which may be expected to vary from one culture to another. Even within the Elema field these factors show considerable diversity, which seems to demonstrate once more that cultural elements may pass on from one setting to another, leaving their original meaning behind them and taking on a new one. It seems that the trait in question is fundamentally the habit of making masks, more or less startling in appearance, to cover the head and body, and these may appear—as *hevehe, kovave, dukduk, tamate,* &c.— in a variety of forms each surrounded by its own complex of ideas and ritual.

The Antiquity of Hevehe

The people of Orokolo Bay are now firm in the opinion that *Hevehe*—or at least that central part of it which surrounds the tall masks, or *apa-hevehe*—dates from the beginning. But a number of informants from various villages of the Houra-Haera have independently maintained that the *apa-hevehe* itself originated with them, and that the Western Elema have received it as a cultural gift.

It seems that the Houra-Haera, i.e. the people of the Lower Vailala bush villages, have proved a strangely fertile source of invention, or at least one important centre of distribution, for the ceremonies now practised on the coast.[1] It is certain that they have not only provided Orokolo Bay with those special *eharo* which have been absorbed into the body of *Hevehe*, but that they are also responsible for the present form of that much more important feature in the cycle, viz. *Hevehe Karawa*. To these subjects we shall return presently. In the meantime, although it must be admitted that we have no more than the Houra-Haera's word for it, there is some suspicion that *Apa-Hevehe* itself has been introduced from that tribe to the Western Elema.

It is interesting to note that *Apa-Hevehe* and the other features which together constitute the whole cycle were not practised by the bush tribes in the hinterland of Orokolo Bay until a few generations back. Old men of Pareamamu can give

---

[1] It is perhaps significant, and at least remarkable, that the Houra-Haera also originated the Vailala Madness movement. See *Vailala Madness*, p. 28.

some detail of the circumstances in which *Apa-Hevehe* was introduced to their villages. It was brought by a Houra-Haera man of Yari, and since his grandson, a contemporary of my oldest informant (who might be 65–70 years of age), is said to be still living, it means that the *Apa-Hevehe* at Pareamamu dates back only some four or five generations at most.[1] Similarly the Muru tribe can recall the names of the men from Arihava who first showed them how to make the tall masks, *apa-hevehe*. One of them, Mava, was the father of that notable village constable, Kori, who was a leading light among the apostles of the Vailala Madness and whom I knew as an old man fifteen years ago. It is plain therefore that *Hevehe* at Muru is of still more recent introduction.

The cycle has obviously been established very much longer than this among the coastal villages of the Western Elema; but with such examples of recent introduction to hand, it must be admitted that we have no convincing reason for assuming that it is, even in Orokolo Bay, of very great antiquity.

Composite Nature of the Cycle

Neither the age of *Hevehe* nor its provenance, immediate or distant, need concern us as of real importance. A much more significant inquiry deals with the composition of the cycle as it exists to-day; and here we are on somewhat firmer ground.

It seems obvious, largely from internal evidence, that the cycle is the result of a process of blending. It is proposed briefly to review this evidence and to adduce some historical details which should place the contention beyond dispute.

The generally accepted theory is that the *apa-hevehe* are the daughters of the *ma-hevehe*; that they come from the sea for a sojourn in the *eravo*; that they are fitted out with their raiment, &c., as the result of repeated visits on the part of

---

[1] I have recorded a statement from a group of informants that Pareamamu previously possessed *Hii-Kairu*, but I do not find this verified elsewhere in my notes, and it may be they were referring to the *Hii* ceremony (see p. 343). But if the note is correct as it stands it proves conclusively the contention that *Hii-Kairu* is an interpolation in the *Hevehe* cycle.

their mother; and that after their masquerade they return
to the sea. This is very simple and straightforward, but it
does not account for all the episodes in the cycle and certain
discrepancies have to be cleared away.

An inquiry into the nature and antecedents of the individual masks points plainly to their association with the
bush rather than the sea; while both at the beginning and
the end of the cycle we find the bush-idea and the sea-idea
in some sort of opposition: the *hevehe* first come from the
bush (at the cane-cutting) before they are brought from the
sea (at the first *Hevehe-Karawa*); and (at the burning) they
appear to go back to the bush before their spirits finally go
down to the sea. It is further significant, as in itself suggesting duality, that there should be two distinct kinds of initiation (to *Apa-Hevehe* and *Hevehe-Karawa*) in one and the same
cycle.[1]

Over and above this there is the difficulty of accounting
for the *eharo* in general (they certainly have no necessary connexion with the sea), and for the whole episode of the *Hii
Kairu* which, together with the bathe, fire-fight, and fire-
presentation, would seem to constitute one complex. There
can be no question that all these form parts of the *Hevehe*
cycle as it stands; but it is more than difficult to discover any
logical reason why they should occupy the places they do
in the sequence of episodes. The absence of any such logical
connexion is more evident still in the case of the special
eharo.

In view of these difficulties we can hardly avoid the conclusion that the *Hevehe* is a composite mass; a number of
separate elements have somehow been fused into a whole.
But in order to confirm this conclusion we may consider
some historical evidence in detail.

There can be no question about the special *eharo*. They
are acknowledged as introductions from the Houra-Haera.[2]
Hii Kairu is not so easily disposed of. But the comparison
between the *Hevehe* of Orokolo Bay and the *Aiaimunu* of

---

[1] If the brief ordeal connected with the fire-presentation (p. 312) can be regarded
as such, then we have a third kind of initiation in the cycle.

[2] See pp. 331, 334, 335n.

Iari may, I think, be taken to prove conclusively that this episode is separable from the whole. For no such episode occurs in *Aiaimunu*. The two cycles correspond in other essential respects, so that, whether one be derived from the other or both from a common source, the absence of anything corresponding to *Hii Kairu* at Iari seems to prove that it is inessential.

But there is another and more important feature of the *Hevehe* cycle which finds no parallel in the *Aiaimunu* of Iari. This is nothing less than *Hevehe Karawa*, and it is on this question that I propose to adduce the historical facts.

In *Natives of the Purari Delta* a chapter[1] was devoted to the ceremony called *Erimunu*, which means *Imunu* of the Sea, or Water. The name is as literal as possible a translation of *ma-hevehe*, and the procedure is a close copy of *Hevehe Karawa*. At the beginning of that chapter I wrote that *Erimunu* was 'a recent acquisition in the Purari Delta'.

'On every hand it is admitted that the ceremony has been acquired within quite recent times from Orokolo. In any Purari village where it is practised, the names of those who introduced it will be remembered; they are either of men lately deceased, or frequently enough of men still living.'

All this has been amply verified in Orokolo and Arihava, where the circumstances surrounding the first visit of *Hevehe Karawa* (later to be known as *Erimunu*) to Maipua can be recalled. Its further progress among the Namau tribes is readily traced, but to this day it has never reached the populous tribe of Iari.

I treated *Erimunu* as a separate ceremony in the Purari Delta: no informant ever gave me any hint that it was associated with *Aiaimunu*, as *Hevehe Karawa* is with *Hevehe*. But this may have been incorrect. I have since learned that at Maipua, the nearest Namau tribe to the Western Elema, the fusion has definitely taken place.

We thus possess evidence to show conclusively that *Hevehe Karawa* has travelled as an independent unit from the Western Elema to the Namau; and there is just the same sort

---

[1] Chapter xv, pp. 182 ff.

of evidence to show that it has reached the Western Elema from the Houra-Haera.

One story, circumstantial enough to be convincing, is as follows: Hore and Hurevari, both of Kaivukavu, Arihava, went to Koialahu to see the burial of their *arivu*, Bira Epe. They 'saw his face' and he was buried; and next day they returned with the *haro eharu*. This (or part of it, perhaps) happened to take the form of an *aroa* fringed with dogs' teeth, and for his own convenience Hurevari sent it on ahead in the care of his wife.[1] But in doing so he had, unwittingly, committed a serious offence. The *aroa* had been one of those ostensibly brought up by *Hevehe Karawa* in a performance of that ceremony at Koialahu; and now, seeing it carried off by a woman, the donors were scandalized. They said they would bring their *Hevehe Karawa* to Arihava in order that Hurevari should learn the ceremony and make no such mistake again. Apparently it was a matter of friendly arrangement: Hurevari was warned to have food and pigs in readiness, and in due course the Houra-Haera party came along the beach by night and the dreadful noises of *Hevehe Karawa* were heard in Arihava for the first time. The pigs were taken away, and next morning the identical *aroa* which had caused the whole to-do was brought forth to be decorated with ornaments by the Houra-Haera visitors and then hung over Hurevari's shoulder.

Other informants have given the names of Hurevari and Hore as above; but there is some dispute as to which *eravo* among those of Arihava and Orokolo was the first to receive this new fashion, and accordingly some further names are mentioned. There is no doubt that the new ceremony was brought from the Houra-Haera on a number of separate occasions by arrangement with separate communities, and all about the same time. One of the first, if not the first, of such arrangements was between Laivi of Arihava and Eroha of Berepa. (Informants from the Western Elema and Houra-Haera have independently given the same names.) The Eroha in question was the father of Evara, of Vailala Madness fame,[2] and grandfather to Kivavia, one of the present

---

[1] See p. 221.   [2] See *Vailala Madness*, p. 17, &c.

government interpreters at Kerema. These facts demonstrate that *Hevehe Karawa* in its present form is not only an addition to the *Hevehe* cycle, but a recent addition.

There appears to have been something like a counterpart of the present ceremony in existence before this time, and there are still very old men in Orokolo Bay who can give some account of it. Instead of the horde of noise-makers there were but two old men, one with a shell-trumpet and one with a drum. The latter was tapped very softly, and it was properly *apa ruru-auka*, a drum with a broken tympanum, whence the ceremony was called *Hevehe Ruruauka*.[1] With these muffled noises the *ma-hevehe* came up from the sea; and (according to Lahoe, the oldest man in Orokolo Bay, who claims to have actually seen the performance in its original form) the cane frames of the *apa-hevehe* were brought into the village the following afternoon in full daylight, to the sound of drums and *puva*. The women, who were of course absent while this was taking place, were supposed to believe that the *ma-hevehe* (called the *hevehe lau*) had come from the sea and was seeking its daughters (*hevehe marita*) *in the bush*.[2] It had now collected them and installed them in the *eravo*. Later the *ma-hevehe* returned to the sea. In the whole course of the cycle it is said to have come up only two or three times.

In the old days, then (and they are not very distant), there was no oft-repeated *Hevehe Karawa*, with its hordes of young men, initiations, killing of many pigs, and lavish presents of ornaments. All this, which now constitutes so important a part of the cycle, is acknowledged to be an introduction, an element from outside which has been incorporated into the whole.

Hevehe *as a System*

It seems that some conclusions of wider application may be drawn from our consideration of the structure and evolution of *Hevehe*. It is evident that the whole thing hangs

---

[1] Another name was *Bevehere Hevehe*, 'The Cold *Hevehe*'.

[2] Lahoe spoke of the *hevehe marita* (i.e. *apa-hevehe*) as *ude 'uvea*, 'in the bush' or 'belonging to the bush.'

together tolerably well—indeed one might almost say surprisingly well. But it is equally evident that there is some
looseness in its construction; there are signs of stratification,
or of a lumping together of various originally separate
elements. These are not completely fused together or
amalgamated. *Hevehe* remains as an aggregation of elements,
and, while these work pretty well together, the whole is not
free entirely from inconsistencies. In short, *Hevehe* as it stands
is not a complete system: it only approximates to one.

It has been shown that new features (and to keep clear of
hypothetical cases we may cite *Hevehe Karawa* and the special
eharo alone) have been added to the cycle. It has received
these largely as mere additions: there is no evidence to show
that the previous structure of the cycle underwent any
significant change in order to adjust itself to them.

It would follow *a priori* that *Hevehe* could also lose some
of its component elements without suffering any significant
change. Nor is there any lack of concrete evidence in support of this contention.

The very last episode of the cycle is a case in point. A
man-killing expedition was no mean undertaking, and it
might be fairly considered that this stirring finale to the
cycle was an important part of it. Yet, though the *Pax
Britannica* has effectively deleted the last scene, the drama
runs through without it. It is a case of lopping off an inessential part: it is subtraction, involving no disorganization.

Another case—a small one but none the less significant—
is found in the use of the bull-roarer at certain moments in
the cycle. According to some exponents it is part of the
cycle; others declare it is not; it may be used, or it may not
be used; in one instance it was intended to use it, but for
some reason it was overlooked.[1] In short, though the bull-
roarer is in itself a highly important object, it seems to make
not a particle of difference whether it is employed in the
Hevehe cycle or not; and, if it is, it can obviously be dropped
at will. It is a case of omission without disorganization.

It has not been possible to see any one *Hevehe* cycle, much
less a number of them, in entirety; and so it has not been

[1] p. 379.

possible to tell whether any parts are ever omitted in current performances. But, to consider the shorter cycle of *Kovave* (of which I have seen a number throughout) as a parallel, it is most significant to note that whole slabs of the ritual can be dropped at will. The brief account given in Chapter VII makes no mention of certain episodes which may appear in some performances of the cycle; while, on the other hand, it describes certain others which are not uncommonly left out of it, e.g. the race, the night-raid, and the ceremony of pushing the *kovave* back into their *eravo*.[1] Such variations do not signify different forms of the cult in different places: they are variations of one and the same cult in one and the same village.

Kovave approaches very nearly to a consistent whole, but it is difficult to regard its various episodes as integral parts of a perfect system when they can be included or omitted at will, merely according to the whims or enthusiasms or convenience of the participants. It is at least likely that in the vastly greater *Hevehe* cycle certain features which appear in the programme of one *eravo* might for perhaps practical reasons be omitted from that of another; and it seems to the writer, hypothetically, that even some of major importance could be deleted without shaking the structure of the whole. Indeed he would go so far as to say that the whole complex of *Hii Kairu*, for instance, including the bathe and fire ceremonies[2] might be abstracted from it, and the cycle still run on to its logical finish.

The deletion of *Hii Kairu*, to pursue this hypothetical instance, would be like an amputation—and needless to say a grievous loss; but it would not amount to the removal of a vital organ.

Less patent but, intrinsically, far more important examples of loss which does not necessarily imply disorganizations are found in the decay of certain pretences, beliefs, or theories that might, prima facie, be thought essential to the continuance of the cycle. An illustration is found in the fading-out of the fiction that the *aroa* in *Hevehe Karawa* is brought up by the *ma-hevehe*; and it was suggested that most

---

[1] pp. 145–6.   [2] See Chapters XIX and XX.

of the pretences of secret organizations must tend in this direction. Yet *Hevehe Karawa*, like other such mysteries, can continue though the fiction which might seem to stand at the very base of it is dissolved away.[1] Similarly the special *eharo*—Ira and Ope and the rest of them—appear in cycle after cycle; yet those who see them, and even those who impersonate them, may be ignorant of their stories and unaware of any significance in the part they play.[2] It is perhaps not too much to say that such part is really devoid of significance as an element in the cycle.

Indeed the *eharo* at large, the totemic dance-masks, must be assumed to have lost their original meaning;[3] and the same might even be said of the *hevehe* themselves.[4] Yet both kinds of mask appear and reappear in successive cycles.

Lastly and generally, even if the contention is sound that every ritual detail in the cycle at large must have, or have had, its mythical counterpart, it is no less true that the links have mostly severed.[5] It is no longer possible, in the majority of cases, to discover the connexion even by research; and it is beyond doubt that it has virtually disappeared from public memory. Nevertheless, the ritual can and does go on without it. It might well be thought that a knowledge of the relevant myths and an appreciation of their connexion with the ritual were essential parts of a system, the myth being the very justification of the ritual. But such is plainly not the case.

If *Hevehe* could be regarded as a completely organized system, then these intangibles should find as definite a place therein as the various acts of ritual themselves. But investigation goes to show, not only that the theoretical bases of such acts have largely crumbled away, but also that, in so far as they continue to exist, they are highly varied and inconsistent. It would surely be a strange misapplication of the word to say that they resolved themselves into a system, or that they occupied a place in a system called *Hevehe*.

Western Elema Culture as a System

The pains taken to show that *Hevehe* itself is not a fully integrated whole are, it is hoped, justified by the intention

[1] pp. 221-2.   [2] p. 337.   [3] p. 289.   [4] p. 262.   [5] p. 341.

of applying the argument to Western Elema culture at large. It is suggested that the *Hevehe* cycle may be viewed as a cultural microcosm. Its system (in so far as it is systematic) and its lack of system (in so far as it is asystematic) are both typical of the larger whole of which it forms a part. It does not perhaps follow from the claims sometimes put forward for the systematic nature of cultural relations at large that the same systematic nature should belong to each and every one of the component parts of a culture; but if we have found that a component so large and important as *Hevehe* falls short of systematic perfection, we may infer that similar and larger imperfections will be found in the culture as a whole. The argument hitherto has dealt with *Hevehe* merely as a specimen.

Cultures vary in their degree of approximation to systematic completeness. Some, remote from the world's affairs and the turbulence of change, have achieved comparative equilibrium. They are virtually static, but it is doubtful indeed whether any are completely so. During the present generation the life of the Western Elema is undergoing somewhat drastic change, a period of cultural rough weather. But it is certain that even in pre-European times the scene was not entirely calm. It is plain that contact with neighbours on east and west brought about changes in the life of Orokolo Bay, and there is some evidence that these were not necessarily ancient ones: nor need we suppose that the people who could, under European influence, initiate a general change so startling as that of the Vailala Madness were unable to initiate previous changes under other influences.

Granted the existence of change, whether fast or slow, and whether by way of acquisition or loss, it plainly follows that all cultures, that of the Western Elema among them, are capable of somehow prolonging their existence. They do so partly by a process of adaptation, but partly by merely persisting. In the writer's view cultural changes do not necessarily involve the amount of disorganization which it is commonly claimed they do.

Some elements are more deeply impacted in the cultural

mass than are others; they depend on others, and others depend on them, to a relatively great extent. Some, on the other hand, are but lightly involved in the mass:[1] they are relatively independent. Their coming may have no great effect on what was there already; and their going—if they happen to go—may cause but little disturbance. This is obviously the case with countless cultural details, admittedly small matters, whose presence or absence is hardly felt by the rest of the culture. But it may be true of what are in themselves large matters; and as an example I quote the case of seclusion. This institution, quite an imposing one as it was, is now moribund if not actually dead; but while deploring that fact in itself I cannot see that it has disorganized the existent culture to any appreciable extent. It has not, to take a specific example, interfered with *Hevehe*; nor can I imagine that the two institutions are in any real sense, directly or indirectly, interdependent.

The Vailala Madness has provided us with all too many examples of cultural loss. It was a sacrifice, partly enthusiastic, but partly also deliberate, of a great deal of the more ornamental parts of Elema culture. Drums, dancing, feathers, long hair, Bull-Roarer, *Kovave*, and *Hevehe* went overboard: a self-reformed people was determined to 'chuck away its b—— New Guinea somethings' and thenceforward to 'stop quiet along village'.

Orokolo and Yogu, as we have observed, stood out; but the reformers made a conquest of Arihava, Auma, and Vailala, and in these three villages, despite some sporadic revivals, the ceremonies are mostly dead. Their death, however, has not brought about the disintegration of the whole culture: far from it. Social organization remains largely as it was. The *eravo* communities (even though no true *eravo* are left) maintain their identity; youths and maidens marry and are given in marriage under the same terms and in the same manner; *aukau* still give ornaments to *arivu*, and *arivu* still give pigs to *aukau*; it may even be said that the older generation maintains its authority. Magicians (of garden,

---

[1] My typist rendered the word as 'mess'—most apt ineptitude, but rather too strong to retain.

sea, and beach), doctors, sorcerers—all these flourish as vigorously as ever; and the knowledge of the myths, to judge from my own informants, is perhaps better in Arihava than in Orokolo.

Some communities in Arihava have in recent years revived the Bull-Roarer and *Kovave*. But against *Hevehe* all three of the village-groups affected by the Madness appear to remain adamant. We shall discuss their arguments against it in an ensuing chapter; the point here is that they can dismiss a thing as great as *Hevehe* from their lives and go on living, otherwise, much as they were. They can restore *Kovave* (as in some cases they have done) without *Hevehe*; and the same is true of the Bull-Roarer. *Hevehe* is in fact wholly separate from either of these two cults,[1] as they are separate from one another. Each is to all intents and purposes an independent unit.

Some time has been spent in demonstrating that *Hevehe* in itself is far from being a fully integrated whole or a fully organized system. It is now submitted that the culture of which it forms a part is likewise far from being a fully organized system.

The writer feels bound to modify his earlier views, expressed fifteen years ago, upon the decay of ceremonies and its effect on Western Elema culture.[2] The decay of ceremonies he has not ceased to deplore, and he is still of the opinion that 'one cannot delete any part of the social life of a primitive people and leave the other parts unaffected'. But it does not seem to him now that the effect must necessarily be so drastic. 'You have only to remove one wheel to stop the watch, or one stone from the social structure to have it tumbling about your ears'—these prophetic figures of speech seem in the light of further reflection (not to mention subsequent events) to have been very wide of the mark.

Cultural Involution

Having proceeded from *Hevehe* considered internally to *Hevehe* as a component of Western Elema culture, we may

---

[1] The one or two optional appearances of the bull-roarer in the *Hevehe* cycle may be ignored in this connexion; so also may the hypothetical association between bull-roarer and *hevehe* in the matter of the latter's origin.   [2] See *Vailala Madness*, p. 64.

now carry the argument a stage farther and briefly consider culture in the abstract.

Far be it from me to suggest that culture is devoid of organization. The whole point of the present argument is that all cultures are organized, but none of them more than partly so. It has been shown that the one under consideration has evolved to some extent by a process of accretion; and in so far as this is the case the various accretions have not all been fused together in such a manner as to become genuinely interdependent and each indispensable to the whole. On the contrary they have formed a whole which remains to some extent loosely constructed: new elements could be introduced, and existent elements dropped out, without necessarily creating disorganization. It is now submitted that every culture partakes of the same nature: each at its best is only a semi-integrated whole.

Of the innumerable elements which go towards its composition some may indeed be so fundamental, so wide in their ramifications, as to be actually essential to its continuance. So, for instance, if the raising of pigs were forbidden at Orokolo (this monstrous hypothesis is used merely for argument) it is almost conceivable that the whole cultural structure might collapse. But other institutions—and they may be well developed in themselves—remain but loosely embedded; they have not become inextricably interwoven with the other elements; they can be detached and the rest go on subsisting together much as they were. In the writer's view, *Hevehe* itself is one of these.

It may be thought that the introduction of saving clauses, like 'much as they were' and so on, vitiates the present argument, implying that associations or connexions really existed but were overlooked. The argument, however, fully recognizes the existence of connexions between cultural elements or between any element and the whole; but it claims that whereas some such connexions are vital and significant, others (and they are very numerous) are fortuitous and without significance. They in no way amount to interdependence.

It may be theoretically true that you cannot change any one part of a culture without affecting the whole, just as it is theoretically true that you cannot drop a pin without shaking the universe. And it is a well-recognized fact, not only of anthropological experience, but of politics, civics, economics, and so on, that changes in one department of life may bring about far-reaching effects in others, where indeed they may be unforeseen and not understood. It is presumably this fact which in the first place gives rise to the conception of the systematic nature of social relations; and this, carried to its logical extreme, has led to the comparison of culture to an organism, or even, with more emphasis on the way it 'works', to a machine.

These are admittedly analogies and no one claims that either comparison is perfect. It is with the same reservations that I take the risk of using another simile which may even shock some theoretical sensibilities. It is suggested, then, that the general fact that all parts of a culture are somehow related, so that you cannot touch one part without affecting the whole, can be expressed, with partial truth at any rate, by comparing it to a pile of rubbish. Every particle therein is in a sense related to the whole and to every other particle: the discarded boot rests on the ashes, the ashes on the potato-peel, the potato-peel on the jam-tin, and so on. Remove that jam-tin, and you may shake the pile to its very base. But it is not a system. The relations between the parts are merely those of juxtaposition or contact, direct or indirect; and, while it must be repeated emphatically that this irreverent simile of the rubbish-heap is not meant to give a full picture of cultural relations, it nevertheless seems to the writer that many of those relations are just of the kind indicated.

It should be remembered that any human culture as a whole, like any component part of it, is the work of human minds—a great many of them, both in the present and through unnumbered generations of the past—reacting to their environment. Since human minds are fallible, both individually and in the mass, it is surely beyond the bounds of probability that they should have achieved a perfect organization among the innumerable elements that go to make up their culture. These minds have thrown in their contributions one after another: some have been important, some negligible; some have affected the main structure (for of course it has one) of the cultural mass, others lie, so to speak, one on top of another; and some of these, function-less survivals, remain as so much cultural rubbish.

Culture is neither a machine nor an organism; nor, of course, is it a pile of rubbish. Without at present seeking any other simile it is enough to say that, having evolved to some extent by a process of accretion, it never succeeds in achieving complete organization, but remains always in part a mere aggregation. It tends by virtue of inertia to remain as it has been. It is a jumble of essentials and inessentials; or (in terms of value) of grain and chaff; good, indifferent, and bad.

It has seemed worth while to develop at some length the thesis to which we were led by examining the structure and evolution of a single institution; but the foregoing argument need not be construed as an attack on Functionalism itself. It presents, rather, an explanation of the writer's reasons for accepting Functionalism only in a modified form.

While, then, according proper recognition to the value of the Functional approach, he is of the opinion that, carried to its extreme, Functional doctrine reveals a fallacy. Instead of being, as that doctrine implies, an organized system, or a fully integrated whole, every culture, past or present, has fallen short of that ideal—as in human nature it is bound to do. The confusions which seem apparent to common sense in social relations — the contradictions, inconsistencies, conflicting loyalties—might be explained away by the claim that all these resolve themselves into a system which is simply beyond human powers to appreciate. But the thesis here advanced is that the apparent confusion is to some extent, and inevitably, real.

The most significant fact about the elements of a culture remains that they are involved with one another; and, if the present thesis is valid, this is partly a matter of organization or system, and partly one of mere aggregation, not without some degree of confusion. It seems that the non-committal word 'involved' may itself adequately cover both aspects;

and therefore the name 'involution' is suggested for a concept of culture which takes them both into account. It may serve, at least as far as the writer is concerned, to cover an acknowledgement of the fact that culture is in part a functional system, and a firm conviction, on the other hand, that it is in part also a sorry tangle.[1]

[1] The thesis of this chapter has been further developed in 'Creed of a Government Anthropologist', Presidential Address, Anthropology Section, Australian and New Zealand Association for the Advancement of Science, 1939.

XXVI

THE VALUES OF *HEVEHE*

Problems of Value

PURE-MINDED anthropologists hold themselves aloof
from questions of value; but this detachment is not so
easily maintainable by government anthropologists. They
have dealings with two classes of people, administrative
officers and missionaries, who frankly concern themselves
with native welfare and who even take upon themselves the
responsibility of deciding whether this or that in native
custom is desirable or undesirable—bluntly, whether it is
good or bad. The anthropologist who desires to be helpful
must not be afraid to enter into their discussions. The
practical issue of the moment, put simply, is whether
Hevehe should continue or not continue. We shall therefore spend some time in debating its various values, since
they must be appreciated before the question can be fairly
answered.

It would be possible perhaps to judge *Hevehe* on its intrinsic merits alone, say as a work of art. Those who have read
the description of it may be enabled to judge for themselves
whether or not it is worth preserving on these grounds.
The writer, having actually seen it in action (which is much
better than reading of it), would go so far as to say that it
was worth preserving merely as a human achievement. But
this is to treat it in abstract. *Hevehe* is more than an artistic
creation: it is still a living institution.

It is more practical to judge the institution in relation to
the people to whom it belongs. Whether *Hevehe* is good
for them is the question that confronts the administrators,
educators, and missionaries who have the natives' interest
in their hands. (The natives' own answers to the question
'Is *Hevehe* good or bad *for us*?' will be considered in due
course. They obviously represent a factor of some importance, more than is often recognized.)

Methods of Evaluation

If a Functionalist undertook to assess the value of *Hevehe* he would perhaps consider it first of all as an essential part of a cultural system and sum up its importance according to the extent of its interactions with other parts thereof. And it might be fully expected that he would not hesitate to advocate its preservation; for he would argue that the disappearance of any such feature would entail the dislocation or total break-up of the system at large.

Now I have no doubt that this point of view possesses a real importance: it cannot be denied that the disappearance of *Hevehe* would make some considerable impression on Western Elema culture as a whole. But, without losing sight of this aspect of the problem, I propose to attack it mainly on other lines. My reasons for doing so are (1) that I cannot agree that the loss of *Hevehe* would affect the total culture so disastrously as the Functional theory would assume; and (2), even if it did, I cannot see that this in itself is a final reason for wishing it to survive.

An intense interest in the internal 'workings' of culture has led Functionalism to what I am bound to think a fallacious conception—an overstatement of the systematic nature of cultural relations; and it has possibly bred too great a reverence for cultures as they exist. The modified view already propounded is that cultures are uncontrolled growths, haphazard agglomerations; and as such they achieve at best only a partial organization. It is maintained further that, as manmade affairs, they represent only the poor best that their makers have been able to achieve. They provide them with a means of living well according to their lights, of satisfying their human needs, more or less imperfectly, in their particular environments. Such a view as this does not incline to any reverence for culture as sacred and inviolable.

It is readily conceivable that higher intelligences would have evolved a culture better fitted to the environment, even if that environment remained as it was; it is certain that, when the environment is drastically altered by European intrusion, the old culture, as a means of living well, becomes both inadequate and unsuitable. It will have to gain something and to lose something in order to bring it into fit relation with the new conditions. The change may be so small that we shall call it the same culture with a difference, or so great that we shall have to call it a new one. In neither case can we expect complete integration, but the altered culture will no doubt manage to shake itself into some sort of going order.

The Elema-European blend (which may of course develop some unique characteristics) may be a worse culture than the old one; on the other hand it may be a better. By what criteria are we to judge? Difficult as it may be to assess, I think its general value is to be reckoned by the degree in which it ministers to the fundamental needs of the human beings to whom it belongs and the degree in which it gives expression to their potentialities. It is the human being that represents the end; the culture, a transient, changeable, imperfect thing, is only the means which he, his fellows, and his forebears have evolved to meet those needs and express those potentialities. The evaluation of Western Elema culture, therefore, or of any constituent part of it such as *Hevehe*, is ultimately in these terms: To what extent and how well does it provide for the needs, and give scope to the potentialities, of the Western Elema people, having regard to their total environment?

It would presumably need at least a triple alliance of anthropology, psychology, and human biology to undertake so formidable an inquiry; and one does not imagine that even their united forces would at present be able to deal with the problem fully or accurately. Indeed there is at present no lack of disagreement as to what the fundamental human needs actually are, while the question of potentialities may be beyond final answering. Nevertheless, I believe this to represent the ultimate method of attack upon that problem of culture-evaluation which anthropology must face if it is to be of practical use in solving the general problem of native welfare.

It will not be thought, because I have questioned its indispensability in Western Elema culture and declined to accept the implied principle of evaluation, that I would willingly see *Hevehe* go. On the contrary some unguarded touches of enthusiasm in description will have revealed well enough that I have proved false to scientific detachment and fallen somewhat in love with it. (It is surprising how many anthropologists hold high this motto of detachment when they refuse to condemn native customs, yet forget all about its existence when they praise them.) Speaking generally I cannot regard it as part of an anthropologist's duty to defend whatever he finds in native culture; on the contrary I suggest that, if he ventures into the realm of values, he should be prepared to adopt a thoroughly critical attitude. But in this particular case, while endeavouring to keep an open mind, I must confess that I have found the issue extremely one-sided: the present summing-up of *Hevehe* is almost entirely in its favour.

General Values of Hevehe

After so long a preamble regarding the methods to be employed in evaluation, the results achieved may seem a little disappointing. I shall attempt no more than to draw attention to some of the human values of *Hevehe*, as they appear to me.

An Objective

In the first place—and, from the practical point of view, most importantly—the cycle has in the past provided the people with an intense interest. It has been an object, something to work for, not only for the responsible community as a whole but for every individual in it. And when we bear in mind the size of the thing, its sheer length, we shall better appreciate the public value of this interest. It is no small thing to have in view the completion of a cycle of ceremonies which will last perhaps for two decades. One would find it hard to discover any parallel to it in our civilization.

Recreation

The interest of *Hevehe* is something different from that of everyday life; it rises high above day-to-day needs and their fulfilment. But we need not explore any sublimities to discover its principal value: it is to its recreative aspect that I should without hesitation give pride of place. Native life is plentifully supplied with rest; but it is marked by a comparative absence of active recreation. In general terms, adults do not play. They have nothing to compare with the varied forms of amusement that beguile the life of a westerner. On the other hand the community can engage in bursts of recreation which are proportionately far more extensive than is common among ourselves. The Western Elema have found such communal recreation above all in the festivities of *Hevehe*. The pleasure they take in it is obvious. The oft-repeated *Hevehe-Karawa* has all the attractions of a rag; the performers put their heart into it, and repetition does not seem to rob it of excitement. There is feasting and crowding together of people; the jollity of rehearsals and initiations; brilliant spectacles and pageantry—enjoyed by the onlookers and more still by the actors; the humour of the *eharo*; and the bliss of the dancing women. It is no cheap dismissal of *Hevehe* to say that this, of recreation, is its greatest value.

Artistry

Another value that must strike every one is the scope it affords for artistry. I need not dwell on the craftsmanship which goes to the manufacture of *hevehe* and *eharo*, or on the skill, taste, and invention shown in decorating them. It need only be said that the artistic gifts of the Western Elema have found their best expression in the making and adorning of masks; and (except for *Kovave*, which is in all respects a lesser creation) it is the *Hevehe* cycle which provides the need for these masks and with it the scope for this peculiar art. The simple, unique, and often charming designs of which some illustrations have been given in Chapter XVI are seen exclusively on the face of *Hevehe* masks.

Dramatic Art

But there is another aspect of *Hevehe* which claims attention on these aesthetic grounds. It appears to the writer that the cycle as a whole possesses some real dramatic interest;

and that interest, despite long intervals of inactivity, contrives to renew itself up to the very end of what may be the longest dramatic performance in history. Every episode is played out with theatrical effect. *Hevehe Karawa*, the monster rising by night from the sea; dancers and *eharo* brilliantly thronging the arena; Yellow Bark-Cloth Boys bursting out of the silent *eravo*; the ethereal form of the first *hevehe* standing at dawn on the threshold; all these and a score of others—fire-fight, procession, slaying of the leader, retreat of the spirits, conjuring of the sea-monster, casting out of Iko—constitute one long dramatic sequence. It is a drama adorned by spectacles, pageantry, and *coups de théâtre*, and abounding in comic relief, but not without its solemn passages and even its moment of tragedy.

Organization and Leadership

However it has come into being—and we may assume that it has grown of itself, without much planning on the part of individual minds—*Hevehe* is obviously a big concern for a small, primitive community to handle. Success comes partly from that gift of tacit organization and partly (though, I think, in less degree) by the energy and leadership of a few individuals. If these faculties of organization and leadership are of value, it is *Hevehe* more than anything else within the range of Western Elema experience that can encourage them.

Constructiveness

And more than any other feature, old or new, it gives scope to the native's constructive powers. One thinks less in this connexion of the masks themselves than of the great building which is meant to house them. The *eravo* is the real triumph of Western Elema material culture; and it stands to *Hevehe* in a special reciprocal relation. The *eravo*, in its true architectural proportions, is unnecessary except for *Hevehe*: *Hevehe* is impossible without the *eravo*. Not a few of the villages of Orokolo Bay are building their men's houses to-day on a new and easier pattern, viz. that of the square-built, ridge-roofed, comparatively low *uvi-eravo*.[1] In some

---

[1] I.e. 'house-*eravo*', one built like a modern ridge-pole house. See p. 4.

few cases this may be merely a temporary measure, the lesser structure serving all ordinary purposes until, with another cycle, the need arises for the *eravo* proper. But all too often the *uvi-eravo* indicates that *Hevehe* has been abandoned; and where this is the case the *uvi-eravo* seems to the writer a symbol, not of progress, but of decadence. If the capacity for making things by hand and the will to undertake large constructive tasks are worth admiring, then *Hevehe* has performed some good service in developing them.

The Group Spirit

Needless to say so great an undertaking as *Hevehe* requires the full strength of the community. That community is used to acting together in many affairs; but in no others are its members so obviously at one as in the performance of their own cycle. It is true that many kinsmen and friends from outside may have a hand in it; but it remains the responsibility of the community itself, and no man stands aside. Again and again has open expression been given to the desire for unanimity of will and action in carrying the cycle through; and with due allowance for individual variation it is remarkable to what extent that unanimity is achieved. *Hevehe* provides a notable means of expression for the Group Spirit: it is a school for the development of mutual support and loyalty

Cultural Pride

For just as every individual, from the Drum-Leader downwards, takes a pride in the particular *hevehe* with which he is associated, so does the community at large take pride in its united effort. It is 'our *eravo*, our *Hevehe*'; and no effort is spared to make a good showing. The reward, for individual or for group, is *lare eapapo*, a 'big name'.

We may not attach a very high spiritual value to pride of this kind, but it seems to the writer that, in the present circumstances of the Western Elema, it possesses a special importance. There is always the danger that European contact may strip the native of pride in himself and what he does

—indeed there is no question that this form of deterioration has been all too common in Orokolo Bay. The Vailala Madness was an epidemic of contempt for the native way of life; and the plague is by no means blotted out. Such self-contempt is not only unjustified, but morally calamitous. There are still many things left to the Western Elema of which they might be proud; and of *Hevehe* they might be proudest of all. It has been the pride of the individual and the pride of the *eravo* community: it could, if it remained, be the pride of the people.

Religious Values

It may have been expected that in an attempt to summarize the values of *Hevehe* the religious ones would come first on the list; but I have ventured already to express the considered opinion that the cycle is neither mainly religious nor deeply religious. Yet obviously this aspect demands consideration.

Hevehe has its bearing upon both of those categories between which Western Elema religious interest is divided—the spirits of deceased human beings and those independent spirits who have been identified with the Immortal Story Folk and the Magic People. The emphasis of the cult, however, is all upon the second category, in which may be included the monstrous beings of river and sea. Some of the spirits are obviously placated from time to time in the *ivaiva*, though this recurrent ceremony is not in strictness part of the cycle. Apart from these acts of placation the religious implications of *Hevehe* are vague. It may be regarded, perhaps, as a great rite of worship or conciliation in which the Story Folk are entertained by the lesser breed of mortals. But this is pure assumption: I have never heard a native give any such general interpretation of the cycle, and I feel sure that most of them would learn of it with surprise. Nor do I recollect hearing in regard to *Hevehe* that general negative argument so commonly advanced in justification of ceremonies, viz. that, if they were not performed, some evil—whether of sickness, hunger, or calamity—would descend on the community. In the absence of even this vague sanction I find it difficult to regard *Hevehe* as predominantly

religious in its purpose. It seems that the religious significance which it may once have possessed has already faded
from memory, and by now *Hevehe* stands mainly on its own
merits. It has followed the familiar course and become an
end in itself.

There remain in it, however, countless points of contact
with the world of spirits. We have seen that the individual
mask-owners in many cases boast or confess a connexion
between their mask and their magic; and so *Hevehe* reaches
out into mythology, whence Elema magic is derived. The
personal names and decorations of the masks; the costumes
and characters of the *eharo*; almost every step and detail in
the ritual—these things together could furnish myriad allu-
sions to the vast other-world of mythology. How far these
may be present to the ordinary native's consciousness it is
impossible to say; but, in so far as they are present, they
may, for aught we know, be the very breath of romance.
Perhaps it is pretty seldom; but we need not suppose that
Elema man has lived by sago alone.

Finally, though *Hevehe* may not lend itself to any specifically religious interpretation, it has nevertheless been supported by a general sanction to which the word may not
unfittingly be applied. It is *birari mai*, 'the fashion of our
ancestors', and in the implied sentiment there is at least
something of religious force.

Wider Social Intercourse

We may now turn to one or two values which should
appeal to those who are directly concerned with peace and
the native's material welfare. It may be said that *Hevehe* has
exerted a powerful influence in drawing together the various
social units of Orokolo Bay and its neighbourhood. It may
be of some importance that such a cultural bond should
unite tribes and peoples over a comparatively wide area; but
the thing of real significance is that the great festivities of
the cycle actually bring the people together in person. The
same effect on a lesser scale belongs to all feasts and festivities, and it is difficult to view it as anything but an argument
in their favour. They afford opportunities for those periodic

expressions of gregariousness in which most natives seem to delight; and in so doing they help to maintain human contact and widen the social horizon. It is sometimes argued by those who are opposed to native feasts in general that, by bringing old enemies together, they not infrequently lead to brawls and bloodshed. But one feels pretty confident that, by and large, festivities serve rather to conciliate the old enemies. It is certain that suspicion and animosity between groups thrives best on isolation, and *Hevehe* has in the past provided the most important of all counteractions against it. At any rate, as far as I have observed them, the tone of the great gatherings has always been one of friendliness and high conviviality.

Food Production

A more utilitarian value of *Hevehe* remains to be mentioned, viz. its effect on food-production. Measured by native standards the quantities of food prepared for one of the major festivities is prodigious. Sago is almost unlimited, and the production of extra supplies means merely extra work in the making, while pigs see to their own multiplication; but the garden products must be planned for. An important stage in the cycle will demand a huge surplus in garden food, and that implies common gardens on a large scale. The notion that feasts mean simply waste of food is erroneous: the food is mostly carried away by guests and consumed subsequently. The result, therefore, is not waste, but plenty.

This is the native's view and I quote an incident to illustrate it. In the first enthusiasm of the Vailala Madness Keuru had discarded the ceremonies; but they afterwards restored them. Asked why they had done so a Keuru man replied—and very significantly—'Because we were hungry.' He went on to explain that gardens (by which he meant common gardens) were not made without some definite purpose. Gardens were made for feasts; and feasts were made for ceremonies. It is obvious that among the Western Elema it is the ceremonies which ultimately supply the incentive for large-scale food-production. *Hevehe* is beyond comparison the biggest, and therefore supplies the strongest incentive.

Functional Values

The foregoing is a random list of virtues belonging to the *Hevehe* cycle as they have appeared to the writer. No doubt others could be excogitated on similar lines. In addition to these the Functionalist might present a whole catalogue of functions, showing how *Hevehe* was bound up with other aspects of the whole culture. Thus it could be demonstrated to uphold the predominance of males and the marked separation between the activities and interests of the two sexes in Western Elema Society; or again the supremacy of the old men, upon which so much depends for the ordering of that society; or again, the independent existence of the *eravo* communities; or the separate identity of the *aualari* groups. Further than this it obviously provides most ample opportunities for those interchanges of duties and gifts by which kinsmen and formal friends are bound together. But any further account of such functions is left to those who attach a greater importance to them. The subject is not pursued here, because it is considered that they represent specific rather than general values, and are dependent on the continuation of a culture which is bound to undergo radical change.

The tone of the present chapter has been entirely in favour of *Hevehe*. It is not in the nature of things, however, that every one concerned should share the views expressed. If they did, the cult would hardly find itself in such grave difficulties. In the following chapter, which deals with its present decline, we shall mention incidentally some of the arguments against it.

XXVII

THE DECLINE OF *HEVEHE*

The Present Situation

WHATEVER we may think about the continuance of *Hevehe*, the people to whom the cult belongs are showing a very strong inclination to drop it. Among all the Western Elema only two main village groups—Orokolo and Yogu—have cycles in progress; and in only one[1] *eravo* is there any prospect of bringing the current cycle to a reasonably early conclusion. In one other the masks are well advanced; but the latest news, at the time of writing, is that the building has collapsed, and I am unable to say what action has been taken.[2] In three others the cycles are still, after twenty-odd years, at a very backward stage; and, all things considered, it seems doubtful whether they will ever be brought to completion.

The real question is whether the natives have the will and spirit to commence all over again. The prevalent attitudes seem to be those of uncertainty and unwillingness. Some— particularly the senior men—express themselves ready to start new cycles in due course if only all will agree to do the same—another example of that desire for unanimity which we have so often noted. It is difficult to see how this proviso could now be fulfilled, even within the boundaries of Orokolo alone; so that, if it were to be regarded strictly, we should have to admit that *Hevehe* was doomed. But it is still remotely possible that, given support from one another, certain of the more conservative *eravo* may pluck up courage.

Taking the Western Elema as a whole, however, the majority of individuals and groups seem set against the renewal of *Hevehe*; and this determination is found not only among those who have embraced the Mission way of life so wholeheartedly as to abandon the other ceremonies, but also

[1] Waiea Ravi.
[2] Meouri Ravi: the ordinary course would be to transfer the masks to a *baupa eravo* and there store them until a new *eravo* had been built. But it is doubtful whether the community concerned will summon the energy needed.

among the more stiff-necked generation among whom the old way of living is largely maintained. The arguments of Mission boys we shall consider later on. In the meantime we may examine those of the population at large. After having considered these arguments, i.e. the ostensible reasons for not wishing to renew *Hevehe*, we may pass on to analyse the real reasons to which its present decline may be attributed.

Native Arguments against Renewal
Death by Sorcery

The commonest of all arguments against *Hevehe* is that it causes deaths among the villagers. The validity of such a belief need not, of course, be seriously considered; but the belief itself amounts to a very powerful force. The supposed agent of death is the sorcerer; the reason, some breach of procedure, a slight upon some member of the *avai*, a too-small pig, a default in paying over the ornaments, or, above all, the witting or unwitting observation of forbidden mysteries. For these shortcomings or misdemeanours, it is thought, the sorcerers are always ready to exact the penalty. When recently a woman of Waiea Ravi died, her husband found a little parcel left conspicuously on the *eravo*-floor near the entrance. It contained two small pig-bones, and wisps of bast and frayed sago—indicating that the woman had spied on the pig-eating after *Hevehe Karawa* and knew too much about the construction of the masks. The husband accepted it as explanation of her death; she had been 'put under the *eravo*'. This is merely an example of the stock explanations of natural death.

We have already seen that the belief in sorcery and the threats of sorcerers are in part responsible for the long delays in the progress of the cycle; we now see that the fear of sorcery is the commonest argument used by the native himself against renewing it. It is a false argument, but unfortunately a very convincing one.

It is thus apparent that sorcery, as a firmly established part of Western Elema culture, can militate against another part of that culture. In some respects, of course, it serves to support *Hevehe*, e.g. in preserving its show of secrecy and safeguarding the prerogatives of the older males. But it would be difficult indeed to maintain that sorcery and *Hevehe* are mutually indispensable. It is certain that sorcery could survive without *Hevehe*—if *Hevehe* must go it is not to be expected that either the belief in sorcery or the practice of it will suffer in the least. On the other hand, it is at least possible, if we could conceive of sorcery as disappearing, that *Hevehe* might survive without it, by virtue of other sanctions and values. However this may be, it is worth reminding those who defend sorcery as a mainstay of primitive society that it can also interfere with a society's way of living; that it can, in fact, clog the cultural workings.

Previous Exposure

There is nothing to indicate that the fear of sorcery in connexion with *Hevehe* is a modern phenomenon: we may assume that it has always been present, and that in the past it served merely to put off or retard the cycles. At the present juncture it might well be overcome as an argument against renewal were it not that manifold other influences are present in its support.

The Vailala Madness of twenty years ago has supplied a special argument which is very commonly quoted in all the villages where it took effect. During its earliest stages the ceremonies—Bull-Roarer, *Kovave*, and *Hevehe*—were willingly exposed and their paraphernalia destroyed. The womenfolk in some cases actually witnessed the pious orgies of destruction, and in general were either disillusioned or found it no longer necessary to maintain the illusion. Consequently the men of to-day declare themselves reluctant to try to create the mystery afresh: they say they would be ashamed; the women would laugh at them.

We shall perhaps be justified in regarding this as an excuse when we consider what happened in the cases of Bull-Roarer and *Kovave*. These lesser ceremonies have been renewed in a number of *eravo* in Arihava, and in those cases the women immediately fell back into their old-time position of pretended ignorance. It is not too much to assume that the same would happen if the men of Arihava could induce themselves to restore *Hevehe*.

Lack of Man-Power

Another argument in common use is the lack of man-power. The native is prone to gross exaggeration of the decline in his numbers : he looks back to the good old times when the population was as thick as the 'tree-leaves'. Then it was an easy matter to carry a cycle through. But now, as he says again and again, the scanty few who remain in his community are simply not up to it.

This contention is not without force, though the trouble lies in dispersion rather than depopulation. On the other hand, it is sometimes, like the others, merely an excuse: Arihava, for instance, is apt to explain the absence of *Hevehe* by pointing to the scarcity of its population, whereas in fact it is more thickly populated than Orokolo, where the cere-monies have survived.[1]

Too Much Trouble

There can be little doubt that the fourth argument com-monly put forward is the really decisive one. It is simply that *Hevehe* means too much trouble. Some men apply the argu-ment to the ceremonies at large. In the old days, they say, they were always preparing for one celebration or another, always busy at mask-making or food-getting; now it is much better—they have plenty of time for making money. (The last can, of course, be taken *cum grano salis*.) But the reference is almost always specifically to *Hevehe*; and it is a significant fact that Bull-Roarer and *Kovave* should have been revived by those who set their face stubbornly against it. The explanation is simply that the *Hevehe* cycle is too long, too big a thing to face. The others last respectively for two or three days and a few weeks; with *Hevehe*, one never knows when it will end. As one man put it shortly, '*Kovave* are small, *Hevehe* are big.'

---

[1] The census figures show an increase in the population of Arihava over the 15 years from 1920 to 1935, viz. from 1,235 to 1,409. This seems to dispose of the argument.

There is, no doubt, some excuse for this attitude: the native's time is not quite so much his own as it used to be. But it is, nevertheless, a dismal reflection that the modern native is unwilling to revive *Hevehe* because it is too big for him.

European Contact

Having dealt with the arguments against *Hevehe*, commonly heard from the natives themselves, we may now consider the various outside causes which are directly or indirectly operating against it.

While it is by no means inconceivable that such a cult as *Hevehe* might die, so to speak, a natural death due to purely native influences, most will be ready to concur in the assumption that its decline is a product of modern times. And these modern causes may be subsumed under the heading of European contact.

The Europeans by whom the Western Elema, as other Papuans, have been affected are roughly divided into three categories—Commercial, Government, and Mission. We shall consider their respective influences in turn.

Commercial Influence

From early days a succession of European traders have been settled in Orokolo Bay—never more, I believe, than three at any time. While remaining on tolerably good terms with the natives they have never, as far as my information and experience allows me to judge, taken a very deep interest in their affairs; nor have they ever interfered to any appreciable extent. They have been very small employers of labour; they have sold trade goods and dealt to some little extent in native ornaments; and they have bought copra, often giving trade goods in advance. But their influence has, on the whole, been very small. Not being members of any powerful organization they have lacked the prestige which might have made it effective. Generally speaking, then, they have been merely white residents, leading a life apart. The breakdown of *Hevehe* is, therefore, no responsibility of the local traders.

The indirect influence of planters and commercial people in other parts of the Territory has been greater, by reason of the drainage of young men who go off under indenture. In comparison with many other districts, indeed, that drainage has not, on the whole, been very serious: the 'Gulf Boys', often ignorantly lumped together as 'Orokolo Boys', have not the best reputation, and, while there are still employers who swear by them, there are more who swear at them and look for labourers elsewhere. Nevertheless, as the natives themselves so often state, the absence of a proportion of able-bodied young men has certainly made it more difficult to keep *Hevehe* alive. To this important extent, therefore, commerce has proved an adverse influence.

Government Influence
Policy of Non-Interference

The influence of the Government has been much more marked. Towards all native customs (except in so far as they are considered harmful or inimical to peace and good order) the policy of the Papuan Government is mainly one of neutrality. With regard to such cults as that of *Hevehe* and *Kovave*, in which no serious harm has ever been demonstrated, the course is, therefore, one of non-interference: they are neither deliberately discouraged on the one hand nor bolstered up on the other.

It is fortunate for the Western Elema that, like other Papuans, they have had this fair, if negative, treatment. It is worth quoting the words of a former magisterial officer to show what might have been.

The late C. A. W. Monckton, in the course of a very brief visit to the Gulf,

'heard of the existence of a secret society called the Kaiva Kuku, the members of which assembled fully disguised in strange masks and cloaks and went through secret ceremonies and ritual; branches and agents of it also existed in every coastal village'.

He recorded his belief that the members of this 'secret society' were,

'a set of blood-thirsty, terrorizing, and blackmailing scoundrels, badly needing stamping out';

and his opinion that the organization was

'bad, and existed merely for the purpose of carrying out unnameable rites and beastliness, this being borne out by the history of all native races among which secret societies were established'.

More explicitly, he inferred that the 'secret societies' of the Gulf were attended by

'bestiality, human sacrifice, incest, and other abominable crimes'.[1]

It is fortunate that early policy was no more inclined than present policy to lend an ear to such counsel. It is at least felt necessary to know something of native institutions before they are condemned, and so the mask-ceremonies of the Gulf have so far escaped; nor, if the present investigations have any value, does it seem likely that the Government will take any future action to discourage them.

Rumours of Abominations

It should be mentioned, incidentally, that rumours of sexual abominations in connexion with *Hevehe* still survive among Europeans. In the course, however, of a most whole-hearted endeavour to learn everything possible about the cult I have discovered nothing to verify them; nor can I imagine when, where, or how they are supposed to take place in the cycle. That sodomy should exist sporadically among the Western Elema is always a possibility; but I can only say I have found no trace of it among them as socially condoned or sanctioned. My informants, closely questioned in the hope of discovering the truth of the matter, hear of it with patent astonishment which speedily turns to uncontrollable laughter. Therefore, while realizing the difficulty of uncovering such a subject as that of unnatural vice, I may set down the opinion that *Hevehe* is entirely free of it.[2]

Nor does it contain anything comparable to those (in our

---

[1] *Some Experiences of a New Guinea Magistrate*, 1920, chap. xii. '*Kaiva Kuku*' is the Motu name for the masks in general.

[2] Sodomy is an accepted part of initiation ceremonies in the Trans-Fly (see author's *Papuans of the Trans-Fly*, pp. 158, 194); and I understand that it exists on the left bank of the Fly also. The eastern boundary of the distribution of the custom is not settled. I have not heard of it in the Delta Division.

view) disgusting features reported of the *Moguru*.[1] The most that can be said of it is that some of the songs are obscurely indecent, and that the *eharo* are in some cases frankly obscene. This obscenity, however, is incidental. Further, it represents a kind of humour which, while broader than we allow ourselves in public, is freely acceptable to Elema society and devoid of shamefulness. It seems, therefore, that the charge of indecency cannot be laid against *Hevehe* as a whole; while, further than that, it seems quite questionable whether, with due regard to differing conventions, we are entitled to instruct the Elema on what constitutes indecency.

Peace and Dispersal

While deliberately refraining from direct interference, however, the Government has been responsible for changes which have at least made the survival of *Hevehe* difficult.

The first business of a Government is to bring about order and peace; and one important effect of these measures is a tendency for the large village settlements to split in pieces. No longer afraid of the Kukukuku, of neighbouring tribes, or of one another, the individuals and small component groups of the main settlements can indulge their spirit of independence and set up on their own. The result in Orokolo Bay has been that the whole beach is spotted with small hamlets, off-shoots from the central *eravo*-communities. These hamlets are far too small to build *eravo* proper and undertake cycles of their own; while the communities which they have deserted complain that the current cycles cannot progress for lack of support. It is this cause more than any other which has reduced Meouri Ravi, for instance, where the cycle was near completion, to a state of dereliction and despondency.

But peace and good order have produced more than local decentralization. Nowadays the young Orokolan has taken to travel; he wishes to see the metropolis of Port Moresby, and so takes a passage on a coastal boat or joins the crowd aboard one of the *bevaia*, the eastward-sailing counterparts

[1] Landtmann, *Kiwai Papuans of British New Guinea*, Macmillan, 1927.

of the Motuan *lakatoi*. There is nearly always an important percentage of young men absent from the villages.

The Tax

Most of them are seeking work in order to pay their tax; and there is no doubt that this, the imposition of a tax, is in effect one of the main obstacles to the continuance of *Hevehe*. It is not in the writer's mind to question the advisability or justness of such a tax, particularly as the money would be obtainable on the spot if the native would devote himself more contentedly to the home industry of copra. But the instability of prices mystifies and annoys him; and, more than that, he seems to regard copra-making as drudgery. All too often he prefers to go abroad and commit himself to a year's indenture in order to earn £6. Half of that sum he may expend on trade luxuries and with the remainder pay his tax for three years. It is thus seen that, by making it safe and convenient for the young men to leave their villages and by providing a specific reason for doing so, the Government has increased the difficulty of carrying *Hevehe* on.

In other respects it seems that Government activities have not been very damaging to the cult. Carrying, the care of tracks, building of rest-houses, &c., do not make frequent claims on the Gulf natives and do not last so long as to amount to serious distraction. Altogether the Government has endeavoured to keep its hands off. Officers are reminded in a circular instruction that 'Unnecessary interference with native life should be avoided'; and such effects as Government action may have had on the survival of the cult are, at any rate, inadvertent and more or less inevitable.

Mission Influence

We cannot always make these excuses when we consider the record of the Mission, to whose effect on *Hevehe* we may finally turn. The London Missionary Society has posted in Orokolo Bay a succession of energetic and capable men who appear, on the whole, to have adopted a sufficiently broad-minded attitude towards native institutions as they found them. Some have expressed and carried out a policy of non-interference; others have been more vigorous in encouraging a new system with which *Hevehe* is regarded as incompatible. But none, as far as my knowledge and information go, have taken direct and active measures against it. Notwithstanding all this it must be assumed that the policy of the Mission has been against the mask-ceremonies, for there exists a long-established tradition that among the youths on the Mission-station, where a large number are assembled and trained for the future, none should wear a mask.

The Native Missionary's Arguments

It is these active, promising boys, their intelligence sharpened by education, who represent the most progressive part of the rising generation. The Mission-station turns out the native teachers and preachers of the present and future; and it is obvious that among them there is an element—I believe a predominant one—of strong hostility against the old ceremonies.

While a European missionary may himself maintain a tolerant and even sympathetic attitude towards such ceremonies, it is a well-known fact of experience that he may find it hard or impossible to restrain the destructive zeal of his young teachers. How that zeal, puritan and iconoclastic, comes into being, it is hard to understand: it is possibly a heritage from that not very distant time when European missionaries made a virtue of the same attitude; or it may be simply the result of semi-educated fanaticism.

However that may be, it is certain that a number of native teachers are convinced in their hearts that the new way is good and the old is bad; and, exerting considerable influence as they do, they are throwing their weight into a campaign against the ceremonies.

We may first consider some of their arguments and then turn to the methods they employ.

Worship of Strange Gods

The first argument may be called a theological one. I made a point of interviewing the most active of the teachers in this campaign, an earnest and well-intentioned man named

Yakopo. Asked what he thought of *Hevehe*, *Kovave*, Bull-Roarer, *hohao*, &c., he said politely that he had done with them; he and his people had thrown them out because they read the Book, where they were told to give over the things of this world. He searched through his Bible, but, understandably nervous, failed to find the place. Then he had recourse to a little hymnal, got out by a past missionary, on the back page of which was a list of the essentials of religion. The first two items on this list were,

Harihu lahua ava va arekaea

and

Hohao harihu heva arekaea,

which may be translated 'Ye shall have no other gods', and 'Ye shall not make any graven image'. *Hevehe*, *kovave*, bull-roarer, and *hohao* were 'other gods', and (the last two at least) 'graven images'. We cannot do other than respect such sincere loyalty even though we may remain out of sympathy with the Divine jealousy of which it is a reflection, and even though we may recognize that some honour is also due to the inarticulate loyalty of those who hold by *Hevehe*.

Lies and Deceit

Another argument is that the ceremonies are bad because they are full of lies and deceit, the reference being to the pretence involved in *Hevehe Karawa* and the supposed living character of the masks. We have observed often enough, however, that the secrets are very open ones. It must demand a higher degree of credulity than would be found in any disinterested person to imagine that the women were really taken in.

Victimization of Women

A third argument is that the ceremonies are bad because they mean the victimization of women—a point much stressed by the preacher. I cannot avoid thinking this an example of priggery: the Orokolans are exhorted to pity the poor women who labour to provide the greedy men with food. One may well be in sympathy with a general desire to raise the status of women, but it is hard to believe that such an argument as the above, so transparently false in sentiment and reason, can be seriously put forward. And yet it is constantly in the preacher's mouth. We have seen the women busy, eagerly expectant, and obviously happy in their preparations for feast after feast; and we have seen the delight with which they hailed their *hevehe* when the Revelation came. It is hard to imagine they feel put upon. I have heard a vivid account of the destruction of the masks at Vailala during the Madness. The door of the *eravo* was thrown open so that the women might see the *hevehe* before they were taken away and burnt. It was a moment when they might have rejoiced at their emancipation; but instead of that they wailed and slashed their cheeks.

Absence of the Spiritual

Another argument used by the native preachers (though it seems unlikely that it could have originated with them) is that *Hevehe* and *Kovave* are things 'devoid of spirit', or 'devoid of the spiritual'.

> *Hevehe kovave ove karia eharu.*

They are, on the contrary, *eharu-bohoava-eharu*—'things of the full belly'. The reference is to the feasts which accompany the celebrations and to the food which is from time to time brought to the *eravo*, ostensibly for the mask-spirits, but really for the men.

One cannot deny that the Western Elema, like most natives at a similar stage of development, attach a very great importance to food; but one does not feel compelled to take exception to this preoccupation when one considers the other motives attached to it—the hospitality, conviviality, pride of production, and so on. At any rate it is questionable whether the abolition of *Hevehe* could do much to remedy it —if it needed a remedy. Those natives who have already dropped the major ceremonies find other excuses for feasting and filling their bellies; and they are not more spiritual. But quite apart from the question of food it seems, after what we have seen of it, a vilification of *Hevehe* to say that it is devoid of the spiritual.

Distraction from Studies

Lastly, there is the more practical contention that the ceremonies distract the young from their studies. As a pupil put it, 'If we dance there is a noise in our ears that prevents us from hearing in church or school.'

There is obviously something in this; but the question is more complex than appears to the native teacher. It involves a balancing of the values of *Hevehe* against those of spelling and arithmetic, and a possibility of compromise which does not occur to his single-mindedness. School education has made rather slow strides in Orokolo Bay, but there is, in some quarters at any rate, a genuine keenness to acquire it— if mainly for utilitarian motives, 'so that we can get good wages'. The possibility of reconciling education with the claims of the existent culture must, however, be left to the last chapter.

Methods of Propaganda

These being the main arguments of the mission reformer, let us see briefly how he puts them into effect. In the villages the offices of teacher and preacher are combined; and while some of these dual functionaries refrain conscientiously from direct attack on the existent way of life, they all, as far as I have ascertained, profess a personal preference for the 'new' way. It is to be expected, therefore, that, though they may be honest in saying that the choice lies with the people themselves, their influence in favour of change is a strong one. Some, however, go very much farther. It is a matter of complaint which I have frequently recorded in my notes that certain school-teachers constantly instruct their pupils to 'throw away' the old fashions and adopt the new ones; and it is alleged that they go to the length of explaining the mysteries, so that the older men profess themselves unable to go on with the ceremonies: they would be ashamed to do so when even the children know all about them. It is evident that such conduct on the part of Mission teachers must in the long run, if not speedily, make the continuance of *Hevehe* impossible.

The same propaganda proceeds in the church. Informants at Vailala have asked, not without bitterness, how they could perform a secret ceremony on Saturday when their wives and daughters would hear all about it from the preacher on Sunday. And young zealots have declaimed against *Hevehe*, with a fearlessness which does them credit, in those open-air services held before the *eravo* itself, the very citadel of the old cult. Thus a fiery young lay-preacher points to the great building and cries, 'You women work and make food for nothing. The *hevehe* hanging there are made by human hands. They do not eat your food. It is eaten by deceiving old men!'

The preacher, sincere in his desire to save, points out that those who adhere to the old ways which God has condemned, must go to the *Ita Heaha*, the 'Bad Place'. Yakopo, the most fanatical and influential of all, assured me gravely that this must be. And his neighbour, the aged Hcpe, a champion of the old order, told me with tears of indignation in his eyes how Yakopo had recently declared that he and his heathen following would never survive death; their souls (the unorthodoxy is no doubt due to a misunderstanding) were to 'burn in the sky'.

The effect of such teaching and preaching is to bring *Hevehe* and the other ceremonies into disrepute with those—and I believe they are in the great majority—who desire co-operation with the Mission. There is a very widespread impression that they are disapproved by God.

It is impossible to avoid the conclusion that the Vailala Madness, which dealt such a shattering blow to the ceremonies, was mainly due to Mission teaching. Needless to say, it was not directly instigated by any missionary; and it is a pleasure to record that the Rev. H. P. Schlencker, who was then in charge at Orokolo, counselled the villages to resist it, and thereby in all probability prevented the Western Elema stronghold from capitulating. But, these things notwithstanding, there remains no doubt that the doctrines of the Vailala Madness were attributable in the long run to Mission teaching.

Nor can it be said that those doctrines differ essentially from the doctrines propounded by some of the more fanatical of native preachers to-day. They may rake up arguments —we have examined them—but the general proposition is that 'Such-and-such is an old fashion, and therefore a bad one'. The young are urged to put such old fashions away from them because *Harihu iki hairihairi*, 'God dislikes them'.

It is easy, instructive, and not without entertainment, to make out lists in various social settings of the practices that have, or have not, the Divine sanction. Some believe that God prefers singlet and calico loin-cloth to the perineal band; others naïvely explain that He approves of clothes only on Sundays. So, in the opinion of some, he may forbid the wearing of feathers; the use of mud and charcoal in mourning; the practice of magic; and even smoking and betel-chewing—though this only for adults. Opinions may differ in respect of these and other things : I have even heard a Christian maintain that God approved of magic. But there is little room among the more ardent native Christians for difference of opinion regarding *Hevehe*, *Kovave*, Bull-Roarer, and the cult of *hohao*. These things have been condemned by God through the mouth of his Western Elema apostles. They are definitely on the black list.

It is evident that those who lend an ear to such teaching cannot profess Christianity and practise *Hevehe* at the same time without hypocrisy, or at least a muddlement of ideas. Many succeed, more or less, in doing so—e.g. the Christian youth who had passed through Bull-Roarer and *Kovave* before his baptism and who expressed the hope that he would yet pass through *Apa-Hevehe* and *Hevehe Karawa*, although he said openly that God did not approve of any of them. But, while many may thus compromise, the rising generation of the faithful is being more completely weaned away. Some youths of Vailala explained to me that they were against *Kovave* (and, of course, *Hevehe*) simply because they were *akore hekai*—the young boys, or the new generation. And a grave Councillor of the same village explained

PLATE 62

1. Yakopo   2. Hepe

The New Order confronts the Old

further that the rising batch of boys would not wish to be initiated because they would 'belong to God'.

Ivo and Lerevea: a Parable

Reference was made earlier to one of the mythical accounts of the origin of *Hevehe*.[1] It is worth bringing up that story again for the sake of its bearing on the present issue. It contains a queer incident which, though apparently, or even obviously, recent, is so deeply embedded that it might seem to belong to the mythical epoch; at any rate my informants think it part of the original.

When Ivo, chief of the Lower People, mounted the wrong ladder in the darkness and thus found his way into the sky, he was entertained there by Lerevea. Looking down with a bird's-eye view next morning he saw his fellows on earth and listened to the adjurations of his host: when he returned he must never steal another man's wife, never shoot his pig, never thieve from his garden; he must not lie with his wife by day in the bush, but only in his house by night; for all these things were visible to those who lived in the sky, and they were often compelled to turn their backs in shame on what they saw.

In due course Ivo was escorted back to earth amid thunder, lightning, and rain. The Sky-People left generous gifts of food and returned, while Ivo was received with joy and surprise by his fellow villagers. Soon after, having first called down the Sky-People to accept a return gift of food, he proceeded to instruct his village in *Hevehe* and to make preparations for a festival.

Now it is, plainly enough, the gist of the tale in its original form that Ivo had learnt how to make *Hevehe* from Lerevea himself; indeed the story is told to explain the origin of the cult. But in this apocryphal version it appears that Ivo brought down with him a further gift, one which he failed to appreciate or understand. Instead of revealing this to his fellow villagers he hid it away in a corner of his house. It was nothing less than a 'book'—*hohoa*, the kind of writing practised by the white man.

[1] See p. 392.

Seeing Ivo busy with his drums, masks, and feathers, Lerevea called down to him: 'That thing I gave you—what are you going to do with it?'

To which Ivo answered, 'I cannot understand it. I do not want it. Don't you see what I am doing?'

'Yes,' answered Lerevea, 'that is your own way; but my gift you have kept hidden.' And he was angry and said that the people on earth would suffer *kakare eapapo*, 'great pain', for following their own courses.

But the *Hevehe* went on, and has continued up to the present time. In the words of my informants it is *overa pupu mai*, an ancient sacred custom, or *birari pupu*, the sacred thing of their ancestors. But Lerevea in the story called it an evil thing and upbraided the Earth-People for clinging to it. His other gift, the book and all book-learning, he gave to the white man.

The application is not far to seek. It is God himself who speaks through the mouth of Lerevea, and thus the sense of Divine disapprobation is already finding a place in the very mythology of *Hevehe*. In the old view *Hevehe* was *birari pupu* and therefore demanded perpetuation. In the new, it is a mere Papuan thing, guilty and contemptible. It is obvious that with a people who are not averse to Christianity the cult cannot prosper greatly while they are taught that God is against it.

XXVIII

THE FUTURE

The Case for Retention

WE have considered the values for *Hevehe* as well as the arguments against it; and, presuming the presentation to have been a fair one, it must seem obvious that the balance is on the credit side. The writer, who would be far from making such a claim for every element in native culture, has, therefore, no hesitation in saying that, if possible, *Hevehe* should be encouraged to continue.

The main reasons for such a recommendation are that the institution has provided the native with an absorbing interest as well as a unique means of expressing himself and of satisfying various social, psychological, and material needs. For this interest and these satisfactions the new way of living, if it means the abolition of *Hevehe*, does not appear to have provided an adequate substitute.[1]

The substitutes, in so far as they represent activities, are church service, school, and games. All these are very valuable; but it seems possible that they might take the form, not so much of replacements in Western Elema culture as of additions to it. In so far as this is already the case—and to a large extent it is, for those who still hold by *Hevehe* engage in all these extra activities—they are an undoubted enrichment of the culture. But if it is felt that *Hevehe* must go in order to make way for them, then, to repeat, the writer maintains that they provide no adequate substitute for its peculiar values. In short, the disappearance of *Hevehe* must mean a serious cultural impoverishment. It would indeed be difficult to devise anything similar out of our own culture to replace it.

Another argument may be adduced for the retention of

---

[1] The native has found some additional substitutes of his own. It seems that the *bevaia* trading expeditions are more frequent than they used to be (see 'Trading Voyages from the Gulf of Papua', in *Oceania*, vol. iii, no. 2); and the cult of deceased kin, made popular by the Vailala Madness, still flickers on, providing occasion for the sacrifice of pigs and feasting.

Hevehe. Apart from any intrinsic value it may possess, it is something of the native's own creation. In a world of change he stands in danger of being overawed and too much humiliated by the power and apparent superiority of the white man. It seems wholly desirable in such circumstances that he should retain something, in fact a great deal, that is distinctively Papuan. Of *Hevehe* he could at least say, 'This is my own!'—and it is assuredly no poor thing of which he need be ashamed, but rather his highest achievement, and one which even the European might admire without compromising his dignity.

For these reasons, therefore, it is suggested that *Hevehe* is worthy of retention. Others, with different ideals of native welfare, may think the opposite. And others again may say that it is no concern of ours at all: it is purely a question for the native himself.

Freedom and Non-Interference

This last is a very strong position. It is remarkable how often we discuss the pros and cons of native customs with a view to deciding whether they should go or stay, forgetting that the native has a mind of his own, and that the choice might not unreasonably be left to him. The concept of freedom, or cultural self-determination, is one which may well cause grievous difficulty to educators; for, while they may recognize it as sacred, they are nevertheless compelled in practice to adopt some policy; and thus, though they may desire the native to make his own choice, they cannot do otherwise than influence it. The educator is thus brought to something of an impasse, the solution of which would seem to lie in such a broad education of his pupils that we could rely upon their choice to be both critical and sound. Granted this, the educator should then, presumably, rest content with the choice, whatever it might be.

Now, if we are agreed upon the subject of cultural self-determination, it will seem that the Western Elema themselves must choose whether they will keep *Hevehe* or have done with it. And it will doubtless be replied that they have already made their choice. The last chapter shows plainly enough that the general vote, so far at any rate, is against it.

It seems, however, to the writer that this is another example of that alleged free choice which is really nothing of the kind. It is rather the inevitable result of long-continued propaganda upon a relatively suggestible people. Some native peoples are more suggestible than others; and it might be said on the whole that the Western Elema have been peculiarly stubborn: after more than forty years of missionary effort they still retain a remarkable attachment to their old customs. But this is only a matter of degree. Even Western Elema resistance must be overcome by such methods in the long run. The freedom of what seems to be their present united choice is spurious. They could not have it otherwise.

If it is right that their choice in the matter of *Hevehe* should be a critical and free one, then, during these last forty years, they should have heard something in its favour—words or gestures of respect, approval, and admiration (where they were undoubtedly due) as well as those of condemnation and contempt. The writer cannot believe that the native's verdict against *Hevehe* has been based on an impartial presentation.

Under these circumstances it seems doubtful whether the attitude of neutrality consistently adopted by the Government is sufficient to meet the case. Were *Hevehe*, together with the other ceremonies, exposed merely to the impersonal and inevitable forces of change, that neutrality would be justified and fair. But, while the Government has remained neutral, the other great influence on native life, viz. the Mission, has, through its native evangelists, persisted in attacking; and against these champions of change *Hevehe* has been fighting a losing battle.

One cannot resist drawing a comparison with events in one of the European countries at the present moment. Two great nations maintain a policy of non-intervention, arguing (apart from practical considerations which may concern themselves) that the factions in Spain must be left to settle their own political differences. Meanwhile two other great nations are allegedly pouring in assistance to ensure that the side they favour wins. This is illustration, not analogy. It may fairly be said that no nation bears direct responsibility for the internal affairs of another, and so intervention is not obligatory. But we admittedly hold the fate of the Papuans in our hands as trustees; we cannot evade responsibility for their cultural future; and so intervention may become a duty. In the personal opinion of the writer, who sees so much to commend in *Hevehe*, a policy of non-intervention may amount to a betrayal of the natives' interests. So long as we remain neutral we are merely standing by while the supporters of *Hevehe* go under to their enemies.

Hevehe *and Education*

While fully in accord with the idea that native institutions should stand or fall according to their merits or their adaptability to new conditions, and the principle that the natives to whom they belong should ultimately decide, the present writer feels strongly that propaganda on one side should, in the interests of a fair fight, be countered by propaganda on the other. Here, however, favourable propaganda has been conspicuous by its absence. It is suggested, indeed, that those who have been responsible for educating the native have often failed in their duty towards him by neglecting to make the most of the cultural material which they have at hand.

Modern theory insists that native education should bear an intelligent relation to existent culture. The notion of abolition and replacement is no longer the guiding principle: it is not the function of the educator to destroy, but to make the most of, what exists already. In the present instance, if we desire to sustain and cultivate the powers and energies of the Western Elema; to foster their aesthetic, imaginative, and creative gifts; to give them scope for organization, leadership, co-operation, and social intercourse; and to permit them to indulge in their self-chosen form of recreation—then we have at our disposal, in *Hevehe*, the very substance by which these ideals may be turned into realities. It provides scope and opportunity for their fulfilment on a scale far grander than does anything they have learnt from the white man. If education values self-expression in the pupil, then the educator will not supplant, but use, the institution in which the Western Elema have expressed themselves most nobly. In short, it seems that the fostering of *Hevehe* might well be an essential part of a sound educational programme.

Compatibility with Christian Faith

The question naturally arises whether *Hevehe* and the minor ceremonies are compatible with the accepted aims of education and evangelization as at present in force. With regard to education in the more restricted sense the questions are those of distraction of interest and loss of time. To the writer it seems that, with due regard to the total environment in which the Western Elema live, the claims of spelling and arithmetic might well make some sacrifice to those of *Hevehe*; while, as for the scholar's time, it is suggested, not that some of it should be spared for *Hevehe*, but rather that sufficient should be *devoted* to that subject as the prime achievement of his people.

Nor does the ideal of evangelization raise any insuperable obstacle. Provided we can dispense with crude and primitive notions regarding 'false gods' and 'graven images' there is nothing in *Hevehe* to render it incompatible with essential Christian belief and conduct. I can see no difficulty in the Christian youth's passing through it from beginning to end; and it is hard to believe how either *Hevehe* or Christianity would suffer in the process. If any one were to suggest that belief in the Immortal Story Folk cannot exist side by side with the belief in God, then I submit that he does not know his native. Fortunately for the evangelist, native logic is not of the kind to be over-particular about consistency: the idea of God can enter into a brain that still gives lodging to many heathen fancies; and so I believe that a sincere convert might pass through *Hevehe* without a sacrifice of faith. On the other hand, since the theological part of *Hevehe* is relatively unimportant, I have no fear of expressing the opinion that conversion to Christianity on the part of those who practise it need not affect its continuance. In short, the two are not, on a liberal view, mutually exclusive; and, in so far as the native has been taught that he must surrender the one before he can embrace the other, he has been confronted by a false antithesis.

I once discussed with three men of Auma the question of whether they could combine the old with the new. One of them said, 'No, God is angry with the people for practising *Hevehe* and *Kovave*, and I am afraid to renew them.' He was voicing the very common opinion which has been brought into being by the teaching of fanatics. The second said he thought he could worship God and wear a mask at the same time. Whether he was sincere, or whether he had examined his heart before answering so boldly, I cannot say, but I believe, nevertheless, that he uttered a truth. The third man, however, gave the most illuminating answer: he said that he did not think at all. This is without doubt a very common attitude. But for the teaching of the evangelists, the ordinary native, a potential convert, would not be aware of any antagonism between *Hevehe* and the new faith. He would hold to both.

I have recorded a conversation with some young men of Hareamavu, the western part of Arihava, where the ceremonies have been completely wiped out. It was the old fashion, they said, still practised in Orokolo, to hold *Hevehe* and *Kovave* in one hand and God's Word in the other; but they held God's Word in both hands. If that is their considered choice, no one will question it; though it is undoubtedly attributable to the influence of one man, the zealous and masterful teacher who resides among them. In Yogu, where the teacher is a mellower person and unaggressive, the people said they wanted church, school, and *Hevehe* —all three. It is not hard to imagine that, under a moderate régime, the three might thrive together.

Practical Suggestions

It remains to make one or two practical suggestions in the hope that the Western Elema may be given a belated chance to continue or revive the *Hevehe* cult if they really wish.

It seems that there are two very substantial obstacles: first the lack of man-power brought about by labour conditions and the tax, second the attitude of the native evangelist and teacher. With regard to the first I have only to suggest that the various individual communities who now shrink from the task of building their own separate *eravo* and embarking on their own cycles might be induced to club together and share the responsibility and the glory. Considering the already mixed composition of the average *eravo*-community, a union of two or three of them is not an inconceivable remedy; and, by distributing the labour, it would at least do something to remove the complaints, on the European side, that *Hevehe* is too great a distraction from other aims, and, on the native side, that it is 'too much trouble'.

As for the second obstacle I would suggest that the destructive influence of certain evangelists and teachers should be brought definitely to an end. While entertaining a proper respect for the zeal of these men, I cannot but believe that their attitude of antagonism towards *Hevehe* and other existent institutions is wholly out of keeping with the principles of native education and, in its effect, thoroughly mischievous.

Further I would suggest that the Mission—if it can agree that *Hevehe* even at this stage should be given its chance—should take some active steps to break down the tradition against it. Instead of the old understanding that no Station youth should go into the village to be initiated, I would go the limit and suggest the very reverse—a new rule that every youth on the Station *must* be initiated. If such a change could meet with Mission approval it would speedily disabuse the native mind of the fatal idea that *Hevehe* is against the will of God.

The able and progressive missionary now in charge at Orokolo places no definite obstacle in the path of *Hevehe*, and has expressed himself ready to allow the Station boys, if they so desire, to undergo initiation. He has, as it seems to the writer, a great opportunity to demonstrate that evangelization and education may proceed hand in hand with the continued functioning of what is best in the old culture.

But, even if it were agreed on all sides that *Hevehe* was worthy to survive, it may be now too late. If that is so, the writer must content himself with having given an account of what strikes him as a cultural achievement of no mean order. There are many more fine things now threatened with extinction in the cultures of Papua and other native countries; and *Hevehe*, if the hope of its renascence is past, may stand at least as a sad and salutary example. Perhaps its fate may have some slight effect upon the solution of similar problems in other settings. This book concludes, then, with the hope, however idealistic, that things like *Hevehe* will elsewhere be given a better chance; that the new order will show a readier disposition to compromise with the old; and that the highest products of a not ignoble past may more often live on into the future.

APPENDIX

TABLE OF RELATIONSHIP TERMS
(MALE SPEAKING)

Females use the same terms as males except in the following cases:

1. They use an additional term *loare* (collect. *loahura*) for brothers on the paternal side. This term is restricted to own brothers and near brothers. For distant brothers in the classificatory sense the general collective term *apo-heare* is used.

2. They use the term *arivu* for the *arivu* of their spouses. For their own brothers' children they use the terms *akore* and *meavore* (according as the brother is older or younger).

3. They do not use the term *ai* for the son of their *aukau*. They call him *akore-apo* or *akore-heare* (according as the *aukau* is older or younger than their own mother).

MOTHER'S PEOPLE

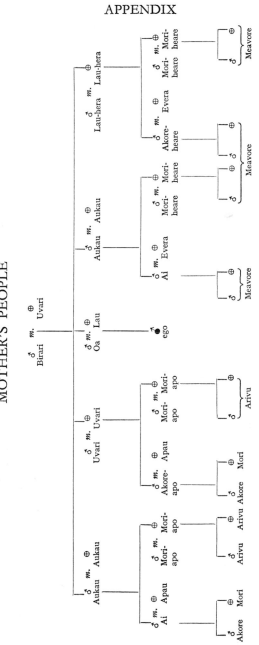

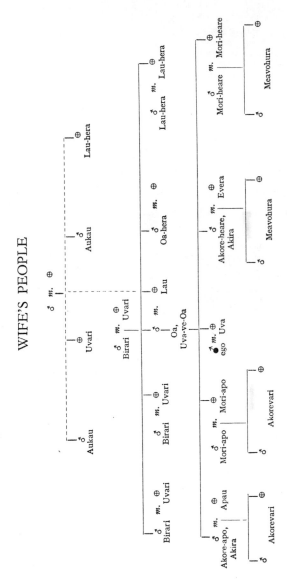

WIFE'S PEOPLE

GLOSSARY

Adidiavu	name of a song.
ahea	hot; heat; magical power.
ai	cross-cousin.
Aiaimunu	'Drum-*imunu*'; the Namau ceremony corresponding to *Hevehe*.
aiape	collective form of *ai*.
aiha	bad-tempered, irascible; supernaturally dangerous.
aitave	crescent pearl-shell ornament.
ake-ape	door (lit. 'track-mouth').
akira	brother-in-law.
akore	son; boy.
akore apo	elder brother (classif.).
akore heare	younger brother (classif.).
amua	chief (*eravo-amua*, *eravo*-chief; *karigara-amua*, village-chief).
apa-haro-haera	Drum-Leader; one of the two men owning the leading *hevehe* masks.
apa eravarava	drum-beaters.
apa-hevehe	drum-*hevehe*, i.e. the tall mask with drum (referred to throughout the book as *hevehe*).
apakora	frontlet of shell disks.
ape	mouth; mouthpiece of mask.
apiapi	ginger.
apuviri	name of a song.
arara	basket-work at rear of *hevehe* mask.
arita	coconut-shell spoon.
arivu	sister's child.
aro	charcoal; blackening of mourner.
aroa	netted string bag.
aruhihi larava	central part of *eravo* interior.
aualari	a totem; a character in the mythology belonging to any one of the *aualari* groups, i.e. the ten main lineal divisions of Western Elema society.
aukahura	maternal kin (collective form of *aukau*).
aukau	maternal uncle.
aukau havahu	maternal uncle proper; i.e. the individual who enters into the gift-exchange relationship with a particular *arivu*, or nephew.
avaha	back; back part of *hevehe* mask.
avai	(1) property, esp. in the form of trees, coconuts, sago palms, &c.; (2) the old men.
baupa eravo	lit. 'decoration *eravo*'; the young men's or boys' house.
be'ure-hevehe	'ground-*hevehe*', i.e. bull-roarer.
bevaia	the Elema trading-vessel.
bevaia haera	organizer, chief man, of trading voyage.
bira	male; husband; man.
bira'ipi	a patrilineal clan of local origin.
bira-kake	age-mate.
birakau	age-group.
birari	grandfather; father's elder brother; ancestor.
dehe	door; tall door of *eravo*.
edoroba	rubbish, remnants.
eharo	lit. 'dance-head'; the fanciful (sometimes totemic) mask used in connexion with the *Hevehe* cycle.
Eharo	the ceremonies in which *eharo* masks are used.
eharu	thing; property; esp. shell ornaments.
eravo	men's house (the personal name of the men's house usually includes the word *ravi*—Avavu Ravi, &c.).

eravo-ve-uvari	the *eravo*-grandmother, i.e. the spiritual guardian of the men's house.
erekai-akore	a 'belted boy', a lad who has not yet assumed the perineal band.
erohore	fisherman's pedestal in water.
eva	the ornaments constituting the bride-price.
evera haera	expert; craftsman.
haera	man; men; people.
hahi	journey; trading expedition.
hapa	young frond of palm, split down the centre, with leaflets hanging as a fringe, used decoratively or as a tabu sign (also carried by novices with gifts of meat attached); effigy of bird or fish used in *eravo* decoration.
hara	plaited coconut leaf, as mat, screen, &c.; coconut-leaf bag; the covering worn for concealment by secluded boys when abroad in village.
harau	a large hollow seed; rattles of same.
harea	sorcery.
harihu	ghost; independent spirit; sorcerer's familiar.
Harihu	Mission word for God.
harihu haera	sorcerer.
haro-eharu	lit. 'head-things' (ornaments); the posthumous gift of shell ornaments to maternal kin of deceased (or, in case of a woman, to her brothers).
havahu	real, proper.
hehe-eapoi	first important mortuary feast.
hevehe	the tall mask; the being or spirit represented by it. (The full expression is *apa-hevehe*, i.e. drum-*hevehe*, but the abbreviated form is used throughout the book. For other meanings of *hevehe* see Chapter IX.)
Hevehe	the cycle of ceremonies centring on the *hevehe* masks.
Hevehe Karawa	the ceremony in which the *ma-hevehe* appears.
hevehe-lau	(1) proprietress, or 'mother', of the *hevehe* mask; (2) the *ma-hevehe*, or sea-monster, as fictional mother of *apa-hevehe*.
hii	fine bark-cloth; perineal band.
Hii	a cycle of ceremonies belonging to the Houra Haera.
Hii Kairu	the episode of the Yellow Bark-Cloth Boys (*Hii kairu-akore*).
hirita	an enclosure walled with palm branches: (1) at rear of *baupa eravo* for seclusion of boys; (2) in front of *eravo* proper during culminating stage of *Hevehe* cycle.
hoaho-akore	young bachelor newly emerged from seclusion.
hohao	carved wooden plaque of anthropomorphic form kept in *eravo*.
hopa	a belt, with *mae* attached, fastened about the chest of the mask-wearer.
hovori-hovori	the sorcerers leading the *ma-hevehe* party in *Hevehe Karawa*.
Horovu Harihu	the Land of the Dead.
hurae	hearth.
Hurava Hakare	name of a song.
idihi-vira	dancers in costume.
iki	liver.
ivaiva	a ceremony of placation involving a food-offering.
ive	one of the central pillars of the *eravo*.
kaia larava	rear end of *eravo* interior.
kaiavuru	*hohao* (q.v.) of importance, with immanent spirit.
Kaiva Kuku	the Motu (?) name for the mask ceremonies of the Gulf in general.
kake	friend; formal friend; namesake.
karigara	village; the settlement of an *eravo*-community.
kariki haera	'handy man'; curator and ceremonial factotum of *eravo*.
keko	bamboo; bamboo pole.
kiriki haera	the slayer.

kora-iru	barks, &c., used as medicines.
kora marita	'tree maidens'; spirits of the trees or bush.
kora papaita	scaffolding in front of *eravo* for climax of *Hevehe*.
korepaka	shield.
koro	bast.
kovave	the conical mask; the being or spirit represented by the mask.
Kovave	the cycle of ceremonies centring on *kovave* masks.
lakatoi	the Motuan trading-vessel.
Laraa	the procession of *hevehe* entering the *eravo* at the end of their month's dancing.
larava	(1) transverse section of the men's house, which is divided into *oropa larava* (front), *aruhihi larava* (centre), and *kaia larava* (rear); (2) a patrilineal kinship group, limited in strictness to association with one hearth in the *eravo*.
lare	name.
lau	(1) mother; (2) story, legend, myth.
love	(1) amaranth leaves; (2) sprig or tuft of feathers.
love hae	a particular kind of *eharo* mask, more or less conventional, decorated with sprigs (*love*) of feathers.
ma	water, sea.
mae	frayed sago leaf, used for women's skirts and mantles of masks.
maea-ihura	'body-cries'.
mahea	(1) boiled sago; (2) the women's stationary dance.
ma-hevehe	the sea-*hevehe*; sea-monster.
maho	magic.
maho haera	Magic People; i.e. people of the myths whose names are used in magic.
maioka	shame; ashamed.
mairai	veranda platform.
Mairava	the Revelation; the ceremony in which the *hevehe* first emerge from the *eravo*.
marupai	charm, of dwarf coconut, carved.
mori	girl; daughter (plur. *marita*).
obo-eva	betrothal price.
okeahi	a formal friend, in gift-exchange relationship with reciprocal *okeahi*.
oro	a certain tree.
oropa larava	front part of *eravo* interior.
ove	soul; ghost.
ove-hahu	independent spirits (particularly of the bush).
pairava	medicinal leaves, &c.; especially those used for purification.
paiva haro	'cane head'; cane framework of *hevehe* mask.
papaa	stew, of boiled sago, &c.
papaita	(1) stairway; (2) ramp of timber leading to entrance of *eravo* or *baupa eravo* for ceremonies.
papaita-ipive-uvari	the grandmother at the foot of the stairs, the *eravo* grandmother.
poilati	'sago-bringers' (?); the masked men who collect food for the guests before the ceremony of the New Door.
pupu	forbidden, untouchable, sacred; tabu sign.
pura	coarse bark-cloth.
puva	shell trumpet.
ravi	men's house (Namau language).
ruru	palm spathe; mask, disguise.
upi	ginger.
uva	wife; wife of formal friend or age-mate.
uvari	grandmother; father's elder sister; ancestress.
uvi-eravo	*eravo* built in modern style, resembling a house (*uvi*).
Yahe	name of a song.
yakea	united shout; cheer.

INDEX